Principles and Theories of Data Mining With RapidMiner

Sarawut Ramjan
Thammasat University, Thailand

Jirapon Sunkpho
Thammasat University, Thailand

A volume in the Advances in Computer and
Electrical Engineering (ACEE) Book Series

Published in the United States of America by
  IGI Global
  Engineering Science Reference (an imprint of IGI Global)
  701 E. Chocolate Avenue
  Hershey PA, USA 17033
  Tel: 717-533-8845
  Fax: 717-533-8661
  E-mail: cust@igi-global.com
  Web site: http://www.igi-global.com

Library of Congress Cataloging-in-Publication Data

Names: Ramjan, Sarawut, 1984- author. | Sunkpho, Jirapon, DATE- author.
Title: Principles and theories of data mining with RapidMiner / authored by
  Sarawut Ramjan, and Jirapon Sunkpho.
Description: Hershey, PA : Engineering Science Reference, [2023] | Includes
  bibliographical references and index. | Summary: "This book is
  academically written as a guide for students and people interested in
  experimenting Data Mining using RapidMiner software. It covers the
  contents related to Data Mining, which consists of Classification, Deep
  Learning, Association Rule, Clustering, Recommendation System and
  RapidMiner Software usage as well as researching case studies on the use
  of data mining techniques in data science. Additionally, this book is
  the foundation of Python programming for data science for young
  scientists who want to understand data mining algorithms. As well as
  starting to write programs that can be applied to other data science
  programs. At the end of this book, authors describe about data
  governance with a case study of the government sector to enable young
  data scientists to understand the role of data scientists as part of
  stakeholders in data governance actions. The authors hope that this book
  is a good beginning for those who would like to develop themselves or
  for those who own data within their organization to meet internal and
  external problems. RapidMiner software is used to analyze data and
  provide guidance for further study in data science at a higher level"--
  Provided by publisher.
Identifiers: LCCN 2022061153 (print) | LCCN 2022061154 (ebook) | ISBN
  9781668447307 (h/c) | ISBN 9781668447314 (s/c) | ISBN 9781668447321
  (eISBN)
Subjects: LCSH: Data mining. | Big data. | RapidMiner (Electronic
  resource).
Classification: LCC QA76.9.D343 R356 2023 (print) | LCC QA76.9.D343
  (ebook) | DDC 006.3/12--dc23/eng/20230123
LC record available at https://lccn.loc.gov/2022061153
LC ebook record available at https://lccn.loc.gov/2022061154

This book is published in the IGI Global book series Advances in Computer and Electrical Engineering (ACEE) (ISSN: 2327-039X; eISSN: 2327-0403)

British Cataloguing in Publication Data
A Cataloguing in Publication record for this book is available from the British Library.

All work contributed to this book is new, previously-unpublished material. The views expressed in this book are those of the authors, but not necessarily of the publisher.

For electronic access to this publication, please contact: eresources@igi-global.com.

Advances in Computer and Electrical Engineering (ACEE) Book Series

Srikanta Patnaik
SOA University, India

ISSN:2327-039X
EISSN:2327-0403

MISSION

The fields of computer engineering and electrical engineering encompass a broad range of interdisciplinary topics allowing for expansive research developments across multiple fields. Research in these areas continues to develop and become increasingly important as computer and electrical systems have become an integral part of everyday life.

The **Advances in Computer and Electrical Engineering (ACEE) Book Series** aims to publish research on diverse topics pertaining to computer engineering and electrical engineering. **ACEE** encourages scholarly discourse on the latest applications, tools, and methodologies being implemented in the field for the design and development of computer and electrical systems.

COVERAGE

- Computer Hardware
- Microprocessor Design
- Electrical Power Conversion
- Power Electronics
- Algorithms
- Applied Electromagnetics
- Computer Architecture
- Digital Electronics
- Programming
- Optical Electronics

IGI Global is currently accepting manuscripts for publication within this series. To submit a proposal for a volume in this series, please contact our Acquisition Editors at acquisitions@igi-global.com or visit: https://www.igi-global.com/publish/.

Titles in this Series

For a list of additional titles in this series, please visit: www.igi-global.com/book-series

NeutroGeometry, NeutroAlgebra, and SuperHyperAlgebra in Today's World
Florentin Smarandache (University of New Mexico, USA) and Madeline Al Tahan (Abu Dhabi University UAE)
Engineering Science Reference • © 2023 • 300pp • H/C (ISBN: 9781668447406) • US $270.00

Energy Systems Design for Low-Power Computing
Rathishchandra Ramachandra Gatti (Sahyadri College of Engineering and Management, India) Chandra Singh (Sahyadri College of Engineering and Management, India) Srividya P. (RV College of Engineering, India) and Sandeep Bhat (Sahyadri College of Engineering and Management, ndia)
Engineering Science Reference • © 2023 • 389pp • H/C (ISBN: 9781668449745) • US $270.00

Artificial Intelligence Applications in Battery Management Systems and Routing Problems in Electric Vehicles
S. Angalaeswari (Vellore Institute of Technology, India) T. Deepa (Vellore Institute of Technology, India) and L. Ashok Kumar (PSG College of Technology, India)
Engineering Science Reference • © 2023 • 342pp • H/C (ISBN: 9781668466315) • US $260.00

Handbook of Research on AI Methods and Applications in Computer Engineering
Sanaa Kaddoura (Zayed University, UAE)
Engineering Science Reference • © 2023 • 632pp • H/C (ISBN: 9781668469378) • US $335.00

Structural and Functional Aspects of Biocomputing Systems for Data Processing
U. Vignesh (Information Technology Department, Vel Tech Rangarajan Dr. Sagunthala R&D Institute of Science and Technology, Chennai, India) R. Parvathi (Vellore Institute of Technology, India) and Ricardo Goncalves (Department of Electrical and Computer Engineering (DEEC), NOVA School of Science and Technology, NOVA University Lisbon, Portugal)
Engineering Science Reference • © 2023 • 246pp • H/C (ISBN: 9781668465233) • US $270.00

5G Internet of Things and Changing Standards for Computing and Electronic Systems
Augustine O. Nwajana (University of Greenwich, UK)
Engineering Science Reference • © 2022 • 308pp • H/C (ISBN: 9781668438558) • US $250.00

Theory and Applications of NeutroAlgebras as Generalizations of Classical Algebras
Florentin Smarandache (University of New Mexico, USA) and Madeline Al-Tahan (Lebanese International University, Lebanon)
Engineering Science Reference • © 2022 • 333pp • H/C (ISBN: 9781668434956) • US $270.00

IGI Global
PUBLISHER of TIMELY KNOWLEDGE

701 East Chocolate Avenue, Hershey, PA 17033, USA
Tel: 717-533-8845 x100 • Fax: 717-533-8661
E-Mail: cust@igi-global.com • www.igi-global.com

Table of Contents

Preface

Welcome to this guide on data mining using RapidMiner software. This comprehensive book is specifically designed for beginners and anyone who wants to explore the world of data mining. The book is structured into 12 chapters, each covering a specific topic in detail.

Chapter 1, "Introduction to Data Mining," gives an insight into the trend and importance of data mining in various industries. Chapter 2, "Data," explains the different types of data that a data scientist should understand before analyzing it using data mining techniques.

Chapter 3, "Software Installation and Introduction to RapidMiner," provides a detailed guide for beginners who want to practice using RapidMiner. Chapter 4, "Data Pre-Processing and Example of Data Classification With RapidMiner," guides a beginner in understanding data pre-processing and how to apply it using RapidMiner.

Chapter 5, "Classification," enables beginners to apply RapidMiner to classify data that answers business questions. Chapter 6, "Deep Learning," introduces the concept of deep learning and provides practice exercises using RapidMiner to apply deep learning techniques for data analytics.

Chapter 7, "Clustering," teaches beginners how to apply RapidMiner to divide data by clustering techniques. Chapter 8, "Association Rule Mining," introduces the creation of association rules from a dataset by RapidMiner.

Chapter 9, "Recommendation System," explains the concept of recommendation systems and how to apply them with RapidMiner. The chapter 10, titled "Case Studies on the Use of Data Mining Techniques in Data Science," furnishes the novice with the author's scrutinized data mining technique outcomes, thus facilitating the application of data mining to research domains.

Chapters 11 and 12, "Python Programming for Data Mining," introduce beginners who want to analyze data with more complex data mining techniques.

This book is ideal for beginners who want to grow in their data scientist career or anyone who wants to address internal and external issues using data in their organization. Get ready to dive into the exciting world of data mining using RapidMiner software with this guide.

Sarawut Ramjan
Thammasat University, Thailand

Jirapon Sunkpho
Thammasat University, Thailand

Chapter 1
Introduction to Data Mining

ABSTRACT

Data mining is a powerful and increasingly popular tool that uses machine learning to uncover patterns in data and help businesses stay competitive. Data scientists are trained to understand business objectives and select the correct techniques for data exploration and pre-processing. After formulating the business question, data mining methods are chosen and evaluated to determine their ability to fit the data set and answer the query. Results are then reported back to the business owner. Data mining is an essential part of modern business, allowing the organization to keep up with the competition and remain successful. With its growing popularity, the need for data scientists is rapidly increasing.

INTRODUCTION

Nowadays, data analysis using data mining is becoming more and more important. The digital ecosystem supports the storage of massive amounts of data either Cloud Technology or Database with large amount of memory. Moreover, these data are generated with users around the world in real time with high the speed communication through Social Networks resulting in a massive growth of data, known as Big Data. Businesspeople around the world can take advantage of it. For instance, to analyze customer purchasing patterns or predict the number of raw materials for production, it requires Data Mining techniques to analyze the patterns and predict the outcomes necessary for entrepreneurs' decision making.

Data analysis for business decision making can be done with various techniques such as Descriptive Statistics and Inferential Statistics. Therefore, the Data Mining technique is not a replacement for traditional data analysis, but it should be considered the development of advanced analysis techniques along with the work of machine learning technology. It supports the processing of large amount of data, Big Data. Consequently, Data Mining has yielded accurate results consistent with business questions.

DOI: 10.4018/978-1-6684-4730-7.ch001

IMPLEMENTATION OF DATA MINING AND CHALLENGES

With the need for problem analysis, it has created a position to be responsible for data analysis, namely Data Scientist. However, the Data Scientists are not solely from experts in digital technology, but they can be any person who owns the data. The medical technicians, who have information on the patients' health and understand the context of medical industry, question asking and the nature of the data, can become a Data Scientist.

Many industries have employed data scientists who are not familiar with the industry or lack experiences in the data they are to analyze. Therefore, the data scientists have to consult the questioners, possibly from the management department, and the experts in order to obtain results consistent with the facts. Therefore, in the scientific work, the data can be applied in various industries as presented in the following examples.

- In the market, to determine the selling price, the consumers can see a model which consists of many sub-models. The prices vary depending on the car's components. However, the consumers can still find similar pricings in all sub-models. For instance, Sub-model 1 costs 1,000,000 baht. The 2nd Sub-model is priced at 1,600,000 baht and the 3rd Sub-model is priced 1,7000,000 baht. It is obvious that the difference between the 2nd and 3rd Sub-models is only 100,000 baht. Such a price setting is caused by dividing customers into 3 groups to suit the number of Sub-models which is three. Data mining techniques are then used to analyze the mid-prices of each customer segment of each Sub-model. Unless the data scientists analyze the data using the techniques, general businesspeople may divide the pricing into 1,000,000 baht, 1,300,000 and 1,700,000 baht for Sub-data respectively. The clustering techniques are, therefore, used to determine the price of car sales to be able to set a suitable price for each target group. And the dealers also get the most profit.
- To forecast the condominium price in Bangkok (Sunkpho and Ramjan, 2020) using data analysis, it was found that variables affecting the prices of the condominium in Bangkok are the distance from the condo to Skytrain and MRT stations, the number of rooms, the number of floors and the age of the condominiums. Data scientists use deep learning techniques to analyze such variables and the prices, and found that the smaller distance from the condo to the sky train and subway stations, the higher the prices are. The more numbers of rooms are, the lower the prices will become. The more floors the condos have, the higher the prices are. And if the age of the condominium is less, its price is high. Therefore, the condominium real estate industries can consider such variables to determine the appropriate prices of the condominium projects.
- To categorize borrowers with the ability to pay debts, Banks have to classify their borrowers. To promote bank services, the borrowers are convinced to extend their loans with attractive offers such as a lower interest rate (Refinance). Data scientists can use data mining techniques to classify the customers by analyzing various variables. Since the banks have information about borrowers such as age, income, loan duration, default rate and the amount of additional loans that have already been approved, they can classify borrowers with the ability to repay their debts, so that they can offer marketing promotions. Banks can increase their interest income further.

From the sample cases, Data scientists do not only need to develop their knowledge on data analysis with data mining techniques, but have to study on statistics, database technology, data visualization and knowledge relevant to the data analytics industry. Although data science offers benefits to a variety of industries, these industries still face dimensional the following challenges (Tanantong, 2020).

Scalability: The size of the data keeps growing from the updates of social network users or from the updates of business partners (Almasoud, Al-Khalifa and Al-Salman, (2019). For example, travel agents from around the world update their booking information through the Global Distribution System (GDS) at the same time and make transactions round the time. As a result, the databases grow larger by users all the time. Therefore, in the perspective of the industries that need to use big data for analysis, the algorithms in data management, accessing information, transferring data over a high-speed network as well as data mining techniques can support large-scale data processing.

High Dimensionality: With information technology, whether in the forms of photos or videos file with a higher resolution, it can detect the nature of obstacles. When combined, these autonomous vehicle pictures can generate huge amounts of high-resolution data (Lawal, Ibrahim, Sani and Yaakob, 2020). Consequently, the data scientists are required to improve their algorithms in Data Exploration and Pre-Processing for more accurate analysis.

Various and Complex Data: Since organizations store information in a data warehouse, the warehouse contains a large number of Attributes and Data Types because the data created by each social network platform varies depending on its design (Berman, 2018). Therefore, it is a great challenge for data scientists to collect those data and select only the attributes useful for the analysis. Moreover, to prepare data from a variety of sources, the data scientists need to optimize data and shape them into the same standards appropriate for each type of data mining technique.

Data Ownership and Distribution: At present, organizations around the world store data through cloud technology with the distributed storage system. As a result, the source of data is spread all over the world as well. Accessing large volumes of data requires high-speed and highly secured public networks (Jiang, Jiang and Wang, 2020). Therefore, the security of data retention and each country's data processing rights have become a challenge for data scientists. In Thailand, where the Personal Data Protection Act is enforced, data scientists cannot take customer data for analysis without consent.

DATA ANALYSIS PROCESS WITH DATA MINING TECHNIQUES

Data Mining Technique is to analyze the data and search for data patterns from large datasets (Bramer, 2016). It is divided into four main categories; Classification, Numerical Prediction, Association Rule, and Clustering. These analytical techniques are not recently emerging but have been used for data analysis in order to obtain results in various forms of decision making. The main difference between data mining techniques and the descriptive and inferential statistical analysis is the use of Machine Learning (ML) techniques (Bell, 2015: Chiarini, Kohli and Forsgren, 2021). As a result, data mining techniques are able to analyze data until the results are closer to the facts. In addition, the development has resulted in a new forms of data processing such as Deep Learning which is suitable for analyzing large volumes of data and non-linear or Association Rule Mining. In turn, data scientists can apply the model to analyze data in accordance with business problems. Therefore, data mining techniques are used in various forms of knowledge discovery. For example, it can be used to analyze tumor patterns that can progress to become cancer. It can analyze the customers who have the ability to pay off loans, suitable for marketing promotions and expansion to new credit lines.

Data analysis process with data mining techniques in the form of Knowledge Discovery Process (Cardona, Gomez and Trujillo, 2014: Kyaw and Limsiroratana, 2019: Gupta, Sahayadhas and Gupta, 2020) consists of:

- **Data Sources:** Data scientists can access multiple data sources at the same time to determine the likelihood that those datasets can be used to analyze in order to obtain the results suitable for answering the questions.
- **Data Store:** Data scientists may collect data sets from a single source, in-house database, multiple sources, business partners and social networks such as Twitter. Data storage can be in a single data or a data set format, formed by merging datasets from multiple data sources.
- **Data Selection and Pre-Processing:** Data scientists can use data processing techniques to select data. For example, the relationship between variables in the data set and the target variables is analyzed by seeking expert advice on the data set. Then the data are prepared for processing with data mining techniques such as missing values, eliminating outliers.
- **Data Mining:** Data scientists need to choose the appropriate data mining techniques in order to obtain results that can be used to answer the questions. In the step, the data scientist can also review whether the data mining techniques are suitable for analyzing the existing datasets and whether it can answer the questions. Unless the dataset and data mining techniques are consistent, the data scientists can consider two scenarios; modifying the new data analysis method to replace the old method but obtaining the results that can be used interchangeably or considering changing the data set suitable for data analysis
- **Interpretation:** The results obtained from the analysis with data mining techniques still seem to be quantitative data or Data Visualization (Samasiri, 2020). Data scientists need to interpret the results so that questioners can understand it. Therefore, when asking those who wish to use the data, Data scientists need to firstly determine whether those questions require data mining techniques, or simply using the raw data to process is enough to answer those questions.

However, the Knowledge Discovery Process is generally used for data analysis. Cross-industry Standard Process for Data Mining: CRISP-DM was developed for the purpose of analyzing business-related data (SPSS Inc, 2000).

- **Business Understanding:** Initially, data scientists work with business questioners; a senior management or a domain expert; to define problems in which data visualization or data mining techniques can be used for answering a set of questions related to the business context. In the medical or sports industries all of which have different contexts, data scientists need to consider the internal environment within the organization such as budgets, human resources that support data analysis and the amount of time to analyze the data. The success of the data analysis should be set so that when it is completed, it can indicate whether the obtained data can be used to answer business questions. Finally, the technology used for both hardware and software analysis can be selected. For example, if the given question requires large data processing, data scientists need to use high-performance hardware computing to shorten the processing time. If they would like to reduce the time to create a model for data analysis, the ready-made software can be applied. But it costs higher compared to the data analysis by programming in open-source languages.

- **Data Understanding:** It is to verify whether existing data sets, either within the business or outside the business, such as customer feedback on social networks, can be used to analyze the data. In this process, the data scientists and the questioners can work together to ensure that the data therein is accurate and consistent with the business context. In turn, it can be used for analysis to answer business questions accurately and consistently. At this stage, the data scientists must consult with the data experts to define the meaning and specify the format of the data type as well as conducting Data Exploration through various tools in the form of visual information in order to check for outliers or incomplete information. Data scientists can then determine the appropriate data cleansing method for data preparation at the next step.

- **Data Preparation:** It is the process by which a data scientist refines a dataset into a format appropriate, for data mining techniques, by eliminating incomplete data, replenishing missing data or combining datasets from multiple sources. At this stage, the data scientist selects the data able to be used for processing the result (Feature Selection). And through the process of understanding the data, data scientists have to choose a method for cleaning the data, such as filling in incomplete data or eliminating empty data as well as modifying the types of data ready for data analysis with data mining techniques such as changing letters into numbers. Then the data scientists will create a data set from the data that has been cleaned to become a ready-to-use dataset for data analysis with data mining techniques.

- **Modeling:** Data scientists choose a data mining technique, Polynomial Regression or Simple Linear Regression, corresponding to the problem set, to get the results that are in line with the needs of business people. The results of the analysis of the data that are closest to the facts can be selected. This is reflected in the processing efficiency of each data mining technique. Once Supervised-Learning data mining technique has been selected, the data scientists need to consider data segmentation in order to teach machine learning the Trian Set. Then, the proportion of the data used in the test was considered (Test Set) before bringing all the data to analyze within the model. In this step, the data scientist can go back and refine the data to be ready for data analysis so that the obtained results are more accurate.

- **Model Evaluation:** Data scientists can select a number of data mining techniques with data analysis capabilities that can be used to serve the same purpose. In other words, to evaluate the model performance, precision of the model is not the only thing to be considered, but also the consistency of the analysis results. In many cases, the data scientists may find that the results obtained from the data analysis may not be consistent with the business questions. The scientists can set the success of data analysis in the business understanding process as a measure of the effectiveness of data analysis.

- **Deployment:** This is to take the results to answer business questions in order to support business decisions. The results can forecast the amount of raw material that should be prepared for the 4th quarter. In this process, the results obtained from the data mining techniques are numerical. This requires the interpretation of results in a format that the general public can understand. Therefore, the data scientists are required to prepare an oral presentation along with the preparation of supporting documents so that business questioners can understand the results obtained from the analysis. Also, during the presentation the data scientists can pose questions from other perspectives. Moreover, in future data analysis projects including providing feedback to the organization on the information, the organization needs to collect and gather data beneficial for future analysis.

From Knowledge Discovery Process and Cross-industry Standard Process for Data Mining: CRISP-DM. This book summarizes the data analysis process with data mining techniques as shown in Figure 1.

Figure 1. Data analysis using data mining techniques

As shown in Figure 1, the process starts with understanding business problems and determining the problems with the management team. Then the survey is conducted and the data are prepared by considering the resources in order to obtain the appropriate answers to the questions. In this step, data scientists need to consult with data experts, especially those who are familiar with the industry. Then the data are prepared for processing with data mining techniques. During processing, the data scientists have to choose a data mining technique, consistent with their answers. Multiple techniques can be selected at the same time and the degree of accuracy of each model is tested to obtain the results. Afterward, the effectiveness of the results is tested by the data experts to reflect whether the results can be used to answer the questions. In the last section, the data scientists make an oral presentation to interpret the analysis results to the executives who are also the questioners.

SUPERVISED LEARNING

Regarding Supervised Learning Data Mining Techniques (Abdul and Starkey, 2020), data scientists need to define the target variables (Data Labelled) used for data analysis. Then the data set is divided into 2 parts. The first part is for teaching machines to learn. The second part is for testing data sets according to established data mining techniques. The data mining techniques that are classified as Supervised Learning are as follows.

Classification

Classification is to categorize the data (Maslan, Mohamad and Mohd, 2020). For example, if doctors want to categorize patients with COVID-19 into 3 categories, asymptomatic patients who show no symptoms, symptomatic patients and severe patients, other variables are required to classify data according to the classification rules as follows.

If the diagnosis = COVID-19 and symptoms detected = symptomatic and symptom level = severe condition, then patient status = severe patient.

If the diagnosis = COVID-19 and symptoms detected = symptomatic and symptom level = mild symptoms, then patient status = symptomatic patient.

If the diagnosis = COVID-19 and symptoms detected = asymptomatic, then patient status = asymptomatic patient.

The classification can only be done only if there is a result of a variable that supports the effect of a classification, such as diagnosis, symptoms, and level of symptoms which are the variables of COVID-19. And the classification outcome is the target variable. Classification rules can be described as Decision Tree (Romero et. al., 2019) to illustrate variables as presented in Figure 2.

Besides classification rules, the nearest neighbor matching method can also be applied (Atanasovski, Kostov, Arapinoski and Spirovski, 2020) by identifying what kind of data it is classified from the nearest information. For example, if the car model data is close to the data of other luxury cars, such car model will be classified as a luxury car.

Figure 2. Decision tree diagram

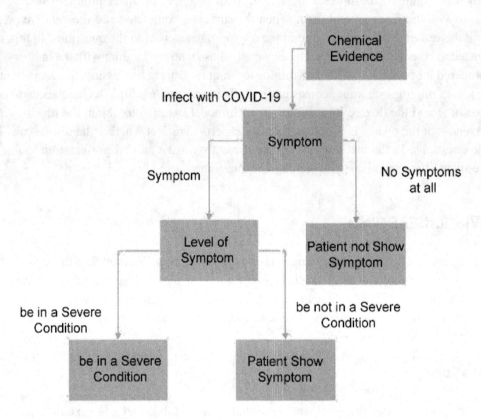

Numerical Prediction

Numerical Prediction is classified as Supervise Learning (Liu et. al., 2021) which requires setting the target variable and analyzing the data from other variables. For example, it can be applied to analyze students' height with Simple Linear Regression. Other well- numerical data forecasting include Neural Networks that can use multiple variables to predict target outcomes, and Deep Learning which is appropriate for data processing with large volumes and non-linearity. Through such processing, the datasets need to be divided; for machine learning and for testing based on numerical forecasting.

UNSUPERVISED LEARNING

Unsupervised Learning is the techniques in which the data scientists do not need to determine the target variables nor to divide the datasets into machine learning and testing parts (Shrestha, Razavi and Prasad, 2020). All data can be processed to achieve the desired results. The data mining techniques classified as Unsupervised Learning are as follows:

Association Rule Mining

Association Rule Mining is used to analyze the relationship of data within a single variable or multiple variables. For example, marketers need to know what Hashtags they should write to present their products on Twitter to match the needs of customers. In response to such a question, the data scientists can use Association Rule Mining techniques to analyze the association rules of these data, as presented in the example (Tanantong and Ramjan, 2021).

Hashtag $_1$, Hashtag $_2$, Hastag$_3$, ..., Hashtag $_n$ => {Supply} or
Hashtag $_1$, Hashtag $_2$, Hastag$_3$, ..., Hashtag $_n$ => {Demand} or
Hashtag $_1$, Hashtag $_2$, Hastag$_3$, ..., Hashtag $_n$ => {Others}

According to the samples, data scientists can perform an analysis of hashtags within Twitter. This allows marketers to determine which hashtags they should use in order to be consistent with the purchasing needs of their customers within Twitter. For example, #SellingBlackpinkConcertTickets, which is a hashtag about selling products, together with #LookingForBlackpinkConcertTickets, which is a Hashtag about the need to purchase products will allow customers to find a group of such Twitter messages faster.

Clustering

Clustering is to group data from 2 or more variables (Reddy and Aggarwal, 2014). Data scientists can take a series of data on the width and length of the pants legs that former customers bought from the factory. Then the number of desired groups is specified as presented in the Figure 3.

Figure 3. Clustering of pant sizes that the factory wants to produce
Source: Tanantong and Ramjan (2022)

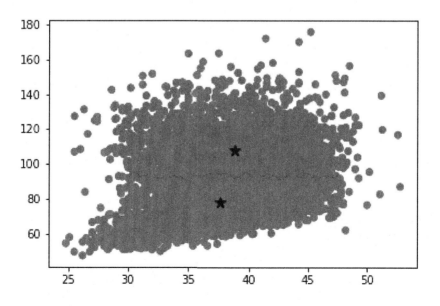

From the figure, the data scientists can take the data on the pant leg width displayed on the x-axis and the pant leg length displayed on the y-axis to create a data point, and the data are then divided into 2 groups. The red color represents Group 1, and the blue represents Group 2. In each group, there is an intersection (Centroid) which the data scientists can use in order to determine the 2 sizes of the pants that the factory should produce.

DATA ANALYSIS TOOLS

In data science, there are tools to analyze huge amounts of data. The steps of the data analysis and data collection are as follows:

Data Collection: In the case that the data scientists are in the organization and required to analyze data, they can access to data sources directly with permission from their organization. But for the scientists who need to use public information such as information from websites or social networks, they can use tools such as the Twitter API for extracting data from Twitter (Hernandez-Suarez et. al., 2018) and Python Web Scraping for extracting data from websites (Nigam. et. al. 2021).

Survey and Data Preparation: If the data scientists develop themselves from people working in the digital field, they can write programs, such as R or Python to explore data. It can develop data visualizations in various ways. The highlight of these languages is that it is an open-source software so the purchase of the software is free of no charge. On the other hand, the data scientists, who once was data experts, may choose to use software packages such as Microsoft Power BI, Tableau or RapidMiner to explore data. Data scientists can then choose to prepare the data through Python by improving the data format, combining data from multiple datasets, removing incomplete data, filling incomplete data or preparing data using models within RapidMiner software. To prepare uncomplicated data, the data scientists can also use Microsoft Excel software.

Data Processing With Data Mining Techniques: Data scientists can still choose to write a program with Python in order to process data from libraries. Python has provided for both supervised learning and unsupervised learning. RapidMiner software can be applied to support modeling in all forms of data mining processing techniques and displaying both statistical data and visual information. Therefore, RapidMiner software has gained popularity and overcomes the limitations of the data scientists who lack programming skills. It assists them to use data mining techniques in their data science work.

Data Presentation: In this process, the data scientists can seek advice from a data expert in order to verify the effectiveness of the processing. The results shown via Python or RapidMiner can be used to be relay to the questioner. The data scientists need to translate the results to infer the answers the questioners need. In other cases, if such questions do not require the use of data mining techniques for analysis, the data scientists can also use a variety of software to develop visual data to answer those questions.

Thus, RapidMiner software is a data science tool that supports every step of the data scientist's work. There are also machines used for processing with complete data mining techniques, and data scientists do not need to write programs. This book is, therefore, use RapidMiner software to demonstrate data processing with various data mining techniques.

CASE STUDY

World-wide educational institutions have recognized the importance of data science, from the survey process, data preparation, data visualization and data mining processing. Not only institutions of higher education, but private-sector academies focus on providing short-term coursework to enable learners to re-skill, transforming themselves to become data scientists. For those who are data scientists can also increase their knowledge and abilities even higher. At present, many universities are using online learning and teaching methods, both in the form of the university itself and partnerships such as *Coursera* or *EdX*. Students can study one subject at a time and receive a certificate. When students complete the compulsory courses, those certificates can be converted into credits to university coursework in order to obtain a degree. There are also data scientists who intend to share their knowledge independently from university teaching. Those scientists can organize their own training courses through online platforms such as *Udemy*.

An interesting difference between the teaching and learning management of universities, the private sectors and independent data scientists is the cost of education. If students are looking for a certificate or a degree from a world-leading university, they may choose to study through an online platform that the university manages itself or through a partner platform. To study in this manner, students need to have a reasonable budget for studying. On the other hand, if students would like to learn without expecting a certificate from a world-class university, they can save money by choosing to study with independent data scientists who provide online courses through online platforms. Surely, on the internet, students still have access to data science resources where data scientists share their passions, a wealth of knowledge and experience through *YouTube* channels.

Therefore, this book introduces interesting courses on self-improvement in data science, especially the courses that are taught through the Online Platform.

UNIVERSITY COURSES TAUGHT THROUGH ONLINE PLATFORM

Nowadays, universities world-wide have become aware of distance learning management. They have developed both graduated and non-graduated courses for students to study through online platforms from anywhere and at any time in the world. Besides, in the countries where English is not the official language, there are also universities that provide courses in their native language having English subtitles for lectures. Therefore, learners are no longer limited in their educational opportunities by language barriers. And what is interesting is the *First Mover Higher Education Institutions*, leading universities of the world, are stepping into the distance education industry. Regardless of where in the world the learners reside, they can study at an internationally standard tertiary institution. Therefore, this section of the book introduces online master's degree programs related to data science work in which readers can start studying a series of courses and collect all the credits.

The Master of Computer Science program offered by the University of Illinois provides a Data Science major in which students gain knowledge of machine learning, data mining, visualization data creation and processing big data with Cloud Server. Students can study courses to earn credits and gradually combine them into a Master of Computer Science for graduation, such as the course of Deep Learning Visuals.

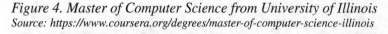

Figure 4. Master of Computer Science from University of Illinois
Source: https://www.coursera.org/degrees/master-of-computer-science-illinois

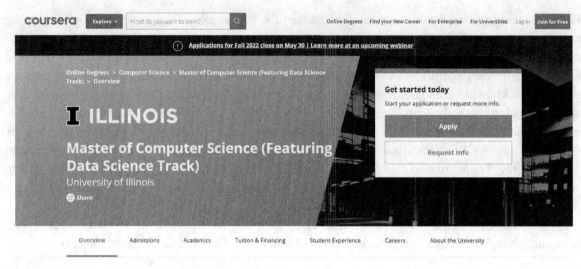

When there is a course improvement, it may result in the students being unable to bring the credits to combine for a Master of Computer Science graduation, but the students can still complete the afore-mentioned subjects to enhance their knowledge. However, for those who are interested in studying for a degree, the University of Illinois offers the following specializations:

- **Machine Learning:** Is a subject on using machine learning to analyze audio data, geography, computer vision, and natural language processing.
- **Data Visualization:** is about creating visual data using *Tableau* program so that data scientists can use the developed visual data for effective presentation. The visualization data can also inter-act to show the details of the data analysis in different dimensions.
- **Data Mining:** Is regarding the analysis of unstructured data and patterns of the data being analyzed.
- **Cloud Computing:** Is about *Cloud* computing technology, infrastructure development and ap-plication development to prepare a Cloud environment suitable for analyzing data from Big Data.

When graduating, the learner will acquire the specific skills which are the ability to process big data in *Cloud* environment, data analysis skills to support decision-making and principles of using data sci-ence for research as well as the use of tools to support data analysis with data science.

Such courses are a broad framework for learning content. If students would like to earn a degree, they will still have to take additional compulsory subjects such as *Cloud* Computing Capstone and Practical Statistical Learning, and will also have to take other elective subjects such as Internet of Things and Methods for Applied Statistics. In all subjects, students must obtain a grade of at least B-level. Students can also complete all course in 1 year or take up to 5 years. Throughout the course, they can connect with teachers and teaching assistants through the Discussion Board.

Eligible applicants to study for a degree must have completed a bachelor's degree, obtaining a minimum 3.20 GPA out of 4.00 and should have a background in object-oriented programming, Data Builder and

Algorithm. However, students who do not have such skills can enroll for these courses on programming fundamentals and data structures. And for those who are from Non-Native English-speaking countries are required to present TOEFL/IELTS results to apply for the course.

Master of Science in Analytics From Georgia Institute of Technology

Figure 5. Master of Science in Analytics, Georgia Institute of Technology Teaching through EdX's online platform
Source: https://www.edx.org/masters/online-master-science-analytics-georgia-tech

The Georgia Institute of Technology's Master of Science in Analytics is a joint program of Georgia Tech's College of Engineering, College of Computing, and Scheller College of Business, with majors focused on three areas: Analytical Tools, Business Analytics and Computation Data Analytics. Students will also be able to choose from the Analytics: Essential Tools & Methods MicroMasters Program to study without expecting a degree. The courses can also be credited toward postgraduate study. It consists of the following courses:

- **Introduction to Analytics Modeling:** Is a related course to understand data, data forecasting and data analysis for business decision making. In this subject, students will understand how to choose the right datasets, algorithms, techniques and patterns in data analysis to support decision-making in solving business problems. Students will learn R language as an analysis tool and practice modeling in data analysis which covers Classification, Clustering, Change Detection, Data Smoothing, Validation, Prediction, and Optimization.
- **Computing for Data Analysis:** Is a course that covers data collection, data storage, data analysis and visualization data. In this subject, students will use data analysis tools including Python, R, and SQL, using the software editor, Jupyter notebooks. Students will gain knowledge in quantitative data analysis that integrates statistical data analysis methods with computer programming by applying those statistics as data processing algorithms.
- **Data Analytics for Business Course:** Provides students with an understanding of real-world business case studies and the application of data analytics techniques to support decision-making to address problems in those case studies. It covers the collection of data, analysis of various forms

of data, exploring patterns of data, bringing the dataset to test according to the hypothesis set. This course also covers the challenges regarding data analytics the business world is facing. In this course, R language is used as a tool to practice experimenting with datasets.

Once students have studied in the Micro Master's course, they can continue to study at the Georgia Institute of Technology through the university's Online Platform.

Figure 6. The Georgia Institute of Technology's Master of Science in Analytics program is offered through the university's online platform
Source: https://pe.gatech.edu/degrees/analytics

In order to earn a degree, students must choose to study major subjects, which are divided into 3 majors:

MAJOR: ANALYTICS TOOL

Section 1: Compulsory Courses

- **Introduction for Computing for Data Analysis:** In this course, students will learn about data analysis, programming, database access, multidimensional array, quantitative data processing and the visual data development from case studies and practices.
- **Introduction to Analytics Modeling:** This course discusses various models and data analysis techniques including Classification, Clustering, Time Series, regression, experimental design for testing data distribution, composition analysis, modeling, preparing Model Validation Data, and selecting features used in Data Analysis.
- **Business Fundamentals for Analytics:** This course is regarding fundamentals of management and business terminology, which provide students with an understanding of the concepts enable businesspeople to work in the business world

Section 2: Advanced Compulsory Courses

- **Data and Visual Analytics:** In this course, students will learn how to create multidimensional visual data by focusing on both theoretical and practical studies with datasets in case studies.
- **Data Analytics in Business:** This course deals with extracting data from business datasets. It covers methodology, process V, and challenges related to data analysis in business.

Section 3: Elective Courses in Statistics – Students Can Choose Two Subjects From the Entire List of Courses

- **Time Series Analysis:** Forecasting data from stored data based on time in each period.
- **Regression Analysis:** This course covers the use of statistics for forecasting data by using Bayesian techniques for data analysis and testing hypotheses.
- **Data Mining and Statistical Learning:** This course covers the use of data mining techniques and statistical principles in data analysis such as K-NN, regression analysis, and neural networks, using R language as a tool for experimenting with data mining techniques.

Section 4: Elective Courses in Practice – Students Have to Choose One Subject

- **Simulation:** It covers the use of models to analyze data for problem solving.
- **Deterministic Optimization:** In this course, students will learn about the concepts of linear algebra and calculus, as well as the concept of calculating suitable values using various techniques.

Section 5: Elective Courses – Students Have to Choose Three Subjects

In this section, students can choose to study subjects in other sections so that the coursework in this section can complete collecting credits. However, there are other subjects in this section for students to choose.

- **Big Data Analytics:** In the Health Industry: Students will learn about the analysis and development of multidimensional visual data, both theory and practice from case studies in the health industry.
- **Database System Concepts and Design:** Students will learn about relational databases, database design and query processing.
- **Machine Learning for Trading:** In this course, students will learn about the challenges of applying Machine Learning to Trading, algorithms for collecting data from market orders, data analysis for trading decisions using Linear regression, KNN and Regression Trees that are appropriate for each case.

Section 6: Applied Analytics Practicum

In this section, students need to develop projects in the Analytics Tool by bringing business problems from the real cases of their work to use as topics in project preparation. Students are required to produce a report explaining the scope of the project, data analysis purposes, project management plan and results in data analysis.

MAJOR: BUSINESS ANALYTICS

Section 1: Compulsory Courses

- **Introduction for Computing for Data Analysis:** In this course, students will learn about data analysis, programming, database access, multidimensional array, quantitative data processing and the development of visual data from case studies and practice.
- **Introduction to Analytics Modeling:** This course discusses various data analysis models and techniques, including Classification, Clustering, Time Series, regression, experimental design for testing the data distribution, composition analysis, modeling, preparing Model Validation data and selecting Features to use in data analysis.
- **Business Fundamentals for Analytics:** This course deals with fundamentals of management and business terminology to provide students with conceptual understandings enable business people to work in the business world.

Section 2: Advanced Compulsory Courses

- **Data and Visual Analytics:** In this course, students will learn how to create multidimensional visual data by focusing on both theoretical and practical studies with datasets in the case studies.
- **Data Analytics in Business:** This course deals with extracting data from business datasets. It covers methodology, process V, and challenges related to data analysis in business.

Section 3: Elective Courses in Statistics – Students Choose Two Subjects From the Entire List of Courses

- **Time Series Analysis:** Forecasting data from stored data based depending on time in each period.
- **Regression Analysis:** This course covers the use of statistics to forecast data by using Bayesian techniques for data analysis and hypotheses test.
- **Data Mining and Statistical Learning:** This course covers the use of data mining techniques and statistical principles in data analysis such as K-NN, regression analysis, and neural networks using R language as a tool for experimenting with data mining techniques.

Section 4: Elective Courses in Practice – Students Have to Choose One Subject

- **Simulation:** This course covers the use of models to analyze data in problem solving.
- **Deterministic Optimization:** In this course, students will learn about the concepts of linear algebra and Calculus, as well as the concept of calculating suitable values using various techniques.

Section 5: Elective Courses – Students Need to Choose Three Subjects

In this section, students can choose to study subjects in other sections so that the coursework in this section can complete collecting credits. However, there are other subjects in this section for students to choose.

- **Digital Marketing:** Students will explore a wide range of digital marketing concepts including mobile marketing, email marketing and social media marketing, and the use of marketing analytics tools such as search engine optimization, pay-per-click advertising.
- **Financial Modeling:** In this course, students will learn about creating spreadsheets using pivot tables, using Excel functions to analyze data, writing VBA. It covers applications in analysis, financial report, cost analysis and pricing. Students therefore can build financial models.

Section 6: Applied Analytics Practicum

In this section, students need to develop projects in the Analytics Tool by bringing business problems from the real cases of their work to use as topics in project preparation. Students are required to produce a report explaining the scope of the project, data analysis purposes, project management plan and results in data analysis.

MAJOR: COMPUTATIONAL DATA ANALYTICS

Section 1: Compulsory Courses

- **Introduction for Computing for Data Analysis:** In this course, students will learn about data analysis, programming, database access, multidimensional array, quantitative data processing, and the development of visual data from case studies and practices.
- **Introduction to Analytics Modeling:** This course discusses various data analysis models and techniques including Classification, Clustering, Time Series, regression, experimental design for testing the distribution of data, composition analysis, modeling, Preparing Model Validation Data, and Selecting Feature used in Data Analysis.
- **Business Fundamentals for Analytics:** This course deals with fundamentals of management and business terminology to provide students with conceptual understanding enable business people to work in the business world.

Section 2: Advanced Compulsory Courses

- **Data and Visual Analytics:** In this course, students will learn how to create multidimensional visual data, focusing on both theoretical and practical studies with datasets in the case studies.
- **Data Analytics in Business:** This course deals with extracting data from business datasets. It covers methodology, process V, and challenges related to data analysis in business.

Section 3: Elective Courses in Statistics – Students Choose Two Subjects From the Entire List of Courses

- **Time Series Analysis:** This course deals with data forecast from stored data based on time in each period.
- **Regression Analysis:** This course covers the use of statistics for data forecast, using Bayesian techniques for data analysis and testing the hypotheses.
- **Data Mining and Statistical Learning:** This course covers the use of data mining techniques and statistical principles in data analysis such as K-NN, regression analysis, and neural networks, using R language as a tool for experimenting with data mining techniques.

Section 4: Elective Courses in Practice – Students Have to Choose One Subject

- **Simulation:** This course covers the use of models to analyze data for problem solving.
- **Deterministic Optimization:** In this course, students will learn about the concepts of linear algebra and Calculus, as well as the concept of calculating suitable values using various techniques.

Section 5: Elective Courses – Students Need to Choose Three Subjects

In this section, students can choose to study subjects in other categories so that the coursework in this section can collect complete credits. However, there are other subjects in this section for students to choose.

- Knowledge-Based AI
- Reinforcement Learning
- Deep Learning

Section 6: Applied Analytics Practicum

In this section, students need to develop projects in the Analytics Tool by bringing business problems from the real cases of their work to use as topics in project preparation. Students are required to produce a report explaining the scope of the project, data analysis purposes, project management plan and results in data analysis.

With a wide variety of majors, learners can choose from categories and majors for flexibility in graduation. Georgia Institute of Technology guarantees the quality of education through EdX's online platform, provided by the Georgia Institute of Technology itself, as it is equivalent to studying on campus by equipping the same faculty teaching onsite at the Georgia Institute of Technology. When students enroll the Master of Science in Analytics course, they receive an orientation from the course director to be well prepared and enabled to write through Online Platform until graduation. The cost of studying is approximately 275 USD per credit, so throughout the course students can budget for approximately 9,900 USD with additional tuition fees of 301 USD per semester.

Figure 7. Master of Science in Digital Business Transformation (Data Science) from Thammasat University
Source: https://www.skilllane.com/academic/tuxsa/datascience

A leading university named Thammasat University is located in a Southeast Asia, Thailand. The university has provided a course in the Master of Science in Digital Business Transformation (Data Science) course. This course is a collaboration between Thammasat University and Online Platform Skilllane, which is an educational Start Up in Thailand in organizing an online master's degree program under the name *TUXSA* in Thai. *TUXSA* also means skill, corresponding to SkillLane's name. The Master of Science in Digital Business Transformation (Data Science) program is under the College of Innovation, one of the faculties of Thammasat University.

In the aforementioned course, various learning styles are provided to grant certificates for each course. Students can choose to study to improve their knowledge or choose to study to collect credits for further study to receive a degree at Thammasat University by registering for the final exam after completing the course content. They can also study to receive a Data Science certificate after gaining 18 credits. Compulsory courses are as follows.

- **Python for Data Science:** In this course, students will learn about the fundamentals of programming using Python, problem analysis, Algorithm of sequential programming, programming for creating conditions, programming for reprogramming the computer, and case studies in the field of data science.

- **Python for Advanced Data Science Applications:** Students will explore the relationship of Python programming to data science, the structure of Supervised-Learning and Unsupervised-Learning, the use of data mining techniques in data analysis, and visual data presentation.
- **Business Intelligence:** In this course, students will learn about the principles of integrating data from various sources, designing indicators to measure business performance, data extraction, feature engineering, dashboard designing, and the use of Microsoft Power BI as practical tools for case study practices.
- **Text Analytics**: This is a course on data mining techniques used to extract text patterns and data from websites, evaluation of the efficiency of the algorithm used to extract the data, Semi-structured and unstructured data relationships for data drilling and limitations of data mining in each model, application of forecasting and data clustering techniques, and evaluating the effectiveness of the results obtained from data drilling.
- **Data Mining Algorithm:** In this course, students will learn about the concept of accessing data within a database and data mining, data extraction from data mining, the use of Decision Tree, classification and clustering, and current data Mining case studies.
- **Advanced Data Mining Algorithms:** This course builds on Data Mining Algorithms, aiming to provide learners with essential data mining techniques including Neural Network, K Nearest Neighbor (K-NN) and Logistic Regression, along with applied case studies, using data mining in different industries.
- **Data Exploration:** Students will learn about the process of exploring data, access to resources, understanding data types and learning about exploring data techniques using R language as an experimental tool along with case studies.
- **Data Preprocessing:** Students will realize the importance of data preparation before using it in data mining analysis, covering data selection, data cleaning, data integration, data reduction, and data engineering.
- **Fundamental of Digital Transformation:** Students will learn about creating digital competence for organizations, designing customer experiences with digital technology, and internal process improvement.
- **Advanced Digital Transformation:** It is a course about modifying business models, change management, engaging people in the organization for change, instilling digital skills for people in the organization, and digital platforms that affect internal processes of the organization.
- **Data Science Capstone Project:** It is a data science project consisting of questioning for data analysis, seeking for data, data mining, data preparation, using models for data analysis, data visualization, and data interpretation.
- **Data Science Research Methodology:** This course prepares students for independent research consisting of Research problems, hypotheses, literature reviews, quantitative data analysis, qualitative data analysis, experimental data analysis, hypothesis testing, interpretation of results, summarizing results, citations, and writing research reports and academic articles.

When students have completed all the courses, they can apply for the Comprehensive Examination and the result is used for admission to the College of Innovation Thammasat University. When becoming students at Thammasat University, they can also take elective courses and conduct independent research to complete their studies. The elective courses are as follows:

- **Business Case for Data Science:** This is a course that discusses the context and the use of data across industries and within organizations, adaptation of the organization to development of data science today, the importance of different data types influencing the growth of a business or organization, the role of data analysts and the challenges and barriers of data science, future trends in data science, the relationship of data and artificial intelligence, and application of artificial intelligence in business.
- **Developing Solution and Engagement:** Students will learn how to apply digital technology to solve problems at organizational and national levels by searching for connections between problems and types of technology in order to analyze, plan, create or use technology to meet the needs and solve problems at organizational and national levels with case studies.
- **Cyber Security Policy:** This course includes contents in Cybersecurity Technology, Encryption, Economics of Cybersecurity, Cyber Security Policy both nationally and internationally, Critical Infrastructure Protection, Disaster Recovery Planning, and Cybersecurity case studies.
- **Cyber Threat and Security:** This course covers internet technology and networking, information technology system security, Internet threats at the malware level, cyber theft, movement for the benefit of the group and cyber warfare, and Privacy and Cyber Surveillance.
- **Digital Leadership:** In this course, students will be prepared to become executives in digital organizations by studying about communication skills, human relations management, conflict resolution, effects of leadership on Team Performance, morality, ethics and leadership, social conduct, environment, and human rights.
- **Digital Organization Behavior:** This course focuses on managing organizations that use digital technology, regarding leadership in the digital age, principles of Agile Management, leadership and risk management, awareness of innovation and creativity, incubating innovation, corporate culture, and optimization in the organization.
- **Design Thinking for Business Strategy and Entrepreneurship:** This course includes contents in design thinking process for developing a successful digital business strategy, and bringing the design thinking process to the opportunity. It starts with identifying stakeholder needs and barriers to create technological advantages that drive business growth, and to develop a digital product strategy to be in line with the market and operating system.
- **Design Thinking for Digital Society Architecture:** It is to apply design thinking processes to design social architecture in the digital era in order to achieve holistic harmony, and to apply the results of the design thinking process to analyze the social overview as well as managing differences in environment and culture that arise from the rapid change through the drive of digital technology.

The curriculum is 100% online where students can do their independent research and contact advisors to ask for advice, and do Defense Exam through online channels. Innovative College staff will schedule exams that are suitable for both the students and the committee.

Regarding qualifications of the applicants, those who have not completed the bachelor's degree can study the aforementioned subjects. However, the students are required to have a bachelor's degree in order to become an official Master degree student. Therefore, for those who are currently studying at high school or bachelor's level, can study various subjects and collect credits beforehand. And once having a bachelor's degree, they can then apply all the qualifications and compulsory courses that have been studied to register a Master degree here.

Figure 8. Data and Policy short-term course hosted by The University of Chicago
Source: https://info.harris.uchicago.edu/summer-scholar-program?hsLang=en

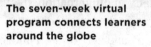

This short course from Harris School of Public Policy, The University of Chicago is delivered through the University's Platform by bringing the Domain of Public Policy as a case study throughout the training. It covers data collection, data cleaning, data analysis and data visualization development to solve the social problems. The program is also suitable for those with no experience in data science, as well as students or professionals who would like to re-skill to become the data scientist profession. The course covers the following contents.

- **Principles of Statistical Data Analysis:** It deals about the use of data analysis tools, a data analysis process that supports the development of public policy, the use of case studies to analyze problems, data analysis method, and interpretation of the results obtained from the data analysis.
- **Basic R Programming Language:** It is suitable for those who have no programming background. It enables learners to enter the basics of programming with R language, data extraction, data cleaning, data analysis and data visualization by using R language to write command sets.
- **Capstone Research Project:** The course prepares teachers to supervise in researches and create networking among students in a project. The project covers the process of research design and public policy analysis. The process is also consistent with the data analysis methods of data science work; data collection, data analysis, data visualization and model policy creation. The trainees will be able to apply the knowledge from the project to analyze the data in other domains.

After completing this course, students will receive an Official UChicago Transcript containing grades for each subject and a Certificate of Credential Completion for each trained subject.

In this course, students can access the videos of each lesson and each course over and over again through The University of Chicago's Platform. Students can also request a consultation with a course assistant through the Q&A. Regarding the Capstone Research Project, students will also have the opportunity to meet and consult with teachers in Live Lectures as well as work in groups with other learners who are attending the same class during the same period.

Regarding qualifications, students must be at least 18 years of age and have completed the first year of a bachelor's degree. Due to the fact that students have to work in groups with others, this course is conducted several times a year. Students can apply for classes according to the cycles. In this course some scholarships are also provided for the applicants who are eligible for scholarships.

Universities worldwide are keen to provide distance learning programs for both degree programs and non-degree programs. And after the COVID-19 crisis, these universities have adapted to teaching in the form of Live Sessions where learners have to access the class via applications. From such events, learners all over the world are acknowledging the effectiveness of video-based learning that is recorded on various online platforms. Thus, the direction of campus education has become a stepping stone in management evolution for university education.

COURSES OF THE INDUSTRY THAT ARE TAUGHT THROUGH ONLINE PLATFORMS

Industry around the world is experiencing a situation where the graduates or those who have graduated from short courses cannot work or do not have skills that meet the needs of that industry. In the data science industry, the digital data leading companies have created their own courses to produce employees to meet their needs. Those who have graduated from those courses can also use the certificate to apply for a job with any company that provides teaching and learning in data science on an online platform.

This book, therefore, provides examples of data science courses provided by the world's largest companies that would like to create skilled workers in line with their operational needs.

IBM Data Science Professional Certificate

IBM is a private company who produces Online Courses, especially in Professional Certificate, in collaboration with Coursera, an online platform in education. The tutors are IBM's data science experts. Learners can choose to earn a certificate for each course of a total of 10 courses, and combine all 10 courses to earn an IBM Data Science Professional Certificate.

The IBM Data Science Professional Certificate aims to help learners understand the concepts of working in data science, developing skills in using data analysis tools, data cleaning, creating visual data and using machine learning for data analysis focusing on the application of Python. This course is also suitable for those with no computer science background or programming skills. Similar to other short-term courses, this course promotes Re-Skill for those who want to transition from other careers to becoming a data scientist. The course consists of the following subjects.

- **Comprehension of Data Science Work:** It discusses the concept of data processing with an ancient Egyptian case study that ties taxation to the amount of water in the Nile to reflect the link between past processing and the value of Processing with today's data science principles.

Figure 9. Certificate in Data Science by IBM
Source: https://www.coursera.org/professional-certificates/ibm-data-science

- **Well-Known Data Science Tools:** There are Jupyter Notebooks, RStudio and GitHub, Computer programming in data science using Python and R. In this course, students also create projects related to data science.
- **Process of Data Science Work:** It discusses how to identify and analyze problems from business case studies including data collection, data analysis, modeling and understanding user feedback after the model is implemented to reflect the effectiveness of the model, which leads to solutions to specific business problems.
- **Use of Python in Data Science and Artificial Intelligence:** It starts with the basics in programming, data structure, data analysis with practice in programming as well as making projects based on the knowledge learned in this course. Python classes in Data Science and Artificial Intelligence can also be integrated into other IBM courses, including the IBM Applied AI Professional Certificate, Applied Data Science Specialization, and IBM Data Science Professional Certificate.
- **Creating a Python Project for Data Science:** This is to bring the data set, a case study, to demonstrate for students in writing a program to analyze data in the form of Dashboard, and when students want to register for this course, they need to pass the courses on the use of Python in data science and artificial intelligence before.
- **Database and SQL for Data Science With Python:** This course discusses the concept of Relational Database, retrieving data from a database by writing SQL statements, building a database in the cloud, and applying SQL statements with Python from Jupyter Notebooks.
- **Python Data Analysis:** Students will learn how to use Python for data exploration, data preparation before data analysis, the use of simple statistics to analyze data, preparation of visual data, data forcast, and data analysis models which covers libraries including Pandas, Numpy and Scipy, Scikit-Lern.
- **Data Visualization With Python:** This course applies storytelling to communication with data visualizations, Python programming for data extraction, understanding the data and the use of such data to support decision, which covers the Matplotlib, Seaborn and Folium libraries.

- **Machine Learning With Python:** This subject discusses a case study of real-world application of Machine Learning, principles of Supervised-Learning and Unsupervised-Learning, Evaluation of model performance, Algorithms of Machine Learning Processing. This course discusses data mining techniques including Regression, Classification and Clustering. The case studies are cancer detection, forecasting economic trends, forecasting the likelihood that users will switch to other product services, and referral systems.

- **Applied Data Science Capstone:** Students will assume the role of a data scientist for a startup company. Students will use the data science processes to analyze data. It includes surveying data, data visualization, data mining model development, evaluation of model performance, and interpreting the analysis results for the company so that the company can take that information into account for operating costs. The course will prepare a data set for learners to analyze.

Google Analytics Professional Certificate

Figure 10. Google Analytics Professional Certificate
Source: https://www.coursera.org/professional-certificates/google-data-analytics

The Google Analytics Professional Certificate course by Google, in partnership with Coursera Online Platform, focuses on building skills for anyone without restrictions on educational qualifications. Learners with no background and degrees in data science can attend such courses. This course covers data collection, data processing, data compiling for presentation and the use of data from the processing to make decisions. The course instructors are data science experts working at Google. Students will also be able to share hands-on experiences from those involved in the data science industry. Upon completion of the course, students can also get a certificate for applying to work with Google companies.

- **Foundations: Data, Data, Everywhere:** In this course, students will learn how to use SQL and R to process data, data science process as well as ecosystem terminology in data science work. This course will bring real case studies about data analysis to develop new products and improve internal processes of the organization used for data analysis. Students will gain experiences to become a Junior Data Scientist. This creates the opportunity to apply for a data scientist job.

- **Ask Questions to Make Data-Driven Decisions:** This course aims to help learners organize their thinking for effective questioning, which leads to the pursuit of resources that can be used for data processing. This course also prepares students to use worksheet software in data processing.
- **Prepare Data for Exploration:** In this course, students will learn how to determine the data sources suitable for analysis, structured or unstructured data types, characteristics of the bias types during data collection which affects the analysis and interpretation of the data processing results, the use of SQL to retrieve data within a database, data filtering, data compilation and data security.
- **Process Dirty for Data to Clean:** In this course, Google experts will use real-world case studies as an experimental tool. Learners will learn how to verify data completeness, data cleaning, the use of SQL for data cleaning and data processing, comprehension of data level probably used for processing after data cleanup, and preparation of data cleaning report.
- **Analyze Data to Answer Questions:** In this course, students will learn about a variety of data analysis methods Feature Engineering process, the use of formulas and functions within Spread Sheet Software and data processing using SQL language.
- **Share Data Through the Art of Visualization:** This course deals with the study of visual data development, creating a story to explain the visual data, practical use of *Tableau* for visualization and filtering, effective presentation, limitations that can arise and effective interaction with the audience.
- **Data Analysis With R Programming:** In this course, students will learn how to use Software Editor, which is R Studio, to write programs with R language, to use commands from the *Tidyverse* library, to comprehend the Data Frame and its implementation, and to develop visual data with R language.
- **Google Data Analytics Capstone: Complete a Case Study:** In this course, students will explore case studies in implementing data science processes in real-world datasets, including asking questions, data analysis, interpretation, visual data development. This course also provides students with interview questions for job vacancies in the field of data science.

Although students can choose to study any subject first, this course is designed for learners to study in an organized sequence in order to prepare students for professional skills in data science. The certificate they have received can be used to apply for a job anywhere, especially at Google company.

It is not a new trend that the industrial sector intends to produce workers that meet their own needs, so teaching and learning through Online Platform has become a new recruitment method. Moreover, due to the COVID-19 crisis spreading around the world, employees do not need to go to work at the company but work from home, so the company can recruit employees to work for them from anywhere. The potential of employees can be improved by taking the courses that the company provides on the Online Platform.

COURSES TAUGHT BY INDEPENDENT DATA SCIENTISTS

At present, there are many online platforms, which is one way to generate income for those who are highly skilled in various subjects and intend to bring their own knowledge to develop into courses for those who are interested. The emergence of this courses has greatly influenced the concept of non-credit education. And as a result, the value of graduate education is dwindling. In addition, the importance of the educational system through higher education institutions has also been decreasing because learners can study through the Online Platform with experts in various subjects. There is no limitation in recruiting and study time is flexible, so student can choose to take only the subjects that they are really interested. In addition, it is open for professionals to produce their own material, which has also become an opportunity for learners to choose instructors with high expertise and good transferability. In turns, the students feel it is worth the tuition fees they have paid.

The data science experts themselves, expectedly data scientists who are not professors in higher education institutions, have foreseen such avenues and produced many courses in data science varied from at the preliminary to higher levels through the online platforms. This book has picked up examples of courses that independent data scientists have developed and published through the online platform, as follows.

Python for Data Science and Machine Learning Bootcamp

Figure 11. Python for Data Science and Machine Learning Bootcamp via Udemy online platform
Source: https://www.udemy.com/course/python-for-data-science-and-machine-learning-bootcamp/

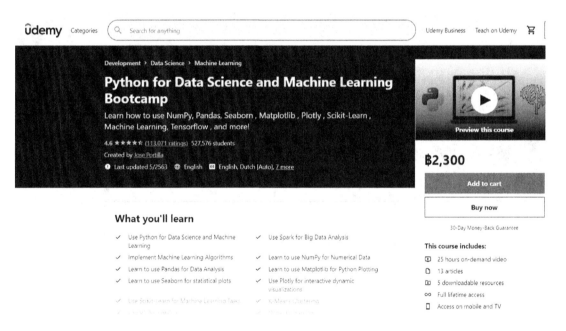

In Python for Data Science and Machine Learning Bootcamp, which produces courses from Jose Portilla through Udemy's online platform, learners will learn about Python programming for data science and machine learning, and apply machine learning algorithms to data processing. It covers critical libraries such as *Pandas* for data analysis, *Seaborn* and *Matplotlib* for visualization, *Plotly* for Interactive Visualizations, *NumPy* for Quantitative Data Analysis, and *Scikit-Learn* library for running commands for data mining techniques including K-Mean Clustering, Logistic Regression, Linear Regression, Random Forest Decision Trees, Natural Language Processing and Spam Filters, Neural Network and Support Vector Machines.

In this course, *Jupyter* is used as a software editor. The instructor also prepares a *Capstone Project* on financial data analysis to allow students to learn Python programming in real situations. The final part of the course also discusses Big Data processing with *Spark*, so students have a glimpse into the application of Python programming in Big Data processing.

However, for this subject, students need to have a good background in programming and the basic commands in Python before they can begin to learn the different types of command sets involved in processing. In the course, teachers have provided more than 100 Clips of teaching materials with detailed command sets.

Data Science and Machine Learning Bootcamp With R

Figure 12. Data Science and Machine Learning Bootcamp with R
Source: https://www.udemy.com/course/data-science-and-machine-learning-bootcamp-with-r/

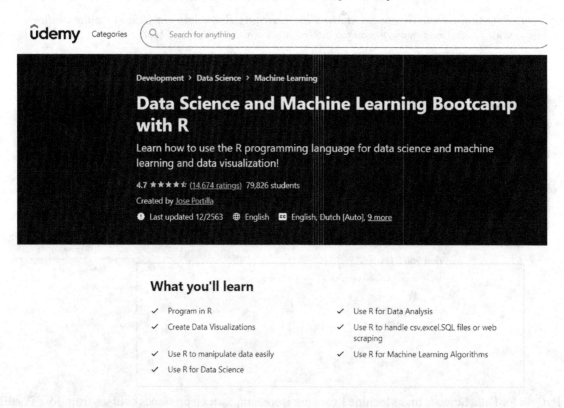

R is considered one of popular computer languages. Data Science and Machine Learning Bootcamp with R is an online course developed by Jose Portilla via Udemy online platform. Students will learn how to get started with installing R Studio and the R Translator, then learn about Matrix, Data Frames, Lists, Fundamentals of R Programming such as structural programming, recursive programming, conditional programming, visual data development, using machine learning for data analysis within R language, Linear Regression, Logistic Regression, K Nearest Neighbors, Decision Tree and Random Forest, Support Vector Machine, K- Mean Clustering, Natural Language Processing, Neural Nets.

Regarding data mining techniques and the development of visual data, instructors also provide a Capstone Project to every lesson so that students can experiment with data analysis from the data set that corresponds to the questions.

Therefore, this course is suitable for those who have no programming experience at all. The teacher will teach the foundation of programming using the R language as an experimental tool, and the application of R language for data analysis through over 100 video clips.

The Ultimate Hands-On Hadoop: Tame Your Big Data

Figure 13. The ultimate hands-on Hadoop: Tame your big data
Source: https://www.udemy.com/course/the-ultimate-hands-on-hadoop-tame-your-big-data/

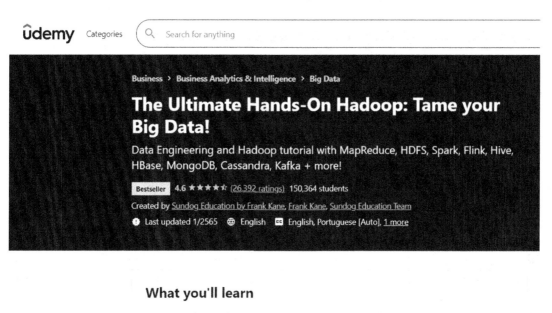

In The Ultimate Hands-On Hadoop: Tame Your Big Data course, developed by Frank Kane from Sundog Education Team on the online platform Udemy, students will learn about designing Distributed Systems for Big Data Management using Hadoop and Data Engineering Technologies, data analysis on Hadoop Cluster, relational data analysis using Hive and MySQL, non-relation data analysis using HBase, Cassandra and Mong DB, data querying, interactive using Dirll, Phoenix and Presto, choosing the right storage technology, understanding Hadoop Cluster Management using YARN, Tez, Zookeeper, Zeppelin, Hue and Oozie, real time Streaming Data management with Kafka, Flume, Spark Streaming, Flink and Storm.

In this course, the instructor provides hand-on lessons with over 14-hours-long video files that will provide students access to Big Data management on Hadoop. From business case studies, the learners are required to have a basic knowledge of programming in Python. Therefore, this course is ideal for Software Engineers and Developers who intend to gain more knowledge in the Hadoop ecosystem and how to use Hadoop to store and analyze data in Big Data, as well as Project or Product Managers who intend to understand Hadoop's architecture. Moreover, Data analyzes or Database administrators can also apply knowledge from this subject to their work as well.

From the example mentioned above, it can be seen that independent data scientists are experts in data science from their own hand-on experience and have the same content transfer skills. Therefore, for those who are already working in the data science industry and studying for a degree, it does not affect their career development as they can choose to study through this online platform.

KNOWLEDGE RESOURCES ON YOUTUBE CREATED BY INDEPENDENT DATA SCIENTISTS

From the case studies mentioned above, all of them are paid educational courses. However, within YouTube there are independent data scientists who are generous to share their knowledge to the public on a non-profit basis. Materials on data science are produced and uploaded on YouTube for anybody to learn. This book has picked up examples of teaching materials on YouTube as follows.

Data Analysis With Python: Full Course for Beginners (Numpy, Pandas, Matplotlib, Seaborn)

The data analysis with Python – Full Course for Beginners (Numpy, Pandas, Matplotlib, Seaborn) is produced by Santiago Basulto of RMOTR and is 4.22- hour-long, covering the topic of an overview of Python in data science, demonstration of using the Pandas library, Seaborn and the SQL language within Python for data analysis, using Jupyter Notebooks as a tool for testing command set, using Numpy for Data Pre-Processing, using the Pandas library for creating and manipulating data frames, and fetching external image datasets into commands.

Therefore, this course is suitable for those who intend to learn about data science and learn to write computer programs and to prepare the data for further data analysis before deciding to continue to more complex subjects.

TensorFlow 2.0 Complete Course: Python Neural Network for Beginners Tutorial

In addition to the introductory courses suitable for those who intend to get started with their data science careers, *YouTube* also offers free and fixed lessons. This course deals with high-level data analysis techniques such as the TensorFlow 2.0 Complete Course – Python Neural Network for Beginners Tutorial, which discusses programming in Python for data analysis using the Neural Network technique. This course was developed by *Tim Ruscica*.

Figure 14. Data analysis with Python: Full course for beginners (Numpy, Pandas, Matplotlib, Seaborn)
Source https://www.youtube.com/watch?v=r-uOLxNrNk8&list=RDLVua-CiDNNj30&index=4

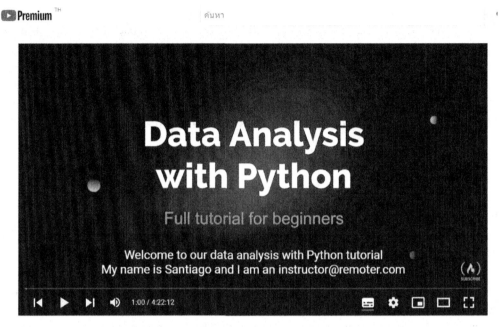

Data Analysis with Python - Full Course for Beginners (Numpy, Pandas, Matplotlib, Seaborn)

Figure 15. TensorFlow 2.0 complete course: Python neural network for beginners tutorial
Source: https://www.youtube.com/watch?v=tPYj3fFJGjk&list=PLWKjhJtqVAblStefaz_YOVpDWqcRScc2s&index=1

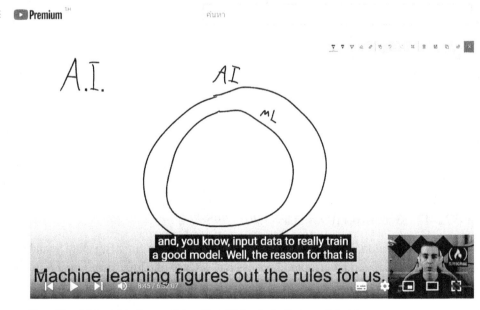

TensorFlow 2.0 Complete Course - Python Neural Networks for Beginners Tutorial

In this course, the content covers Principles of Machine Learning, Introduction to TensorFlow, Core Learning Algorithm, Neural Networks with TensorFlow, Convolutional Neural Networks, RNNs, Reinforcement Learning with Q-Learning.

According to the content, this course is suitable for anyone who has a background in Python programming and intend to practice Python programming to apply machine learning. In each lesson, the teacher explains the steps and commands in detail so that students can apply their knowledge to any other data set.

As is obvious, YouTube has free-of-cost contents available for both beginners and advanced data science students. Teachers may only expect learners to press Like, Share and Subscribe. And it is a good start for those who are not financially ready but would like to improve themselves.

CONCLUSION

Industries in the world see benefits from using data mining techniques to respond to business inquiries. Therefore, it is necessary to provide an environment conducive to data analysis such as creating a data scientist and purchasing software and hardware to facilitate big data processing. Data mining techniques are divided into Supervised Learning, which includes numerical classification and forecasting; and Unsupervised Learning model, which includes analysis of correlation and segmentation rules. RapidMiner software is popularly used because it can support every step of data analysis where the data scientists can create models for data preparation and analysis without writing any program.

EXERCISE QUESTIONS

1. Give an example of the application of data mining techniques in various industries.
2. Describe challenges of Scalability on Data Mining Processing.
3. Explain the meaning of Supervised Learning.
4. Explain the meaning of Unsupervised Learning.
5. Explain the differences of data analysis by program writing and using software packages.

REFERENCES

Abdul Aziz, A., & Starkey, A. (2020). Predicting Supervise Machine Learning Performances for Sentiment Analysis Using Contextual-Based Approaches. *IEEE Access : Practical Innovations, Open Solutions*, *8*, 17722–17733. doi:10.1109/ACCESS.2019.2958702

Almasoud, A. M., Al-Khalifa, H. S., & Al-Salman, A. S. (2019). Handling Big Data Scalability in Biological Domain Using Parallel and Distributed Processing: A Case of Three Biological Semantic Similarity Measures. *BioMed Research International*, *2019*, 1–20. doi:10.1155/2019/6750296 PMID:30809545

Atanasovski, M., Kostov, M., Arapinoski, B., & Spirovski, M. (2020). K-Nearest Neighbor Regression for Forecasting Electricity Demand. *2020 55th International Scientific Conference on Information, Communication and Energy Systems and Technologies (ICEST), Information, Communication and Energy Systems and Technologies (ICEST), 2020 55th International Scientific Conference On*, 110–113.

Bell, J. (2015). *Machine learning: hands-on for developers and technical professionals. John Wiley & Sons.*

Berman, J. J. (2018). Principles and practice of big data: preparing, sharing, and analyzing complex information (2nd ed.). Academic Press/Elsevier.

Bramer, M. (2016). *Principle of Data Mining* (3rd ed.). Springer-Verlag London Ltd.10.1007/978-1-4471-7307-6

Cardona, J. A. S., Gomez G, C. H., & Lopez Trujillo, M. (2014). Knowledge discovery process in the open government Colombian model. *2014 9th Computing Colombian Conference (9CCC), Computing Colombian Conference (9CCC), 2014 9th*, 96–102. 10.1007/978-1-4471-7307-6

Chiarini, T. M., Kohli, R., & Forsgren, N. (2021). Theories in Flux: Reimagining Theory Building in the Age of Machine Learning. *Management Information Systems Quarterly*, *45*(1), 455–459.

Gupta, A., Sahayadhas, A., & Gupta, V. (2020). Proposed Techniques to Design Speed Efficient Data warehouse Architecture for Fastening Knowledge Discovery Process. *2020 IEEE Third International Conference on Artificial Intelligence and Knowledge Engineering (AIKE)*.

Hernandez-Suarez, A., Sanchez-Perez, G., Toscano-Medina, K., Martinez-Hernandez, V., Sanchez, V., & Perez-Meana, H. (2018). *A Web Scraping Methodology for Bypassing Twitter API Restrictions.* Academic Press.

Jiang, S., Jiang, T., & Wang, L. (2020). Secure and Efficient Cloud Data Deduplication with Ownership Management. *IEEE Transactions on Services Computing*, *13*(6), 1152–1165.

Kyaw, K. S., & Limsiroratana, S. (2019). Case Study: Knowledge Discovery Process using Computation Intelligence with Feature Selection Approach. *2019 17th International Conference on ICT and Knowledge Engineering (ICT&KE), ICT and Knowledge.*

Lawal, M. M., Ibrahim, H., Sani, N. F. M., & Yaakob, R. (2020). Analyses of Indexing Techniques on Uncertain Data With High Dimensionality. *IEEE Access : Practical Innovations, Open Solutions*, *8*, 74101–74117. doi:10.1109/ACCESS.2020.2988487

Liu, Y.-Y., Li, L., Liu, Y.-S., Chan, P.-W., Zhang, W.-H., & Zhang, L. (2021). Estimation of precipitation induced by tropical cyclones based on machine-learning-enhanced analogue identification of numerical prediction. *Meteorological Applications*, *28*(2). Advance online publication. doi:10.1002/met.1978

Maslan, A., Mohamad, K. M. B., & Mohd Foozy, F. B. (2020). Feature selection for DDoS detection using classification machine learning techniques. *IAES International Journal of Artificial Intelligence*, *9*(1), 137–145. doi:10.11591/ijai.v9.i1.pp137-145

Nigam, H., Biswas, P., Raj, J. S., Iliyasu, A. M., Bestak, R., & Baig, Z. A. (2021). *Web Scraping: From Tools to Related Legislation and Implementation Using Python.* Academic Press.

Romero, M. P., Parry, J., Prosser, A., Upton, P., Rees, E., Tearne, O., Arnold, M., Chang, Y.-M., Brunton, L. A., Stevens, K., & Drewe, J. A. (2019). Decision tree machine learning applied to bovine tuberculosis risk factors to aid disease control decision making. *Preventive Veterinary Medicine*, 175. PMID:31812850

Samasiri, P. (2020). Visual representations of different family structures using an interactive data exploration technique. *2020 1st International Conference on Big Data Analytics and Practices (IBDAP), Big Data Analytics and Practices (IBDAP), 2020 1st International Conference On*, 1–5.

Shrestha, R. B., Razavi, M., & Prasad, P. W. (2020). An Unsupervised Machine Learning Technique for Recommendation Systems. *2020 5th International Conference on Innovative Technologies in Intelligent Systems and Industrial Applications (CITISIA), Innovative Technologies in Intelligent Systems and Industrial Applications (CITISIA), 2020 5th International Conference On*, 1–9.

SPSS Inc. and International Consortium Publish CRISP-DM 1.0; Free Document Offers Step-By-Step Guidance for Data Mining Projects. (2000). *Business Wire*.

Sunkpho, J. & Ramjan, S. (2020). Predicting Condominium Price in Bangkok Using Web Mining Techniques. *Srinakharinwirot Research and Development (Journal of Humanities and Social Sciences), 12*(24).

Tanantong, T. (2021). *Data Mining*. Retrieved from: https://www.skilllane.com/courses/tuxsa-Data-Mining-Algorithms/chapter

Tanantong, T., & Ramjan, S. (2021, April-June). An Association Rule Mining Approach to Discover Demand and Supply Patterns Based on Thai Social Media Data. *International Journal of Knowledge and Systems Science, 12*(2), 1–16. doi:10.4018/IJKSS.2021040101

Tanantong, T., & Ramjan, S. (2022). *Data Visualization for Data Science* (1st ed.). Thammasat Press.

Chapter 2
Data

ABSTRACT

The initial step for a data scientist when addressing a business question is to identify the data type, as not all types can be employed in data mining analyses. Accordingly, the data scientist must select a suitable data type that corresponds to the data mining technique and classify the data into categorical and continuous types, regardless of the source of the data. Quality control is a significant factor for the data scientist, particularly if data collection was poorly administered or designed, leading to issues like missing values. Once the data scientist has acquired a relevant dataset, they should inspect the outliers associated with each feature to make sure the data is suitable for analysis. Observing outliers through data visualizations, such as scatter plots, is a common practice among data scientists, highlighting the crucial role of data type determination.

INTRODUCTION

Though the Administrators or Domain Experts in each industry see how necessary to use data analysis to solve problems or to drive the organization, though they and are aware of the advances in data analysis using data mining techniques, they cannot link the existing data to individual data processing techniques. In many cases, it was found that the development of data visualization is sufficient for data analysis to answer questions without the need for data mining techniques. On contrary in some cases, the organizations do not have enough data to be analyzed to respond to the determined questions.

The main reason is that administrators or domain experts in the organization lack understanding of which data can be used and how the questions should be asked in order to gain useful data. Many organizations have developed their domain experts to become data scientists and trained them in a wide range of data analysis. The positions of data scientists are necessary as they can use the existing data to analyze and solve problems in a timely manner. For example, in the medical industry, patient data can be used to analyze the treatment. The use of data in each form of data analysis is therefore an important point for data science students.

DOI: 10.4018/978-1-6684-4730-7.ch002

ATTRIBUTE

The attributes of the data are used to define the scope of the Data Object. For instance, the data attribute is gender, and data object is male, female, or genderless. Data attributes are also used in different contexts (Inmon and Lindstedt, 2015). When data scientists write programs, data attributes are viewed as variables and considered as features. Data scientist collects data in a dataset consisting of a feature that stores multiple records. In data science, these records are called "Instance". The structure to store Feature, Data Objects, and Instances, is as follows (Gru¨tter, 2019: Angiulli & Fassetti, 2021).

Table 1. The example of feature, data object, and instance

First Name	Last Name
Jirapon	Sunkpho
Sarawut	Ramjan
Kom	Campiranon

In Table 1, there are totally 2 features consisting of first name and last name. The first name features are Jirapon, Sarawut and Com while the last name features are Sunkpho, Ramjan and Campiranon, respectively. When data objects from multiple features are combined, they become the Instances. From Table 1, there are 3 Instances consisting of Jirapon Sunkpho, Sarawut Ramjan and Kom Campiranon, respectively.

Data Dimensionality: Is the number of features within a dataset (Li, Horiguchi and Sawaragi, 2020). In data science, it focuses on analyzing the data in various fields without focusing on storing data from the beginning. The number of dimensions is an issue that the data scientist must consider in order to select only the features that can support the analysis. Therefore, the data scientists need to reduce the number of dimensions to have the features necessary for data analysis. This allows data scientists to reduce the time and digital resources required to process massive instances of datasets.

Resolution: Is a measure used to store Data Object in each Feature. In Data Science (Wang et al., 2019), when data scientists collect datasets from multiple sources, there is often a problem with storing the same data across multiple measures. For example, Feature height from dataset A is collected in centimeters, whereas Feature height from dataset B is stored in inches. Therefore, before implementing those datasets, data scientists must perform Attribute Transformation or changing the shape of the Data Object to be in one form or another

DATA TYPE

Different data mining and visualization techniques use different types of data. It may use only one type of data or a combination of different types. It is a great challenge for Data Scientists to analyze the data to identify whether it is consistent with the data mining techniques and to answer the determined questions. The data can be divided into 2 types.

Categorial Data

Categorial Data is the counted data considered as quantitative data without continuity. It also includes Nominal Scale and Ordinal Scale. Each category has different uses (Van et al., 2005).

1. **Nominal Scale:** Is the data collected as grouping (Andrews and Messenger, 1973), such as gender, including female, male, and other genders. When data scientists use nominal scale in data analysis, they can compare data of the nominal scale; males and females as presented in the example.

Figure 1. Example of data visualization with nominal scale

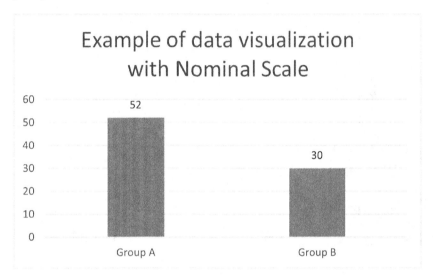

As seen in the figure, data scientists can compare the Nominal Scales to describe the data with Mode or the most duplicated data. For example, the data ranged 0-5, mode 3 means the number 3 is most chosen. The data ranged 6-10, mode 7 means that the number 7 is most chosen. Data scientists should not use nominal scale to calculate by adding, subtracting, multiplying, dividing or averaging. For example, if the data show that there are 7.5 males, it does not make sense in data analysis because in reality there cannot be 7.5 people. Moreover, turning letters into numbers cannot give those numbers real values to be calculated. If Bang Rak District is valued as No. 1 and Sathorn District as No. 2, then 1 plus 2 equals 3 means nothing in data interpretation. In many cases, the nominal scale data can be used with other data types to process visualization data as in the example.

As obvious from the figure, the Nominal Scale is the survival rate and the mortality rate of smokers developed into visualization in the form of histogram which shows the range of the living and the dead in the x-axis, and the frequency of the living and the dead in the y-axis.

2. The Ordinal Scale represents abstractions with ordinal numbers (Yager, 2020). Intention is an individual emotion. Data scientists can represent that emotion as Likert Scale ranging from 1 to 5. For example, "no intention to buy" is represented by number 1 while "probably buying" is represented by number 2 with the intensity of buying intent being from weak to intense at number 5. When

emotion is represented by numbers, data scientists can therefore draw conclusions. If the respondents choose number 4 the most, this emotion cannot be determined in average value. Number 4.5 cannot be interpreted as what the level of purchase intention is. However, data scientists can apply ordinal scale called Supervised-Learning such as Regression in data analysis, by responding to the determined problems. For example, the purchase intention on product A has a significant influence on the purchase intention on product B.

Figure 2. An example of the application of the nominal scale with other data

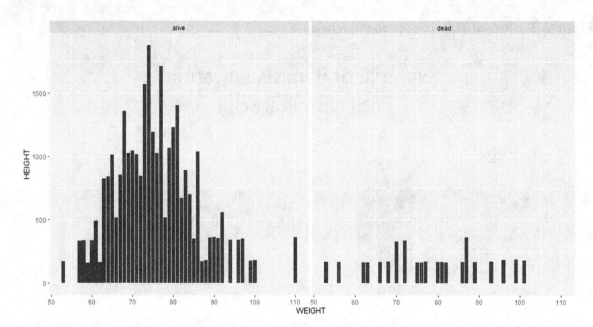

Continuous Data

Continuous data is the data presented with real numbers (Mesner and Shalizi, 2021), such as financial data and temperature data. These data can be used for calculating the average such as the data on average salary for employees who have been in the company for more than 5 years. Data scientists can develop visualizations from continuous data as follows.

According to the figure, data scientists create a scatter plot from continuous data where the data in the x-axis represents the temperature, and the y-axis represents the amount of ozone. The data of both features are real numbers. It does not matter whether the original data that the data scientist imports from the sources or outside are Categorical Data or Continuous Data, data scientist should consider the objectives of the data analysis. Then, data scientists can select the suitable mining techniques for analyzing the data. The desired data can then be selected.

Figure 3. Example of visualization from continuous data

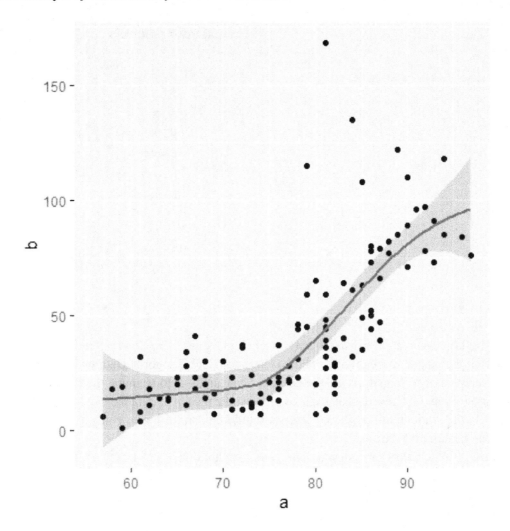

DEFINITION OF DATA TYPES WITHIN THE RAPIDMINER SOFTWARE

This book applies RapidMiner software as a tool to experiment data analysis using different data mining techniques. According to the academic classification, data is divided into Categorial Data and Continuous Data. But RapidMiner provides a method for defining each data type as follows.

In the example, the data types within RapidMiner have been divided as the following:

Polynominal: Is the data that can be in both alphabets and numbers. Data scientists can import Categorial Data and define it as Polynominal, such as gender. However, data scientists need to consider the data through each type of data mining techniques. Alphabetic and integer data cannot always be processed with the same data mining techniques, although they can also be designated as Polynominals.

Binominal Data: Is a type of data that have only two values; "No" can be replaced with number 0, and "Yes" with the number 1.

Figure 4. Examples of data types within RapidMiner

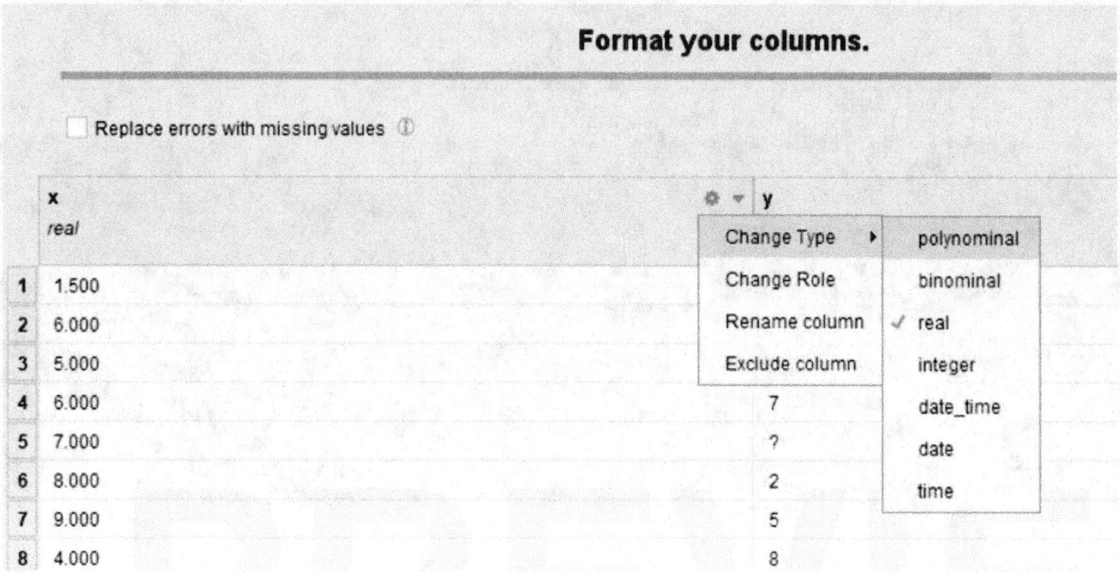

Real Data: Is a real number such as temperature, height, or distance. However, there are certain types of data analysis techniques that can analyze both Continuous and Categorial Data such as Linear Regression. The examples of such analysis are the Ordinal Scale analysis to examine the correlation between different variables, and the real data analysis to forecast the results of data having 2 or more variables.

Integer: Is the whole number. Data scientists should be careful not to convert letters into integer number in the quantitative data analysis.

Date_time: Is a period of time; day, month, year, and duration.

Date: Means date, day, month and year.

Time: Means a period of time.

All of Date_time: Date, and Time data are used to analyze time-controlled data such as Time Series technique.

Therefore, accurate determination of such data types will affect the selection of appropriate techniques. It also affects the development of data visualization as well.

DATA QUALITY

To process data with data mining techniques, the data set must be qualified for the analysis. Data mining technique is only a processing tool, but data scientists must survey and prepare the data in consideration of the quality of the data in many areas in order to obtain accurate results.

Bias: Is a careful selection of data analysis to reduce the high concentration of opinions among the samples (Carlson, Livermore and Rockmore, 2020). Thailand's public data system is operated by state-owned energy enterprises. If data scientists would like to study the needs of citizens or the level of satisfaction the citizen has upon the government, and they cannot collect data from people in the whole country, the random methods must be used to collect the data. However, if the scientists only randomly collect data from people living in Bangkok and surrounding areas, the randomization causes biases that the data cannot represent the whole nation.To reduce bias, the appropriate proportion of the population must be concerned. For example, Chiang Mai Province has a denser population than Loei Province, so data scientists cannot do random sampling with equal numbers because when the data of all provinces are put together, it would not be sure whether such information can be used to represent Thailand. In other cases, the proportion of the actual data is not related to the sample number. For example, data scientists randomize only 60 percent of samples to analyze data on debt defaults; however, the real data shows that there is only 40 percent. It means that from randomization, data scientists receive 20 percent more than the real data.

Outlier: Refers to an abnormal Data Object (Li et al., 2019: Jyothi et al., 2020). When a data object has an outlier, either negatively or positively, the feature average is distorted. Data scientists can use survey processes to visualize data patterns in order to detect outliers by creating a Scatter Plot visualization.

Figure 5. Exploring data objects that are outlier

As seen in the figure, Scatter Plot takes the Data Object from the Feature (Shao, et al., 2017). Total Population which is presented on the x-axis, and the features showing the number of murders is shown on the y-axis. From the visual data, data scientists should firstly consider whether the value is really outlier or no, by consulting with data experts in order to verify whether the value is abnormal or different from most data. This is to avoid a data entry error.

Missing Value: Is an empty Data Object within a Feature (Montesdeoca et al., 2019). It can occur for many reasons. When the users do not fill out information either on paper or digital forms, it is possible that the data collection tools asking for what the users do not have data. For example, if the person filling out the information is a male but the tools require him to inform the frequency of menstruation, then, the user may skip filling those questions. This causes missing value. In another example, if the applicant is a student with no income, but the salary information must be filled, the user will skip filling out the information as well.

Once a Missing Value has occurred, the Data Scientist can do 3 approaches as follows:

1. When the missing value is between 0 and 14%, data scientists can remove the instance.
2. In the case that the missing value is between 15 and 40%, data scientists can add the possible data to replace the missing values. If the feature is continuous, data scientists can replenish the mean value obtained from calculating all data objects to replace the missing value. Data scientists should be concerned of the type of data before calculating the replenished value to replace the Missing Value. The replenished value cannot be the average.
3. If the missing value is 41% or more, data scientists should consider refraining the use of feature in data analysis because the data is not large enough to represent any data in the analysis.

Duplicate Data: Is data redundancy (Song, Yu, and Bao, 2019). In data science, this can happen when combining more than two data sets. For example, it occurs when there is more than one instance to indicate the same data while the only difference is the data owner's email address. When data scientists combine the same data collected from two data sets, there is a duplication of data. In such a case, data scientists take data into the preparation process in order to reduce data redundancy.

Inconsistency Data: Is inaccurate data (Johnny and Trovati, 2020). Such cases can occur, when the users fill out the wrong information in the first place; such as the use of negative numbers for human height or a typo in the name. This can be prevented by designing an online form that alerts the user to the misinformation before the user can enter it.

CASE STUDY

Among the vast amount of data, a number of people including beginner data scientists are confused about what kind of data can be used for analysis, what type of problems requires only data summaries, what type of problems requires only Classic Statistic, what type of problems requires data mining techniques to process. Therefore, This chapter presents a collection of case studies on the use of data in various aspects.

Becoming a Data-Driven Decision-Making Organization: Seven Challenges Facing Not-for-Profits (Hume & West, 2020)

Among the trends in Digital Transformation, organizations are aware of the use of data in decision-making in both the public and private sectors. However, there are some articles that address 7 challenges of non-profit organizations in using data to make decisions.

1. **Selecting the Right Data for Analysis:** Amidst the overwhelming data, organizations need to first review what is the purpose of corporate data analysis. The organization can, then, collect and store data in order to identify methods for collecting or acquiring the data. If the data cannot be obtained from within the organization, it is necessary to determine the external sources. However,

if an organization realizes that acquiring or storing data is not worth the investment, it can review whether there are other sources of data to be analyzed.

2. **Selecting the Right Analytical Tool:** There are a number of software to be used to analyze the data. Many organizations start their data analysis with popular spread sheet software such as Microsoft Excel that can take datasets for compiling, calculating, and developing data. It is considered a standard tool that most employees have been trained since high school. Thus, organizations can save a lot of training costs on such software. For organizations that expect more complex data analysis results, the use of database data for data analysis and create more professional visual data, they can use the software like Business Intelligence which can take data from the database to be analyzed, preparing financial reports from the Accounting Database, and analyzing the data source before processing it into the software such as Microsoft Power BI or Tableau.

BI is not only used for analyzing historical data but also for the future decision-making, such as product price setting, which is calculated from the average product price in the market. To process in such a manner, the scientists can use competitor price data to analyze in the form of time series to show price trends and market segmentation where competitors have placed their brand positioning. However, the afore mentioned software is still difficult to access, especially for the employees who have no experience in data science. So, it's important that organizations take action to explore the tools in the market and then study which tools are suitable for your organization's work and worth the investment. In addition, when selecting the tools, organizations must also plan for the installation and maintenance cost of those tools in terms of procuring hardware and the amount of software sufficient for the number of personnel.

3. **Team Building for Data Analysis:** While the businesses offer a high rate of paid for data scientists, the non-profit organizations have a limited budget. So, training and appointing a Domain Expert in a process with similar capabilities as a data scientist becomes an attractive and more budget viable option.

However, when recruiting people, non-profit organizations can select people with potential to be improved, such as those who graduated in information technology or finance, and those who have fundamental knowledge sufficient for building up to become a data scientist in the future.

4. **Centralization of Data:** In the real situation, organizations, especially those in smaller, less tech-savvy organizations, tend to store data that is random and scattered. Consequently, data integration has become a huge challenge for organizations, especially in the organizations that lack experience in structured data integration. This data integration becomes another factor for selecting both hardware and software for future data analysis.

5. **Making Accurate Data:** Although data scientists have many technical methods to analyze data, they will never be able to process data properly if the original data is not correct. Before bringing data into the Database or Data File, the accuracy of the data is to be concerned first. Many organizations often try to pass this responsibility on to their IT staff. But the person who should understands the data accuracy is the one who is directly responsible for bringing the data into the system, such as the financial department. Therefore, the organization needs to provide a Check List of the validation of data as a tool for personnel to verify whether the data entered the system is correct or not. For example, email addresses should be separated by @ sign.

6. **Creating a Culture of Change:** To create a culture of change to drive the use of data as a basis for decision-making, the board of directors needs key policymakers to drive it. This may start from allocating a budget to invest in Digital Infrastructure by taking into account the balance between hardware and software investment along with recruiting or developing personnel to use those technologies. Organizations may start with small projects involving data analytics to pilot other agencies. Therefore, the most important driver in creating a culture of change is a group of people who lead an organization.

7. **Initiating an Informed Decision:** The use of data for decision-making does not focus on visualization. But it is the use of the results obtained from visualization to support or drive organizational decision-making, such as creating a Trend Chart comparing Return of Investment from Classic marketing versus Digital Marketing from 2009 to 2022 to make decisions on whether the organization should invest more on human resources and budget into marketing.

From the seven challenges, non-profit organizations realized that even if they do not require business or market share expansions like any other normal business organizations, they cannot neglect the use of data in decision-making, starting with investing in enhancing their computing capabilities with sufficient Digital Infrastructure. It is to increase the employee skills to support data processing. It also benefits from driving the organization with the use of data, analysis of effective strategies to drive the organization towards its vision.

Market Analysis From Banking Customer Data (Torrens & Tabakovic, 2022)

Customer financial transactions through Banking Apps provide a valuable dataset for analyzing market data. The bank can analyze customer patterns to develop effective marketing strategies. Machine learning itself is a modern tool to learn customer patterns. Therefore, the bank has applied machine learning to analyze market data to develop the bank to become a Data Driven Organization.

Therefore, the Bank should aims to collect data on customers' financial transactions, which reflect their behavior in using money through online channels. The customer behavior on websites or social networks show different insight data from their behavior in online shopping through the Bank's Apps. When the customers like to consume something, they often subscribe to social network channels such as YouTube Channel or Instagram, but the bank's data only show what the customers pay on a daily basis, such as shopping for everyday things at the superstore. Incidentally, advertising within Digital Banking Apps may not display billboards like other online services, but it has to focus on accumulating points to use in other services, such as accumulating credit card points.

The variables used in the data analysis, therefore, cover the nature of the customer's spending. It can tell higher amount of money spent to buy a particular product than others, the use of money to buy the same product from multiple sellers or competitors, and where customers conduct financial transactions through Digital Banking Apps. Based on the variables reflecting the frequency of using this money, banks can divide customers into high and low purchasing power groups as well as being able to distinguish which customers do not have behavior in conducting transactions through Digital Banking Apps.

The dataset can be used for analysis with K-Mean Clustering in order to use the collected data to determine an objective marketing strategy, including increasing brand loyalty, increasing the digital spending level of customers of low purchasing power customers, increasing the spending frequency of current customers, and retaining existing customers.

Banks can use the Supervised-Learning techniques, Linear Regression Algorithm, Logistic Regression Algorithm, or Random Forest, to predict the likelihood of customer spending. In this case, the bank used a dataset from 150,000 customers transacting over a period of 12 months to train the model and then predict the possibilities with various data mining techniques until it is found that the most efficient technique is Random Forest. The bank can also group its data analysis according to the type of industry in which customers purchase goods through bank financial transactions. In this case, the bank analyzes and segments them into Gastronomy, shoes, sports, cosmetics, and tourism and also found that Random Forest is the most effective method of forecasting the use of money to buy products from various industries.

Thus, this is another case study where banks can use existing datasets to analyze data to develop marketing strategies. Other businesses can also group data with interesting variables for data analysis too.

Analyzing Data from Big Data Generated by Production Systems to Support Decision-Making (Rogers & Kalinova, 2021)

In the manufacturing industry, there are many processes to increase efficiency, such as controlling the production standard, reducing losses from manufacturing errors, shortening the production process, and minimized human-controlled production. Currently, the Internet of Things Technology (IoT) is applied to detect actions occurring in each production process, detecting the amount of liquid or gas in a pipeline. And from the application of such technology, the industry has received real time data and it creates a data set as Big Data. From such Big Data, the manufacturing industry can analyze the data in a variety of perspectives, which include forecasting whether each machine has reached its maintenance interval, improving the productivity of marketing audience analysis production, streamlining business processes to retain customer groups, lowering the cost of raw materials in production, and optimizing security during the production process.

To answer the above question, the manufacturing industry also has to do digital planning to support future data analysis. It includes the adoption of mobile devices such as tablets or mobile devices to display real-time data analysis, provision of software used for data analysis such as inventory management, movement of raw materials in production, preparation of a semi-automated production process using robots, preparation of sensor technology to collect data in real-time, the use of data systems to control production, and the use of models to forecast data and plan for future technological changes that can be used in conjunction with manufacturing systems such as AI or Blockchain.

By implementing a large number of data processing technologies, the manufacturing industry is able to reduce the number of human-machine control. It can also control the production process from a distance via a remote system. Companies can collect data from those devices and analyze them to solve problems in the manufacturing process, such as discovering defective equipment or loss analysis from the production process. Mobile analytics data visualization can be done in a dashboard style. Using a dashboard, data users can compare data collected through IoT with Key Performance Indicators to reflect process efficiency.

With this sensor technology, companies can also manage their inventory by checking whether the amount of raw materials left in the production or the product is at the level that needs to be ordered more or produced in order to control storage costs. Such data analysis can also be performed throughout the Digital Supply Chain so that the end customer needs are delivered to the raw material suppliers.

The manufacturing sector also faces the challenge of equipping staff with expertise in IoT technology and data analytics skills, as well as developing senior management understanding of how to ask questions suitable for further analysis. Above all, the board of directors of each company need to formulate a digital strategy to drive the organization towards a Data Driven Organization.

The Challenges of Being a Data Driven Organization (Bean, 2022)

Organizations worldwide are aware of being a Data Driven Organization. Those companies have adapted hard by adopting new technology, improving processes within the delivery of products and services through reliance on technology, and even trying to change the corporate culture until being able to compete over competitors. The biggest challenge, however, is that large companies or even government agencies, which are long established, have a large number of senior employees having been working within the company. Those employees not only tolerate changes in technology or new ways of working, but also have political power within the company to resist any form of change. The emergence of the COVID-19 crisis has caused the companies around the world to change he way they work. Senior employees are in a state of compromise, relying on technology and digitization to proactively change the way they work. On the other hand, consumers have various options to receive information. Therefore, consumers can also consider choosing the best quality information to support their decision making. With data collection technologies such as IoT and high-performance data processing technologies, today companies can bring large data sets to be processed. No more data sampling techniques are needed because today's digital resources are powerful enough to analyze data.

Among organizations that are trying to adapt to become a Data Driven Organization, the success factor of the organization turns is none other than the inspiration of leaders to be a Data Driven Organization instead of technological change. The main obstacle to organizational change is the resistance, which arises from the organizational culture. Leaders can often start by cultivating people in the organization to realize the value of data and initiate the management of corporate assets. To ensure that organizations have policies and measures to protect personal data has become the global pressure from government laws, increasingly vigilant about securing personal data to their citizens.

The solution for organizations that are trying to become a Data Driven Organization is that leaders must have an innovative character. Among many models of data mining techniques, leaders need to create a question-frame where data analysis initiatives differ from competitors in order to obtain answers that competitors cannot access, and dare try and make mistake in order to create an experience of learning from failures.

Relevance of Big Data, AI, and Robotics (Curry et al., 2022)

Europe has initiated the establishment of associations related to Big Data, AI and Robotics to strengthen Europe's international competitiveness. The association has faced a variety of challenges, prompting the association itself to analyze the weakest elements in ecosystem for the promotion of Big Data, AI and Robotics until these elements were met: Unpredictable European Policies and Measures Society's confidence in Big Data, AI and Robotics, knowledge and skills in Big Data, AI and Robotics, digital utilities that still need to be developed, technological complexity and investment with a very high budget in digital. These elements have promoted Big Data, AI and Robotics in Europe, as well as differentiating research studies in each field and not leading to a better understanding of how to apply Big Data, AI and Robotics in both business and technology.

The Big Data, AI and Robotics Association has become an intermediary to connect those elements, advocate research policy and share knowledge to connect stakeholders in terms of research and technology implementation in more complicated environment. Therefore, the Association has developed a framework for creating an ecosystem that facilitates such action, with the following components: Principles of Rights and Values of Big Data, AI and Robotics in Europe, the Value of Big Data, AI and Robotics to Business, Society and Citizens Policies, Regulations, Assurances and Standards for Big Data, AI and Robotics. These principles create an innovative ecosystem used to promote the creation of knowledge and skills in Big Data, AI and Robotics, and the ecosystem also promotes research and application of Big Data, AI and Robotics.

By building an ecosystem of Big Data, AI and Robotics and innovations, Big Data, AI and Robotics will promote the growth of Europe's technology for decision support and help Europe lead the way in science and innovation related to AI, Data and Robotics and its application, as well as to build confidence in European citizens to implement such technology.

CONCLUSION

The dataset is made up of a combination of features which store data objects internally. And each dataset can contain multiple instances. Using such data to analyze with data mining techniques, data scientists need to first survey the data in order to identify the data type first. Each data mining technique requires the use of different types of data. Additionally, in response to some types of problems, only data visualization can be used without analyzing the data with data mining techniques. However, even in data visualization development, data scientists also need to understand the data types in order to accurately display the data and answer the determined questions.

EXERCISE QUESTIONS

1. Explain and give examples of Category Data.
2. Explain and give examples of Continuous Data.
3. In RapidMiner software, what types of data can the continuous data be defined as?
4. Explain about the bias data and give examples.
5. Describe data objects that are outliers.

REFERENCES

Andrews, F. M., & Messenger, R. C. (1973). *Multivariate nominal scale analysis; a report on a new analysis technique and a computer program.* University of Michigan.

Angiulli, F., & Fassetti, F. (2021). Uncertain distance-based outlier detection with arbitrarily shaped data objects. *Journal of Intelligent Information Systems*, *57*(1), 1–24. doi:10.100710844-020-00624-7

Bean, R. (2022). Why Becoming a Data-Driven Organization Is So Hard. *Harvard Business Review Digital Articles*, 1–6.

Carlson, K., Livermore, M. A., & Rockmore, D. N. (2020). The Problem of Data Bias in the Pool of Published U.S. Appellate Court Opinions. *Journal of Empirical Legal Studies*, *17*(2), 224–261. doi:10.1111/jels.12253

Curry, E., Heintz, F., Irgens, M., Smeulders, A. W. M., & Strmigioli, S. (2022). Partnership on AI, Data, and Robotics. *Communications of the ACM*, *65*(4), 54–55. doi:10.1145/3513000

Grütter, R. (2019). A framework for assisted proximity analysis in feature data. *Journal of Geographical Systems*, *21*(3), 367–394. doi:10.100710109-019-00304-3

Hume, E., & West, A. (2020). Becoming a Data-Driven Decision Making Organization: Seven Challenges Facing Not-for-Profits. *The CPA Journal*, *90*(4), 32.

Inmon, W. H., & Lindstedt, D. (2015). *Data architecture: a primer for the data scientist : big data, data warehouse and data vault*. Morgan Kaufmann/Elsevier.

Johnny, O., & Trovati, M. (2020). Big data inconsistencies and incompleteness: a literature review. *International Journal of Grid and Utility Computing*, *5*, 705. 10.1504/IJGUC.2020.110057

Jyothi, P. N., Lakshmi, D. R., & Rao, K. V. S. N. R. (2020). A Supervised Approach for Detection of Outliers in Healthcare Claims Data. *Journal of Engineering Science & Technology Review*, *13*(1), 204–213. doi:10.25103/jestr.131.25

Li, J., Horiguchi, Y., & Sawaragi, T. (2020). Data Dimensionality Reduction by Introducing Structural Equation Modeling to Machine Learning Problems. *2020 59th Annual Conference of the Society of Instrument and Control Engineers of Japan (SICE), Instrument and Control Engineers of Japan (SICE), 2020 59th Annual Conference of the Society Of,* 826–831.

Li, K., Li, J., Liu, S., Li, Z., Bo, J., & Liu, B. (2019). GA-iForest: An Efficient Isolated Forest Framework Based on Genetic Algorithm for Numerical Data Outlier Detection. *Transactions of Nanjing University of Aeronautics & Astronautics*, *36*(6), 1026–1038.

Mesner, O. C., & Shalizi, C. R. (2021). Conditional Mutual Information Estimation for Mixed, Discrete and Continuous Data. *IEEE Transactions on Information Theory*, *67*(1), 464–484. doi:10.1109/TIT.2020.3024886

Montesdeoca, B., Luengo, J., Maillo, J., García-Gil, D., García, S., & Herrera, F. (2019). A first approach on big data missing values imputation. *IoTBDS 2019 - Proceedings of the 4th International Conference on Internet of Things, Big Data and Security*, 315–323. 10.5220/0007738403150323

Rogers, S., & Kalinova, E. (2021). Big Data-driven Decision-Making Processes, Real-Time Advanced Analytics, and Cyber-Physical Production Networks in Industry 4.0-based Manufacturing Systems. *Economics, Management, and Financial Markets*, *16*(4), 84. doi:10.22381/emfm16420216

Shao, L., Mahajan, A., Schreck, T., & Lehmann, D. J. (2017). Interactive Regression Lens for Exploring Scatter Plots. *Computer Graphics Forum*, *36*(3), 157–166. doi:10.1111/cgf.13176

Song, J., Yu, Q., & Bao, R. (2019). The Detection Algorithms for Similar Duplicate Data. *2019 6th International Conference on Systems and Informatics (ICSAI), Systems and Informatics (ICSAI), 2019 6th International Conference On,* 1534–1542.

Torrens, M., & Tabakovic, A. (2022). A Banking Platform to Leverage Data Driven Marketing with Machine Learning. *Entropy (Basel, Switzerland), 24*(3), 347. doi:10.3390/e24030347 PMID:35327858

Van der Ark, L. A., Croon, M. A., & Sijtsma, K. (2005). *New developments in categorial data analysis for the social and behavioral sciences.* Lawrence Erlbaum Associates Publishers.

Wang, J., Sato, K., Guo, S., Chen, W., & Wu, J. (2019). Big Data Processing With Minimal Delay and Guaranteed Data Resolution in Disaster Areas. *IEEE Transactions on Vehicular Technology, 68*(4), 3833–3842. doi:10.1109/TVT.2018.2889094

Yager, R. R. (2020). Ordinal scale based uncertainty models for AI. *Information Fusion, 64,* 92–98. doi:10.1016/j.inffus.2020.06.010

Chapter 3
Software Installation and Introduction to RapidMiner

ABSTRACT

Licensed and open-source data mining software has made it easier for data scientists to process and analyze large datasets. Python and R are popular open-source tools used for teaching data mining techniques, including data classification and clustering. However, one of the main challenges for domain experts looking to upskill in data science is computer programming. Licensed software such as RapidMiner provides a solution to this issue, as it is designed for data mining processing without requiring computer programming skills. RapidMiner allows data scientists to bring their data sets and mining models into an analysis process that includes all data science mechanisms. It also offers various supporting models for data pre-processing and creates data visualizations during data exploration. After data mining, RapidMiner displays easy-to-interpret results, enabling data scientists to effectively explain the answer to a business question to stakeholders. With its user-friendly interface, RapidMiner is an excellent choice for those without a technical background in programming.

INTRODUCTION

RapidMiner software is very popular in data science work, and has been used in data scientist development trainings (Chisholm, 2013: Klinkenberg & Hofmann, 2014: Kotu & Deshpande, 2014). The scientists can learn about various data mining techniques and apply those concepts in data analysis with RapidMiner without writing any program. Moreover, RapidMiner software supports every step of the data science field work. Data scientists can import datasets into RapidMiner software to promptly explore data through the feature visualizations. In data preparation, the scientists can use models within the RapidMiner software to customize their data ready for analysis with various data mining techniques. RapidMiner software provides the sample data sets for the scientists to use in experimenting data during their trainings as well.

DOI: 10.4018/978-1-6684-4730-7.ch003

RAPIDMINER SOFTWARE INSTALLATION

Professors and learners of data mining techniques who would like to use RapidMiner software as a tool to study and experiment for data analysis can download RapidMiner software at the following this link, https://rapidminer.com/, which will take you to the download page as seen below (Chavan, 2020: Soft, 2020: Vasudevan, 2021).

Figure 1. RapidMiner software download

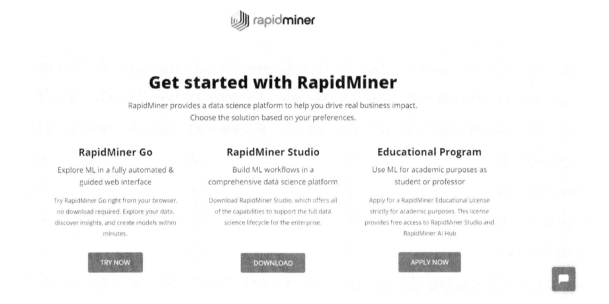

As seen in the figure, select Apply Now at RapidMiner in the form of Education Program, then fill in the details to verify your identity, as seen below.

From figure 3.2, select Educational Purpose, and then fill in your first and last names, educational institution name, the role of the software user consisting of teachers and students, email address and password (Naparat, 2020). Then press the button Register.

As seen, my.RapidMiner.com will send an e-mail requiring the user to confirm the software download request. The user, then, should verify the e-mail.

From the picture, once the email is verified, my.RapidMiner.com will download the software as shown in the picture down here.

From the figure, check the type of operating system inside the computer. In the case of Windows operating system where there are 2 types; 32 Bit and 64 Bit, select the correct download according to the operating system. And in the case of MAC OS or Linux operating system, choose to download according to the operating system. Once the download is completed, you will receive a file for the software installation.

When double clicking on the Installation File, the start screen will appear. Then press the Next > button to go to the next step.

Figure 2. Filling out the information to verify your identity

Apply for an Educational License

If you are a student or professor at an accredited university, you qualify for a 1-year, renewable educational license of RapidMiner Studio and RapidMiner AI Hub.

RapidMiner's Educational License is not available for commercial, non-profit organizations, or funded research.

If you remain eligible, you may extend your 1-year license by contacting us.

What are you using Rapidminer for?

○ Commercial purposes (e.g. business evaluation, not-for-profit)
◉ Educational purposes (e.g. educator, student)

First name:

Sarawut

Last name:

Ramjan

University:

Thammasat University

Role:

Instructor ⌄

Email address:

sarawutr@staff.tu.ac.th

Create a password:

Your password should be at least 8 characters long

....

Confirm your password:

....

Register

Already have an account? Sign in here.

Figure 3. Sending an e-mail for confirmation

We've sent a confirmation email to sarawutr@staff.tu.ac.th. Click on the confirmation link in the email to activate your account. If you can't find an email from inquiries@rapidminer.com, please check your Spam and Junk mails.

You can also resend the verification email.

From the figure, read the License Agreement and press I Agree to go to the next step.
At this step, select the file location to install the software. Then press the Install button.
After completing the software installation process, press **Finish** to start using RapidMiner software.

Figure 4. Confirmation (verify) of software download via electronic mail

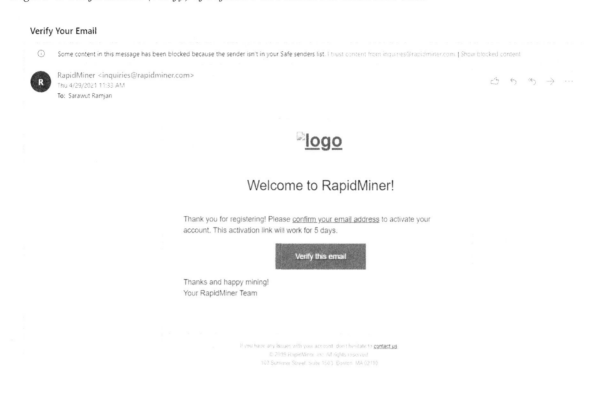

Figure 5. RapidMiner software download

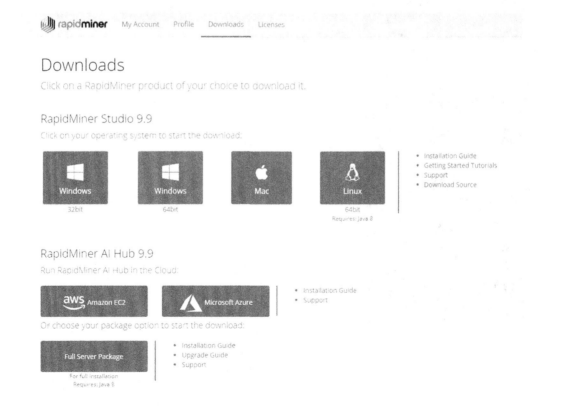

Figure 6. RapidMiner software installation

rapidminer-studi
o-9.9.0-win64-ins
tall

Figure 7. Starting software installation

Figure 8. License agreement

GETTING START WITH RAPIDMINER SOFTWARE

Data scientists can begin their RapidMiner software usage by logging into RapidMiner software. A window will appear; then, the data scientists can begin modeling by selecting Blank Process as follows.

When entering RapidMiner software, there are 5 components; 1. Main Menu 2. View 3. Repository 4. Operator and 5. Parameter. Each component supports the users as seen in the image below.

The users can create files, which stores the models within the RapidMiner software called **Process**. It is to access each file stored within the computer, record the process, and process the data mining from the menu and the icon in the Main Menu section.

Data scientists can create data mining models in the Design section. When processing the model, the results of the data analysis can then be checked in the Results section.

Data scientists can import the datasets to analyze into RapidMiner software by importing the data. The scientists can access the recorded processes and retrieve the ready-made datasets provided by RapidMiner software, so that data scientists can create models from the dataset (RapidMiner, Inc., 2020).

Data scientists can choose different types of data mining techniques from **Operators**. These techniques are diagrammatic with arrangement and connection to each part according to the designed processing algorithm.

Figure 9. Selecting file location

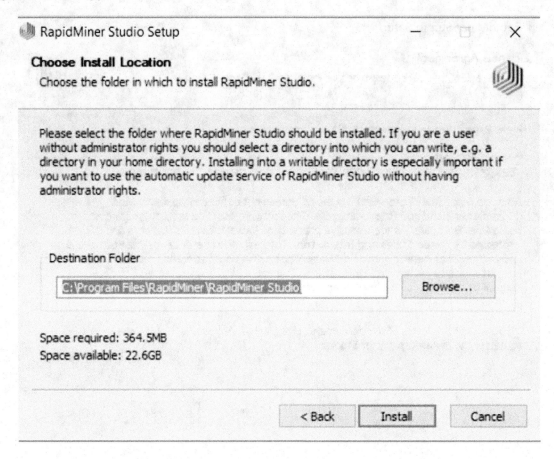

To take each piece of the data mining models to arrange and connect, data scientists can customize the default parameters in order to control processing operations for more accurate data analysis. Data scientists can practice using RapidMiner, starting with a sample dataset called **Iris** to create a process:

In the figure, data scientists run through the repository by accessing the folder where the sample dataset, named Iris, is stored, and then import the Iris dataset into modeling. The data scientists then draw a line to connect the output from the Iris dataset to the Result. When executing, you will receive the result of processing as shown in the image below.

From the data set, data scientists can start exploring the data by examining the patterns of the data in the Statistics section:

From the figure, data scientists can begin exploring the data via statistics, which provides a detailed breakdown of the data in every feature. From the sample, Iris dataset consists of 7 features, with the target variables holding information of the Irish flower species, as well as the other features. The sizes of the Irish flowers are listed in statistics as it also shows the smallest, the largest value and the average values. And from the initial examination of the data, data scientists are able to explore the nature of data with greater details through the development of visualization (Ironfrown, 2016: Global Mindset University, 2020: Tuition, 2021).

Figure 10. The installation is completed

Figure 11. Getting started with RapidMiner software

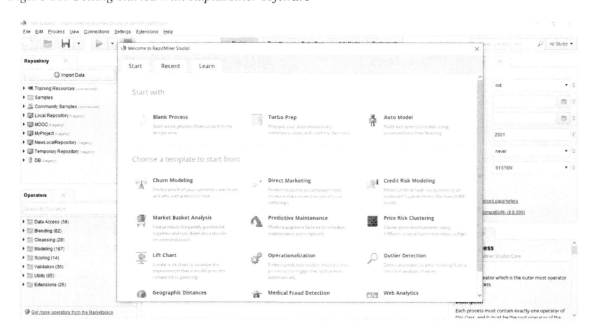

Figure 12. Main menu

Figure 13. View

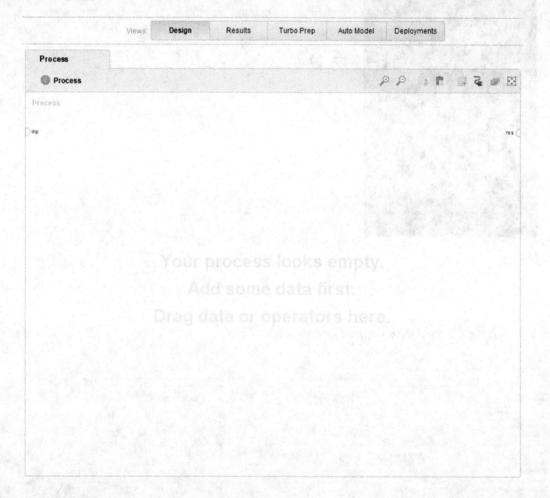

From the figure, data scientists developed a box plot visualization by selecting to display the data from features named a1, a2, a3, and a4, respectively. From the visual data, the scientists receive the information about the least value being 25%, the moderate value being 75%, and the largest value for each feature. Data scientists can also customize the visualization display format for exploring the data quickly.

Figure 14. Repository

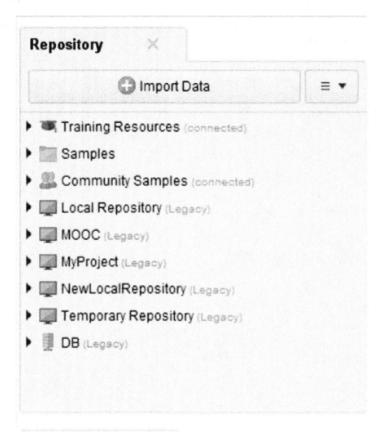

Figure 15. Operators

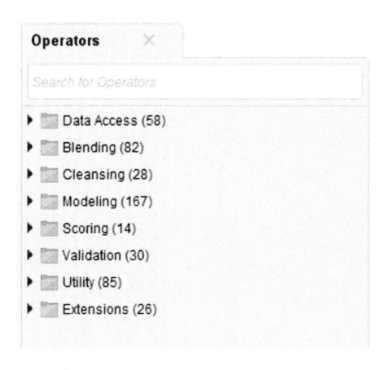

Figure 16. Parameters

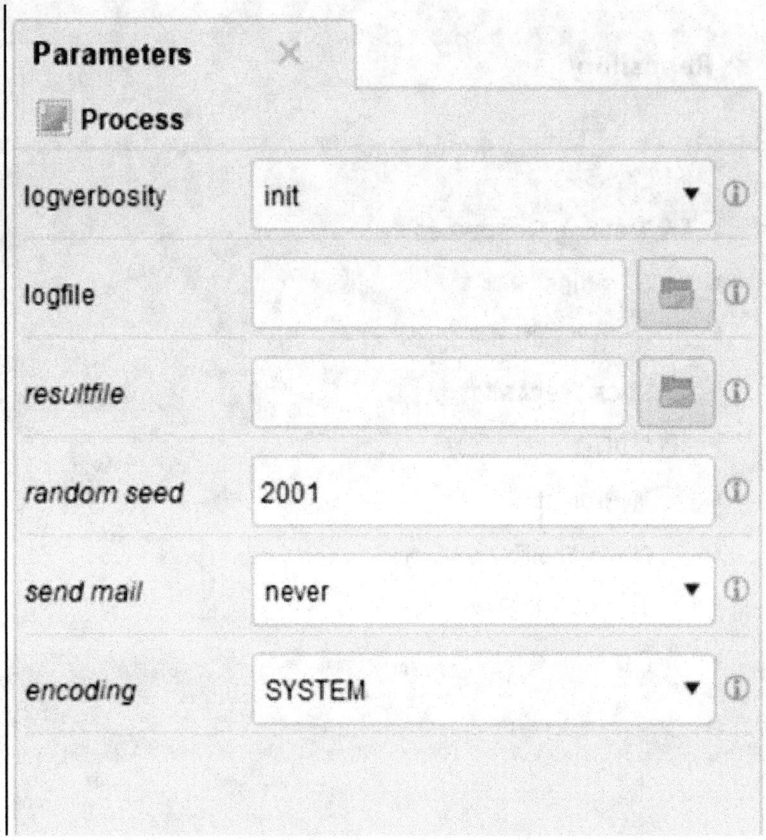

Parameters ✕

Process

logverbosity	init ▼
logfile	📁
resultfile	📁
random seed	2001
send mail	never ▼
encoding	SYSTEM ▼

Figure 17. Importing the data set into the Process

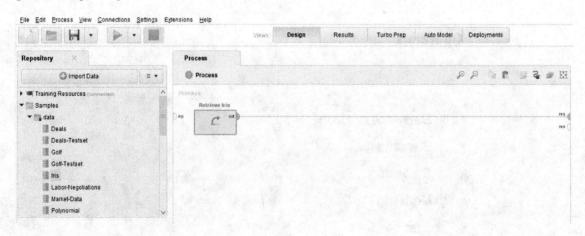

Figure 18. Results of the Iris dataset

Row No.	id	label	a1	a2	a3	a4
1	id_1	Iris-setosa	5.100	3.500	1.400	0.200
2	id_2	Iris-setosa	4.900	3	1.400	0.200
3	id_3	Iris-setosa	4.700	3.200	1.300	0.200
4	id_4	Iris-setosa	4.600	3.100	1.500	0.200
5	id_5	Iris-setosa	5	3.600	1.400	0.200
6	id_6	Iris-setosa	5.400	3.900	1.700	0.400
7	id_7	Iris-setosa	4.600	3.400	1.400	0.300
8	id_8	Iris-setosa	5	3.400	1.500	0.200
9	id_9	Iris-setosa	4.400	2.900	1.400	0.200
10	id_10	Iris-setosa	4.900	3.100	1.500	0.100
11	id_11	Iris-setosa	5.400	3.700	1.500	0.200
12	id_12	Iris-setosa	4.800	3.400	1.600	0.200
13	id_13	Iris-setosa	4.800	3	1.400	0.100
14	id_14	Iris-setosa	4.300	3	1.100	0.100
15	id_15	Iris-setosa	5.800	4	1.200	0.200
16	id_16	Iris-setosa	5.700	4.400	1.500	0.400
17	id_17	Iris-setosa	5.400	3.900	1.300	0.400
18	id_18	Iris-setosa	5.100	3.500	1.400	0.300

ExampleSet (150 examples, 2 special attributes, 4 regular attributes)

Figure 19. Exploring data models with statistics

Name		Type	Missing	Statistics			Filter (5 / 6 attributes)	
id		Nominal	0	Least id_99 (1)	Most id_1 (1)	Values id_1 (1), id_10 (1), ...[148 more]		
label		Nominal	0	Least Iris-virginica (50)	Most Iris-setosa (50)	Values Iris-setosa (50), Iris-versicolor (50), ...[1		
a1		Real	0	Min 4.300	Max 7.900	Average 5.843		
a2		Real	0	Min 2	Max 4.400	Average 3.054		
a3		Real	0	Min 1	Max 6.900	Average 3.759		
a4		Real	0	Min 0.100	Max 2.500	Average 1.199		

Figure 20. Development of box plot visualization data

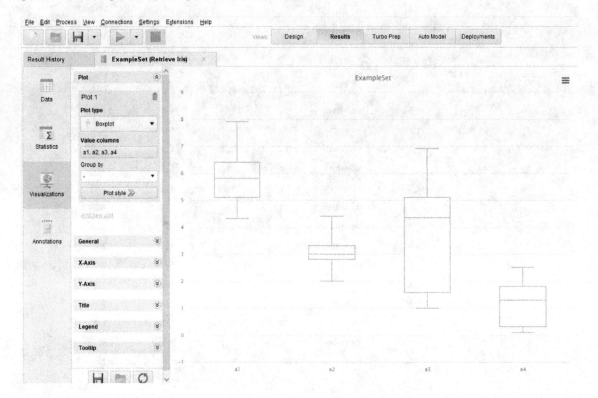

CASE STUDY

The Selection of Software for Data Science Processing (Abbasnasab Sardareh et al., 2021)

Although the industries worldwide are waking up to prepare for Big Data processing by recruiting large numbers of data scientists, one challenge is choosing the right software for data processing. The software packages have hidden complex statistical formulas within, whereas data scientists can simply mouse-click on a tool to allow the software to perform the required processing. However, industries and data scientists specializing in statistical processing still need someone who has expertise in each field to be able to ask sharp questions and choose the right processing method to answer them. Therefore, the industries are facing problems in transforming Domain experts, who lack experience in statistical computing, into data scientists. For instance, domain experts in social sciences such as education, sustainability are not skilled at calculating with statistical formulas (But, of course, they specialize in qualitative data analysis and not always at quantitative data analysis. Some are very proficient.) Normally, those who are beginners in statistics need to know about descriptive analysis, data visualization, hypothesis testing by t-test, ANOVA, Regression analysis, and chi-squared. It has become an important variable that data scientists use when selecting appropriate software. For some software brands, users can click the mouse to instruct the software to process the data set. It is a package that the software has provided processing feature. But for some brands, the users need to write a set of instructions to execute the data set in exchange for processing it in such a way or called "Customization". Therefore, one brand of data processing software cannot meet all the needs of the users.

SPSS is a widely used statistical data processing program and is often the default software for data scientists to study data processing. SPSS is capable of processing quantitative data into statistical results such as Regression Analysis, and able to process data in Graph format. However, SPSS is a high-priced licensed software. Many universities around the world, therefore, prefer to purchase them for their students to use as a site license. SPSS is a software package that requires data scientists to prepare clean datasets before they are importing into SPSS. The scientists can click the command buttons to allow SPSS to process data as needed.

R programming language is a Free Software that data scientists can use for processing data sets through writing instruction sets. Within the R language, there is a library where the data scientists can run a ready-made instruction set to process, such as creating a Data Visualization with Customization, or data processing with some data mining techniques such as K-NN. However, an interesting point is that data scientists using the R language to process data are required to have programming skills in a computer language before.

The variables data scientists take into account when selecting the software can be divided into 2 variables, consisting of the variable for data processing and for usage. Regarding processing, the data scientists focus on computing capabilities in data science tasks, including a user-friendly user interface, a number of statistic features covering statistical data processing, tools to create Data Visualization that are commercially beautiful and valuable in data analysis. It also supports for Data Pre-Processing within one software without relying on other software to pre-process the data before importing the data into the software. In terms of usability, data scientists focus on processing speed and simple steps per processing time, and simplicity in writing a set of instructions for processing.

CONCLUSION

Data scientists can learn how to use RapidMiner for data mining by installing the Education Program RapidMiner software, designed for teachers and students to be able to take sample datasets and sample models to practice analyzing data in different ways. The software also supports other steps in the data analysis, such as creating data visualizations for exploring data in various formats. RapidMiner software is a data analysis tool which the data scientists can use in their research by going beyond the limitations of computer programming skills. However, RapidMiner software is a tool that supports data analysis in the form of models, so data scientists need to study and understand how data mining techniques work in order to be able to choose a sample data set appropriate for the processing of each data mining technique.

EXERCISE QUESTIONS

1. Install RapidMiner software on your computer.
2. Retrieve the Iris dataset and develop the visualization data in histogram and boxplot from that dataset.
3. From number 2, describe the survey results from the visualization.

REFERENCES

Abbasnasab Sardareh, S., Brown, G. T. L., & Denny, P. (2021). Comparing Four Contemporary Statistical Software Tools for Introductory Data Science and Statistics in the Social Sciences. *Teaching Statistics: An International Journal for Teachers, 43*.

Chavan, A. (2020). *RapidMiner Installation on Windows*. Retrieved 15 December 2021 from https://www.youtube.com/watch?v=4RpepmDH-7s

Chisholm, A. (2013). *Exploring Data with RapidMiner: Explore, Understand, and Prepare Real Data Using Rapidminer's Practical Tips and Tricks*. Packt Publishing.

Global Mindset University. (2020). *RapidMiner Data Exploration demo | Data Analysis - Using the Iris Data | Data Mining*. Retrieved 15 December 2021 from https://www.youtube.com/watch?v=EfQkqcj3MIk

Ironfrown. (2016). *RapidMiner Stats (Part 5): Boxplots*. Retrieved 15 December 2021 from https://www.youtube.com/watch?v=IJ180B4ZiLo

Klinkenberg, R., & Hofmann, M. (2014). *RapidMiner: data mining use cases and business analytics applications*. CRC Press.

Kotu, V., & Deshpande, B. (2014). *Predictive analytics and data mining: concepts and practice with RapidMiner*. Elsevier Ltd.

Naparat, D. (2020). *Data Mining with Rapidminer - Getting RapidMiner Educational License*. Retrieved 15 December 2021 from https://www.youtube.com/watch?v=hBxjN1YYXXU

RapidMiner, Inc. (2020). *How to Import Data into a Repository | RapidMiner Studio*. Retrieved 15 December 2021 from https://www.youtube.com/watch?v=DS-tYhgA5lA

Soft, N. (2020). *RapidMiner Tutorial For Beginners | Download & Install | Introduction to RapidMiner*. Retrieved 15 December 2021 from https://www.youtube.com/watch?v=im11NBJfjhM

Tuition, D. (2021). *RapidMiner Tutorial, Learn Data Cleaning, Data Visualization & Data Analysis with Rapidminer*. Retrieved 15 December 2021 from https://www.youtube.com/watch?v=r27eUHJtIFs

Vasudevan, S. (2021). *Rapid Miner Installation - Step by Step explanation*. Retrieved 15 December 2021 from https://www.youtube.com/watch?v=Wp42fV4q66Y

Chapter 4
Data Pre-Processing and Example of Data Classification With RapidMiner

ABSTRACT

In this book, the focus is on data mining with RapidMiner. However, it's important to note that there are other essential steps to consider when delving into the realm of data mining. This chapter serves as an introduction to the process of data pre-processing using RapidMiner, allowing readers to practice with a data set example available on the platform. With RapidMiner, data pre-processing begins with exploring the data visually and then selecting the features that will be analysed with each data mining technique. Managing missing values in a feature is also a crucial step in this process, which can be achieved by either eliminating or replacing them with appropriate values. In addition, RapidMiner allows data scientists to detect outliers and normalize features easily using diagram design, without requiring any computer programming skills. To help readers become familiar with the tools offered by RapidMiner, a classification technique will be demonstrated step-by-step in the book.

INTRODUCTION

RapidMiner is a tool supporting throughout the process of data science work (Mat, Lajis & Nasir, 2018). Data scientists can import data sets into RapidMiner software in order to prepare the data ready for processing with various data mining techniques (Dai et al., 2016: Samsani, 2016: Phan, Wu & Phan, 2021). In Missing Value Management and Outlier Management, when the data is available, data scientists can use various data mining models, either Supervised Learning or Unsupervised Learning (Cai et al., 2016: Mandhare & Idate, 2017: Susanti & Azizah, 2017: Abu-Soud, 2019). Processing algorithms are designed through model connections, and then the result of data processing is executed. To connect such models, the need for computer programming is unnecessary. Therefore, the scientists can quickly modify models at each step and perform reprocessing to improve the model's processing accuracy.

DOI: 10.4018/978-1-6684-4730-7.ch004

DATA PRE-PROCESSING USING RAPIDMINER SOFTWARE

To import datasets into a data mining model with RapidMiner software, data scientists can manipulate the data with Microsoft Excel. For example, Attribute Transformation is done to change the shape of the data before it is imported into RapidMiner software. They can also choose the operator within Rapid-Miner as well. An experiment can be performed to prepare the data as follows:

Figure 1. Using the Titanic sample dataset

Data scientists can choose to use the Titanic sample dataset for experimentation. After the dataset is imported into the process, data scientists connect the dataset's output to the Result section, and execute the model. The result is as follows.

Figure 2. Titanic dataset details

Row No.	Passenger ...	Name	Sex	Age	No of Sibling...	No of Parent...	Ticket Numb...	Passenger F...	Cabin	Port of Emi
1	First	Allen, Miss. E...	Female	29	0	0	24160	211.338	B5	Southampt.
2	First	Allison, Mast...	Male	0.917	1	2	113781	151.550	C22 C26	Southampt
3	First	Allison, Miss....	Female	2	1	2	113781	151.550	C22 C26	Southampt
4	First	Allison, Mr. H...	Male	30	1	2	113781	151.550	C22 C26	Southampt
5	First	Allison, Mrs...	Female	25	1	2	113781	151.550	C22 C26	Southampt
6	First	Anderson, Mr...	Male	48	0	0	19952	26.550	E12	Southampt
7	First	Andrews, Mis...	Female	63	1	0	13502	77.958	D7	Southampt
8	First	Andrews, Mr. ...	Male	39	0	0	112050	0	A36	Southampt
9	First	Appleton, Mrs...	Female	53	2	0	11769	51.479	C101	Southampt
10	First	Artagaveytia,...	Male	71	0	0	PC 17609	49.504	?	Cherbourg
11	First	Astor, Col. Jo...	Male	47	1	0	PC 17757	227.525	C62 C64	Cherbourg
12	First	Astor, Mrs. Jo...	Female	18	1	0	PC 17757	227.525	C62 C64	Cherbourg
13	First	Aubart, Mme....	Female	24	0	0	PC 17477	69.300	B35	Cherbourg
14	First	Barber, Miss....	Female	26	0	0	19877	78.850	?	Southampt
15	First	Barkworth, Mr...	Male	80	0	0	27042	30	A23	Southampt
16	First	Baumann, Mr...	Male	?	0	0	PC 17318	25.925	?	Southampt
17	First	Baxter, Mr. Qu...	Male	24	0	1	PC 17558	247.521	B58 B60	Cherbourg
18	First	Baxter, Mrs. J...	Female	50	0	1	PC 17558	247.521	B58 B60	Cherbourg

As seen in the data set details, the dataset consists of 1,309 records, and the missing values appear within the dataset. Within RapidMiner, a question mark is used to represent the Missing Values. When data scientists access the Age statistics section, it reveals the details of the Missing Values, as shown below.

Figure 3. The missing value details of age

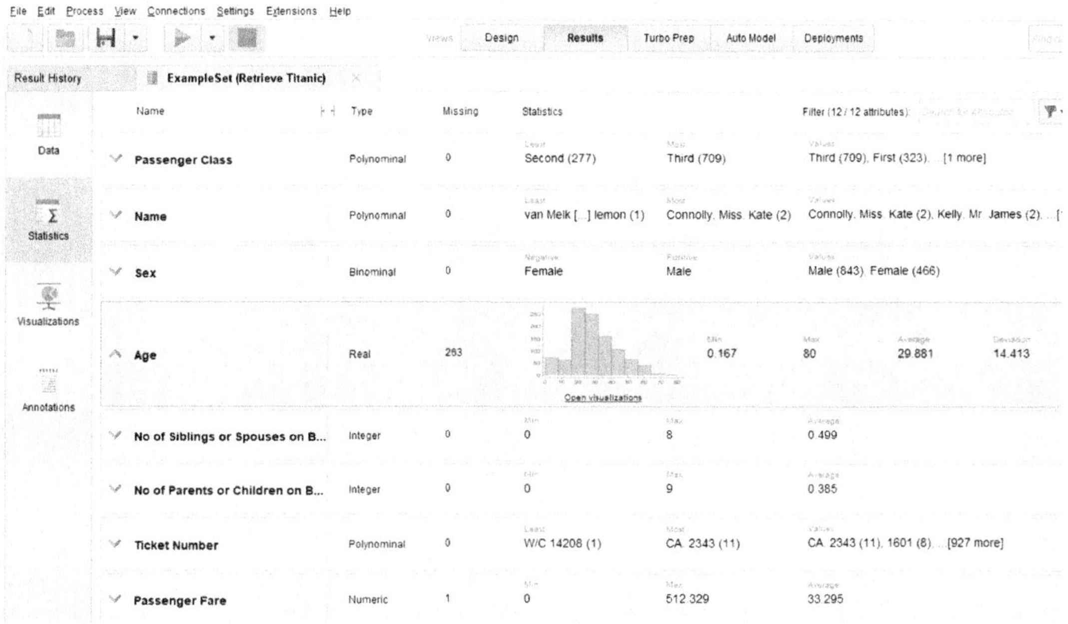

When looking at Age, there are 263 Missing Values. But to analyze the data, Age is required. Data scientists need to deal with the missing values in some ways. Data scientists can then press the Open Visualizations button to display the visual information as seen below.

From the figure, data scientists can consider the data distribution with histogram visualization which displays data of age ranges on the x-axis, and displays the data of the frequency on the y-axis. When considering the Titanic dataset, data scientists focus on the characteristics of the survivors and casualties from the Titanic shipwreck. Therefore, data scientists are necessary to consider the features useful for data analysis. And when considering from the datasets, some features should be excluded. This is due to 2 reasons. Firstly, the features on Passenger Names, Ticket Numbers and Ports of Embarkation which inform about passenger's destination should be eliminated because it does not affect the survival rate. And the other reason is that some data, namely Cabin Numbers and Life Boat Numbers, have a large number of missing values, which affects the accuracy of the data analysis. The data scientists can use an operator called Select Attributes to remove unwanted features from the data set as shown in the picture.

As obviously seen in the picture, data scientists connect models in the dataset to the Select Attribute, and then connect the Select Attribute to the Result. Meanwhile, the data scientists determine the parameters by selecting the Attribute Filter Type as the subset, then selecting the Select Attributes, and then selecting only the features they want. This process is called Feature Selection.

Figure 4. Visualization of age data

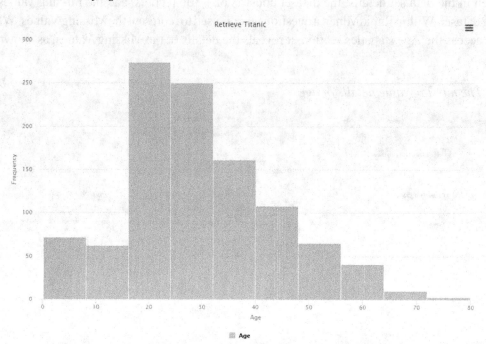

Figure 5. Select attributes

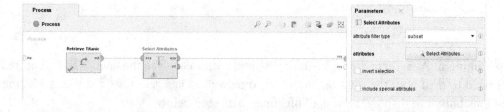

As a result of Feature Selection, when executing a model within the dataset, only the selected features are left. This is to prepare the data before processing with data mining techniques as shown in the picture below.

To operate the Feature Selection using models within the RapidMiner software, data scientists can select the features and also preserve the original dataset. However, within the datasets there can be missing value data. Therefore, data scientists can use the Operator named Replace Missing Value to manipulate the missing values.

Data scientists can manipulate the missing values for a specific feature by setting the Attribute Filter Type as the subset and select the Select Attributes. From the sample, the scientists select Age, then determine the default value as Average. Therefore, the missing value data within Age will be replaced by the mean as shown in the figure.

When manipulating the missing value data, data scientists must consider the outlier data. As seen in the example, the feature is called Passenger Fare or unusually expensive ticket prices which can be considered from the visual information as follows.

Figure 6. Feature selection

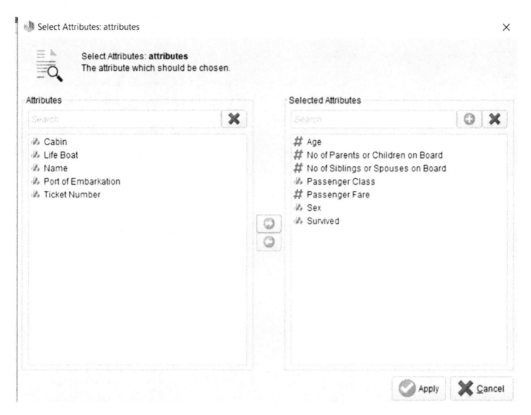

From visual histogram data, data scientists can observe a range of data that do not clump with other data, and have a low frequency. Therefore, such data may be considered as outlier, and can be manipulated using a model named Detect Outlier (Distances) as follows.

In the figure, data scientists can examine the outlier data and obtain the results from execution as seen below.

About the added feature, Outlier, data scientists can determine whether the data is an Outlier or not. If it is, the feature shows True, and if it is not, the feature shows False.

To determine Parameter in Number of Neighbors is to compare the data with 10 other numbers. If there is difference, it will be outlier. Number of Outliers refers to the amount of data that the data scientists consider as Outlier. In this case, the scientists can determine 100 outliers. After validating the outlier data, the scientists can remove the outlier from the dataset using a Filter Examples model.

Once the Filter Examples are imported into the Process, data Scientists define the conditions for removing the Outliers from the Data Set by assigning Parameters in the Filters section, and select the Outliers to equal False.

When the model is executed, the dataset has the outlier value as false, in order to store only the data that are not outlier.

Data scientists can then standardize data by Normalization as seen in the example. Data scientists need Normalization Feature called Age. The scientists can modify the age to range from 0 – 1. To normalize model, it can done as follow.

Figure 7. Data sets from feature selection

Row No.	Passenger ...	Sex	Age	No of Sibling...	No of Parent...	Passenger F...	Survived
1	First	Female	29	0	0	211.338	Yes
2	First	Male	0.917	1	2	151.550	Yes
3	First	Female	2	1	2	151.550	No
4	First	Male	30	1	2	151.550	No
5	First	Female	25	1	2	151.550	No
6	First	Male	48	0	0	26.550	Yes
7	First	Female	63	1	0	77.958	Yes
8	First	Male	39	0	0	0	No
9	First	Female	53	2	0	51.479	Yes
10	First	Male	71	0	0	49.504	No
11	First	Male	47	1	0	227.525	No
12	First	Female	18	1	0	227.525	Yes
13	First	Female	24	0	0	69.300	Yes
14	First	Female	26	0	0	78.850	Yes
15	First	Male	80	0	0	30	Yes
16	First	Male	?	0	0	25.925	No
17	First	Male	24	0	1	247.521	No
18	First	Female	50	0	1	247.521	Yes

ExampleSet (1,309 examples, 0 special attributes, 7 regular attributes)

Figure 8. Manipulating with missing value

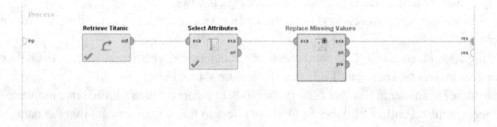

From the figure, data scientists can choose the type of data processing by adjusting the parameters, as presented below.

In the figure, data scientists select the Attribute Filter Type as the Subset, then press the Select Attribute button and the feature named Age. Then select Method to adjust the value within Age to be Rang Transformation in order to adjust the age data to range from 0 – 1. The result of executing is shown in the picture.

Therefore, in the process of surveying and preparing data, the scientists must explore data through visual data first. The missing value and outlier data are then manipulated with further processing (Luengo et al., 2020).

Figure 9. Determining parameter for replacing missing value

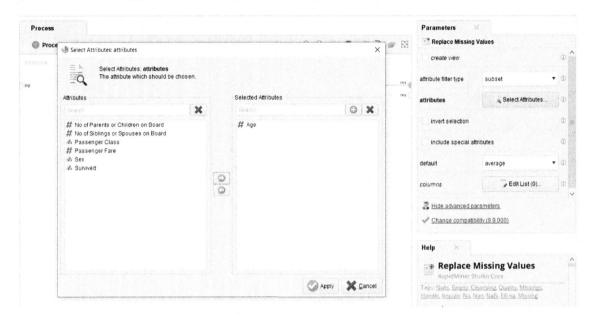

Figure 10. Titanic data set after manipulating the missing value

Row No.	Age	Passenger ...	Sex	No of Sibling...	No of Parent...	Passenger F...	Survived
4	30	First	Male	1	2	151.550	No
5	25	First	Female	1	2	151.550	No
6	48	First	Male	0	0	26.550	Yes
7	63	First	Female	1	0	77.958	Yes
8	39	First	Male	0	0	0	No
9	53	First	Female	2	0	51.479	Yes
10	71	First	Male	0	0	49.504	No
11	47	First	Male	1	0	227.525	No
12	18	First	Female	1	0	227.525	Yes
13	24	First	Female	0	0	69.300	Yes
14	26	First	Female	0	0	78.850	Yes
15	80	First	Male	0	0	30	Yes
16	29.881	First	Male	0	0	25.925	No
17	24	First	Male	0	1	247.521	No
18	50	First	Female	0	1	247.521	Yes
19	32	First	Female	0	0	76.292	Yes
20	36	First	Male	0	0	75.242	No
21	37	First	Male	1	1	52.554	Yes

ExampleSet (1,309 examples, 0 special attributes, 7 regular attributes)

Figure 11. Exploring the outlier data

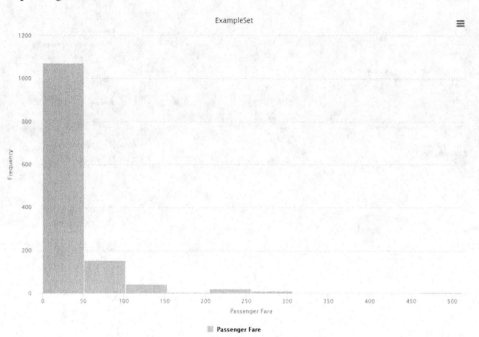

Figure 12. Outlier inspection

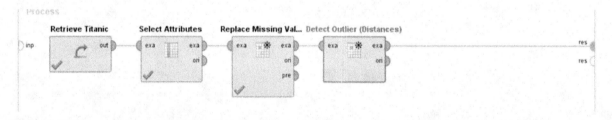

EXAMPLES OF DATA CLASSIFICATION WITH RAPIDMINER SOFTWARE

In data classification, data scientists pick up problems in data analysis from executives or data experts (Başarslan & Argun, 2018: Zuo & Guo, 2019). The problems are then defined, which is to determine the data sources and the datasets in order to find answers to the questions. A good example of classification is a case study of classification of the Titanic wreck survivors. Data scientists can choose to use sample datasets within the RapidMiner software, including pre-prepared datasets to teach machine learning and the original dataset containing target variables. Using datasets for teaching and testing follows the principles of data analysis, which is classified as Supervised Learning. The process is as seen below.

Data scientists analyze data using the Titanic Training dataset, which is a sample dataset within RapidMiner software. It is used to testify various forms of data analysis, as seen in the example. The scientists use the Decision Tree model, a technique for classifying data on the deaths and survivors of the Titanic wreck (Yang, 2019). The obtained result is seen in the following models.

Figure 13. Outlier data display

Row No.	outlier ↓	Passenger ...	Sex	Age	No of Sibling...	No of Parent...	Passenger F...	Survived
1	true	First	Female	29	0	0	211.338	Yes
2	true	First	Male	0.917	1	2	151.550	Yes
3	true	First	Female	2	1	2	151.550	No
4	true	First	Male	30	1	2	151.550	No
5	true	First	Female	25	1	2	151.550	No
10	true	First	Male	71	0	0	49.504	No
11	true	First	Male	47	1	0	227.525	No
12	true	First	Female	18	1	0	227.525	Yes
15	true	First	Male	80	0	0	30	Yes
17	true	First	Male	24	0	1	247.521	No
18	true	First	Female	50	0	1	247.521	Yes
24	true	First	Female	42	0	0	227.525	Yes
25	true	First	Female	29	0	0	221.779	Yes
28	true	First	Female	19	1	0	91.079	Yes
29	true	First	Female	35	0	0	135.633	Yes
33	true	First	Female	30	0	0	164.867	Yes
36	true	First	Female	45	0	0	262.375	Yes
43	true	First	Female	59	2	0	51.479	Yes

Figure 14. Determining the number of outliers

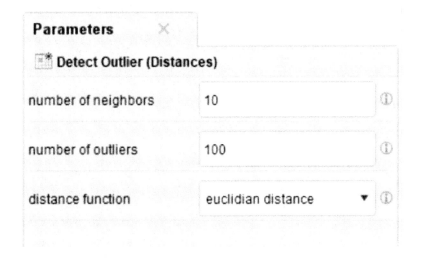

Figure 15. Removing outlier data from the datasets

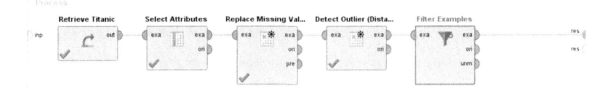

Figure 16. Defining conditions in order to remove outliers from datasets

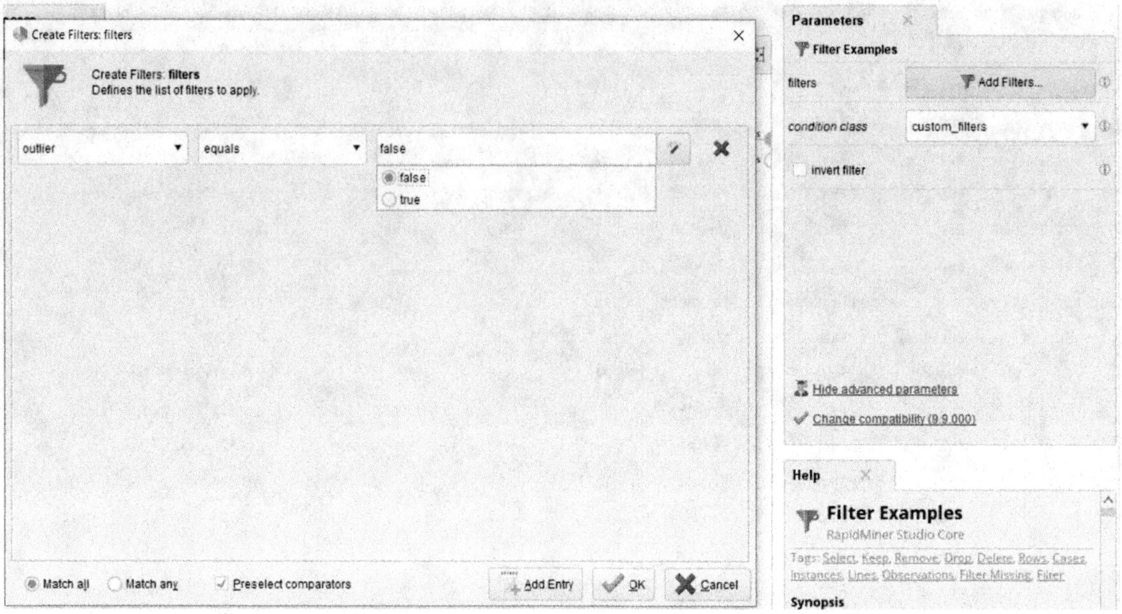

Figure 17. Datasets where the outlier data are removed

Row No.	outlier	Passenger ...	Sex	Age	No of Sibling...	No of Parent...	Passenger F...	Survived
1	false	First	Male	48	0	0	26.550	Yes
2	false	First	Female	63	1	0	77.958	Yes
3	false	First	Male	39	0	0	0	No
4	false	First	Female	53	2	0	51.479	Yes
5	false	First	Female	24	0	0	69.300	Yes
6	false	First	Female	26	0	0	78.850	Yes
7	false	First	Male	29.881	0	0	25.925	No
8	false	First	Female	32	0	0	76.292	Yes
9	false	First	Male	36	0	0	75.242	No
10	false	First	Male	37	1	1	52.554	Yes
11	false	First	Female	47	1	1	52.554	Yes
12	false	First	Male	26	0	0	30	Yes
13	false	First	Male	25	0	0	26	No
14	false	First	Male	25	1	0	91.079	Yes
15	false	First	Male	28	0	0	26.550	Yes
16	false	First	Male	45	0	0	35.500	No
17	false	First	Male	40	0	0	31	Yes
18	false	First	Female	58	0	0	26.550	Yes

ExampleSet (1,209 examples, 1 special attribute, 7 regular attributes)

Figure 18. Normalization

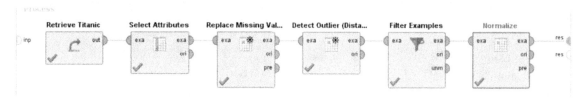

Figure 19. Assigning parameters to normalize

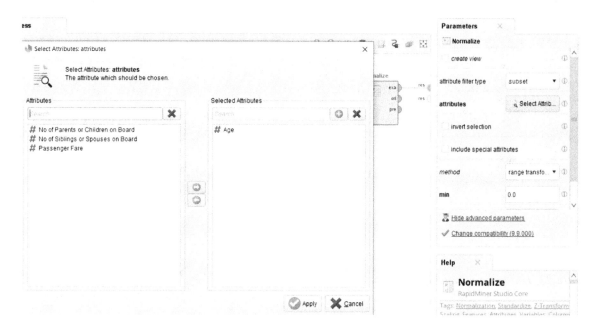

Based on the figure, data scientists set the parameter as 5 leaf nodes. The analysis shows that the mortality rate is higher in males than females. Data scientists then need to test the model's performance using the dataset. The scientists use the Titanic dataset as an example. The original dataset tests and determines the target variables as Survived in order to analyze the data.

From the picture, in order to test the performance of the model, the scientists determine target variables using the Set Role model, and then set Survived as a label or target variable. The data can be then analyzed using machine learning capabilities with the Apply Model.

From the picture, data scientists can use the Decision Tree that have been taught. The taught machine can test the Titanic dataset to identify which passengers died or survived. The results obtained from the test are as follows.

The scientists can compare the actual data, used to teach the machine learning, to classify the data whether each passenger survived or died. To test the classification accuracy, data scientists can use the Performance model.

After analyzing the data, data scientists can test the classification accuracy of machine using the Performance model and obtain the following results.

Figure 20. Dataset which are normalized

Row No.	outlier	Age	Passenger ...	Sex	No of Sibling...	No of Parent...	Passenger F...	Survived
1	false	0.685	First	Male	0	0	26.550	Yes
2	false	0.900	First	Female	1	0	77.958	Yes
3	false	0.556	First	Male	0	0	0	No
4	false	0.757	First	Female	2	0	51.479	Yes
5	false	0.341	First	Female	0	0	69.300	Yes
6	false	0.370	First	Female	0	0	78.850	Yes
7	false	0.426	First	Male	0	0	25.925	No
8	false	0.456	First	Female	0	0	76.292	Yes
9	false	0.513	First	Male	0	0	75.242	No
10	false	0.527	First	Male	1	1	52.554	Yes
11	false	0.671	First	Female	1	1	52.554	Yes
12	false	0.370	First	Male	0	0	30	Yes
13	false	0.356	First	Male	0	0	26	No
14	false	0.356	First	Male	1	0	91.079	Yes
15	false	0.399	First	Male	0	0	26.550	Yes
16	false	0.642	First	Male	0	0	35.500	No
17	false	0.570	First	Male	0	0	31	Yes
18	false	0.828	First	Female	0	0	26.550	Yes

ExampleSet (1,209 examples, 1 special attribute, 7 regular attributes)

Figure 21. Data analysis using decision tree

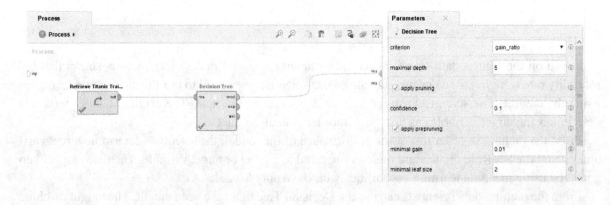

In the figure, the efficiency of machine learning classification is 78.76 percent, and the error is 21.24 percent. In data analysis by classification, data scientists can use RapidMiner software to analyze data through modeling without any need for programming (Ghous and Kovács, 2020). The scientists can use the useful datasets for data analysis to teach machine learning. This will lead to efficient data testing. This book introduces various data mining techniques to test, in order to obtain the results to the questions by using RapidMiner as a data analysis tool.

Figure 22. Results from decision tree analysis

Figure 23. Target variables (label)

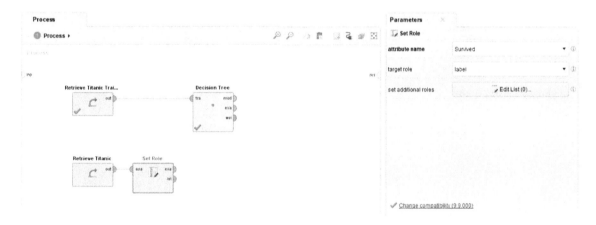

CASE STUDY

Automated Data Preparation (Zagatti et al., 2021)

Preparing the data before processing with data mining techniques starts with exploring whether the data is complete and consistent with the original dataset. Later, data scientists need to understand the nature of the data on whether it can actually be used for analysis to answer the questions. At this stage, the scientists can also create Attribute Transformations to change the format of the data so that it can be used for processing or collecting data from a variety of sources before then making Standardization to make the same data in different storage formats. The distribution of the data is then analyzed to determine how suitable it is to analyze. If the mean of the data is the outlier data, data scientists need to deal with those outliers. If the data is missing values, data scientists need to deal with those missing values as well. As is obvious, it requires a lot of the skill of a data scientist to pre-process the data. In addition, if the data scientist is not a Domain Expert who specializes in the data set, then it is necessary to rely on Domain Expert to analyze and interpret the results of data pre-processing at every step, which is even more complex. Although today's data pre-processing software such as Auto-Sklearn can be used for automated data cleaning, the aforementioned instruction set still cannot deal with data in the manner of categorical data. On the other hand, within RapidMiner provides an Auto Model to support scientists to perform a wide range of data mining models by traversing complex data mining techniques but the Auto Model does not cover all Data Pre-processing. Therefore, no matter what software a data scientist uses in data processing, in Data Pre-Processing, the scientists still have to use their own abilities and rely on Domain Experts.

Figure 24. Using the apply model

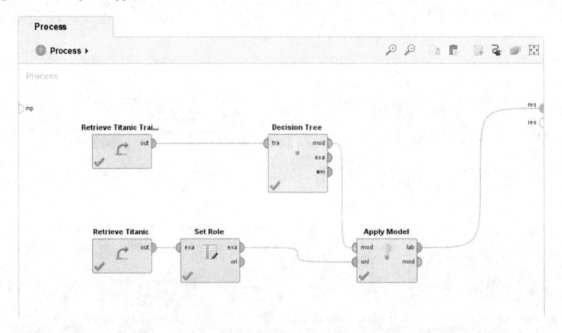

In 2021, there was a research article suggesting the use of meta-learning for the preparation of Data Pre-processing in an automated format (Zagatti et. al., 2021) to help optimize data pre-processing so that data scientists can encounter diverse and complex datasets. The technique uses a method of learning from the current dataset and then forecasting the data to complete the dataset. This algorithm starts with filling the data by adding mean, median, and frequency values into the missing value data. This research report uses One-Hot Encoding technique to turn those data into numbers. In the next step, this algorithm rescales all data to the same standard by Standardization in order to convert all data to $0 - 1$. This research has selected several datasets suitable for testing the efficacy of the algorithm and then measuring the efficiency of data cleaning using the Random Forest technique. Then, the new data set is forecasted using k-NN technique.

Figure 25. Results from decision tree data analysis

Row No.	Survived	prediction(S...	confidence(...	confidence(...	Passenger ...	Name	Sex
1	Yes	Yes	0.756	0.244	First	Allen, Miss. E...	Female
2	Yes	No	0.185	0.815	First	Allison, Mast...	Male
3	No	Yes	0.756	0.244	First	Allison, Miss...	Female
4	No	No	0.185	0.815	First	Allison, Mr. H...	Male
5	No	Yes	0.756	0.244	First	Allison, Mrs. ...	Female
6	Yes	No	0.185	0.815	First	Anderson, Mr....	Male
7	Yes	Yes	0.756	0.244	First	Andrews, Mis...	Female
8	No	No	0.185	0.815	First	Andrews, Mr...	Male
9	Yes	Yes	0.756	0.244	First	Appleton, Mrs...	Female
10	No	No	0.185	0.815	First	Artagaveytia, ...	Male
11	No	No	0.185	0.815	First	Astor, Col. Jo...	Male
12	Yes	Yes	0.756	0.244	First	Astor, Mrs. Jo...	Female
13	Yes	Yes	0.756	0.244	First	Aubart, Mme. ...	Female
14	Yes	Yes	0.756	0.244	First	Barber, Miss...	Female
15	Yes	No	0.185	0.815	First	Barkworth, Mr...	Male
16	No	No	0.185	0.815	First	Baumann, Mr...	Male
17	No	No	0.185	0.815	First	Baxter, Mr. Qu...	Male
18	Yes	Yes	0.756	0.244	First	Baxter, Mrs. J...	Female

Figure 26. Model performance test

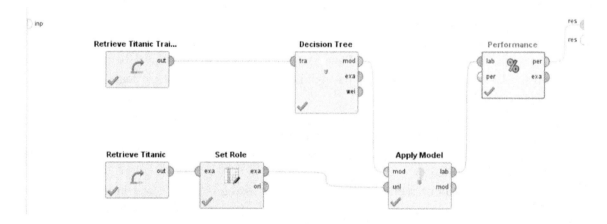

It can be seen that Data Pre-Processing is a challenging process that combines both data mining techniques, and the expertise of data scientists and Domain Expert. Data science requires a lot of practices and experiences.

Figure 27. Model accuracy

accuracy: 78.76%

	true Yes	true No	class precision
pred. Yes	338	116	74.45%
pred. No	162	693	81.05%
class recall	67.60%	85.66%	

Extracting Data from Social Media for Analysis (Zadeh et al., 2021)

Amidst the transition from data warehouse collection, data scientists are facing with Big Data collection. More and more businesses are gearing up to be data-driven organizations and have discovered that social media is the source of the big data. Businesses can access data sources on social media and collect them to extract only the parts they need for data pre-processing. It is then analyzed with data mining techniques to obtain results consistent with business problems. There are a number of tools from different vendors that support Big Data analytics such as IBM or Cloudera.

In 2021, there was a research on extracting data from social media for data analysis (Zadeh, Zolbanin & Sharda, 2021). The researchers aimed for creating a tool to support data analysis courses, especially the Big Data for teachers to use as a teaching tool for students. The researchers have used a lot of tools to create a framework to be used as a teaching tool, including 1. InfoSphere BigInsights from the IBM which has a Big Data processing environment based on Hadoop, 2. JSON Query Language (JAQL) to process semi-structured data, 3. BigSheets that supports Data Exploration and Data Visualization on Big SQL, 4. Annotation Query Language (AQL) for Text Analytics to analyze semi-structured and unstructured text data, and 5. Big R for processing data on Hadoop.

Such a research has been carried out Five datasets out of 180. All datasets were tested and 5 datasets were selected, from the Accuracy, for experimentation. For example, the Titanic dataset or the Bike Buyers dataset consists of 1. Missing Value Dataset and Categorial Dataset, 2. Missing Value Dataset and non-Categorial Dataset 3. Non-Missing Value Dataset and Categorial Dataset 4. Non-Missing Value Dataset and non-Categorial Dataset, and 5. Missing Value Dataset only for numeric features and Features that are Categorial Data.

The study selected five datasets for the experiment because this research aims to test the efficiency of the model in extracting data from social media during the data pre-processing process. With the use of a variety of tools such as Auto-sklearn, the researchers compared the extraction efficiency from several methods with Accuracy value.

From such efforts, it can be seen that the Data Pre-Processing is diverse, and in many cases data scientists need the right tools for each dataset and each data analysis purpose. No machine perfectly fits all, so data scientists need to study and apply them for each task.

CONCLUSION

Data science work starts with questions asked by executives from the business sectors or data experts in other industries, such as the medical industry or agricultural industry. After receiving those problems, the scientists seek information sources consisting of internal data or data from outside the organization. Then, the dataset is taken to survey the data in order to determine whether the dataset can answer the questions via the process of data pattern analysis, Missing Value analysis and Outlier analysis. Then, the data is prepared for analyzing with data mining techniques; such as manipulating the Missing Value, manipulating the Outlier and Data Normalization. Data techniques can be used to respond to the questions. Data scientists can also examine how accurate the model is. During the process, the data scientists can also return to data preparation for more accurate data analysis. Once the have been obtained, the scientists can use the results to present to the questioners. In this whole process, the scientists can use RapidMiner software to support work from the start.

EXERCISE QUESTIONS

1. Manipulate the Missing Value using the Titanic dataset.
2. Manipulate the Outliers using the Titanic dataset.
3. Classify the data with the Decision Tree model using the Titanic Trained dataset.
4. Test the classification efficiency of the data using the Titanic dataset with the Titanic Trained dataset.

REFERENCES

Abu-Soud, S. M. (2019). A Novel Approach for Dealing with Missing Values in Machine Learning Datasets with Discrete Values. *2019 International Conference on Computer and Information Sciences (ICCIS)*, 1-5. 10.1109/ICCISci.2019.8716430

Başarslan, M. S., & Argun, İ. D. (2018). Classification Of a bank data set on various data mining platforms. *2018 Electric Electronics, Computer Science, Biomedical Engineerings' Meeting*, *2018*, 1–4.

Cai, S., Sun, R., Hao, S., Li, S., & Yuan, G. (2016). An efficient outlier detection approach on weighted data stream based on minimal rare pattern mining. *China Communications, 16*(10), 83-99.

Dai, H., Zhang, S., Wang, L., & Ding, Y. (2016). Research and implementation of big data preprocessing system based on Hadoop. *2016 IEEE International Conference on Big Data Analysis (ICBDA)*, 1-5. 10.1109/ICBDA.2016.7509802

Ghous, H., & Kovács, L. (2020). Efficiency Comparison of Python and Rapidminer. *Multidiszciplináris Tudományok*, *10*(3), 212–220. doi:10.35925/j.multi.2020.3.26

Mandhare, H. C., & Idate, S. R. (2017). A comparative study of cluster based outlier detection, distance based outlier detection and density based outlier detection techniques. *2017 International Conference on Intelligent Computing and Control Systems (ICICCS)*, 931-935. 10.1109/ICCONS.2017.8250601

Mat, T. M., Lajis, A., & Nasir, H. (2018). Text Data Preparation in RapidMiner for Short Free Text Answer in Assisted Assessment. *2018 IEEE 5th International Conference on Smart Instrumentation, Measurement and Application (ICSIMA)*, 1-4.

Phan, Q.-T., Wu, Y.-K., & Phan, Q.-D. (2021). An Overview of DataPreprocessing for Short-Term Wind Power Forecasting. *2021 7th International Conference on Applied System Innovation (ICASI), Applied System Innovation (ICASI), 2021 7th International Conference On*, 121–125.

Samsani, S. (2016). An RST based efficient preprocessing technique for handling inconsistent data. *2016 IEEE International Conference on Computational Intelligence and Computing Research (ICCIC)*, 1-8. 10.1109/ICCIC.2016.7919591

Susanti, S. P., & Azizah, F. N. (2017). Imputation of missing value using dynamic Bayesian network for multivariate time series data. *2017 International Conference on Data and Software Engineering (ICoDSE)*, 1-5. 10.1109/ICODSE.2017.8285864

Yang, F.-J. (2019). An Extended Idea about Decision Trees. *2019 International Conference on Computational Science and Computational Intelligence (CSCI)*, 349-354. 10.1109/CSCI49370.2019.00068

Zadeh, A. H., Zolbanin, H. M., & Sharda, R. (2021). Incorporating Big Data Tools for Social Media Analytics in a Business Analytics Course. *Journal of Information Systems Education*, *32*(3), 176–198.

Zagatti, F. R., Silva, L. C., Dos Santos Silva, L. N., Sette, B. S., Caseli, H. de M., Lucredio, D., & Silva, D. F. (2021). MetaPrep: Data preparation pipelines recommendation via meta-learning. *2021 20th IEEE International Conference on Machine Learning and Applications (ICMLA), Machine Learning and Applications (ICMLA), 2021 20th IEEE International Conference on, ICMLA*, 1197–1202.

Zuo, L., & Guo, J. (2019). Customer Classification of Discrete Data Concerning Customer Assets Based on Data Mining. *2019 International Conference on Intelligent Transportation, Big Data & Smart City (ICITBS)*. 10.1109/ICITBS.2019.00093

Chapter 5
Classification

ABSTRACT

In the world of data mining, classification reigns supreme as a popular technique for supervised learning. Its ability to identify patterns in data by dividing it into training sets and utilizing machine learning makes it an essential tool in answering critical questions related to data. For instance, classification can aid businesses in identifying customers with high purchasing potential. One of the standout features of classification is k-nearest neighbors (k-NN), which allows data to be classified according to the training data set. Decision trees are also commonly used to support decision making by producing easily interpretable diagrams. RapidMiner is an outstanding data mining tool that can employ a range of classification techniques, including k-NN, decision trees, and naïve Bayes. In this book, readers can follow a step-by-step guide to using these techniques with RapidMiner to achieve effective data classification.

INTRODUCTION

Data classification is the intension to classify or identify the data such as the classification of customers who are likely to change mobile phone companies. The results obtained from the analysis are the Discreate or Categorial Data, which indicates the cluster or the type of data (Vichi, Ritter & Giusti, 2013). In data science, this group of data is referred as a Class Label. To have a variable target is to classify data using the principle of Supervised-Learning in data processing by dividing the data into 2 parts (Mishra, & Vats, 2021). Part 1 is for teaching machines to learn, and part 2 is to test the performance of the model. The data classification techniques are processed as follows.

As seen in the figure, data scientists can use Classification Algorithm such as K-Nearest Neighbor (k-NN) or Decision Tree to create Classification Model using Training Data to teach the machines to learn in order to obtain the needed results from data classification (Liu, 2021: Mladenova, 2021). Then, Test Data is used to apply the model to test the model's accuracy performance. The test data and the results obtained from the classification are compared.

DOI: 10.4018/978-1-6684-4730-7.ch005

Figure 1. Data analysis with classification

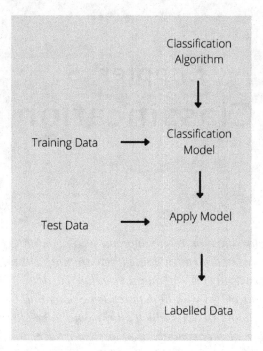

GENERATING TRAINING AND TEST DATA SET

The main principle of Supervised-Learning is to divide the data into 2 parts, consisting of Training Data Set and Test Data Set.

Holdout Method

To divide the data set by Holdout Method, the data is divided into 2 parts including Training Data Set 70% and Test Data Set 30%. However, if the Holdout method is used in cases where the data set is small and is still allocated for model testing, the model lacks the opportunity to learn the nature of the data and ultimately reduces the processing accuracy.

Cross Validation

Cross Validation method is to determine the number of rounds of division into k cycles by dividing the data into 2 parts in every cycle (Mnich et al., 2020). For example, the number of data division is determined and k is equal to 4. Therefore, in Round 1, Cross Validation will identify the part 1 data as a Test Data Set, and parts 2 – 4 as Training Data Set. In the second round, Cross Validation will indicate the part 2 data as Test Data Set, and parts 1 and 3 – 4 as Training Data Set. In the third round, Cross Validation will determine the part 3 as Test Data Set, and Parts 1 - 2 and 4 as Training Data Set. And finally in the fourth round, Cross Validation will set the part 4 data as Test Data Set, and Part 1 - 3 as Training Data Set, as seen below.

Figure 2. Cross validation

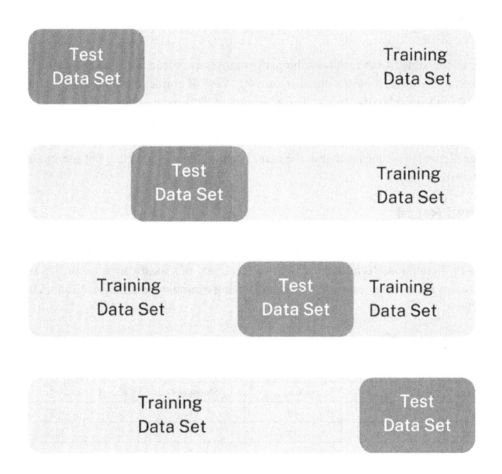

CROSS VALIDATION

This processing allows the Classification Model to be taught and tested within the entire dataset. As a result, even though the data scientists have received the data set with less instances, they can teach the machine learning very well. To test the Classification Technique accuracy, the data set is divided into k number of rounds. The mean precision of all rounds is taken to compute in order to obtain a precision value, the representative of the processing of the data set for each round.

Model Accuracy

Data scientists can measure the efficiency of data classification using the Confusion Matrix which presents not only the number of the correct classification, but also the number of misclassifications as seen in the following example (Görtler et al., 2021).

Table 1. Confusion matrix

		Predicted Value	
		Yes	No
Actual Value	Yes	40	10
	No	30	20

According to the table, if the results of the performance, evaluated with the Confusion Matrix, are obtained as seen in the table, it means that there are 40 "Yes" of correct classification, "True Positive", and there are 10 of the misclassifications, "False Negative". This means there are 50 "Yes" in the actual data, but the model can correctly recognize only 40. On the other hand, there are 30 "No" of the correct classification, which is then called "False Positive", and there are 20 of data misclassification, which is called "True Negative". It means that in the actual data, there are 50 "No", but the model is able to correctly recognize only 20.

Precision and Recall

To assess the data accuracy, precision can also be used to show the accuracy of classification for data such as Soaps or Shampoos. Recall is to present the accuracy of classification according to the actual data, such as Soaps and Shampoos as seen in the following example (Khan, & Ali Rana, 2019).

Table 2. Precision and recall

		Predicted Value		Recall
		Soap	Shampoos	
Actual Value	Soap	40	10	80%
	Shampoos	30	20	40%
Precision		57%	66%	

From the table, data scientists can determine the accuracy of the data classification with 2 measurements. First is Precision. It shows the accuracy ratio of each class as Soap has 57% accuracy. It is calculated by taking 40 to divide by 70. The total classification of the Soap and Shampoo data shows the accuracy of 66%, which is calculated by dividing 20 by 30, which is the proportion of all classifications of Shampoos. The other measurement is Recall, the real data that is accurately classified. The accuracy corresponds to the actual data of Soap is 80%, which is calculated by dividing 40 by 50. And the accuracy of the actual Shampoo data is 40 percent, which is calculated by 20 divided by 50.

OVERFITTING AND UNDERFITTING

In processing with data mining techniques, data scientists can encounter problems with the outcomes in two ways:

1. **Overfitting:** When the data set used to process and the result share a very close relationship, the results obtained from forecasting or classification are very accurate (Junaidi et al., 2021). It was, however, found that the results of forecasting or classification show very low accuracy when testing the model.
2. **Underfitting:** When the results from teaching machines and the model test have very low accuracy, the obtained results, when tested, shows low accuracy (Zhang, Zhang, & Jiang, 2019).

To figure out these two issues, the scientists need to use the Cross Validation technique so that the model can learn the entire dataset. And the performance of data forecasting or classifying can be tested until the problems regarding both overfitting and underfitting can be eliminated. Then, the scientists can apply that processing to the test which has higher accuracy.

INCREASING ACCURACY OF MODEL DATA CLASSIFICATIONS

For Data Pre-Processing, data scientists will do Data Exploration to explore the outlier data and manipulate them by considering cutting them along with the Domain Expert's advice (Song et al,. 2021). Missing Value data are explored in order to fill them with other values. If there is a small number of missing values, some missing values are considered being eliminated. Or if there is a large number of missing values, it should be considering not using the dataset. Attributes that are not useful for data analysis, such as ID card numbers are considered too so that the dataset has only the attributes that can be used to analyze the data accurately. Interchangeable attributes such as gender titles, Mr. or Miss, and male and female are also considered. These two types of data categories can be used interchangeably in order to create high-precision modeling and reduce too many computing resources. Data scientists can consider choosing either of them to analyze. Generalization is the arrangement of data into a suitable format such as grouping revenue into continuous data, ranging 15,000 – 20,000 baht, so that the data are suitable for the classification techniques.

K-NEAREST NEIGHBOR (K-NN)

K-Nearest Neighbor (k-NN) is a data mining technique in terms of Classification with the characteristics of Supervised-Learning, which is used to divide the data into 2 parts; to teach the machine learning and to test the data classification (Rahman et al., 2021) The k-NN also aims to classify the data. For example, data scientists have data to teach machines to learn about each type of film, such as drama or comedy. The scientists, then, bring the test data into the model to allow k-NN to determine what form the film matches. The process is illustrated as follows (Nuttavut Thongjor, 2017).

Table 3. Data used for teaching machine learning before processing with k-NN

Movies	Crying Scenes	Comedy Scenes	Types
Ant's Tear	10	2	Drama
The Mourning Land	8	3	Drama
The Slavery	9	5	Drama
Happy Lettuce	2	15	Comedy
Cat Adventure	3	13	Comedy
Golden Age Amour	9	4	Drama

On the tables, data scientists can input data into models to teach machine learning about movie genres in order to classify data in the film "Golden Age Amour" by calculating the distance of the film and other movies. Then, the k-NN technique will classify "Golden Age Amour" in the same category as the movies with similar distances. It can be calculated according to the following formula

$$Distance = \sqrt{\left(Crying\,Scenes - the\,Data\,Classification\,required\,Crying\,Scenes\right)^2 + \left(Comedy\,Scene - the\,Data\,Classification\,required\,Comedy\,Scenes\right)^2}$$

Data scientists are able to calculate the distances from "Golden Age Amour" to the other films and shows in the following results:

Table 4. the distances of "Golden Age Amour"

Movies	Crying Scenes	Comedy Scenes	Distance	Types
Ant's Tear	10	2	2.23	Drama
The Mourning Land	8	3	1.41	Drama
The Slavery	9	5	1	Drama
Happy Lettuce	2	15	13.03	Comedy
Cat Adventure	3	13	10.81	Comedy
Golden Age Amour	9	4	?	

From the table, when k equals 3, it means there are 3 films with similar distances to "Golden Age Amour", which are Ant's Tear, The Mourning Land and The Slavery. Golden Age Amour, when processed with k-NN technique, is therefore classified as a drama. The scientists can use the k-NN technique to classify data by calculating the nearest distance in order to classify the data from data similarity. The number of k can determine the amount of data used to consider the similarity.

DECISION TREE

Decision Tree is used for data classification (Puspitasari et al., 2021) The results come in the form of a tree diagram. Data scientists have to divide the data into two parts, the data for teaching machine learning and the data for testing. The tree is formed from the results of each test attribute that data scientists use as the condition for data analysis. The tree diagram shows the results by branching in relation to the results in the root analysis, where the leaf node of each branch is the classes or the results. To use the results obtained from Decision Tree analysis, data scientists can take into account the decision-making conditions.

Figure 3. Data classification with decision tree

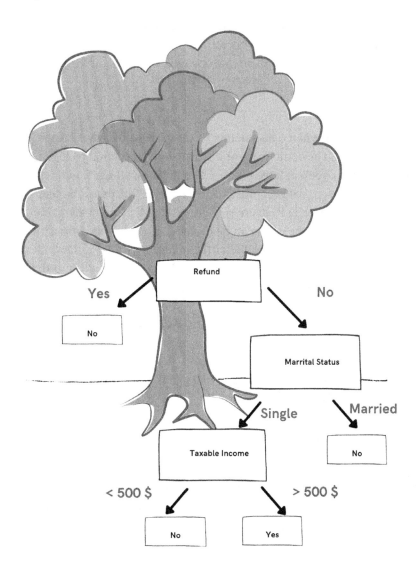

In the diagram, data scientists create a Decision Tree from the attributes consisting of Refund which means the tax refund, Marital Status which is the tax payer marital status, and Taxable Income which is the amount of income that has reached tax threshold. Cheat means to enter false data in order to receive a tax refund. Each attribute contains the following data.

Table 5. Examples of data used in determining the classification

Refund	Marital Status	Taxable Income	Cheat
No	Married	499$	?

From the sample data, data scientists need to know whether the instance is from someone who falsifies the data in order to obtain a tax refund. It can be determined from the Decision Tree, that the person who has requested a tax refund is not eligible for a tax refund if the person is married and has taxable income less than $500. The instances can tell whether someone falsifies the data in order to obtain a tax refund.

Creating a Decision Tree

Creating a decision tree begins when data scientists consult a Knowledge Expert on which attributes should be used in the analysis. The complexity of the decision tree should be taken into account. Therefore, the scientists should not choose a large number of attributes, which would result in the complexity of data classification. In addition, data scientists can also select attributes by using Information Gain, which can be calculated in 2 ways: 1. Reduction of Impurity Measure is the value that each class that can divide into classes. The better the class can be divided, the better the Impurity Measure value will be lower. 2.Entropy is data uncertainty. The better the ability to divide a class, the lower the Entropy. To select attributes to create a decision tree, it can split the decision path in order that data scientists can consider the classification of data in some ways. This book will calculate Information Gain from Entropy as shown in the example below.

There are totally 14 instances, with the label being voluntary resignation divided into 5 times of no resignation, and 9 times of resignation. Data scientists can calculate Entropy by the following formula.

$$\text{Entropy} ([9,5]) = - (5/14) \log_2 (5/14) - (9/14) \log_2 (9/14)$$
$$= 0.94$$

From the calculations, data Scientists have obtained the Entropy of 0.94, which is very high. It means that the Information Gain is at the level that should be improved for more capabilities in data classification. Therefore, data scientists can calculate the Entropy of each Attribute to compare data classification performance along with labels, starting from an attribute named high, moderate and low Work Experience. The data in each category is related to the voluntary resignation information as shown in Table 7.

According to data relationship, scientists must calculate the Entropy for each type of data as follows.

$$\text{Entropy (High Work Experience, 2 resign, 3 no resign)} = - (2/5) \log_2(2/5) - (3/5) \log_2(3/5)$$
$$= 0.97$$

Table 6. Examples of information gain data sets

Work Experience	Education	Family Status	Marital Status	Voluntary Resignation
High	Ph. D.	High	Single	No resign
High	Ph. D.	High	Married	No resign
Moderate	Ph. D.	Moderate	Single	Resign
Low	Master	High	Single	Resign
Low	Bachelor	High	Single	Resign
Low	Bachelor	Moderate	Married	No resign
Moderate	Bachelor	Moderate	Married	Resign
High	Master	High	Single	No resign
High	Bachelor	Moderate	Single	Resign
Low	Master	Moderate	Single	Resign
High	Master	Moderate	Married	Resign
Moderate	Master	High	Married	Resign
Moderate	Ph. D.	Moderate	Single	Resign
High	Master	High	Married	No resign

Table 7. Relationship of work experience data with voluntary resignation data

High Work Experience	Resign	Resign	No Resign	No Resign	No Resign
Moderate Work Experience	Resign	Resign	Resign	Resign	-
Low Work Experience	Resign	Resign	Resign	No Resign	No Resign

In addition, when calculated with the same method for data of Moderate Experience and Low Experience, the entropy values are obtained as 0 and 0.97, respectively. The entropy of the three data types can be calculated for the average for the labeled data as follows:

$$\text{Average Entropy} = (5/14)0.97 + (4/14)0 + (5/14)0.97$$
$$= 0.693$$

Data scientists obtain the Entropy value of the label classification from an attribute named Experience at 0.693. The scientists can do this calculation on the rest of the attributes, and then the entropy of each attribute is subtracted from the total entropy of the data set, in order to obtain Information Gain. For example, if the total Entropy of this data set is 0.94 – 0.693, which is the Entropy of the Work experience attribute, the Information Gain value is 0.247. Therefore, when calculating Information Gain together with other Attributes that have been computed for Entropy, such datasets have Information Gain values for each Attribute as presented in Table 8.

Table 8. Information gain values from the sample dataset

Work Experience	0.247
Education	0.029
Family Status	0.152
Marital Status	0.048

Based on the Information Gain value, data scientists can select the Work Experience Attribute, which has the greatest Information Gain value as the first node, to be able to classify the data effectively in either direction.

Pruning the Tree

In cases data scientists use a dataset consisting of a large number of attributes, which may or may not be related. This results in the creation of a large decision tree which contains a large number of Branches and Leaf Nodes (Karthik & Krishnan, 2021). Moreover, when the data are tested on the model, it has low accuracy that causes overfitting. Therefore, it is necessary for the scientists to prune the tree in order to create the decision tree from the attributes useful for decision-making and small enough to use as a decision-making criterion. Data scientists can determine the highest level of Information Gain that they can tolerate, so that the level of leaf node within the Decision Tree has appropriate number without the complexity. In other cases, the scientists can determine the minimum number of Branches and Leaf Nodes by defining values in both the Information Gain form and the number of Branches and Leaf Nodes. The scientists can define parameters within RapidMiner software, which will be later presented in the next section.

Strengths and Weaknesses of Decision Tree

Decision Tree is a data mining technique used for data classification. It is easy to understand and suitable for analyzing small or Low Dimensionality to enable easy-to-classify decision trees. Data scientists can select only the attributes that affect the consideration with Information Gain analysis or consulting with Domain Expert to obtain reasonable classification conditions. However, if the scientists choose a large number of attributes to create a decision tree, it will result in a large number of leaf nodes and a complexity in classifying the data. Also, if the inappropriate attributes are selected, it will result in a classification error.

NAÏVE BAYES

Naïve Bayes is a data mining technique based on Bayesian Classifier, using probability to classify data within the entire dataset (Rabiul Alam et al., 2021) For example, if we have seen a patient with symptoms similar to COVID-19 infection, we can use probabilities to calculate the percentage of the possibility of COVID-19 infection. The main principle of Naïve Bayes is data analysis based on the principle of probability. Data scientists can classify the data from existing data sets by importing the data sets into the

Table 9. The instances the scientists need to classify with naïve Bayes

Work Experience	Education	Family Status	Marital Status	Voluntary Resignation
High	Master	High	Married	?

Naïve Bayes model to teach the machine learning. Then, the model is tested and the data are categorized. This book uses an example to analyze whether the data sets, including work experience, education, family base, status and voluntary resignation, can tell the employees' voluntariness to resign. The formula based on Bayes Theorem is presented as follows:

P refers to Possibility
C refers to Data Class
A refers to Attribute

$$P\left(C|A\right) = \frac{P\left(A|C\right)P\left(C\right)}{P\left(A\right)}$$

From the formula, data scientists can classify the data according to the instances as seen in the following example.

From Table 10, the sample datasets can be taken from Table 7 to analyze the probability whether employees with such data will decide to resign or not.

P (resign| E) = P (work experience= high | resign) x
P (education = master | resign) x
P (family status = high | resign) x
P (marital status = married | resign) x

$$P \text{ (resign) /P (E)} = \frac{\frac{2}{9} * \frac{3}{9} * \frac{3}{9} * \frac{3}{9} * \frac{9}{14}}{P\left(E\right)}$$

= 0.0053/P(E)

P (no resign| E) = P (work experience = high | no resign) x
P (education = master | no resign) x
P (family status = high | no resign) x
P (marital status = married | no resign) x

$$P \text{ (no resign) } /P \text{ (E)} = \frac{\frac{3}{5} * \frac{1}{5} * \frac{4}{5} * \frac{3}{5} * \frac{5}{14}}{P\left(E\right)}$$

$= 0.0206/P \text{ (E)}$

As in the example, data scientists use the datasets from Table 7 to classify the data, divided into 9 employees who voluntarily resigned and 5 employees who voluntarily did not resign out of the total of 14. Therefore, the scientists can use Bayes Theorem to analyze the probability according to Table 27 to classify whether such employees will resign or not. The probability for resignation is analyzed as 0.0053, and the probability of not leaving is 0.0206. Therefore, data scientist could choose the highest probability level, which is no resignation. The scientists can apply Naïve Bayes to classify data by relying on the data set imported into the model. The results obtained from the Naïve Bayes model is in the form of probabilities, which can be used to classify the data.

OTHER METHODS FOR CLASSIFICATION

In addition to the classification techniques discussed in Sections 1–4, data scientists can use other models to perform classification.

Support Vector Machine (SVM): It is a coefficient calculation used to classify data. The coefficients are created as a line in the data classification (Hyperplane). Each calculation can create multiple lines to classify data. But a good line to be used to classify the data must have the nearest distance, from the line to the data. So, they can split the data appropriately. The classified data are then called Support Vector (Jamalludin et al, 2021).

Artificial Neuron Network: ANN is one of the Classification Techniques by which data scientists can divide the data sets into 2; one is for teaching the machines to learn about the data types and datasets, and the other one is used to test whether the ANN model is able to classify the data precisely. The ANN technique also optimizes the data to be factual by adjusting the weight of each node within the model. The accuracy of ANN classification is high (Fadlil, Umar, & Gustina, 2019).

Logistic Regression: According to the concept of Linear Regression, if data scientists need to forecast data with results that are split into two values, or other results that are Category Data, the data scientists need to use Logistic Regression to predict it. Therefore, Logistic Regression is used to classify data by forecasting the likelihood of an outcome as classified (Thangakumar & Kommina, 2020). For example, the prognosis of a patient's chances of COVID-19 infection or not is similar to the other classification techniques. Data scientists need to consult a Domain Expert to select attributes that can be used to classify data effectively.

DATA CLASSIFICATION WITH RAPIDMINER SOFTWARE

The data classification experiment using RapidMiner software covers three methods: k-NN, Decision Tree and Naïve Bayes:

k-NN Data Mining Technique

Data scientists can perform k-NN data mining classification experiments using Golf datasets within RapidMiner.

Figure 4. Sample dataset: Golf

By bringing a sample dataset named Golf into that model, within the datasets are the attributes "Play" which stands for playing golf, "Outlook" for weather, "Temperature", "Humanity", and "Wind". These attributes can be used to classify the data and tell whether to play golf or not to play golf. Within the data set, there are instances as follows:

Figure 5. Details of golf dataset

Row No.	Play	Outlook	Temperature	Humidity	Wind
1	no	sunny	85	85	false
2	no	sunny	80	90	true
3	yes	overcast	83	78	false
4	yes	rain	70	96	false
5	yes	rain	68	80	false
6	no	rain	65	70	true
7	yes	overcast	64	65	true
8	no	sunny	72	95	false
9	yes	sunny	69	70	false
10	yes	rain	75	80	false
11	yes	sunny	75	70	true
12	yes	overcast	72	90	true
13	yes	overcast	81	75	false
14	no	rain	71	80	true

Then the data scientist can right click, select Insert Building Block and select Nominal Cross Validation to divide the data into Train Set and Test Set.

Figure 6. Using nominal cross validation

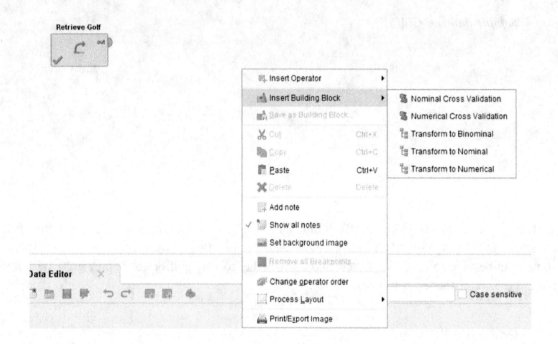

Figure 7. Bringing cross-validation into the model

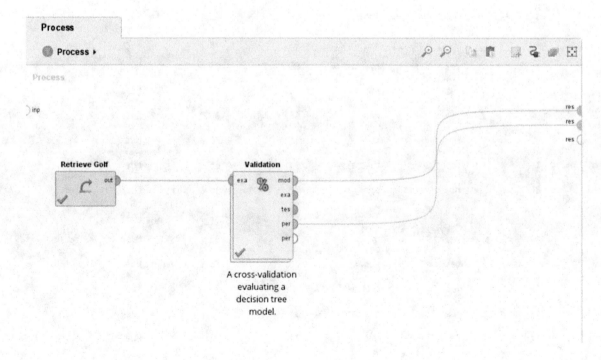

Then, data scientists make a connection between the Golf dataset and Validation, and connect the results of machine learning to the results of model performance testing. Within Validation, the Decision Tree data mining technique is set as default.

Figure 8. Default validation

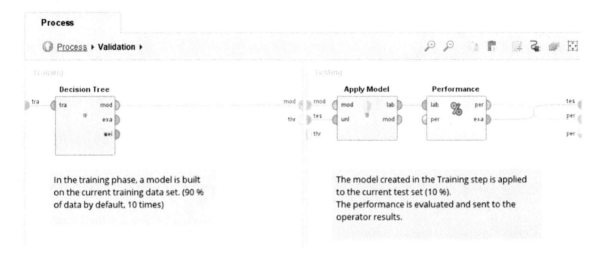

Meanwhile, the data scientists replace the Decision Tree model with the k-NN model as follows.

Figure 9. Using the k-NN technique for data classification

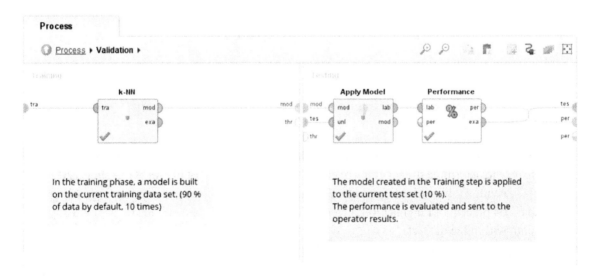

To use the k-NN model, data scientists are required to determine the k number, or the number of distance analysis. From the example, k is set as 3.

Figure 10. Setting k number

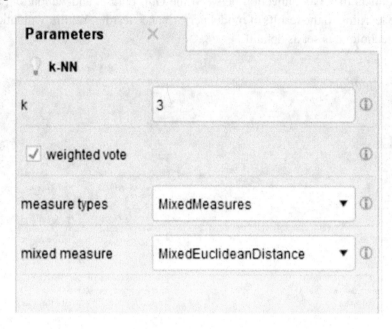

Afterwards, data scientists are able to perform data processing experiments with the k-NN data mining technique and then obtain the following results.

Figure 11. Results of data processing with k-NN data mining technique

accuracy: 55.00% +/- 43.78% (micro average: 57.14%)

	true no	true yes	class precision
pred. no	1	2	33.33%
pred. yes	4	7	63.64%
class recall	20.00%	77.78%	

In the figure, it shows RapidMiner software renders data using precision and recall techniques. The scientists are able to determine the accuracy of each class. The data on Not Playing Golf shows 20 percent accuracy, and Playing Golf is 77.8% accurate. Accuracy of classified data of Not Playing Golf is 33.33 percent, and 63.64 percent of Playing Golf. Overall, the accuracy is 55 percent due to the relatively small amount of data within the dataset.

Data Classification Using Decision Tree

Based on the previous datasets which are Golf and Cross Validation, when data scientists need to analyze data using Decision Tree, they can use Nominal Cross Validation, which default is set to the Decision Tree as seen below.

Figure 12. Using the decision tree defaulted to nominal cross validation

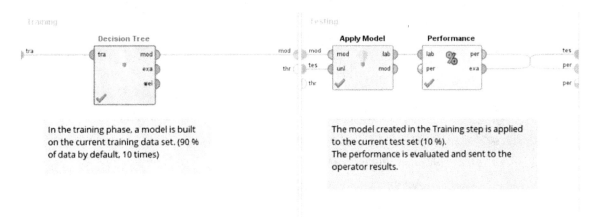

Figure 13. Adjusting parameters to create decision tree model

Data scientists can adjust the Criterion's parameter to Information_gain in order to select the most suitable attributes to create a Decision Tree. The result of processing is as follows.

Figure 14. Results from decision tree processing

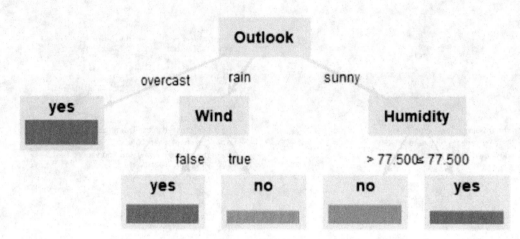

Data scientists can use the results of Decision Tree processing to determine the data, by deciding whether to play golf or not.

Data Classification Using Naïve Bayes

After data scientists have conducted data classification experiments with k-NN and Decision Tree, another technique that can be used to classify data with RapidMiner software is Naïve Bayes, by using the Golf and Nominal Cross Validation datasets as seen below.

Figure 15. Data classification using naïve Bayes

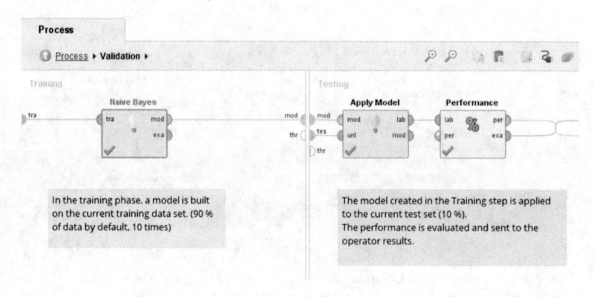

After processing the data with the Naïve Bayes technique, the results of the classification of the data are obtained as shown in Figure 16.

Figure 16. Results from naïve Bayes processing

accuracy: 50.00% +/- 47.14% (micro average: 57.14%)

	true no	true yes	class precision
pred. no	1	2	33.33%
pred. yes	4	7	63.64%
class recall	20.00%	77.78%	

Data scientists can classify the data by the probabilities of each class. In this experiment, the data analysis accuracy is 50.0.

CASE STUDY

Comparison of Data Classification Efficiency to Analyze Risk Factors That Affect the Occurrence of Hyperthyroid Using Data Mining Techniques (Hongboonmee & Trepanichkul, 2019)

Classification Technique is a Data Mining Technique widely used in many industries. There have been many theories developed to support the principles of data analysis with such techniques such as ANN or Decision Tree. In the medical industry, there are many transactions involving patients. Moreover, healthcare professionals are also keen on using data mining techniques for diagnosis and treatment as well as for research purposes. For example, data scientists, who may be hospital personnels or doctors themselves, can collect data on people with diabetes, then use Classification Technique, the Supervised-Learning, to train machines to learn and be able to identify whether patients are likely to develop diabetes or not.

In 2019, there was a study on a trial comparing the effectiveness of data analysis to classify hyperthyroid disease (Hongboonmee & Trepanichkul, 2019). Data were collected from 323 patients from a hospital in Thailand. The experiment was conducted with tClassification techniques, consisting of artificial neural networks, naive bayes and decision tree. The purpose of this research is to create native apps to be installed on smart phones in which users can fill data. It can then analyze their risk of Hyperthyroid. The data set used to teach machine learning consists of features such as gender, age, fatigue, building palpitations, mood swings, normal weight gain or loss, sweating, physical weakness, trembling hands, insomnia, bulging eyes, and the neck size. The Data Object in each feature has the characteristics of Boolean, Yes and No, and the result of the Hyperthyroid Disease Risk Analysis is a Label, which contains the Data Object on Risk Level in Numerical Data.

Such an experiment Datasets were taken into Train model, which consists of artificial neural networks, naive bayes and decision trees, and then it was found that the most effective technique was artificial neural networks. The research also tested on what features influence on the risk of having Hyperthyroid. If the model's accuracy is reduced, then that feature does not affect the classification of risks. It also found that the features influencing the risk of Hyperthyroid are gender, mood swings, and physical exhaustion. The feature age shows the least influence on model performance, which means that Hyperthyroid disease can occur in people of any age. Then, the researchers brought the Classification Model to develop Native Apps, installed on the smart phone, and then the performance of the system is tested among the users in order to reflect the classification performance of the installed native apps.

From such research, it is obvious that The Classification Technique can be used for classifying data and responding to questions. It is also imperative that data scientists test a variety of datasets that have been compiled with various Data Mining Technique in order to test the analytical efficiency before analyzing the data and interpreting the results. The research also shows that data scientists can perform individual data analyzes, data analysis using Python, R or even RapidMiner, or deploying the model from the experiment to allow data users to access data analysis through various applications.

Breast Cancer Prediction and Detection Using Data Mining Classification Algorithms: A Comparative Study (Keles, 2019)

Breast cancer has long been a deadly disease. The medical industry is trying to spread information about breast cancer self-diagnosis so that patients can be quickly identified. Early illness of cancers, if discovered early, it can be cured with a success rate of 90–95%.

In 2019, there was a Breast Cancer Prediction and Detection Using Data Mining Classification Algorithms: A Comparative Study (Keles, 2019) using a variety of data mining techniques to test the effectiveness of breast cancer identification. This research reviewed the literature and found that many other studies have attempted to create data analysis models to identify cancer, tumor and normal tissues using the Decision Tree, the Neural Network and the Decision Tree and k-NN. The research used a total of 6,066 instances of datasets related to past breast cancer diagnoses. 5,405 instances were used to train the model to learn, and 601 instances were used for testing the performance, as well as to optimize the model training. The study also used the Cross Validation Technique, which divides the dataset into 10 parts each of which is applied to train and test models. This allows the model to be trained from 10 datasets and tested by 10 datasets to bypass the constraints of that dataset, which has too few instances of data in train and test models.

From the experiment, the top five data mining techniques that perform best in diagnosing cancer biopsies are Random Forest, Random Committee, Bagging, SimpleCART, and IBK.

In Case Study 1 and 2, the readers will find that even after the scientists have been asked for data analysis and can analyze the suitable data mining techniques, the Classification Technique, the scientists have a large number of algorithms within the Data Mining Technique that can be used in response to data mining, classification or even other types of data mining techniques. Therefore, a method that data scientists can use is to bring up those techniques and experiments to find the most effective techniques.

However, the fact that such techniques are highly effective at analyzing data at a time does not mean they are always the most efficient. They vary depending on the datasets that the data scientists teach the machines to perform. The greater the amount of data a machine learns, the more likely it is to learn and this will result in a more efficient machine's ability to classify data, resulting from more learning in the same way.

Analysis of Work Suitable for Personality With Classification Technique (Sharma et al., 2021)

Classification Technique can be used in disease diagnosis and applied to analyze data to answer other questions. In 2021, there is a study called Data Mining Classification Techniques to Assign Individual Personality Type and Predict. Job Profiles (Sharma et al., 2021) which conducted an experiment on analyzing jobs that match each human personality type using Classification techniques such as Random Forest.

In many situations, people often cannot find work needs that are appropriate for their personality. The research reviewed the literature on Classification techniques that may be used to classify jobs that fit the personality of the target audience. The techniques were Logistic Regression, KNN, Support Vector Machine, Naïve Bayes Classifier, Decision Tree Classifier and Random Forest Classifier. Then, the most suitable algorithms for processing were compared and a random forest was selected. This research then defines the features that can be used for personality analysis, consisting of living life with internal data objects which are extraverted and introverted; decision making with data objects which are planning or using traits; intuition Actions with data Objects which are judgement and empathy. When analyzing personality, data scientists can analyze all the features into 16 personality types to match the job characteristics suitable for each personality type. For example, a planner personality is suitable for a management position.

To create a processing system that can match the jobs with the personality of each user, this research uses the Django Framework to develop a system in the form of a web application using Python to write a set of instructions for processing data using the Random Forest technique.

From the case study, the reader can see that besides using Classification Technique to process datasets to answer case-by-case questions, data-processing instructions can be embedded into applications in the same manners as the case studies have used the Django Framework to develop Web Applications, capable of processing with data mining techniques, Classification. Therefore, for young data scientists who are studying software used for processing Big Data, data scientists should learn more about software that help develop applications.

Using Classification Technique Together With Intrusion Detection System Technology to Classify Threats

Classification itself is also applied in other applications such as network security, especially in networks full of massive amounts of data traversing public infrastructure such as streaming media. In such cases, the Intrusion Detection System: IDS is used to detect potential threats. The network system can detect information or behaviors that are abnormal and can then alert Network Technicians of such threats. This is different from other security solutions such as firewalls that detect threats in a statistic manner. IDS can detect threats entering the network in real time, consistent with streaming media data.

Application of Classification Technique, combined with real-time detection of incoming threats to the network with IDS, can enhance the detection of potential threats. Machine learning can learn the threats entering the network and then detect all information in real time so that IDS can alert Network Technicians to deal with that threat in a timely manner. By 2020, there was a research called Data mining Classification Techniques for Intrusion Detection System (Sharma et al., 2020) that studied the conductivity of Classification Technique applied to increase the efficiency of work for IDS. The researchers used Principle Component Analysis: PCA technique to arrange the composition of the feature used for the experiment. Data classification was performed using Random Forest, J48 Decision tree, Random tree and Naïve bayes. The research used a dataset called NSL-KDD, a dataset on network attacks, for experimentation. The results showed that Random Forest showed the highest accuracy for classifying attack data.

Back in 2015, there was another study, Efficient Intrusion Detection System Using Stream Data Mining Classification Technique (Desale, Kumathekar & Chavan, 2015). The same dataset, NSL-KDD, was used in the experiment, using the Hoeffding algorithm, which features a decision tree learning algorithm, and the Naïve bayes technique for data classification experiments to encourage threat detection of IDS more efficiently. From the experiment, it was found that the Naïve bayes technique had the highest data classification accuracy.

Therefore, data scientists can apply Classification techniques not only in the medical or financial industry, but also in other applications, such as network security, the process of applying different data science applications. All of the Dataset acquisitions are on the principles, collection and extraction of datasets, preparing a dataset, selecting a data mining technique to answer the set questions by performing a variety of experiments and techniques with the highest efficiency and accuracy in data analysis and interpretation of results.

CONCLUSION

Data mining techniques is Unsupervised-Learning. The scientists need to divide the dataset into two parts: one for teaching machine learning and the other one for testing the performance of the model. This book has given examples of 3 data mining techniques, namely k-NN, Decision Tree and Naïve Bayes. For k-NN, data are classified by calculating the distances between the required data and the data used in the analysis. It is to classify the type of data to be analyzed with the data near it. The Decision Tree technique is a diagram based on Information Gain or Attribute Analysis, which is suitable for data classification that allows data scientists to take the data to classify and consider together with the Decision Tree. So that they will obtain the appropriate data classification results. The last section the book brings up is Naïve Bayes. With this technique, the scientists can take the required data to analyze and process together with the dataset. This is to perform a probabilistic analysis of data classification. Data scientists can use RapidMiner software, such as k-NN, Decision Tree or Naïve Bayes, for a quick classification by bringing the desired data set into the model. Then the Cross Validation model is used to divide the data into 2; for teaching machine learning and for testing the efficiency of data classification.

EXERCISE QUESTIONS

1. Explain the difference between Clustering and Classification.
2. Describe Cross Validation and its application in RapidMiner software.
3. Explain the concept of k-NN.
4. Describe the result consideration from the Decision Tree obtained from the data analysis.
5. Search for the researches using Classification in data analysis, and then make a brief summary.

REFERENCES

Desale, K. S., Kumathekar, C. N., & Chavan, A. P. (2015) Efficient Intrusion Detection System Using Stream Data Mining Classification Technique. *2015 International Conference on Computing Communication Control and Automation*, 469-473. 10.1109/ICCUBEA.2015.98

Fadlil, A., Umar, R., & Gustina, S. (2019). Mushroom Images Identification Using Order Statistics Feature Extraction with Artificial Neural Network Classification Technique. *Journal of Physics: Conference Series, 1373*(1), 012037. doi:10.1088/1742-6596/1373/1/012037

Görtler, J., Hohman, F., Moritz, D., Wongsuphasawat, K., Ren, D., Nair, R., Kirchner, M., & Patel, K. (2021). *Neo: Generalizing Confusion Matrix Visualization to Hierarchical and Multi-Output Labels.* Academic Press.

Hongboonmee, N., & Trepanichkul, P. (2019). *Comparison of Data Classification Efficiency to Analyze Risk Factors that Affect the Occurrence of Hyperthyroidusing Data Mining Techniques. Mahanakorn University of Technology (MUT).*

Jamalludin, M. D. M,, Fajar Shidik, G., Zainul Fanani, A., Purwanto, & Al Zami, F. (2021). Implementation of Feature Selection Using Gain Ratio Towards Improved Accuracy of Support Vector Machine (SVM) on Youtube Comment Classification. *2021 International Seminar on Application for Technology of Information and Communication (ISemantic), Application for Technology of Information and Communication (ISemantic), 2021 International Seminar On*, 28–31.

Junaidi, A., Ferani Tanjung, N. A., Wijayanto, S., Lasama, J., & Iskandar, A. R. (2021). Overfitting Problem in Images Classification for Egg Incubator Using Convolutional Neural Network. *2021 9th International Conference on Cyber and IT Service Management (CITSM), Cyber and IT Service Management (CITSM), 2021 9th International Conference On*, 1–7.

Karthik, M. G., & Krishnan, M. B. M. (2021). Detecting Internet of Things Attacks Using Post Pruning Decision Tree-Synthetic Minority Over Sampling Technique. *International Journal of Intelligent Engineering & Systems, 14*(4), 105–114. doi:10.22266/ijies2021.0831.10

Keles, M. K. (2019). Breast Cancer Prediction and Detection Using Data Mining Classification Algorithms: A Comparative Study. *Tehnicki Vjesnik - Technical Gazette, 26*(1), 149.

Khan, S. A., & Ali Rana, Z. (2019). Evaluating Performance of Software Defect Prediction Models Using Area Under Precision-Recall Curve (AUC-PR). *2019 2nd International Conference on Advancements in Computational Sciences (ICACS), Advancements in Computational Sciences (ICACS), 2019 2nd International Conference On*, 1–6.

Liu, L. (2021). Design of Human Resource Management Information System Based on Decision Tree Algorithm. *2021 Global Reliability and Prognostics and Health Management (PHM-Nanjing), Reliability and Prognostics and Health Management (PHM-Nanjing), 2021 Global*, 1–6.

Mishra, A., & Vats, A. (2021). Supervised machine learning classification algorithms for detection of fracture location in dissimilar friction stir welded joints. *Frattura e Integrita Strutturale, 15*(58), 242–253. doi:10.3221/IGF-ESIS.58.18

Mladenova, T. (2021). A Feature-Weighted Rule for the K-Nearest Neighbor. *2021 5th International Symposium on Multidisciplinary Studies and Innovative Technologies (ISMSIT), Multidisciplinary Studies and Innovative Technologies (ISMSIT), 2021 5th International Symposium On*, 493–497.

Mnich, K., Polewko-Klim, A., Kitlas Golinska, A., Lesinski, W., & Rudnicki, W. R. (2020). Super Learning with Repeated Cross Validation. *2020 International Conference on Data Mining Workshops (ICDMW), Data Mining Workshops (ICDMW), 2020 International Conference on, ICDMW*, 629–635.

Mohan, L., Jain, S., Suyal, P., & Kumar, A. (2020). Data mining Classification Techniques for Intrusion Detection System. *2020 12th International Conference on Computational Intelligence and Communication Networks (CICN)*, 351-355.

Nuttavut Thongjor. (2017). *Understanding the data classification: k-Nearest Neighbours*. Retrieved 9 August, 2021, from https://www.babelcoder.com/blog/articles/k-nearest-neighbors

Puspitasari, D. I., Riza Kholdani, A. F., Dharmawati, A., Rosadi, M. E., & Mega Pradnya Dhuhita, W. (2021). Stroke Disease Analysis and Classification Using Decision Tree and Random Forest Methods. *2021 Sixth International Conference on Informatics and Computing (ICIC), Informatics and Computing (ICIC), 2021 Sixth International Conference On*, 1–4.

Rabiul Alam, M. G., Hussain, S., Islam Mim, M. M., & Islam, M. T. (2021). Telecom Customer Behavior Analysis Using Naïve Bayes Classifier. *2021 IEEE 4th International Conference on Computer and Communication Engineering Technology (CCET), Computer and Communication Engineering Technology (CCET), 2021 IEEE 4th International Conference On*, 308–312.

Rahman, B., Hendric Spits Warnars, H. L., Subirosa Sabarguna, B., & Budiharto, W. (2021). Heart Disease Classification Model Using K-Nearest Neighbor Algorithm. *2021 Sixth International Conference on Informatics and Computing (ICIC), Informatics and Computing (ICIC), 2021 Sixth International Conference On*, 1–4.

Sharma, M., Joshi, S., Sharma, S., Singh, A., & Gupta, R. (2021). Data Mining Classification Techniques to Assign Individual Personality Type and Predict Job Profile. *2021 9th International Conference on Reliability, Infocom Technologies and Optimization (Trends and Future Directions) (ICRITO)*, 1-5.

Song, H., Fu, Y., Saket, B., & Stasko, J. (2021). Understanding the Effects of Visualizing Missing Values on Visual Data Exploration. *2021 IEEE Visualization Conference (VIS), Visualization Conference (VIS), 2021 IEEE, VIS*, 161–165.

Thangakumar, J., & Kommina, S. B. (2020). Ant colony optimization based feature subset selection with logistic regression classification model for education data mining. *International Journal of Advanced Science and Technology, 29*(3), 5821–5834.

Vichi, M., Ritter, G., & Giusti, A. (2013). *Classification and data mining*. Springer Verlag.

Zhang, H., Zhang, L., & Jiang, Y. (2019). Overfitting and Underfitting Analysis for Deep Learning Based End-to-end Communication Systems. *2019 11th International Conference on Wireless Communications and Signal Processing (WCSP), Wireless Communications and Signal Processing (WCSP), 2019 11th International Conference On*, 1–6.

Chapter 6
Deep Learning

ABSTRACT

Neural network and deep learning techniques are essential tools for data scientists when analyzing big data for forecasting and classification. In supervised learning, data sets are divided into training sets and test sets, and neural network repeatedly adjusts the weight of data to better represent the actual data. This book offers a practical guide to performing a neural network experiment with RapidMiner, which readers can follow step-by-step. For big data, especially non-linear data, deep learning can be employed. This chapter introduces two types of deep learning: convolutional neural networks (CNN) for picture analysis and recurrent neural networks (RNN) for sequential or time series data. The book provides a demonstration of both techniques using RapidMiner, making it accessible to readers who wish to deepen their understanding of these powerful tools.

INTRODUCTION

In the early days when people first mentioned artificial intelligence, there was a lot of motivation to develop artificial intelligence capable of human-like responses. However, the challenge for the era was that artificial intelligence computing required high-performance computing technology and large volumes of experimental data, resulting in the gradual advancement of artificial intelligence. Now in the era of high-performance computing technologies such as GPUs with a high-speed network (Telikani, Shahbahrami, & Gandomi, 2021), data scientists are able to use data mining techniques to operate on high-performance computing technologies and collect big data for experimentation using techniques that are suitable for such processing. Deep learning technique is used to analyze unstructured data consisting of images, sounds, and text (Fernando et al., 2021: Hongyi Zhu, Samtani, Brown, & Hsinchun Chen, 2021). There are two types of deep learning: Convolutional Neural Networks and Recurrent Neural Networks (Lakshmi Devi & Samundeeswari V, 2021: Snineh et al., 2021). The deep learning model modulates the pre-configuration of data for processing in conjunction with neural network techniques. Artificial Neural Networks (ANNs) is a data mining technique that offers both classification and numerical predictions, which is considered supervised learning (Thankachan, Prakash & Jothi, 2021). Data scientists must first teach machines to learn before testing the data. In the case data scientists classify data with

DOI: 10.4018/978-1-6684-4730-7.ch006

Copyright © 2023, IGI Global. Copying or distributing in print or electronic forms without written permission of IGI Global is prohibited.

other data mining techniques, the data are classified by a linear plane. On the contrary, using neural networks, data scientists can classify data that are closely attached to facts with a Non-Linear Function. The neural network is, therefore, used in 2 ways: first, Pattern Recognition, such as user face recognition for identification or authentication for accessing the phone (Ghorpade & Koneru, 2021), and finally Forecasting such as forecasting the trend of stock prices (Chinnarasri, Nonsawang & Supharatid, 2012).

This book discusses the principles of artificial neural network and deep learning in both CNN and RNN formats as follows:

ARTIFICIAL NEURAL NETWORK: ANN

Conceptual Work of Artificial Neural Network: ANN

Artificial Neural Networks simulate human brain activities by having each node represent a brain cell, and connect each node to form a network which will then be used for processing (Chow and Cho, 2007: Aggarwal, 2018). The neural network therefore consists of 4 parts. 1. Input Neural is used to support the data which will be analyzed with the model. The number of input nodes depends on the number of variables or features used to analyze the data. 2. Output Neural is the result obtained from processing. It can have one or more results depending on data analysis questions. 3. Hidden Layer is each layer of nodes that enhance the processing efficiency of the neural network, and 4. Links is the connection of each node. Each Link calculates Weights, which must be passed on to the next node. Therefore, the neural network optimizes the nodes, so that the scientists can analyze the responses from the dataset imported into the model. The primary model of the neural network is Perceptron. The model is designed to analyze data with input neural and output neural without creating hidden layers to predict numbers. To teach machines learning and to test data with a neural network both focus on adjusting the weights of each link, known as the Back Propagation Artificial Neural Network (BP-ANN) (Ramirez-Hernandez et al., 2020: Guo, Zhang and Chen, 2021) with the process as follows.

1.	Artificial Neural Network model estimates the analysis results.
2.	The results are compared to the actual results that the scientists have taught to the machine learning in order to analyze Error.
3.	The model takes the error to adjust the Weights in each layer in order to achieve a tightness between the analyzed value and the actual data. This process is repeated until the error values reach the acceptable level.

Iterating to adjust such Weights is to teach machine learning and increase the accuracy of data analysis. Iterating each time is called Epochs. Data scientists put 1,000 records into a neural network model, and the number of Epochs is 500, there will be 500,000 times of iteration to teach the machine learning. Therefore, the greater the number of data and the number of nodes within the model is, the more time and digital processing the data scientists need. From the working process that requires computation to analyze all the data, the neural network model is suitable for numerical data. Therefore, if data scientists need to analyze text data in the data preparation process, it is necessary to convert letters into numbers before entering the data into the model.

Figure 1. Artificial neural network

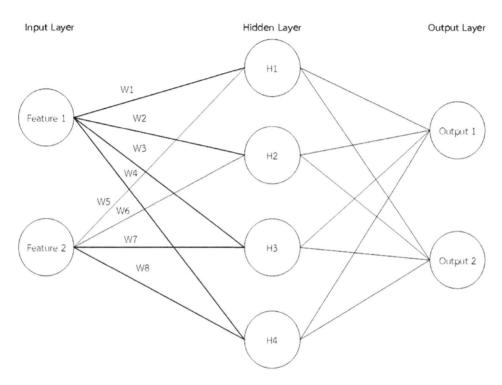

DATA ANALYSIS WITHIN ARTIFICIAL NEURAL NETWORK

Calculating the Output of Artificial Neural Network

Within the neural network, two weights are used to adjust the accuracy of the analysis; 1. Weight from Input and Hidden Layer nodes, and 2. Weight from nodes that act as bias. Within every layer, it consists of 1 node that is additional bias.

From the figure, the neural network and the output calculation use following formula.

$$Y = b + W_1 X_1 + W_2 X_2 \ldots \ldots \ldots W_n X_m$$

where Y refers to Output
    b refers to Weight from Bias
    X_m refers to the number of Features
    W_m refers to Weigh from Feature

According to the formula, the artificial neural network calculates the output values by getting the sum of all input values multiplied by the weight of each node, and adding them to the bias values for each layer. The artificial neural network then uses an Aviation function to adjust the Linear data into Non-Linear data which is between 0 – 1. The data obtained from the computation are closer to the facts until the computed output is obtained.

Figure 2. Components of weight

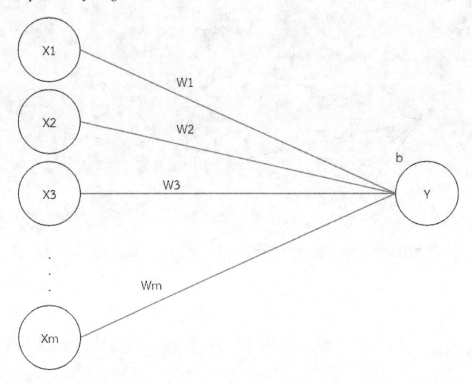

Data scientists can train computations within the artificial neural network to teach machines to learn, as in the following example.

Feature A = 0.4 where Weight = 0.3
Feature B = 0.6 where Weight = 0.5
Output = 0.8

From the data calculated with 0.4*0.3+0.6*0.5+0.8 = 1.22, the value is then adjusted to be Non-Linear by Logistic Activation Function using the formula f(x) =1/(1+e^(-(x))). From the sample data, it can be calculated as 1(1/+e-1.22) = 0.77.

When comparing the output from the neural network 0.77 with the actual value 0.8, the neural network re-adjusts the weight to bring the result as close to the facts as possible by performing the calculation.

$$w_j^{(k+1)} = w_j^{(k)} + \lambda \left(y_i - y_i^{-k} \right) x_{ij}$$

where i is the sequence of the records within the dataset
   k is the number of iterations
   j is the Feature *sequence*
   $w_j^{(k)}$ *is* Input *of* Weight brought into j *iteration*
   y_i *is the actual* Output *value of each record*

y_i^{-k} *is the predicted value of each record in each iteration cycle*

x_{ij} *is the* Feature *initial data in each record*

λ *is the* Learning Rate, being between $0 - 1$. *The closer to 1, the higher learning rate. The closer to 0, the lower the learning rate.*

According to the formula, data scientists can adjust the Weight in order to obtain results that are closer to the actual value as presented in the following example.

Feature A = 0.4 where Weight = 0.3
Feature B = 0.6 where Weight = 0.5
Output = 0.8
Learning Rate = 0.5

From the example, the output is calculated as 0.77 and when compared to the actual value, it is 0.8. Therefore, the Weight is adjusted by

adjusting Weight for Feature A which is 0.3+0.5*(0.8-0.77) *0.4 = 0.306
adjusting Weight for Feature B which is 0.5+0.5*(0.8-0.77) *0.6 = 0.509
adjusting Weight for Output which is 0.8 + 0.5*(0.8-0.77) = 0.815

The artificial neural network performs calculations to adjust Weight and repeats the number of cycles, the data scientist has set, until the error is at the required level in order to provide the most accurate data.

Hidden Layer and Stopping Conditions

In case the neural network does not have a hidden layer, the output can be used to adjust the weight of the input node to make the values obtained from the model as close to the actual value as possible. But in the case of the artificial neural network has a hidden layer, the value of the output in the next layer must be adjusted, as shown in the example below.

In the figure, Weight from node D to node F is 0.5, and node F has an error of 1.2. Weight can be adjusted by 1.2 * 0.5 = 0.6. Weight from node D to node G is 0.2, and node G shows Error value as 0.4. The Weight can be adjusted by 0.2 * 0.4 = 0.08, so node D can then adjust all Weight by 0.6 + 0.80 = 0.68. After adjusting the Weight through iterations or the error is set in the specified point, Neural network models will then stop computation to teach machines to learn, which is known as Stopping Conditions. Data scientists can perform calculations to obtain the appropriate error level to stop calculations in weight adjustments. Data scientists can calculate the Total of Sum Square Error by subtracting each actual output by the value obtained from the forecast. The result is then squared of 2, and the calculated results for each output are then combined as an error level appropriate for stopping the weight adjustment.

Figure 3. Adjusting the hidden layer weight

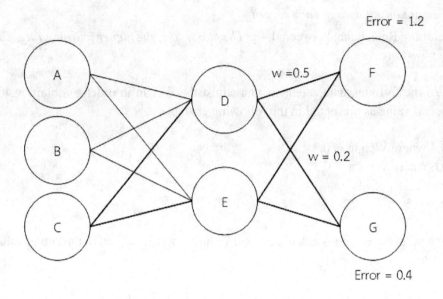

ANALYZING DATA WITH ARTIFICIAL NEURAL NETWORK USING RAPIDMINER SOFTWARE

Data scientists can take the desired dataset to analyze both classification and numerical forecasting into RapidMiner software, and then create the artificial neural network model as seen in the following figure.

Figure 4. Starting neural net

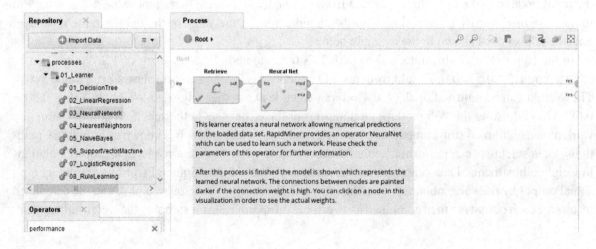

Data scientists can begin using Artificial Neural Network model with the sample process within RapidMiner software called _NeuralNetwork. The process prepares an entire numerical dataset, and uses a Neural Net model to extract those data. Data scientists can define parameters as follows:

Figure 5. Parameters of the neural network

From the figure, data scientists can determine the number of hidden layers. The Training Cycle is then specified to determine the number of times of machine teaching. The learning rate is the machine learning rate that ranges from 0 to 1, and the Momentum is the indication of how much the Weight calculated in the previous round, which will affect the weight adjustment in the current round. The scientists will then decide whether to adjust the learning rate over time. If yes, select Decay. Regarding Shuffle, it is the sequence in which the input data is imported into the new model. About Normalization, it is to normalize the data between 0 – 1. Finally, Error Epsilon is to determine the model to stop analyzing when the Error value is less than a predetermined value. After that, the scientists can execute the model. The results are as follows.

Figure 6. Execute results of artificial neural network

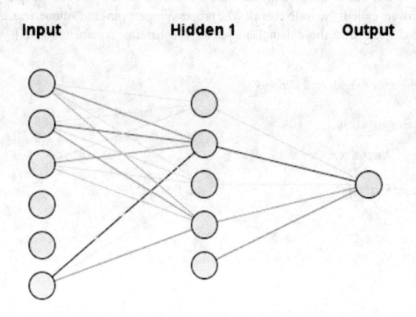

In the figure, the input node corresponds to the number of features used in the data analysis. The sample has 5 features. The neural network generates 5 input nodes, and there are additional bias nodes. The output node corresponds to the target variable. In the example, there is a feature that represents 1 node target variable. The scientists can adjust and increase the number of hidden layers in order to increase the analysis complexity for the artificial neural network.

Figure 7. Adding a hidden layer to artificial neural network

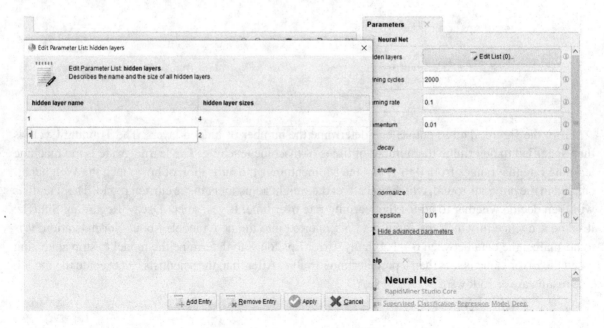

Data scientists can press Edit List button to add hidden layers by specifying the number of hidden nodes. From the figure, the scientists define 2 hidden layers. Layer 1 has 4 hidden nodes, and layer 2 is determined to have 2 hidden nodes. The result of execution is as follows:

Figure 8. Adding hidden layers

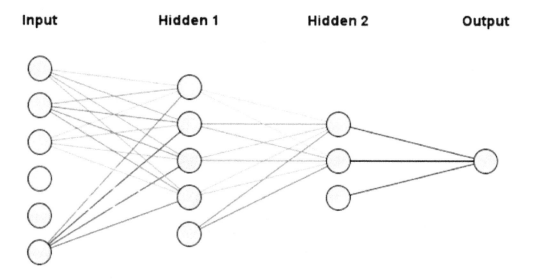

In the figure, when data scientists set the nodes in layer1 as 4. The additional bias nodes are added, and in layer 2 it is set to have 2 additional bias nodes. When data scientists need to classify the data using artificial neural networks, they can conduct an experiment using a sample dataset within the RapidMiner software called Iris, which contains data about the sizes of the Iris flower petals. The experiments can be carried out to identify the Iris flower species from the data set.

Figure 9. Iris classification experiment

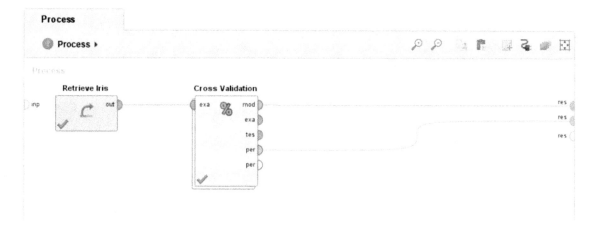

In this figure, data scientists take the Iris data into the process, then the Cross Validation model is used to divide the data into two parts; the data used for teaching machine learning and the data for the Iris species classification test. The result of these 2 parts, the neural network model and the neural network model's classification efficiency, are then connected Within Cross Validation.

Figure 10. Processing results with neural net

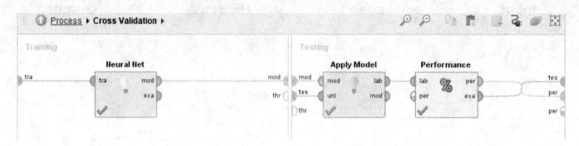

In the figure, the Cross Validation model teaches the machine to learn the data about the width and the length of the Iris petals with the Neural Net model in order to identify Iris flower species, and build a neural network. Then the Apply Model is used to generate the results of the classification of the Iris flower based on the width and length of the petals. In the last section, the accuracy of Iris flower species classification is analyzed.

Figure 11. Neural network for Iris flower species identification

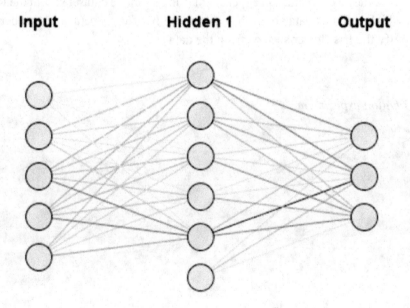

As shown in the figure, the artificial neural network is made up of 4 input features, which are the width and length of the Iris flower. There is 1 hidden layer consisting of 5 nodes, 3 output nodes (3 Iris flower lines). The accuracy of data classification is as follows.

Figure 12. Accuracy of data classification with artificial neural network

accuracy: 97.33% +/- 3.44% (micro average: 97.33%)

	true Iris-setosa	true Iris-versicolor	true Iris-virginica	class precision
pred. Iris-setosa	50	0	0	100.00%
pred. Iris-versicolor	0	47	1	97.92%
pred. Iris-virginica	0	3	49	94.23%
class recall	100.00%	94.00%	98.00%	

After analyzing accuracy of Iris data classification, it is found that the artificial neural network has an accuracy of 97.33%. Data scientists are able to modify the number of hidden layers to increase the complexity of data processing for the artificial neural network. However, the number of hidden layers that can be used for high-precision data analysis depends on the nature of the dataset, and the accuracy does not vary with the increasing number of hidden layers. Therefore, it is necessary that data scientists prepare the data ready for the analysis, and conduct various data analysis experiments for the most accurate data analysis results.

DEEP LEARNING

Convolutional Neural Networks (CNN)

Convolutional Neural Network (CNN) supports large data analysis, especially image data (Sriwiboon, 2020). Therefore, CNN is used in the work related to the artificial intelligence to analyze image-related data, such as the route classification of autonomous vehicles through camera images. Knowledge of CNN starts with the research on cat's vision, which uses the visual method as parts. These parts are then combined into a whole picture, with the cat's brain focusing only on each part of the picture. Data scientists develop data by converting images into numerical format, and then CNN technique is used to classify images into parts similarly to cat's brain. If the images have been compiled in the form of numbers and as features, data scientists can use artificial neural network processing techniques for classification such as images of cats, dogs or elephants. However, those images need to be modeled. The scientists can use CNN techniques to prepare those data as in the following process.

Feature Extraction: It is to transform the images into the number format. Data scientists focus on the features associated with the images; such as the elephant image which has distinctive features such as ears and ivories. Data scientists use a filter matrix to count whether each part of the image has data that correspond to the features of interests.

Filter Matrix: It is used to check patterns in each part of the images in order to obtain features. To check each part of the image, the convolutional operation method is used to obtain the number format data used to represent each feature. There is a method for calculating according to the example below.

In the case that the data scientists receive a 10 x 10 image as input (Original Image), then assigns a 3 x 3 filter matrix size, and set the Filter Matrix to check the format of the image at a time, 1 row and 1 column. Moving the Filter Matrix is called Stride. Sizes of Feature Map can be calculated as = (N - F) / Stride + 1.

N = 10 x 10
F = 3 x 3
Stride = 1
Size of Feature Map = (10 - 3) / 1 + 1 = 8

Therefore, after the convolutional operation, the image size will be reduced from 10 x 10 to 8 x 8, which will store only the necessary parts, such as cat images. The Filter Matrix examines the cat's eyes and nose only. After the convolutional operation, it will store only the specific parts of the eyes and noses, so that it can remember whether the images are cat images.

In this convolution process, the ReLU algorithm is used. When the convolutional operation is negative, the ReLU algorithm adjusts the value to 0, so that the data is a non-linear function, which is close to the facts of data classification.

Data scientists use a filter matrix to detect the data patterns, and allow the features to store only the unique images with Convolutional Operation. The next process is Pooling which is to reduce the size of the data. Data scientists can use either Max Pooling which is the selection of the largest number in each image data segment or Average Pooling which is to take all the numbers in each image data segment to create an average to analyze the data. The example of Max Pooling and Average Pooling is as follows.

Table 1. Sample data set for max pooling and average pooling

4	3	8	7
1	7	8	1
9	6	3	2
3	4	0	4

From the sample dataset, the scientists can do Max Pooling, covering 2 rows and 2 columns, and select the highest value of Data Objects. The result is as follows.

Table 2. Results from max pooling

7	8
9	4

From the Max Pooling table, the size of the dataset can be reduced by selecting only the largest value each time. And based on the results of Max Pooling, the data scientists can also choose to use Average Pooling from the same dataset.

Table 3. Results of average pooling

3.75	6
5.5	2.25

Feature Extraction, therefore, uses the algorithm of Convolutional Operation along with Pooling to extract image-specific data before transferring it to the artificial neural network for classification as shown in the figure.

Figure 13. CNN performance

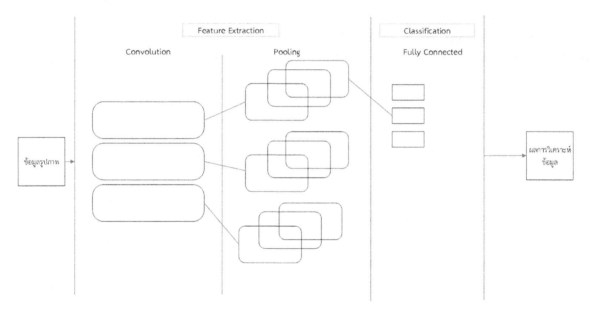

From the picture, the image data is verified and converted into the form that can be used for processing through the feature extraction process. To do this, v Convolution along with Pooling is used to collect only the distinctive features of the image. Then flattening is done to adjust the format of the matrix data into vector. This process is called Fully Connected, which is to put the data parts together in a feature, ready to use in classification process with the artificial neural network. When required to classify data, the scientists need to consult with an image related professional to determine which distinctive feature can be used to classify data from the images. The size of the Filter Matrix, the data format and Stride frequencies are to be considered in order to design the resolution of data extraction appropriate for the questions. When considering the CNN technique suitability, it is suitable for analyzing unstructured data such as images or sounds. For example, it is used to classify cancer-causing tumors from X-Ray images. With the CNN technique that analyzes the data by extracting the data into parts, the result is that each data part shows no relation. Therefore, the data scientists focus on analyzing the relationship of the data, CNN techniques may not be suitable for such problems. The scientists need to provide digital resources with high-performance computing and large datasets to teach machines to learn. This amount of data affects the efficiency of the model's classification.

RECURRENT NEURAL NETWORKS (RNN)

In the case that the problems focus on analyzing the relationships of Sequential Data and Time Series (Sabau et al., 2021) such as Language Translation, Natural Language Processing (NLP) and Image Captioning in daily life, RNN is used in the Search Engine. When the user search for a word, the search engine will suggest the texts related to the text. The RNN model has taught the machine to learn from search queries entered by users around the world until it can analyze the relationship of the data used by users who search through the search engine.

The main characteristics of RNN include: 1. The ability to support data import with the inequitable data size into the neural network, 2. The ability to verify the relationship between data objects, and 3. The ability to arrange the data in sequence such as the arrangement of the sentence structure by RNN processing. The RNN architecture is as follows.

Figure 14. RNN architecture

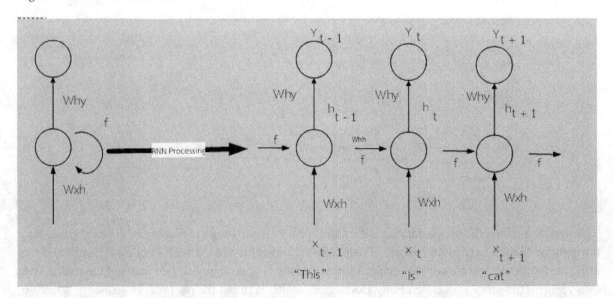

In the figure, the RNN processes the data to analyze the relationship between the data objects. When the data is imported into the network (x), the RNN technique calculates the resulting value (y) by taking the input from the previous step and coprocessing it. It is calculated within the network as follows:

$$Y_t = W_{hy}h_t$$
$$H_t = f(h_{t-1}, x_t)$$
$$H_t = \tanh(W_{hh}h_{t-1} + W_{xh}X_t)$$

The y value, or the result in the current step, is calculated from the Why, which is the Weight of the node multiplied by the ht value. The ht value is derived from ht-1, which is the value from the previous step. The xt value is the input at the current stage. The tanh function is then used to convert the value from – 1 to 1, resulting in a non-linear function. Thus, the RNN algorithm can analyze the relationship of the data by combining the values from the previous data, and analyzing it until the result has become continuity of correlated data.

However, when the data set is imported into a model for correlation analysis, if the correlated data objects have a large storage distance, this results in discrepancies in the analysis of the sequence arrangement. Therefore, data scientists can use the Long Short-Term Memory (LSTM) which has the ability to memorize values from the previous step, that are very distant from the current node, to compute with the current node in order to obtain the result from proper sequence arrangement.

USING CNN DEEP LEARNING TECHNIQUES WITH RAPIDMINER SOFTWARE

To use deep learning techniques with RapidMiner, though within the software has prepared the basic models such as Deep Learning H2O, data scientists are required to install the Deep Learning ND4J extension in RapidMiner when they want to process CNN and RNN models.

Figure 15. Installing extensions

As shown in the figure, to install extensions, data scientists can select the Extensions menu and then select Marketplace (Updates and Extensions).

When entering the RapidMiner Marketplace, the scientists then search for ND4J and press Search. When seeing the extensions related to the machine learning model, then, select all 3 extensions namely ND4J, Deep Learning and Image Handling by clicking on the extension selecting for Installation and press Install Packages. After completing the installation process, data scientists need to restart the RapidMiner software.

To develop models with CNN deep learning techniques, this book has used a sample image dataset from website https://storage.googleapis.com/tensorflow/tf-keras-datasets/mnist.npz. The dataset is MNIST – JPG - Training, which contains a total of 10,000 instances (Beohar and Rasool, 2021: LeCun, Cortes and Burges, 2021) as seen in the example.

Figure 16. Searching for extensions and installing it

Figure 17. Sample data within the experimental dataset

From the image data set, data scientists can use RapidMiner software to model CNN machine learning. The process is as follows.

In the figure, the data scientists have brought the MNIST – JPG – Training dataset into the model using Read Image Meta Data, and then split the data into two parts with Split Data. The data are divided into 2 parts; 80% for teaching machines, and 20 percent for testing the accuracy of the model. Then, the data for the machine learning is imported into the pre-process image to be transformed into Tensor object in the form of vector, in such a way that Deep Learning (Tensor) model can process. The data from the Pre-Process Image and from the Deep Learning (Tensor) are then entered into the Group Model (Generic), which enables the Pre-Process Image to be co-processed with the Deep Learning (Tensor). The accuracy of the processing is then proven with the Apply Model (Generic). The Append model is then used to compare the datasets from forecasting before sending them to the Performance in order to show the accuracy of all data classification processing.

Figure 18. Model of CNN learning techniques

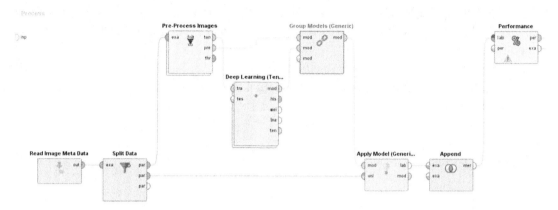

Within Deep Learning (Tensor), data scientists can use models to define CNN-based processing consisting of Convolutional Operation, Pooling and Fully-Connected as seen in Figure 19.

From the figure, data scientists can define each section of the parameters to determine CNN processing as shown in Figure 20.

Figure 19. Setting convolutional operator model, pooling, and fully-connected

Figure 20. Setting parameters to add convolutional layer

Data scientists determine the Size of Feature Map to a frequency of 12, covering the important area on the image by setting the Number of Activation Maps to 12. The size of the Filter Matrix can be set as 5 x 5, and the Filter Matrix move is also set in order to detect every 1 row and 1 column by setting the Stride Size to 1 x 1.

In Figure 21, the scientists can select the method to reduce the data size by setting the Pooling Method to Max, then scale the Filter Matrix by setting the Kernel Size to 2 x 2, and shift the Filter Matrix for detection every 1 row and 1 column with Stride Size of 1 x 1.

Figure 21. Setting parameters to add pooling layer

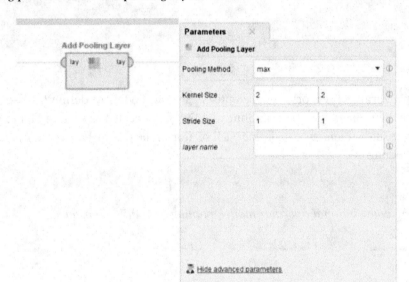

Figure 22. Setting parameters to add fully-connected layer

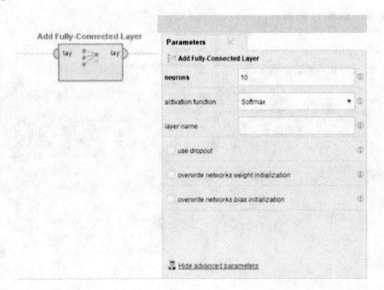

When classifying the data, the number of Neurons must be equal to the number of data types. In this case, the image data is 0–9. So, if there are 10 data types in total, the data scientists have to set the number of Neurons to 10 and the Activation Function into Softmax format by setting Parameter to add Fully-Connected Layer. It is to adjust the data into feature forms that can be used for processing with the artificial neural networks.

In each part of the model, data scientists can define parameters so that the model performs the processing appropriate for the questions.

Figure 23. Setting parameters to read image meta data

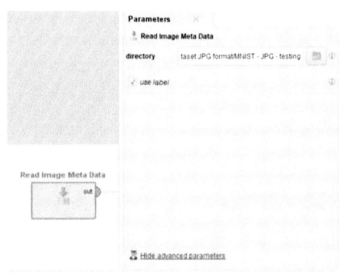

Data scientists can use Read Image Meta Data to bring image data into models by setting the Directory to point to the data source by selecting the folder button, and accessing the source address of the dataset. Then the target variables are set by selecting Use Label. The data set used in this experiment has 0-9 Sub Folders, so the target variables for each Sub Folder is then set according to the folder name, 0-9.

Data scientists can divide data into two parts; one for teaching machine learning, and the other for testing; by setting in the Partitions section, and then pressing the Edits Enumeration button.

Data scientists can determine the proportions of the data by selecting Add Entry, then setting Part 1 to 0.8 and Part 2 to 0.2. After that, the scientists can determine parameters to Pre-Process Images by setting Path as Path.

Then, data scientists can define a model within Pre-Process Images in order to manipulate with image data as follows:

Meanwhile, a parameter for Deep Learning (Tensor) is determined, which also processes the data with Convolutional Operation, Pooling and Fully-Connected.

In the figure, data scientists define Epochs as 30, which is the number that the data set teaches the machine to learn. Then, within Deep Learning (Tensor), the structure of the processing can be defined as follows.

Figure 24. Setting parameters to split data

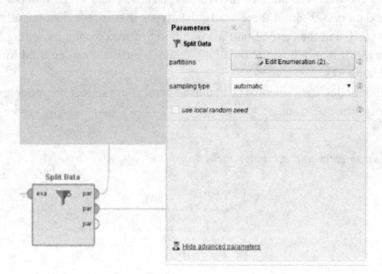

Figure 25. Partition setting to divide the dataset

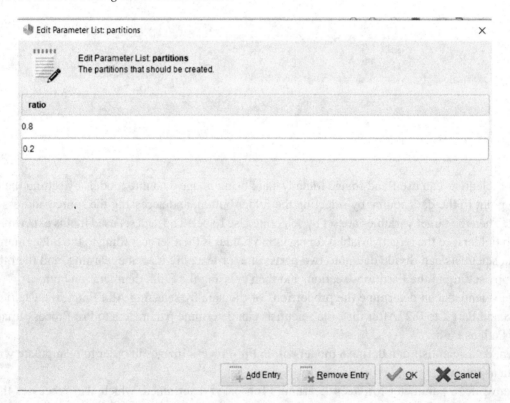

After the scientists have defined the parameters to the Add Convolutional Layer, Add Pooling Layer, and Add Fully-Connected Layer as in the previous step, the data scientist can add the Add Fully-Connected Layer before the last step. And the number of Neurons is set to 100 to reduce the data from the Add

Pooling Layer before sending it to Add Fully-Connected. The number of Neurons is set as 10 according to the number of data types which is 0 – 9. Once a deep learning model has been created, and parameters have been assigned to every model, data scientists can execute the model. The result is as follows.

Figure 26. Setting parameters to pre-process images

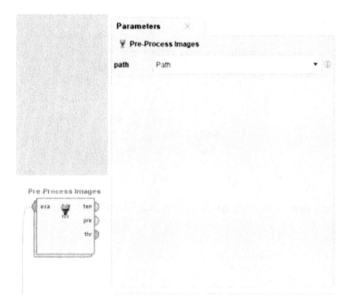

Figure 27. Path setting within pre-process images

Processing results show a comparison between facts and results obtained by classification using a CNN-type deep learning model. For example, the real data is the number 7, and the result of the classification of the data is the number 7. However, this experiment has used a data set with only 10,000 instances; 8,000 instances to teach machine learning, and 2,000 instances to test the model. It results in 10.30 percent of teaching machine learning efficiency, and the numbers that have been correctly classified is only 7 out of 10 categories.

Figure 28. Setting parameters to deep learning (tensor)

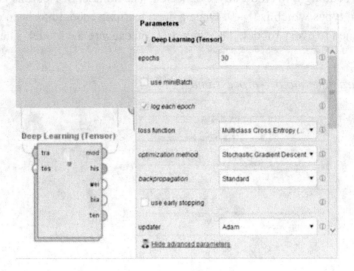

Figure 29. Determining the number of neural for each add full-connected layer

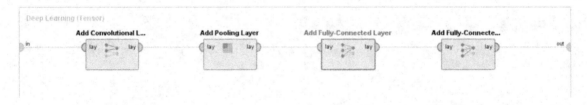

Figure 30. Processing result

Row No.	label	prediction	confidence(0)	confidence(1)	confidence(2)	confidence(3)	confidence(4)	confidence(5)	confidence(6)	confidence(7)	confide
1428	7	7	0.072	0.087	0.087	0.092	0.098	0.096	0.112	0.130	0.124
1429	7	7	0.072	0.087	0.087	0.092	0.098	0.096	0.112	0.130	0.124
1430	7	7	0.072	0.087	0.087	0.092	0.098	0.096	0.112	0.130	0.124
1431	7	7	0.072	0.087	0.087	0.092	0.098	0.096	0.112	0.130	0.124
1432	7	7	0.072	0.087	0.087	0.092	0.098	0.096	0.112	0.130	0.124
1433	7	7	0.072	0.087	0.087	0.092	0.098	0.096	0.112	0.130	0.124
1434	7	7	0.072	0.087	0.087	0.092	0.098	0.096	0.112	0.130	0.124
1435	7	7	0.072	0.087	0.087	0.092	0.098	0.096	0.112	0.130	0.124
1436	7	7	0.072	0.087	0.087	0.092	0.098	0.096	0.112	0.130	0.124
1437	7	7	0.072	0.087	0.087	0.092	0.098	0.096	0.112	0.130	0.124
1438	7	7	0.072	0.087	0.087	0.092	0.098	0.096	0.112	0.130	0.124
1439	7	7	0.072	0.087	0.087	0.092	0.098	0.096	0.112	0.130	0.124
1440	7	7	0.072	0.087	0.087	0.092	0.098	0.096	0.112	0.130	0.124
1441	7	7	0.072	0.087	0.087	0.092	0.098	0.096	0.112	0.130	0.124
1442	7	7	0.072	0.087	0.087	0.092	0.098	0.096	0.112	0.130	0.124
1443	7	7	0.072	0.087	0.087	0.092	0.098	0.096	0.112	0.130	0.124
1444	7	7	0.072	0.087	0.087	0.092	0.098	0.096	0.112	0.130	0.124

Figure 31. Accuracy of data processing

accuracy: 10.30%

	true 0	true 1	true 2	true 3	true 4	true 5	true 6	true 7	true 8	true 9	class prec...
pred. 0	0	0	0	0	0	0	0	0	0	0	0.00%
pred. 1	0	0	0	0	0	0	0	0	0	0	0.00%
pred. 2	0	0	0	0	0	0	0	0	0	0	0.00%
pred. 3	0	0	0	0	0	0	0	0	0	0	0.00%
pred. 4	0	0	0	0	0	0	0	0	0	0	0.00%
pred. 5	0	0	0	0	0	0	0	0	0	0	0.00%
pred. 6	0	0	0	0	0	0	0	0	0	0	0.00%
pred. 7	196	227	206	202	196	178	192	206	195	202	10.30%
pred. 8	0	0	0	0	0	0	0	0	0	0	0.00%
pred. 9	0	0	0	0	0	0	0	0	0	0	0.00%
class recall	0.00%	0.00%	0.00%	0.00%	0.00%	0.00%	0.00%	100.00%	0.00%	0.00%	

CNN type deep learning techniques are suitable for analyzing big data for classification and teaching machine learning. Therefore, data scientists need to use GPU Processing to reduce the time spent on processing. Moreover, processing a large number of instances, and using a large amount of data can promote more accuracy in a CNN-type deep learning model.

THE USE OF RNN DEEP LEARNING TECHNIQUES WITH RAPIDMINER SOFTWARE

Once data scientists encounter difficulties analyzing data to predict outcomes from time series data, they can use RNN. In this paper, the following samples are taken from RapidMiner software for testing.

The sample model is a forecast of oil prices. Within the data set, the features are the sequence of oil price changes, rate of change, date of change and oil prices. There are 10,000 instances. Daily oil price and each sequence of the change depend on the price of the previous day.

Based on the datasets, data scientists can use RNN to forecast oil prices from the continuous and correlated data. The models can be created according to the example.

From the sample model, the Gas Station dataset is imported into the model. Then, the nominal data are changed to numerical with Nominal to Numerical, so that they can be processed by artificial neural network techniques. The data are then divided into two; one for teaching machine learning, and the other for testing the performance of the model with the Filter Example Range. Then the Normalize model is used to adjust the numbers in the data set for teaching machine learning as between 0 – 1. The data is then imported into Example Set to Tensor to change the data format into the form of vector that can be processed with Deep Learning (Tensor). The data used for model testing are imported into the Apply Model to test the performance. They are then imported into Example Set to Tensor in order to change into Vector form. Then, the data used for teaching the machine and the data for performance testing are then processed with the Apply Model. Then, the results are imported into the Append in order to present the accuracy. Within Deep Learning (Tensor), the model connection is defined according to the RNN technique:

Figure 32. Sample model of RNN deep learning

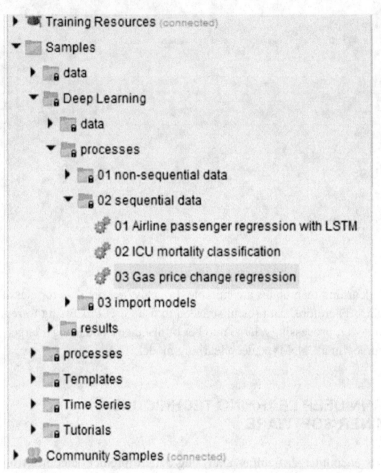

Add LSTM Layer model is implemented so that the model can take the results of previous data to process along with the current data. It can also remember the processing results which are distant from the current data, so that the model can predict the results by the data relationship sequence precisely. Then, Add Fully-Connected is used to compile the data into features that can be processed with the artificial neural networks. The result of data processing is presented as follows.

In the figure, data scientists can forecast oil prices by using Time Series data to analyze correlation from previous data. LSTM technique is used to co-process the distanced data to increase the efficiency. However, the data analyzed with the sample models show accuracy in Root Mean Squared Error form at 0.546 as shown below.

As presented in the figure, the Root Mean Squared Error value is 0.546. It is highly probable that the model has predicted incorrectly due to the use of only 10,000 instances for machine learning. Therefore, when the scientists receive problems that require processing with RNN to find data relationships and sequences, having sufficient data is another condition that needs considering.

Figure 33. Gas station dataset within RapidMiner software

Row No.	id	change	date	price
1	2	0	2016/08/26	1269
2	3	150	2016/08/26	1269
3	4	-120	2016/08/26	1419
4	5	40	2016/08/26	1299
5	6	-40	2016/08/26	1339
6	7	-10	2016/08/26	1299
7	8	-20	2016/08/26	1289
8	9	80	2016/08/26	1269
9	10	-60	2016/08/26	1349
10	1	90	2016/08/27	1289
11	2	-30	2016/08/27	1379
12	3	-40	2016/08/27	1349
13	4	-30	2016/08/27	1309
14	5	60	2016/08/27	1279
15	6	-40	2016/08/27	1339
16	7	0	2016/08/27	1299

Figure 34. Sample model of RNN deep learning

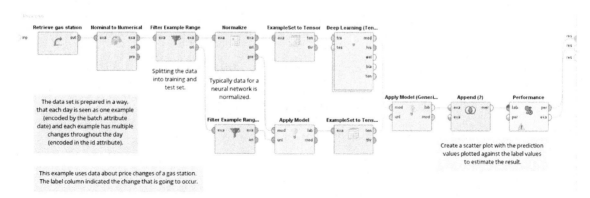

Figure 35. RNN connection

Figure 36. Results from CNN deep learning processing

Row No.	label	prediction	price
1	-0.421	0.115	-0.688
2	-0.000	0.151	-1.198
3	0.316	0.170	-1.198
4	-0.105	0.107	-0.815
5	-0.211	0.136	-0.943
6	-0.316	0.182	-1.198
7	-0.000	0.250	-1.580
8	1.579	0.251	-1.580
9	-0.737	-0.058	0.332
10	0.105	0.042	-0.561
11	-0.632	0.031	-0.433
12	0.421	0.171	-1.198
13	0.737	0.081	-0.688
14	-1.158	-0.070	0.204
15	-0.526	0.182	-1.198
16	0.316	0.285	-1.835
17	-0.105	0.225	-1.453

Figure 37. Root mean squared error values from oil price forecast

root_mean_squared_error

root_mean_squared_error: 0.546 +/- 0.000

CASE STUDY

Risk Assessment of International Business Organization Operation Using Deep Learning Techniques

Any business organization usually encounters risks due to uncontrollable external factors such as currency fluctuations or the threat of war that prevents sellers from producing inputs to deliver. In countries that need foreign investors to spend in their businesses and make profits until they can return the capital to investors, the risk assessment is an important issue to guarantee the return to the investors. Internationally operating companies are all investing and soliciting foreign investors to invest in different ventures. Risk assessments are therefore necessary for those companies. In 2020, a research called Enabling Legal Risk Management Model for International Corporation with Deep Learning and Self Data Mining (Wang). & Chen, 2022) has used the Deep Learning Technique to classify data on legal-related risk issues. The research adopted deep learning data mining techniques including Gradient Lifting Regression Tree, BP Neural Network and Support Vector Machine for experiments Performing.

The research has set the finance failure or the opration failure as the target lebel. The results were divided into 4 levels, namely Giant early warning, Major early warning, Medium early warning and Light early warning. From the experiment, it was found that the BP Neural Network had good performance as it identifies the similar level of risk (Actual output) to the determined risk level (Expected output). Thus, this case study is a good example for data scientists in business and financial institutions who deal with the huge amount of data on a daily basis. The risk is one factor organizations are all aware. And data scientists, themselves, either financial experts or non-financial experts, need to study risk assessment frameworks to identify features that may be useful in their assessment in cases the organization has never collected data useful for risk analysis. other case studies, data scientists still need to rely on Domain Expert to locate the dataset, and experiment with a variety of algorithms that are most effective in data analysis.

Acquiring New Customers for E-Commerce Using Deep Learning Technique

In China, which has a vast territory and a large number of cultivation areas in line with the growth of e-commerce, agricultural products are produced. This has created economic value through selling the agricultural products to consumers all over China and worldwide through the e-Commerce Platform. Bringing e-Commerce to help sell agricultural products also allows farmers to cross through middlemen as they can sell products directly to manufacturers. Each time the consumer receives the product that is less expensive and the farmer earns more profit. However, in order to increase the value of agricultural products sales, marketing and finding factors affecting customer purchase through e-Commerce Platform, has become a challenge for agriculture in China. In 2022, a research called E-Commerce Marketing Optimization of Agricultural Products Based on Deep Learning and Data Mining (Yang, Zheng & Sun, 2022) compiled datasets using the questionnaire tool to collect data from 10 respondents who are farmers in rural China and sell their products through the e-Commerce Platform. The multi-stage sampling method with 95% confidence was selected. Once completeing the data collection process, the study received a return of 293 questionnaires, which means this study had datasets of 293 instances.

From data collection. it was found that the percentage of respondents selling agricultural products in wholesale and retail was at 55.7%, wholesale only at 23.5% and retail only at 16.7%, when sold on the e-Commerce Platform. The problem on selling products are high-priced products at 26.3%, low-quality products at 65.8%, low customer confidence in the brand at 78.4%, lack of variety at 36.4%, and inefficient after-sales service at 53.7%. The dataset was then split into a Train Set and a Test Set for experimental use. In this research, data mining techniques used in experiments are Logistic regression, Decision tree, GBDT, Neural networks. From such research, it was found that the utilization of Big Data will enhance the User Experience as the e-Commerce Platform can present diverse product information. And it ensures buyers, even if it is from a seller who sells agricultural products wholesale. It also allows buyers to identify the brand of the product based on the user experience. The buyers tend to buy from the same seller whom they have had experience in the purchase before. It is called "brand loyalty" to the products. This will gradually increase the opportunity to sell more products. Big Data also extends to sending marketing messages to customers with a history of purchase orders.

From the agricultural product purchasing behavior through the e-Commerce Platform, where all data is collected into Big Data, sellers can also identify whether general product visitors have the opportunity to change to a buyer.

From the case study, it can be seen that the research is not in the nature of collecting data scattered within the organization or from the Social Network, but the questionnaire tools are carefully designed to collect data without data collection bias. Collecting data in this manner helps data scientists reduce the time to do data pre-processing. It is also designed to provide data that can be used to answer questions honestly. Therefore, for data scientists who analyze data similar to such research, the development of questionnaires is an alternative to data collection. In cases the organization does not have data that reflects customer behavior or the existing data need to go through the Data Pre-Processing process until loosing its original pattern, data scientists can design a similar collection of data to overcome that problem.

Using Deep Learning to Forecast Customer Demand in the Apparel and Fashion Industry (Giri, & Chen, 2022)

Today, customers can browse through the website and place an order so that they can be delivered to their homes quickly. However, the biggest challenge for apparel business owners is the rapid change in the needs and tastes of customers. Mass production is at risk of being left in the warehouse because they cannot be sold due to the very short life of each fashion. In the apparel business, it is necessary to find a method for calculating the cost of production that is suitable for the lifespan of fashion. Efforts have been made to forecast such costs and establish pricing to convince the customers to buy in order to drain the manufactured goods. In the apparel business, products have become so widespread that customers wear similar clothes.Then the price will decrease accordingly to allow the remaining inventory to be discharged.

Traditionally, the clothing industry has used customer order history to identify the styles of clothing in each season. However, datasets related to the order history fail to classify patterns of things that never exist, consistent with the fact that new fashions are unprecedented in the world. Therefore analysis of such data was not possible to reflect the needs of customers that will occur in the future. What the clothing industry can do is to bring in other data, data from Social Media to see trends in popularity of customers as well as other features such as colour, size, and shape, which go far beyond the analysis of customer purchase history.

In 2020, Chandadevi Giri and Yan Chen (Giri, & Chen, 2022) developed a model to analyze the fashion needs of customers using deep learning so that the model can classify the data. Classification is based on massive amounts of clothing images from past orders and social media in the context of European fashion.

The researchers have divided the dataset into two groups. The first was numerical data from customer order history such as order quantity and order frequency. The second group was the images of the clothes consisted of shirts, skirts and sweaters. The clustering technique is then used to classify the data from the customer's order history, and combine the image feature to the result from data defined as the target variable. In other words, machine learning determines how each fashion image corresponds to a group of orders. To indicate the consistency, the researchers used the k-NN technique to analyze to which group of order histories the input was close.

The dataset was then taught to machine learning. In the process of testing the model's performance, the researchers inserted newly designed fashion images into the model to test how effective the model was able to classify groups of orders. After the experiment, the researchers suggest that, in the practical case, the fashion industry should have a large amount of data to train the machines to have the opportunity to find a large amount of data enable the machine to classify the data more effectively.

What's interesting about the case study is that researchers are not only using current data to develop and test models, but also applying data that machine learning has previously encountered. The experiment on whether machine learning is going to classify the data correctly has developed the model for real industry use. Deep learning is also applied in a variety of industries and young data scientists should not ignore the small problems that can be used to solve problems to benefit each industry as well.

Using Deep Learning to Speed Up and Collect Massive Data from IoT Devices Used for Remote Diagnosis of Alzheimer's Disease (Hannah et al., 2022)

In medical industry, AI, especially image data such as X-ray film, biopsy photographs has been used to diagnose diseases. Especially in the COVID-19 situation, telehealth counseling has become increasingly popular. Patients can use devices such as tablets to seek medical advice from doctors. Such services can also reduce the spread of the disease and infection from going to the clinic or hospital.

Alzheimer's disease is one of the diseases that affect the elderly and can also be diagnosed through telemetry. In this case, the medical industry can also use artificial intelligence to obtain patient-related data to diagnose whether or not a patient has Alzheimer's disease or stage. The transmission of such data to the digital medical system has resulted in the effectiveness of artificial intelligence in diagnosing Alzheimer's disease. In 2020, researchers have proposed a conceptual framework for optimizing remote diagnosis of Alzheimer's disease by applying deep learning to support the speeding up of large-scale data transport (Hannah et. al., 2022). Data transmission through the block chain is to secure patient data, which should be confidential as it is personal data that must be transmitted to the digital medical system. The experiment has used data collected from the device, IoT deployed at patient homes, transmitted through a block chain to digital medical systems. The tests aims for measuring complete data, transport efficiency, transmission delay and energy efficiency across a variety of methods.

Therefore, it is obvious that deep learning can also be applied for other types of data such as in the medical industry where deep learning is used to support the efficiency of transporting large amounts of data over long distances. And it is also applied in a variety of industries as well.

CONCLUSION

Artificial Neural Network data mining technique is efficient for Data Classification. Data scientists can use features within a dataset to classify data. The features are assigned as a label by machine learning functionality. Therefore, data scientists can use existing data sets to teach machine learning to create an artificial neural network. The results are then generated from the data sets that are used to test the model in order to obtain accurate results. The scientists can also test the accuracy each time, and also apply the artificial neural networks to classify data in other datasets, such as analyzing borrowers with bank refinance capabilities, based on the datasets of debtors who have ever borrowed from the banks. There are two types of deep learning techniques: CNN and RNN. CNN is suitable for analyzing problems that require data classification. This book puts forward an experiment to classify images starting from numbers 0 to 9 using tools within the RapidMiner software including Convolutional Operator, Pooling and Fully to classify data along with an artificial neural network. For the experiment with RNN, this paper uses a sample model within RapidMiner software to predict oil prices from time series data sets in order to analyze correlations and sequences of the data. From the experiments of both CNN and RNN, it has been found that the amount of data used to teach the machine learning affects the efficiency, accuracy of data classification and prediction of learning techniques. In addition, processing a large amount of data also requires GPU Processing to reduce time. When data scientists need to use deep learning techniques to analyze problems, on-premises digital resources are one thing the scientists need to prepare for the implementation of data mining techniques used for Big Data processing.

EXERCISE QUESTIONS

1. Download the sample data sets from the Internet for the purpose of classification.
2. From No. 1, do Feature Selection, then manipulate the Missing Value and Outlier.
3. From No. 2, use the artificial neural network model to classify the data and show the model accuracy in the analysis.
4. Define the problems of data analysis that requires processing with CNN
5. From No. 4, find a suitable data set for data analysis.
6. From No. 5, develop an analysis model using RapidMiner software.
7. From No. 6, summarize the results of the experiment and the accuracy of the analysis.
8. Define problems for data analysis that requires processing with RNN.
9. From No. 8, find a suitable data set for data analysis.
10. From No. 9, develop an analysis model using RapidMiner software.
11. From No.10, summarize the results of the experiment and the accuracy of the analysis.

REFERENCES

Aggarwal, C. C. (2018). *Neural networks and deep learning: a textbook*. Springer. doi:10.1007/978-3-319-94463-0

Beohar, D., & Rasool, A. (2021). Handwritten Digit Recognition of MNIST dataset using Deep Learning state-of-the-art Artificial Neural Network (ANN) and Convolutional Neural Network (CNN). *2021 International Conference on Emerging Smart Computing and Informatics (ESCI), Emerging Smart Computing and Informatics (ESCI), 2021 International Conference On*, 542–548.

Chinnarasri, C., Nonsawang, S., & Supharatid, S. (2012). *Application of Artificial Neural Networks for River Stage Forecasting in Hatyai. King Mongkut's University of Technology Thonburi.* KMUTT.

Chow, T. W. S., & Cho, S.-Y. (2007). *Neural networks and computing: learning algorithms and applications.* Imperial College Press. doi:10.1142/p487

Fernando, T., Gammulle, H., Denman, S., Sridharan, S., & Fookes, C. (2021). Deep Learning for Medical Anomaly Detection - A Survey. *ACM Computing Surveys*, *54*(7), 1–37. doi:10.1145/3464423

Ghorpade, V. G., & Koneru, V. S. (2021). Pattern recognition neural networkmodel for experimental based compressive strength graded self compacting concrete. *Materials Today: Proceedings*, *43*(Part 2), 795–799. doi:10.1016/j.matpr.2020.06.175

Giri, C., & Chen, Y. (2022). Deep Learning for Demand Forecasting in the Fashion and Apparel Retail Industry. *Forecasting*, *4*(2), 565–581. doi:10.3390/forecast4020031

Guo, C., Zhang, M., & Chen, H. (2021). Suitability of low-field nuclear magnetic resonance (LF-NMR) combining with back propagation artificial neural network (BP-ANN) to predict printability of polysaccharide hydrogels 3D printing. *International Journal of Food Science & Technology*, *56*(5), 2264–2272. doi:10.1111/ijfs.14844

Hannah, S., Deepa, A. J., Chooralil, V. S., BrillySangeetha, S., Yuvaraj, N., Arshath Raja, R., Suresh, C., Vignesh, R., YasirAbdullahR, Srihari, K., & Alene, A. (2022). Blockchain-Based Deep Learning to Process IoT Data Acquisition in Cognitive Data. *BioMed Research International*, *2022*, 1–7. doi:10.1155/2022/5038851 PMID:35187166

Lakshmi Devi, R., & Samundeeswari, V., V. (2021). Detection and Automated Classification of Brain Tumor Types in MRI Images using Convolutional Neural Network with Grid Search Optimization. *2021 Fifth International Conference on I-SMAC (IoT in Social, Mobile, Analytics and Cloud) (I-SMAC), I-SMAC (IoT in Social, Mobile, Analytics and Cloud) (I-SMAC), 2021 Fifth International Conference On*, 1280–1284.

LeCun, Y., Cortes, C., & Burges, J. C. C. (2021). *The MNIST Database of Handwritten Digits.* Retrieved from: http://yann.lecun.com/exdb/mnist/

Ramirez-Hernandez, J., Juarez-Sandoval, O.-U., Hernandez-Gonzalez, L., Hernandez-Ramirez, A., & Olivares-Dominguez, R.-S. (2020). Voltage Control Based on a Back-Propagation Artificial Neural Network Algorithm. *2020 IEEE International Autumn Meeting on Power, Electronics and Computing (ROPEC), Power, Electronics and Computing (ROPEC), 2020 IEEE International Autumn Meeting On, 4*, 1–6.

Sabau Popa, C. D., Popa, D. N., Bogdan, V., & Simut, R. (2021). Composite Financial Performance Index Prediction — A Neural Networks Approach. *Journal of Business Economics and Management*, *22*(2), 277–296. doi:10.3846/jbem.2021.14000

Snineh, S. M., Amrani, N. E. A., Youssfi, M., Bouattane, O., & Daaif, A. (2021). Detection of traffic anomaly in highways by using recurrent neural network. *2021 Fifth International Conference On Intelligent Computing in Data Sciences (ICDS), Intelligent Computing in Data Sciences (ICDS), 2021 Fifth International Conference On*, 1–6.

Sriwiboon, N. (2020). Improvement the Performance of the Chest X-ray Image Classification with Convolutional Neural Network Model by Using Image Augmentations Technique for COVID-19 Diagnosis. *The Journal of King Mongkut's University of Technology North Bangkok, 31*(1).

Telikani, A., Shahbahrami, A., & Gandomi, A. H. (2021). High-performance implementation of evolutionary privacy-preserving algorithm for big data using GPU platform. *Information Sciences, 579*, 251–265. doi:10.1016/j.ins.2021.08.006

Thankachan, T., Prakash, K. S., & Jothi, S. (2021). Artificial neural network modeling to evaluate and predict the mechanical strength of duplex stainless steel during casting. *Sadhana, 46*(4), 1–12. doi:10.100712046-021-01742-w

Wang, G., & Chen, Y. (2022). Enabling Legal Risk Management Model for International Corporation with Deep Learning and Self Data Mining. *Computational Intelligence and Neuroscience, 2022*, 6385404. doi:10.1155/2022/6385404 PMID:35432517

Yang, H., Zheng, Z., & Sun, C. (2022). E-Commerce Marketing Optimization of Agricultural Products Based on Deep Learning and Data Mining. *Computational Intelligence and Neuroscience, 2022*, 2022. doi:10.1155/2022/6564014 PMID:35634060

Zhu, H., Samtani, S., Brown, R. A., & Chen, H. (2021). A Deep Learning Approach for Recognizing Activity of Daily Living (Adl) for Senior Care: Exploiting Interaction Dependency and Temporal Patterns. *Management Information Systems Quarterly, 45*(2), 859–895. doi:10.25300/MISQ/2021/15574

Chapter 7
Clustering

ABSTRACT

Clustering is employed to divide a data set into an appropriate number of groups. Clustering is a form of unsupervised learning, which means a data scientist can bring labelled features of interest into the mining model. Furthermore, after dividing the data set, the data scientist can label each cluster. In business, clustering is used to analyze a customer or product segment that matches a target market. This chapter introduces clustering techniques including k-means, hierarchical clustering, and DBSCAN as well as techniques to indicate the efficiency of the clustering analysis. Data scientists can assess the efficiency of clustering analysis in two ways. Firstly, subjective measurement is where a data scientist consults a domain expert to confirm the efficiency of the cluster analysis, and secondly, data scientists can use objective measurements that test the efficiency of the cluster analysis result based on calculations. This chapter demonstrates cluster analysis adoption with RapidMiner so that readers can follow the process step-by-step.

INTRODUCTION

Clustering is Unsupervised-Learning data mining technique (Govindaraj et al., 2020: Abbas et al, 2021). Data scientists are able to group the quantitative data without defining the target variables (Labeled) nor dividing the dataset into 2 parts to teach the machine learning. Clustering technique gather similar data into one group and bring dissimilar data into another group. Therefore, clustering can be applied in a wide range of industries, such as customer segmentation according to customer purchasing behaviors (Punhani et al., 2021). The customers in the same group tend to have similar purchasing behaviors and expected prices. Clustering is applied in order that the business sectors can design marketing plans suitable for each group of customers. It can also diagnose the stage of cancer in each patient from the sizes of the tumors growing in the patient's organs (Kumar, Ganapathy & Kang, 2021).

Although the process of data science provides computational methods to obtain the optimal number of clusters, to specify the number of clusters depends on the objectives of the analysis. Data scientists need to consult with domain experts to gain the exact number of clusters to be analyzed. For example, clustering the sizes of shirts that will be produced by analyzing the clustering data from the purchase

DOI: 10.4018/978-1-6684-4730-7.ch007

history datasets. In this way, data experts can advise on a number of clusters of shirt sizes that are appropriate, such as small, medium, and large.

Clustering can be used to analyze the centroid of the data in each cluster. It can be applied to set the car sales price from the purchase history. Each car model can be produced in many specifications. After the analysis, the car dealers can set various prices of each specification under the same car model by using the data in each group. For example, Model A car with the entry-level specification is 1,300,000 baht. Model A car with the intermediate specification is 1,600,000 baht. Model A car with the highest specification is 1,700,000 baht. As mentioned in the example, the price determination is from the analysis using clustering technique. Data scientists can perform a centroid analysis to each group of data according to the customer purchasing behavior.

K-MEANS CLUSTERING

Once data scientists are asked about the nature of the data, such as the purchasing behavior of each group of customers, they need to find a consistent data set to answer those questions (Ginting, 2021: Puspasari et al., 2021). The dataset initially received is characterized as Unlabeled Data, the data which has not yet been clustered nor defined for its name or meaning. Therefore, these data sets can be clustered and defined according to the objectives of the data analysis, such as definition of the customers; the middle-class or the wealthy.

K-Means Clustering Algorithm

Clustering data can be done by bringing 2 Data Objects; the shirt width and the shirt length; to create a Data Point; the sizes. Data scientists can develop a display in the Scatter Plot format to see the intersection at the data point created from the 2 data objects, and then colorize each data point according to clusters. For example, the yellow data point represents the medium size, and the brown data point represents the large size.

Figure 1. Unlabeled data and data after clustering

To cluster data using the K-Means algorithm, data scientists can import the quantitative datasets into the K-Means model, then determine the number of clusters, and perform clustering analysis. The process is as follows.

1.   Determine the number of clusters into k variables. For example, k = 2.
2.   K-Means model randomly places 2 zero points into the data set, assuming that the 1st center is C0, and the 2nd center is C1.

Figure 2. Clustering data with k-means

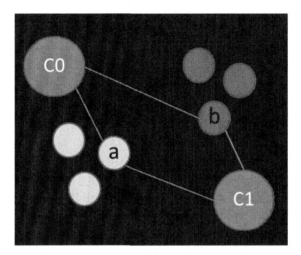

3.   K-Means model will then calculate the distances from each data point to the center. For example, it will be calculating the distance between center C0 and data point a, and calculating the distance between center C1 and data point a. Meanwhile, K-Means calculates the distance between center C0 and data point b, and calculates the distance between center C1 and data point b. When data point a is closer to C0 than C1, data point a is then clustered in Cluster 0. Similarly, when the distance between data point b is closer to C1 than C0, then data point b will be clustered in Cluster 1.
4.   When the data points are grouped in the cluster form, K-Means will then calculate the average distance from the center point of each cluster to all data points, and then move the position of the two centers again. Then, it will perform the calculation in step 3 and compare the average distance from the center to the data points of each cluster from the average of the previous calculations. If the mean varies or greater than 0, the clustering has not yet been completed. So, K-Means will repeat the process over and over so that the data point is positioned closest to the center of each cluster. In case the average is equal to the previous round, or equal to 0, clustering process is considered completed, and K-Means will no longer relocate the center point.

CALCULATING DISTANCES BETWEEN THE DATA POINTS WITHIN K-MEANS CLUSTERING

The distances between the data points and the center of each group within a K-Means cluster can be calculated in two ways: Manhattan Distance and Euclidean Distance.

1. **Manhattan Distance:** Is a method for calculating distances in quantitative data by subtracting the data objects from each instance, and adding the results of all data objects together as presented in the example (Haviluddin et al., 2020).

Table 1. Examples of datasets for Manhattan Distance calculation

Name	Age	Bank Balance	Credit Rating
Jirapon Sunkpho	50	550	3
Sarawut Ramjan	38	520	2

From the Manhattan Distance table, the Data Object from Instance named Jirapon Sunkpho will be diminished by the Instance named Sarawut Ramjan, starting from the Data Object named Age. 50 decreased by 38 equals 12. The Bank Balance Data Object will then be subtracted. The Subtraction is 550 diminished by 520 equals 30, and the Data Object from Credit Rating is subtracted, being 3-2=1. Then all of the calculated results are added as $12 + 30 + 1$ equals 43, which is the distance between the instances named Jirapon Sunkpho and Sarawut Ramjan.

The Manhattan Distance method is, therefore, used in data clustering techniques to group the purchasing behavior or to classify data to segment products. The Manhattan Distance method calculates the distances between data objects in four directions: left, right, top and bottom.

2. **Euclidean Distance:** Within the data set, there is movement of data objects while clustering data in multiple directions. Therefore, data scientists also need to use Euclidean Distance to calculate distances between data objects in various (Bayram & Nabiyev, 2020).

Table 2. Examples of datasets for Euclidean Distance calculation

Name	Age	Bank Balance	Credit Rating
Jirapon Sunkpho	50	550	3
Sarawut Ramjan	38	520	2

From the sample data set, to calculate the distance between the instances named Jirapon Sunkpho and Sarwut Ramjan, the data object of each instance can be calculated as follows:

$$dis\left(x,y\right)=\sqrt{\left(50-25\right)^{2}\left(550-520\right)^{2}\left(3-2\right)^{2}}$$

$$dis\left(x,y\right)=39.06$$

The distance between the two instances is 39.06. In the case the data objects are literal, and data scientists can replace the identical data with the number 1, and the different data with the number 0 before calculating with the usual Euclidean Distance method. This is called Mix Euclidean Measure Distance.

Regarding segmentation using K-Means, data scientists are required to take into account outliers, which are used to calculate the distance between the data point and the center. Therefore, data scientists need to prepare data (Data Pre-Processing) before segmenting them.

However, data scientists are supposed to consider the nature of clustering in the data set before determining the appropriate number of clusters. For example, most of the customer's purchasing behavior data is clustered into two groups, each group having a high-density data point. If data scientists define three groups, the third group may contain only a small number of data points that are insignificant to use as they do not reflect the results that support decision-making.

HIERARCHICAL CLUSTERING

Hierarchical Clustering is a principle that supports the decision making of data scientists (Rezaeijo, 2021: Zhou et al., 2021). To determine the number of data clusters, there are 4 methods for calculating the distance between the data clusters; 1. Calculating the distance from the Data Point in each group that is the closest to each other, 2. Calculating the distance from the Data Point in each group with the farthest distance, 3. Calculating the distance from the average distance of each group, and 4. Calculating the distance between the centers of each group.

Agglomerative Clustering Algorithm is a clustering method that supports Hierarchical Clustering.

1. Bring Data Object with 2 or more variables to create Data Points which can be displayed through the Scatter Plot in order to see the location of the created Data Points such as the number of customers and food sales. Then the customers can be clustered.

Table 3. Sample data for agglomerative clustering algorithm (Munlika, 2019)

Number of Customers per Day (X)	Food Sales (Y)
120	100
59	50
86	70
35	20
105	90

From the table, the data scientists can develop the visualization data to explore the data on the distances between the data points as shown below.

Figure 3. Creating a scatter plot to explore shopping trends

2. Clustering analysis can be done by choosing a method to calculate the distance from the nearest Data Points in each round to cluster the data with the same distances in each group. It can be created as a Proximity Matrix showing the distance between the Data Points as well as the number of clusters as follows:

Figure 4. Proximity matrix, the result of calculating the distance of every pair of data points

	1	2	3	4
2	78.87332			
3	45.34314	33.60060		
4	116.72618	38.41875	71.42129	
5	18.02776	60.95900	27.58623	98.99495

As seen in the figure, to calculate the distance between each data point within the Proximity Matrix, data scientists can divide the data into clusters. In the example, Cluster 1 is Instances 1 and 5, which share the same distances between data points, 18.02. And Cluster 2 is Instances 2 and 3, which are the distances between the data point, 33.60. The third cluster is Instance 4, which covers the 2nd and 3rd instances. Therefore, in the example, there are 4 clusters, which segment the data of the number of customers per day together with food sales. When considering the data, it is found that the original data, grouped into each cluster, shares similar volumes. The graph below presents the segmentation as follows.

Figure 5. Clustering with hierarchical clustering

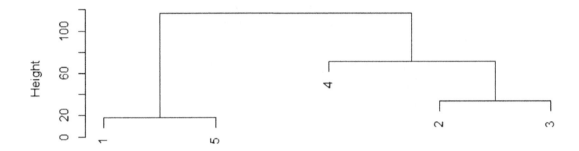

In the figure, the data are clustered by calculating the nearest distance to the nearest of data point, clustering from the nearest data point first and then to the distance that covers all clusters (Peungvicha, Tubtiang, & Sattayaaphitan, 2019). From the picture, data scientists can decide to cluster the data in either of these ways.

1. The cluster consists of cluster 1 that covers instances of the 1st and 5th instances, and cluster 2 covering the 2nd, 3rd and 4th instances.
2. The cluster consists of cluster 1 covering the 1st and 5th instances, cluster 2 that covers the 2nd instance, and cluster 3 covering the 2nd, 3rd and 4th instances.

However, clustering with Hierarchical Clustering has limitations. If the data scientists are unable to pre-process the original data sufficiently and the outlier remains, the data is computed for clustering with other data too. This results in discrepancies in Hierarchical Clustering. Moreover, by calculating the distances between every data point within the datasets, data scientists need to provide sufficient resources as Big Data manner in order to be clustered with Hierarchical Clustering method.

DBSCAN

In some cases, when data scientists survey data by creating a scatter plot and have found that the data is highly distributed. Data scientists can use DBSCAN to cluster their data (Wafa et al, 2021). DBSCAN will determine the center radius (Eps) from every data point, and determine the minimum number of the Data Points that must be within the radius (MinPts). Therefore, DBSCAN aims to determine the density of data within each cluster with the following algorithm.

1. DBSCAN assigns all data points as the center by analyzing the data points that are within the range of Eps whether the number exceeds MinPts or not. If the data points are greater than the MinPts, then the central data point is considered the Core Point. For example, if MinPts is 4, DBSCAN will analyze whether there are more than 4 data points within the radius. And if so, it will assign the center data point as core points and do the same for all data points within the datasets for determining data cluster.
2. In the case DBSCAN analyzes and have found that within the radius of Eps, the number of data points is not greater than MinPts, it will set the Data Points as Border Points. The border points are then clustered within any Core Point to combine into one cluster.
3. If a Data Point is found near the Core Point more than 2 locations, it will cluster those data into one group.
4. If it is found that within the Eps radius from the central Data Point is fewer numbers of Data Points than the MinPts, and Data Points at the center does not cling to the Core Points, any Data Point will be designated as Noise.

Figure 6. Clustering data with DBSCAN

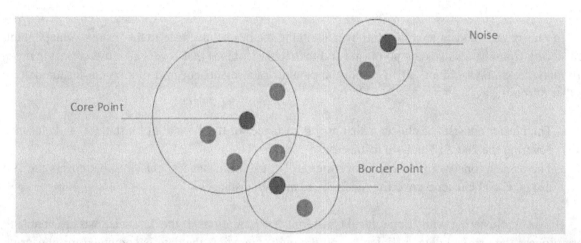

In the figure, the data scientists have set the MinPts value to 4. When the radius within the radius of Eps meets 4 center data points, then the data points are assigned as the core point. And DBSCAN will get the data cluster 1. Then, when setting the center within the Eps radius again, only 2 Data Points can be found from the center. Such center points are designated as Border Points and then grouped into Cluster 1. When the center is set within the radius of Eps again, only 2 Data Points are found, and the cluster is not grouped with other Core Points, so the center point is considered Noise. To determine the Eps or radius from the data point set as the center, data scientists can determine the Eps configuration based on the distance from the center to other data points within the most frequent dataset. It means within most datasets, the distance from the center to the data point is equal to that value. For example, when analyzing the data, it is mostly found that the distance from the center to the data point is 0.8. The data scientists can assign Eps to 0.8, and take all the distances to create a histogram for analyzing the greatest distance frequency.

ANALYZING THE EFFICIENCY OF DATA CLUSTERING

It can be done in two ways, 1. Subjective measurement, which is an assessment from data experts. Experts may consider the data with their experience along with the results of data visualization, and 2. Objective Measurement, which is to consider from the numbers that show the efficiency of data clustering. Each cluster must be clearly grouped, and within each cluster there must be consistent data. To analyze efficiency, the details are as follows.

1. **Subjective Measurement:** Is to present visualization data to data professionals to help assess the efficiency of data clustering. Visual data from data mining techniques can be used for data classification such as Decision Tree or visualization data resulting from cluster analysis. Data clustering must be consistent with the context of the industry. For instance, after clustering the data, data scientists can develop a data visualization that uses color to represent each cluster. Cluster 1 is represented by red, and Cluster 2 is represented by blue. Also, in each cluster there is a Centroid which shows the center of the data in each cluster. Data professionals can determine whether data clustering is accurate, reasonable and consistent with the business context. For example, data clustering of customer pants sizes is divided into 3 clusters, consisting of sizes S cluster, L and XL. It is considered accurate if each cluster has clear and reasonable data on width and length of pants. Therefore, the customers can purchase pants using their individual size.

2. **Objective Measurement:** Uses numbers to analyze the performance of three types of clustering; Dunn Index, Davies-Bouldin Index and C-Index.

   a. Dunn Index determines the minimum distances of the Data Point to the Data Point in other clusters (Intercluster) divided by the maximum distances of the Data Points within the Intracluster (Ben Ncir, Hamza, & Bouaguel, 2021).

$$d = \frac{d_{min}}{d_{max}}$$

From the formula, d_{min} *is* the minimum distance of the Data Point to the Data Point in other clusters. d_{max} is the maximum distance of the data point within the cluster.

The result shows that the larger the number, the better the clustering efficiency. This means that the distance between the clusters is large, making the clusters are further separated. And when the distance between the data points is less, the data within the Cluster is well grouped.

   b. Davies-Bouldin Index is the analysis of data clustering using data from the centroids of every cluster. The algorithm is as follows (Wijaya, 2021)

   i. Calculate the average distance from the Centroid to all Data Points within the same Cluster.

   ii. Calculate the average distance from each centroid of each cluster to the other cluster's centroids.

   iii. Take the average distance from the Centroid to all Data Points of Cluster 1 to add with Cluster 2 and divide by the distance between the Centroids of the 1st Pair.

   iv. Continue this algorithm until all pairs are complete, and then select the result from the most valuable pair. Then, take the above result to divide by the total numbers of clusters.

The results can reflect the efficiency. The lower the values are, the further the clusters can be separately grouped. Each pair should have a considerable distance between the Centroids, and within each cluster there is good clustering of data. And the distance between Centroid and Data Point within the same cluster is small.

c. Index is an analysis of clustering efficiency, which can avoid discrepancies from data points, the noise as follows:

$$c = \frac{S - S_{min}}{S_{max} - S_{min}}$$

when, S is the sum of the distances of each data point within the same cluster

S_{min} is the sum of the smallest distances of each data point from all clusters

S_{max} is the sum of the largest distances of each data point from all clusters

When calculating the results are between 0 – 1, small results mean good clustering efficiency. If the sum of the distances between the largest data points shows a high value, it means that they are clustered separately from each other, and if the lowest distance between the data points is small value, it means that the data points within each cluster is clustered appropriately.

DATA CLUSTERING USING RAPIDMINER SOFTWARE

To use the K-Means clustering software, RapidMiner in clustering, this book uses the Irish flower data set to group the Irish flower data of each cultivar including Setosa, Vesicolor and all Virginega, totaling150 instances. K-Means is classified as Unsupervised-Learning where data scientists can import the datasets into the model without labelling the target variables nor teaching the machine. The experimental process is as follows.

Figure 7. Importing the Irish flower dataset into the model

In the figure, data scientists can import the Irish flower dataset within the RapidMiner software into the model for experimentation. The Irish flower dataset contains the following information.

Figure 8. Irish flower data set

Row No.	id	label	a1	a2	a3	a4
1	id_1	Iris-setosa	5.100	3.500	1.400	0.200
2	id_2	Iris-setosa	4.900	3	1.400	0.200
3	id_3	Iris-setosa	4.700	3.200	1.300	0.200
4	id_4	Iris-setosa	4.600	3.100	1.500	0.200
5	id_5	Iris-setosa	5	3.600	1.400	0.200
6	id_6	Iris-setosa	5.400	3.900	1.700	0.400
7	id_7	Iris-setosa	4.600	3.400	1.400	0.300
8	id_8	Iris-setosa	5	3.400	1.500	0.200
9	id_9	Iris-setosa	4.400	2.900	1.400	0.200
10	id_10	Iris-setosa	4.900	3.100	1.500	0.100
11	id_11	Iris-setosa	5.400	3.700	1.500	0.200
12	id_12	Iris-setosa	4.800	3.400	1.600	0.200
13	id_13	Iris-setosa	4.800	3	1.400	0.100
14	id_14	Iris-setosa	4.300	3	1.100	0.100
15	id_15	Iris-setosa	5.800	4	1.200	0.200
16	id_16	Iris-setosa	5.700	4.400	1.500	0.400
17	id_17	Iris-setosa	5.400	3.900	1.300	0.400
18	id_18	Iris-setosa	5.100	3.500	1.400	0.300

ExampleSet (150 examples, 2 special attributes, 4 regular attributes)

Figure 9. Using k-means clustering

149

In the figure, data scientists use the K-Means Clustering model to cluster the data by setting the number of clusters to 3. The distance between the data points can be calculated using the Euclidean distance method. The results of the initial clustering are as follows.

Figure 10. The number of data objects organized in each cluster

Cluster Model

```
Cluster 0: 50 items
Cluster 1: 38 items
Cluster 2: 62 items
Total number of items: 150
```

From the figure, the data sets are divided into 3 clusters as defined. Cluster 0 has a total of 50 Data Objects, Cluster 1 has a total of 38 Data Objects, and Cluster 2 has a total of 62 Data Objects. In each cluster, there are clustered data as seen through visual information below.

Figure 11. Data results after k-means clustering

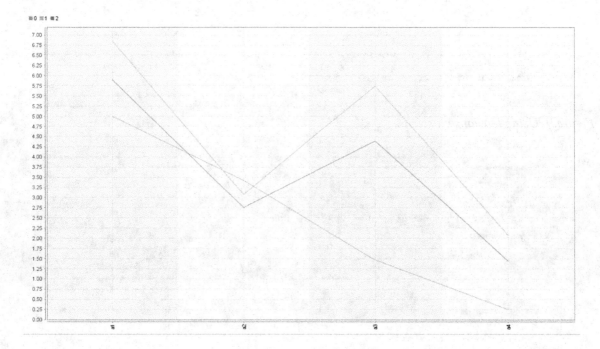

As seen, data scientists can take the visualization data to consult with a data specialist in order to assess the effectiveness of the data clustering, considering the distance between clusters, obviously separated and clustered within the cluster. The Irish flower cultivars are clearly divided into 3. And the sizes of flowers and sepals in each species totally differ.

However, to reconfirm the efficiency of data clustering, data scientists can also perform additional analysis.

Figure 12. Measuring clustering efficiency with cluster distance performance

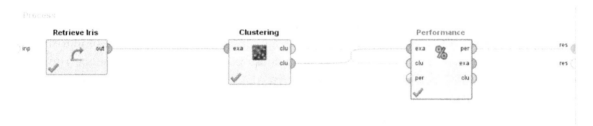

In the figure, data scientists apply Cluster Distance Performance to assess the efficiency of data clustering. The average distance between the data objects within the cluster is evaluated. The average distance between the Centroids in each cluster, and the overall performance are as follows.

Figure 13. Evaluation of clustering efficiency result

In the figure, when using Cluster Distance Performance model to assess the efficiency of clustering, the following results are obtained. The average distance between the centroids in each cluster is 0.52. The average distance between data objects within cluster 0 is 0 0.30. The average distance between data objects within cluster 1 equals 0.62, while the distance between data objects within cluster 2 is 0.64. Last but not least, the efficiency calculated by Davies Bouldin method is 0.66.

From all the results, each pair of clusters have good distances between the Centroids, meaning the clusters are appropriately separated from each other. And within each cluster, the distance between

Centroid and Data Object is not too high, which means there is a moderately grouping effect. When calculating with Davies Bouldin method, the results reflect the efficiency of clustering at a moderate level.

CASE STUDY

The Smart Travel Route Design With Clustering Analysis Algorithm (Lou, 2022)

China has achieved a lot of success in the tourism industry since its opening. However, in 2022, tourism in China is beginning to reach its saturation due to the lack of analysis of tourist routes. The analysis of tourist routes is the planning of visits to various attractions to meet the specific expectations of tourists, such as health tourism. The attractions along the route are places related to the health of tourists, such as natural hot springs and therapeutic spas, which are approved and maintained by the tourism industry related government agencies. To design of the tourist route, it is important to take into account the circumstances surrounding each period; rainstorms or earthquakes that may occur. It then produces an action plan that tour operators can implement.

In 2022, a study called Analysis of the Intelligent Tourism Route Planning Scheme based on the Cluster Analysis Algorithm (Lou, 2022) conducted a study on the analysis of tourist routes by dividing the tourist routes into 3 scales, namely large, medium and small scales. For the small scale, tour operators need to analyze the needs of tourists in each form, aiming to provide tourists with whether it's a city tour or the historical and cultural tour in each locality. Tour operators and travel agents can consider the tourist types by their interests. The tourists' preferences can be categorized as shopping, recreational tourism, adventure tourism and historical and cultural studies.

To analyze such tourist routes, there is a great challenge of providing tourist destinations that meet the expectations and various tastes of tourists to come together on the same route. Therefore, there has been researches aimed at using Big Data for in-depth data analysis. However, if data scientists get travel datasets from a time-consuming travel together with a not-so-good experience to tourists, they will not be able to answer the question. Such datasets simply cannot provide insight to data scientists because data scientists themselves cannot expect how complete the datasets they receive will be. Therefore, there is a number of researches trying to suggest improving the algorithms for data processing so that the incomplete data can be used to process the data by using the ant colony algorithm together with the travel route design. There are also a number of studies that have used a particle swarm algorithm to design a travel route with the shortest time frame by choosing the attractions that are close to each other so that tourists can experience travel at the lowest travel costs. Therefore, designing the route in such a way will allow tourists to travel qualitatively with a small amount of time and save the cost of the tour operator. However, the variables that affect the traveler's experience are not only attractions and duration of travel, but the age range of tourists between teenagers and the elderly in the same group is also a challenge for tour operators and travel agents to design travel routes as well. A research analysis was conducted on the tourist personalization route guidance system.

Regarding the condition of China's tourism industry today, although the design of tourism routes is a principle and standard, accepted all over the world, in the real situation in China, most tour operators and travel agents do not apply those principles to the design of tourist routes because each locality has so many variables and needs that those principles cannot be applied for route design. Therefore, tour operators and travel agents use the experience of their staff as a resource to design travel route. Therefore, tourist routes often face congested traffic conditions because Staff are just familiar with those routes on the journey. On the other hand, China's attractions focus on recreational tourism and sightseeing. As a result, when designing tour routes, tour operators and travel agents do not have many options to meet the different expectations of each group of tourists. Designing a good tourist route should also take into account the delivery of experiences about Food, accommodation, cultural values, the convenience, and the distance between the tourist's accommodation and the attractions.

Cluster analysis techniques are, therefore, used for the design of tourist routes that not only manage the tourist attractions under the routes and timeframes, but also bring cultural values that meet the expectations of tourists. Clustering focuses on segmenting data. The data in each cluster can be distinguished from the properties used in the data analysis. Clustering in data science is similar to processing with other data mining techniques. It begins with selecting datasets that are useful for answering the set questions and attribute transformation for a selected data set to become a feature used for processing with data mining techniques. Then only the features that are useful for data analysis are selected. This may include performing data cleaning, such as eliminating outlier data objects or adjusting the measurements of each feature to be consistent, called the standardization. The data is then analyzed with Cluster analysis, which is Data Mining in an Unsupervised-Learning manner, and then interpret the results.

The research selected techniques corresponding to experiment cluster analysis in 4 methods: density-based cluster analysis algorithm, division-based cluster analysis algorithm, hierarchical cluster analysis algorithm, and k-means cluster analysis. It was found that using k-means cluster analysis is easier to interpret the data obtained from the analysis. It takes less time to process the dataset and low complexity. However, with k-means cluster analysis, outlier data still affects the efficiency of processing and interpreting the results. The research has, therefore, improved the algorithm for further processing by identifying a group (class) of the city as a tourist destination and calculating the distance between those classes, together with calculating the distance of the Data Object related to expectations and personalization of tourists. The key principle is that the smaller the distance, the more data objects are grouped together. The distance between both the attractions and the tourist-related data objects were processed together by k-means clustering until it is possible to cluster the attractions suitable for each type of tourist. By improving the algorithm in this process, tour operators and travel agents are able to use the analyzed attractions to create a travel itinerary that meets the tourists' expectation.

Therefore, besides clustering in the various ways that this book has already mentioned, Data scientists can also make improvements to processing algorithms to make Clustering Analysis flexible and suitable for different objectives and environments.

Using Cluster Analysis to Segment Customers Based on the Nature of Engagement Created by Social Media Influencers on YouTube (Erdoğmuş & Arslan, 2022)

Social media creates dynamic relationships between brands and customers, so some customers can use that relationship to influence the perceptions of other customers, which we call influencers. Influencers can spread their opinions about the products and services they've tried or reach their followers. Advertisers and marketers believe in the influencers' ability to communicate about a brand to their target customers. However, choosing the right influencer for customers and brands has also become a challenge for marketers. The metrics used for choosing an influencer on a social network are the number of Like, Share, and Subscriber as a measure of the effectiveness of each influencer's brand communication. Understanding the influencer's target audience will help influencers design the right content and marketing for their followers.

These issues become a challenge for brand managers to understand the phenomenon of social media and how to take advantages from the engagement that influencers generate to their followers. For the influencers, understanding their target audience can help influencers design the right content and marketing for their followers. YouTube is one of the most popular social media platforms worldwide and is used to publish content and engage your influencer's customers to help them make the purchase of products and services reviewed by the influencer.

The idea of engagement is to create a two-way relationship between the brand and the consumer. That means the consumer influences how the product and service preferences meet their expectations, and the brand expects their customers to have a positive attitude towards their own brand, which is reflected through the use of the brand's products and services. When it comes to online engagement, the brand can review the behavior and attitude that customers have towards the brand through review, like, dislike, follow, share, comment, subscribe, participate in online games. The brand manager can categorize customers on social media based on the nature of their engagement into 6 categories: those who do not use social media, those who travel and watch media on social media, those who interact with influencers on social media, those who surf on social media surfers to collect information on purchasing decisions, those who use social media to review products and services via social media, and finally those who create social media contents.

When it comes to social media motivations, the users benefit from choosing to consume content and use content on social media, interacting with people on social media, searching for content on social media for educational purposes, exploring content on social media for news or new topics, content, killing their boredom, consuming content for entertainment, accessing to social media to separate time from day-to-day operations, creating one's own content to be accepted by others on social media, entering the online world to distance themselves from offline society, building relationships with others in the online community, using social media as a medium to communicate with people in society anywhere and anytime, and exploiting social media such as presenting themselves to be known in the hope of marketing results. These uses are all due to the motivation for using social media, and when specifically mention to YouTube, the main motivation of users is to consume entertainment media, where users may both upload their own video files to communicate to other users and choose to consume content created by other users.

In 2022, there was a research called "Engaging with Social Media Influencers on YouTube: A Cluster Analysis" (Erdoğmuş & Arslan, 2022, which attempted to segment customers based on the type of engagement that YouTube influencers generate using a cluster analysis technique. The research used a questionnaire as a tool to gather information about YouTube users' motivation to engage with influencers. Then K-Mean cluster analysis techniques were used to analyze the data. The results showed that customers can be divided into 3 groups: 1. Customers with positive behavior: This group of people use YouTube for entertainment and often don't press the dislike button on YouTube and don't pay attention to the amount of people who press dislike. They also often don't press the unsubscribe channel on YouTube and often press Like and Share more than other customers. 2. Passive group: These people still use YouTube for entertainment. But their behavior is more like content consumption than interacting or communicating with influencers and other users. There is a chance for this group of people to click unsubscribe channel on YouTube. 3. Users who access YouTube for entertainment and search for information about goods and services solely without any interaction: They often consider the quantity of likes and dislikes in making decisions about purchasing goods and services.

Therefore, influencers and marketers or brand managers should pay attention to creating content and storytelling for positively behaved customers who are interested in following the influencer in order to establish their own social status, make other users interested and purchase goods and services based on the influencer's recommendations. For customers who seek information about products and services on YouTube, behaviors caused by positive behaviors of other users such as like or subscriber result in their decision to purchase goods and services from influencers.

According to the results of the study, data scientists who analyze marketing data can also consider features that may respond to the analysis of market data. It's not limited to demographics. Based on case studies, segmenting customers by engagement level requires a combination of data analysis across multiple features, and it can be demonstrated that if a data scientist wants to analyze data that is deep in a particular science, it is important to analyze data that is deep in a particular science. Understanding only quantitative data analysis or advanced data mining techniques cannot enable data scientists to obtain data of an Unseen or hidden relationship nature. When a data scientist goes into a particular department or organization, to find knowledge in the domain will help data scientists develop themselves to be proficient in data analysis.

Using Cluster Analysis to Analyze After-Sales Service (Hyrmet & Arbana, 2021)

Digital transformation requires multiple variables, and among those driving variables is creating positive customer experiences and creating new business models that meet customer expectations. Organizations that are aware of digital transformation will focus on tightening internal processes and reducing duplication of work between departments, and creating an environment within the agency ecosystem that facilitates innovation, including enhancing the digital maturity of the organization through data governance.

In order to consider digital transformation, organizations need to consider it in a variety of dimensions. 1. In terms of digital strategy, organizations need to take into account the formulation of vision and data governance and strategy implementation to drive the organization towards the vision. 2. In the dimension of creating the ability to deliver a positive customer experience, organizations must perform customer segmentation analysis, using data from social networks to analyze data and improve products and services in line with customer and subscriber expectations. Organizations can use forecasting techniques to formulate marketing strategies, as well as create flexible customer service processes. 3. Technological dimensions involve planning the use of technology, integrating the use of technology into the business model of the organization. 4. Operational dimensions aim to consider the development of internal processes, the implementation of technology for responding to management strategies, as well as increasing efficiency and productivity from improved processes. 5. In terms of organizational management, the organization must focus on changing the corporate culture to be in line with the organization's performance. Digital Transformation communicates such changes throughout the organization, providing training to develop employees to be ready for the adoption of digital technology for their operations and managing knowledge to inherit and transfer valuable skills and knowledge within the organization, independent of employee entry and exit.

As a result of the organization's digital transformation efforts, after-sales service is another service that organizations need to consider in order to create a service strategy that affects the satisfaction of their customers. Therefore, in 2021, Hyrmet & Arbana conducted research using Cluster analysis to segment customers based on their experiences gained from the after-sales service so that the data can be used to develop an appropriate an after-sales service strategy.

The research report seeks to study a variety of data mining techniques, Classification or Clustering, that can be used for segmenting customers based on their experiences provided by the service. It was found that the Clustering technique is suitable for analysis in response to research. Within the Clustering Technique, there are many consistent methods, K-Mean Clustering, farthest-first algorithm, Canopy, clustering algorithm, Density-based group of clustering algorithm, and Filtered clustered Determining. To consider which algorithm is suitable for that task, the researcher begins with an understanding of the business by considering the types of businesses that need to provide the after-sales services by retailers, freight forwarders and factories who sell inputs. Then, the touch points that customers encounter to receive after-sales services, including call center, freight forwarding, and product repair and maintenance, are considered. After that, the researcher has searched for the Data Set for the experiment which is consistent with the research objectives. The Data Set consists of the following Features:

- Product Warranty
- The nature of the maintenance service of the goods is divided into the provision of services provided by the supplier and the outsource to the partnership.
- Image of products and services
- Characteristics of after-sales service
- Types of products such as furniture, domestic products, imported products
- Product life
- Maintenance and maintenance periods
- The sum of the amount of time for the maintenance, guarantee. The sum of such periods must be 0.

After that, we used Feature Selection techniques to reduce features that were not useful for data analysis. A total of three used methods are Correlation-based attribute evaluations, information gain attribute evaluations, and wrapper attributes evaluation each of which yielded results by reducing the number of different features. The remaining features were then processed with cluster analysis techniques across all four of the methods studied. The farthest-first algorithm showed the highest accuracy, which took a short time in processing.

Based on the analysis of such data, businesses need to plan for digital transformation in a variety of dimensions to consider gaps they can use digital technology to improve processes in order to deliver a positive customer experience. The data mining techniques that are suitable for data analytics are then selected so that organizations can use the results to determine products and services and deliver value to customers to meet customer expectations.

Improving the Efficiency of Cinematic Review Data Analysis With the Use of Cluster Analysis (Xu et al., 2022)

On the site for movie review, viewers can freely press reviews to score a movie without any pressure, as well as write textual comments to criticize the movie they've watched. The review scores and comments have become a variable that makes it possible for other viewers who haven't watched the movie to decide whether to watch or not watch it. Marketers are using reviews and comments to make viral content. The variables that affect the decision to watch a movie consists of: Cinematic content, the source of the content related to the film, the genre of the film, and the timing of its release. Analyzing data from review scores and comments has become an issue for data scientists to understand audience behavior in order to use the results to promote marketing. Data analytics and data visualization are another way to help marketers understand data patterns. A good movie is often made with a large number of elements, such as a sensible plot, the actors' performances, spectacular scenes, and the soundtrack. Data scientists can extract comments that correspond to keyword-based data analysis, such as stories or events. Similarity of word groups should be classified into one group. The data pre-processing is a way for data scientists to extract groups of words that are characterized as big data and then analyze it with cluster analysis. Data scientists can use Binary Classification, Decision Tree or Naïve bays, to identify which words are keywords.

In 2022, there was a research study on data analysis for marketing promotion of movies with movie review data (Xu, Chen, & Yang, 2022). The audience's satisfaction level corresponds to the real human emotions that are ambiguous and cannot be classified as right and wrong or black and white. Then, the keywords within the dataset is extracted; positive comments or negative comments. In accordance with the application of Fuzzy Logic theory, it can be determined that each keyword is classified in a comment type; the comments that are rather bad, the comments that are objectively based on the facts, the comments that do not express either positive or negative emotion, Comment in a good way and the comments that go in the way of admiration or delight in the movie Therefore, another prerequisite of such research is the application of Sentiment Analysis to enable machines to determine whether a keyword is a positive or a negative comment.

In the process of dividing keyword data with the K-Clustering Technique, researchers or data scientists have also apply Principle Component Analysis: PCA to reduce the number of data dimension to increase data division efficiency and display data through data visualization.

The research used clustering techniques to break down keyword data in the form of data visualization so that marketers could understand audience emotions and experiences reflected in the form of comments and film ratings, and could use that information to further improve film production and marketing promotion. The research also applied both Fuzzy Logic and Sentiment Analysis in the data pre-processing to increase the data processing efficiency of the clustering technique and attribute Transformation to make data ready for processing with data mining techniques.

CONCLUSION

Clustering is used to classify quantitative data and applied in various ways, such as customer segmentation and classification of diseases. Data scientists can import quantitative data into RapidMiner software, and use data mining techniques such as K-Means Clustering or DBSCAN to cluster the data. In a good data clustering, the data within each group should be clustered, but each cluster should be clearly separated from each other. Within RapidMiner software, it provides a model together with the use of visualization data to assess the efficiency of clustering by data experts.

EXERCISE QUESTIONS

1. Briefly describe the K-Means Clustering algorithm.
2. Explain the difference between Manhattan Distance and Euclidean Distance calculations.
3. Explain how to interpret results from Centroid.
4. Give examples of problems suitable for data analysis with K-Means.
5. Search for a study using K-Means Clustering to analyze the data and summarize it briefly.

REFERENCES

Abbas, A., Prayitno, P., Butarbutar, F., Nurkim, N., Prumanto, D., Dewadi, F. M., Hidayati, N., & Windarto, A. P. (2021). Implementation of clustering unsupervised learning using K-means mapping techniques. *IOP Conference Series. Materials Science and Engineering*, *1088*(1), 012004. doi:10.1088/1757-899X/1088/1/012004

Bayram, E., & Nabiyev, V. (2020). Image segmentation by using K-means clustering algorithm in Euclidean and Mahalanobis distance calculation in camouflage images. *2020 28th Signal Processing and Communications Applications Conference (SIU), Signal Processing and Communications Applications Conference (SIU), 2020 28th*, 1–4.

Ben Ncir, C.-E., Hamza, A., & Bouaguel, W. (2021). Parallel and scalable Dunn Index for the validation of big data clusters. *Parallel Computing*, *102*, 102. doi:10.1016/j.parco.2021.102751

Erdoğmuş, Z. İ., & Arslan, M. K. (2022). Engaging with Social Media Influencers on Youtube: A Cluster Analysis. *Istanbul University Journal of the School of Business Administration*, *51*(1), 359–373.

Ginting, S. W., Hartati, R. S., Sudarma, M., & Swamardika, I. B. A. (2021). Clustering of Earthquake and Volcanic Eruption Trauma Survivor Groups using K-Means Algorithm. *2021 International Conference on Smart-Green Technology in Electrical and Information Systems (ICSGTEIS), Smart-Green Technology in Electrical and Information Systems (ICSGTEIS), 2021 International Conference On*, 69–73.

Govindaraj, V., Thiyagarajan, A., Rajasekaran, P., Zhang, Y., & Krishnasamy, R. (2020). Automated unsupervised learning-based clustering approach for effective anomaly detection in brain magnetic resonance imaging (MRI). *IET Image Processing*, *14*(14), 3516–3526. doi:10.1049/iet-ipr.2020.0597

Haviluddin, I. M., Putra, G. M., Puspitasari, N., Setyadi, H. J., Dwiyanto, F.A., Wibawa, A. P., & Alfred, R. (2020). A Performance Comparison ofEuclidean, Manhattan and Minkowski Distances in K-Means Clustering. *2020 6th International Conference on Science in Information Technology (ICSITech), Science in Information Technology (ICSITech), 2020 6th International Conference On*, 184–188.

Hyrmet, M., & Arbana, K. (2021). The Data Mining Approach: A Case Study - Clustering Algorithms for After Sales Service. *10th Mediterranean Conference on Embedded Computing (MECO)*, 1-6.

Kumar, P., Ganapathy, G., & Kang, J.-J. (2021). A Hybrid Mod K-Means Clustering with Mod SVM Algorithm to Enhance the Cancer Prediction. International Journal of Internet. *Broadcasting and Communication*, *13*(2), 231–243.

Lou, N. (2022). Analysis of the Intelligent Tourism Route Planning Scheme Based on the Cluster Analysis Algorithm. *Computational Intelligence and Neuroscience, 2022*, 1–10. doi:10.1155/2022/3310676 PMID:35800698

Munlika, H. (2019). *Machine Learning with Clustering Model.* Retrieved June 17, 2021, from https://medium.com/tniuniversity/%E0%B8%81%E0%B8%B2%E0%B8%A3%E0%B8%97%E0%B8%B3-machine-learning-%E0%B8%94%E0%B9%89%E0%B8%A7%E0%B8%A2-clustering-model-2a3c392e7faa

Peungvicha, P., Tubtiang, A. & Sattayaaphitan, T. (2019). Clustering of Jewellery Purchasing Behaviour through Social Network. *Journal of Humanities and Social Sciences, Rajapruk University, 5*, 212-224.

Punhani, R., Arora, V. P. S., Sabitha, S., & Kumar Shukla, V. (2021). Applicationof Clustering Algorithm for Effective Customer Segmentation in E-Commerce. *2021 International Conference on Computational Intelligence and Knowledge Economy (ICCIKE), Computational Intelligence and Knowledge Economy (ICCIKE), 2021 International Conference On*, 149–154.

Puspasari, B. D., Damayanti, L. L., Pramono, A., & Darmawan, A. K. (2021). Implementation K-Means Clustering Method in Job Recommendation System. *2021 7th International Conference on Electrical, Electronics and Information Engineering (ICEEIE), Electrical, Electronics and Information Engineering (ICEEIE), 2021 7th International Conference On*, 1–6.

Rezaeijo, S. M., Hashemi, B., Mofid, B., Bakhshandeh, M., Mahdavi, A., & Hashemi, M. S. (2021). The feasibility of a dose painting procedure to treat prostate cancer based on mpMR images and hierarchical clustering. *Radiation Oncology (London, England), 16*(1), 1–16. doi:10.118613014-021-01906-2 PMID:34544468

Wafa, H. A., Aminuddin, R., Ibrahim, S., Mangshor, N. N. A., & Wahab, N. I. F. A. (2021). A Data Visualization Framework during Pandemic using the Density-Based Spatial Clustering with Noise (DB-SCAN) Machine Learning Model. *2021 IEEE 11th International Conference on System Engineering and Technology (ICSET), System Engineering and Technology (ICSET), 2021 IEEE 11th International Conference On*, 1–6.

Wijaya, Y. A., Kurniady, D. A., Setyanto, E., Tarihoran, W. S., Rusmana, D., & Rahim, R. (2021). Davies Bouldin Index Algorithm for Optimizing Clustering Case Studies Mapping School Facilities. *TEM Journal, 10*(3), 1099–1103. doi:10.18421/TEM103-13

Xu, B., Chen, C., & Yang, J.-H. (2022). Application of Cluster Analysis Technology in Visualization Research of Movie Review Data. *Computational Intelligence and Neuroscience, 2022*, 1–11. doi:10.1155/2022/7756896 PMID:35880060

Zhou, Y., Yan, S., Wang, C., Zheng, K., & Zhu, L. (2021). Position Monitoring System Based on Hierarchical Clustering. *2021 26th IEEE Asia-Pacific Conference on Communications (APCC), Communications (APCC), 2021 26th IEEE Asia-Pacific Conference On*, 111–114.

Chapter 8
Association Rule

ABSTRACT

Businesses are increasingly seeking to understand consumer behavior and purchasing habits in order to analyze the relationship between different products purchased by customers. By leveraging the association rule mining technique, businesses can identify complementary products and bundle them together to increase sales. This chapter provides an overview of association rule mining, a form of unsupervised learning that enables data scientists to analyze the relationship between data items in a dataset. The chapter explains the Apriori algorithm, a feature of association rule mining, and highlights how data scientists can collaborate with domain experts to achieve business objectives such as product matching and testing the efficiency of association rule results. Readers can follow a step-by-step guide to experience the association rule mining technique using RapidMiner, enabling them to develop their understanding of this valuable analytical tool.

INTRODUCTION

In business sectors, there is a need to sell multiple products at the same time. For example, superstores often offer several products to their customers, such as offering soap along with shampoo. This kind of product matching is done by analyzing the association rules on customer purchasing behavior (Ren, 2021: Yingzhuo & Xuewen, 2021), which is the customers who buy soap often buy shampoo as well. Therefore, association rules are used to process large data sets to analyze the correlation rules hidden within the data (Paruechanon & Sriurai, 2019: Hong & Nan 2021: Salman & Sadkhan, 2021). The technique is also used to analyze the correlation rules that can occur together; for example, when a car is broken, it can lead to an accident while driving. In processing big data with the association rules, data scientists may be given a number of rules. Data scientists, therefore, are necessary to analyze the benefits and efficiency of association rules in practical applications in industries. Data mining techniques are not only used to analyze business data, but it has also been applied in many industries such as medical diagnosis, Web Mining and Bioinformatics (Toumi, Gribaa, & Ben Abdessalem Karaa, 2021).

DOI: 10.4018/978-1-6684-4730-7.ch008

ASSOCIATION RULE

In analyzing data with Association Rule, data scientists can use the following format (Zhang & Zhang, 2002).

Soap -> Shampoo

From such an association rule, it means that when customers buy soap, they will also buy shampoo. Another metric used for association rule analysis is Confidence, which is the percentage of the availability of rules-based data within the dataset. For example, if the Confidence value is 60 percent, and within the dataset there are 30 instances of soap purchases out of the total 100 instances, it means there is 60 percent of shampoo purchase data, or there are 18 times that soap along with shampoo are purchased.

Another measure is Support, which refers to the percentage of compliant data in the entire dataset. For example, a Support value of 2% means that the entire dataset has compliant instances, which is there are 2 instances of buying soap along with shampoo out of all 100 instances.

To analyze association rules with Confidence and Support values, data scientists can calculate the values of both as in the following example.

The store has a total of 100,000 customer purchases. Of all the data, the total number of milk purchases is 40,000 times, and the total number of fruit purchases is 15,000. Of all the 40,000 milk purchases, the number of purchases of milk along with fruit is 10,000 times. Confidence is calculated, and it results as 25%, which means there is the frequency of buying fruit together with milk at 25 percent. And the Support value is 10 percent which means that the frequency of buying fruit along with milk is at 10 percent of the total data. After analyzing the association rules, data scientists will obtain association rules consisting of a large number of Confidence and Support values. Therefore, the data scientists need to determine the Support and Confidence Threshold in order to measure whether each association rule can be used in analysis. For example, when data scientists define Support and Confidence Thresholds as 50%, after analyzing the data the Confidence and Confidence Thresholds must not be less than 50% to be considered a Strong Association.

The data ready for analysis with association rules are usually in Boolean format. For example, to buy equals 1, and not to buy equals 0. The analysis of association rules based on Boolean can be performed as in the following example.

Table 1. Example of correlation rule analysis from Boolean data

Frequency of Each Purchase	Soap	Shampoo	Detergent	Dishwasher
1st Purchase	1	1	0	0
2nd Purchase	1	0	0	1
3rd Purchase	1	1	0	0
4th Purchase	1	1	1	1

From the table, the association rules can be analyzed with Confidence and Support values as follows.

Soap -> Shampoo having 75% of Support value and 75% of Confidence value
Soap -> Dishwasher having 50% of Support value and 50% of Confidence value
Shampoo -> Detergent having 25% of Support value and 33% of Confidence value
Soap, Shampoo, Detergent -> Dishwasher having 25% of Support value and 100 percent of Confidence value

From the association rules analyzed in the table, the number of Attributes is called Itemset. {Soap, Shampoo} is a 2-Itemset. And {Soap, Shampoo, Detergent, Dishwasher}is a 4-Itemset.

Each dataset has a Frequency, or the itemset. For example, if Frequency is 2%, then the frequency of {soap, shampoo}, which is 2-Itemset, is 2 times out of 100 total data. So, it is equal to Support, which is also the frequency of association rules from all datasets. Data scientists need to determine the value of Frequent Item Set, which should be greater than or equal to Support and Confidence Thresholds, so that the data set contains sufficient Itemset to be used in the analysis with the association rule technique.

APRIORI ALGORITHM

With the Apriori algorithm, the data analysis process begins with the creation of all possible Frequent Item Sets from the data set (Baby & Reddy, 2021: Hodijah & Setijohatmo, 2021). Then, only the Frequent Item Sets with Confidence and Support values greater than or equal to Support and Confidence Thresholds can be used to determine affinity rules. The procedure is as shown in the example.

Table 2. Data analysis sample set with Apriori algorithm

Frequency of Each Purchase	Soap	Shampoo	Detergent	Dishwasher	Body Lotion
1st Purchase	1	0	0	1	1
2nd Purchase	0	0	1	1	0
3rd Purchase	1	0	0	1	0
4th Purchase	1	1	1	1	0
5th Purchase	1	1	0	1	0
6th Purchase	1	0	0	1	0
7th Purchase	0	0	1	1	0
8th Purchase	1	0	0	0	0
9th Purchase	1	1	0	1	0
10th Purchase	1	1	0	1	0

Based on the sample data set, the Support and Confidence Thresholds value is 20 percent when using Apriori Algorithm in association rule analysis. All possible correlation rules are analyzed from the entire dataset starting with a 1-ItemSet with the frequency of each data as follows.

Table 3. Analysis of datasets starting with 1-ItemSet

ItemSet	Frequency
Soap	0.8
Shampoo	0.4
Detergent	0.3
Dishwasher	0.9
Body Lotion	0.1

By setting the Support and Confidence Thresholds at 20 percent, the ItemSet consisting of Soap, Shampoo, Detergent and Dishwashing Liquid has a Support and Confidence Thresholds value greater than 20 percent, and can be created as a 1-ItemSet. In the next step, Apriori Algorithm will create 2-Item data sets as follows.

Table 4. Analysis of the 2-ItemSet datasets

ItemSet	Frequency
{Soap, Shampoo}	0.4
{Soap, Detergent}	0.1
{Soap, Dishwasher}	0.7
{Shampoo, Detergent}	0.1
{Shampoo, Dishwasher}	0.4
{Detergent, Dishwasher}	0.3

According to the Apriori Algorithm table, the frequency of the 2-ItemSet is generated from the number of instances appearing in the frequency of two orders at the same time. For example, soap and shampoo are brought together 4 times, so the frequency is 0.4. Only the 2-ItemSets can be created from the 1-Itemsets with Support and Confidence Thresholds greater than 20%.

Then consider selecting only 2-ItemSet values greater than 20% consisting of {soap, shampoo} {soap, dishwasher} {shampoo, dishwasher} and {detergent, dishwasher}. Then Apriori Algorithm will create 3-Item data sets.

Table 5. Analysis of the 3-ItemSet

ItemSet	Frequency
{Soap, Shampoo, Dishwasher}	0.4

From the table, the 3-ItemSet is created by the frequency of appearing the 1-ItemSet within the same instance up to 3 times, considering the first 1-ItemSet. Based on that dataset, the first 1-ItemSet is Soap, and has 4 Instances consisting of Soap, Shampoo and Dishwasher, so Apriori Algorithm creates a 3-ItemSet consisting of {soap, shampoo, Dishwasher} with a Support and Confidence Thresholds greater than 20 percent.

The Apriori Algorithm then creates a 4-ItemSet. However, creating a 4-ItemSet starts with a 3-ItemSet with the same first two data. But in that case, there is only one 3-ItemSet left, Apriori Algorithm will stop creating ItemSet.

By creating the Frequent Item Set, Apriori Algorithm creates an association rule from a 3-ItemSet by creating a Non-Empty Subset from a 3-ItemSet, and then creating an association rule. The Support and Confidence Thresholds value is set as more than 55 percent.

Table 6. Creating association rules

Non-Empty Subset	Association Rule	Confidence	Strong Association Rule
{Soap, Shampoo}	Soap, Shampoo -> Dishwasher	0.4/0.4 = 1	Yes
{Soap, Dishwasher}	Soap, Dishwasher -> Shampoo	0.4/0.7 = 0.57	Yes
{Shampoo, Dishwasher}	Shampoo, Dishwasher -> Soap	0.4/0.4 = 1	Yes
{Soap}	Soap -> Shampoo, Dishwasher	0.4/0.8 = 0.5	No
{Shampoo}	Shampoo -> Soap, Dishwasher	0.4/0.4 = 1	Yes
{Dishwasher}	Dishwasher -> Soap, Shampoo	0.4/0.9 = 0.44	No

From the table, the association rule is created from a 3-ItemSet. Firstly, all the data are taken to create a total of 6 Subsets called Non-Empty Sets, and then the relationship rules are created from those Subsets. For example, Sub set 1 consists of soap and shampoo. Then the association rule is created from the data within the Set, which is dishwasher. The association rule is soap, shampoo -> dishwashing liquid, which means every time the customers buy soap and shampoo, they will also buy dishwashing liquid too. Confidence value of soap and shampoo is then analyzed from the frequency. If the frequency of purchasing soap and shampoo at the same time is 4 times, and the frequency of purchasing soap, shampoo and dishwashing liquid all together is 7 times, the Confidence value is 0.4 / 0.7 = 0.57, which exceeds the Support and Confidence Thresholds value, being 55 percent. Therefore, the association rule of soap, shampoo -> dishwashing liquid is a Strong Association Rule.

The association rules that could not be analyzed are soap -> shampoo, dishwasher, and dishwasher -> soap, shampoo, which shows a Support and Confidence Thresholds below 55 percent.

By analyzing the data to create association rules with the Apriori Algorithm, the appropriate data for analysis should be Categorial Data such as product type, gender and address. If data scientists use data other than Categorial Data in Apriori Algorithm analysis, they must perform Attribute Transformation to provide the data in the format suitable for data analysis with such techniques.

RULE INTERESTINGNESS

When data scientists perform association rule analysis from existing datasets, they need to consider the benefits of analytical results in order to make decisions in business or industries (Bing, Yiming & Lee, 2001: Glass, 2013: Greco, Słowiński & Szczęch, 2016). The measurement can be divided into 2; 1. Subjective Measure, which refers to the use of domain expert's opinions or recommendations to decide which association rules are useful for decision-making such as having physicians to decide on the association rules of cancer risk factor variables, 2. Objective Measure, which refers to the use of quantitative analysis data to reflect the efficiency of the correlation rules obtained from data mining analysis. Data scientists can use Objective Measures to analyze performance as follows:

The Support value is the frequency with which data appears in the entire dataset. Confidence value is the frequency of having rules-compliant data within the dataset.

In cases where the Support and Confidence values are greater than or equal to the Support and Confidence Thresholds values, the association rules are considered appropriate to support decision-making. In cases when data scientists obtain error during Data Pre-Processing. For example, Product A is sold with Product B, resulting in every instance within the data set appearing the frequency of Product A and Product B. The Confidence and Support values of A -> B are very high, but they do not have any significant analysis because it is already a product that must be sold together.

Therefore, the metric that can solve this problem is Lift. Lift must be greater than 1, so that the rule of relationship can be used to support decision making.

Table 7. Sample datasets for processing life values

Soap	1	1	1	1	0	0	0	0
Tooth Paste	1	1	0	0	0	0	0	0
Shampoo	0	1	1	1	1	1	1	1

From the table, you can create an association rule consisting of Support values and Lift values as follows.

Table 8. Association rules from the sample datasets

Association Rule	Support	Lift
Soap -> Tooth paste	25.00%	2.00
Soap -> Shampoo	37.50%	0.86
Tooth Paste -> Shampoo	12.50%	0.57

As in the table, the relationship rule of soap -> shampoo has a support value of 37.50%, and that of toothpaste -> shampoo is at 12.50%.

However, the lift value of the relationship rule of soap -> shampoo is at 0.86, and that of the relationship of toothpaste -> shampoo is at 0.57. The lift values of both rules are less than 1, meaning it has insignificant relationship to support decision. When looking back into the dataset, it has been found that every time they buy soap or toothpaste, customers tend to buy shampoo as well. It means that regardless the type of purchase, shampoo must be purchased too. Therefore, the aforementioned association rules have no implications for supporting the decision because it is a fact that already exists.

Another metric that data scientists can use to consider in conjunction with lift is conviction. Conviction should be greater than 1 as it is calculated as the Confidence of the first data divided by the Support of the second data. If the result is 1, it means the frequency that shows that the data from the entire dataset of the first data is equal to the frequency of the second data in the association rules. Therefore, it means that the two data are not related to each other. Data scientists can calculate Lift and Conviction values as follows.

There is a sales dataset of 10,000 instances, which represents the frequency of 10,000 purchases.

Soap 4,000 pieces
Shampoo 8,000 pieces
The frequency of purchasing soap along with shampoo is 3,000 times.
The relationship rule has come out as Soap-> Shampoo
Support Value is 3,000 / 10,000 = 30%
Confidence Value is 3,000 / 4,000 = 75%

Lift value can be calculated by taking the Confidence value of the frequency of buying soap together with shampoo divided by the Support value of the shampoo frequency, which is 0.75 / 0.8 = 0.94.

Conviction can be calculated by taking the Support value of the shampoo frequency that appears in the entire data set, subtracting the number 1, and then dividing by the Confidence value of the frequency soap purchase with shampoo and subtracting it by the number 1, which is $(1 - 0.8) / (1 - 0.75) = 0.8$.

Calculations show that if lift value is less than 1, this indicates that the association rule has no significance for its use in decision support. Therefore, such association rules should not be used to make business decisions.

ANALYZING ASSOCIATION RULES WITH RAPIDMINER SOFTWARE

In the data analysis experiment using the association rules, this book uses a sample dataset called shopping.csv, which stores data on purchases. Data scientists have to import a data named shopping.csv into RapidMiner software. The data objects within the dataset are also Boolean. True means Purchase, and False means no purchase. The dataset includes 13 Attributes and 786 Instances.

Therefore, data scientists have to determine each attribute into Binomial values. In Unsupervised-Learning processing, data scientists do not need to define the target variables as shown in the figure.

Meanwhile, the data scientists create the model by importing the shopping.csv dataset into the FP-Growth model, which is used to analyze association rules aiming for creating a tree diagram, and reduce the creation of a large number of Frequent Item Sets in Apriori algorithm. Then the min support value is determined. RapidMiner is already set as 0.95, so reset it as 0.2 as shown in the picture.

Figure 1. Importing the shopping.csv dataset into RapidMiner software

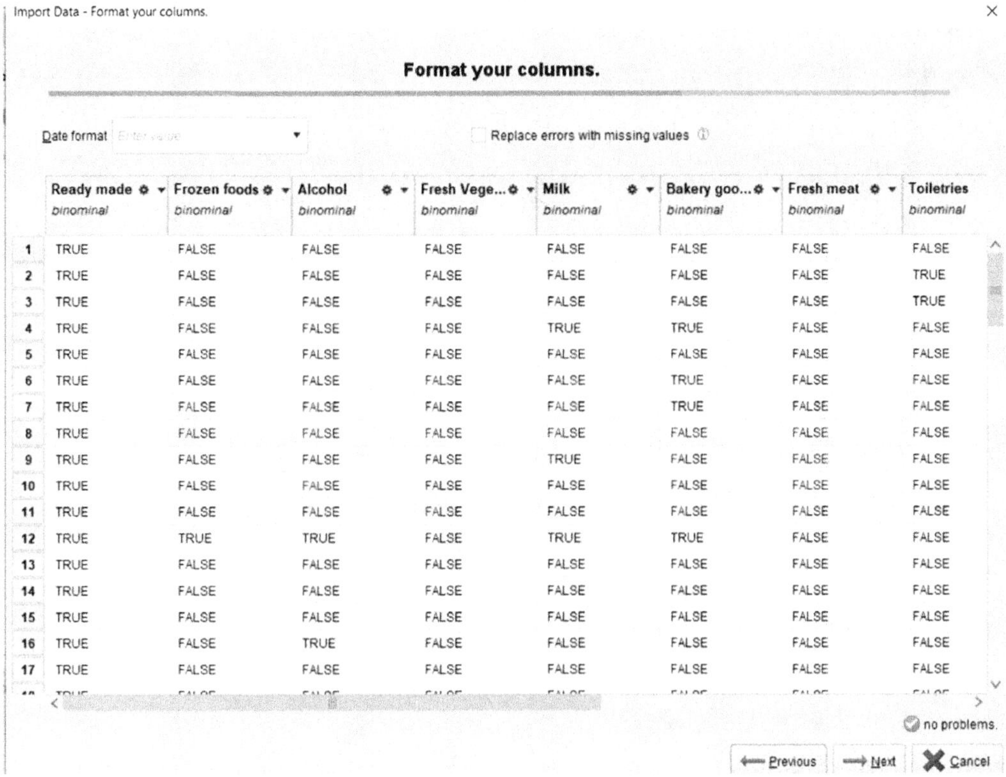

In the figure, data scientists can connect a model from shoppoing.csv into the FP- Growth model, and configure min support at 0.2.

In this figure, the association rule technique is analyzed using the shopping.csv dataset. RapidMiner software has created Item Sets ranging from 1-ItemSet to 4-ItemSet. Every Item Set represents a Support value, or the number of frequencies where the data appear.

However, when considering all the attributes within the data set, there is still the data irrelevant with the frequency of customer purchases. Data scientists have to connect to Select Attributes model in order to select specific attributes related to the frequency of customer purchases.

Data scientists use the Select Attribute model to select only Attributes related to the frequency of customer purchases by specifying the Parameter as a Subset and then selecting Select Attributes by selecting the Attributes; Children, Gender and Working into the box on the right.

After defining the parameters, the data scientists can select Invert Selection so that the RapidMiner software knows it is to use the remaining Attributes that are not the ones chosen for the data analysis. The result after selecting Attribute is as follows.

After the data scientists have selected only the attributes needed to analyze the data, RapidMiner can use the association rule technique to create more Frequent Item Sets, being up to 5-ItemSet.

Once the Frequent Item Set has been created, the data scientists will take all Item Sets to create association rules using the Create Association Rules model, which connects the FP-Growth model to the association rule display as shown below.

Figure 2. Beginning data analysis with the association rule technique

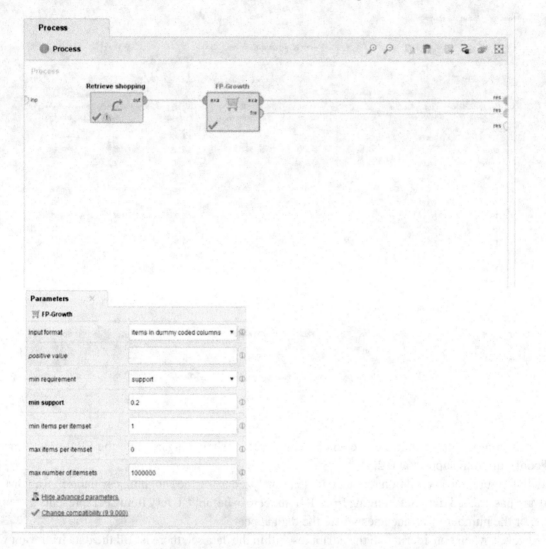

To use the Create Association Rules model to create association rules, data scientists can choose a measure of the efficiency of the strong and valuable association rules to support decision making by defining Parameters as follows.

From the figure, the data scientists can select measures such as Confidence, Life, and Conviction. The minimum value of min confidence can be set. The result is as follows.

From the figure, the data scientists can determine the outcome of the rule. For example, in Association Rule No. 5, when a customer buys Fresh Vegetables, they also buy Tinned Goods. The Confidence value is 0.81, which is considered a reliable relationship rule based on a quantitative measure.

Figure 3. Results of data analysis by association rule technique

Size	Support	Item 1	Item 2	Item 3	Item 4
1	0.525	Snacks			
1	0.508	Ready made			
1	0.462	GENDER			
1	0.455	Tinned goods			
1	0.429	Bakery goods			
1	0.402	Frozen foods			
1	0.394	Alcohol			
1	0.347	CHILDREN			
1	0.188	Milk			
1	0.168	WORKING			
1	0.099	Toiletries			
1	0.083	Fresh Vegetables			
2	0.277	Snacks	Ready made		
2	0.268	Snacks	GENDER		
2	0.232	Snacks	Tinned goods		
2	0.196	Snacks	Bakery goods		
2	0.188	Snacks	Frozen foods		
2	0.176	Snacks	Alcohol		
2	0.167	Snacks	CHILDREN		

No. of Sets: 101
Total Max. Size: 4

Min. Size: 1
Max. Size: 4
Contains Item

Update View

Figure 4. Selecting only the Attribute needed for data analysis

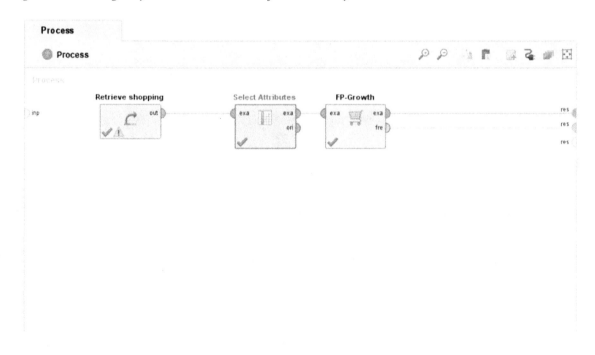

Figure 5. Determining parameters to select attribute models

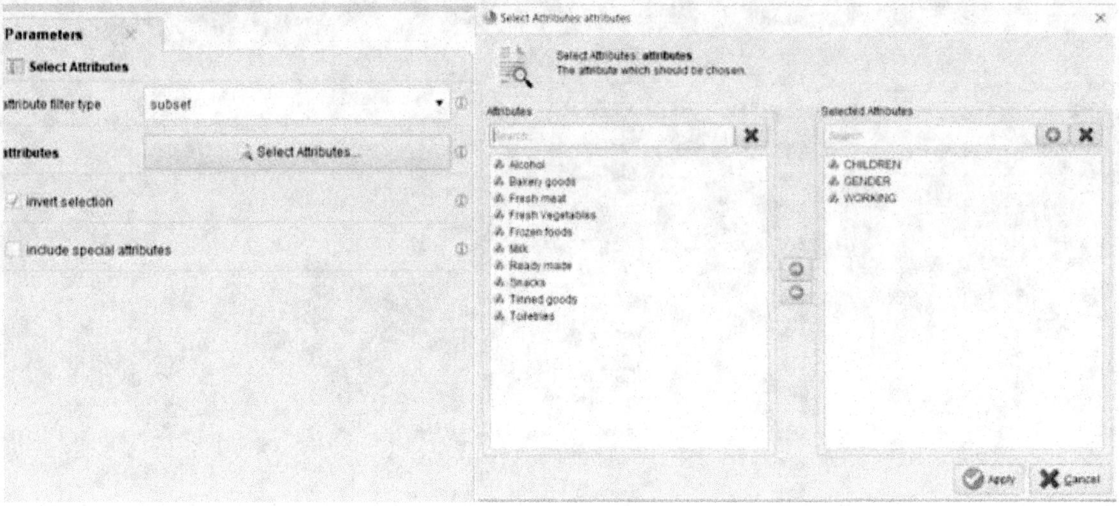

Figure 6. Results after selecting attributes

No. of Sets: 83	Size	Support	Item 1	Item 2	Item 3	Item 4	Item 5
Total Max. Size: 5	1	0.525	Snacks				
	1	0.508	Ready made				
Min. Size: 1	1	0.455	Tinned goods				
Max. Size: 5	1	0.429	Bakery goods				
Contains Item:	1	0.402	Frozen foods				
	1	0.394	Alcohol				
Update View	1	0.188	Milk				
	1	0.099	Toiletries				
	1	0.083	Fresh Vegetables				
	2	0.277	Snacks	Ready made			
	2	0.232	Snacks	Tinned goods			
	2	0.196	Snacks	Bakery goods			
	2	0.188	Snacks	Frozen foods			
	2	0.176	Snacks	Alcohol			
	2	0.064	Snacks	Milk			
	2	0.239	Ready made	Tinned goods			
	2	0.173	Ready made	Bakery goods			
	2	0.191	Ready made	Frozen foods			
	2	0.182	Ready made	Alcohol			

Figure 7. Creating association rules using create association rules

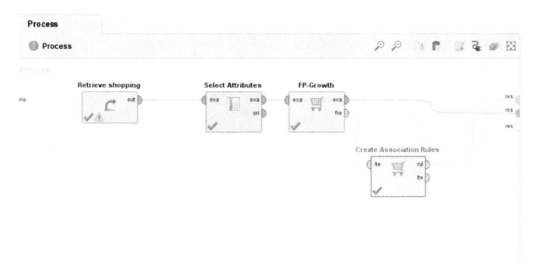

Figure 8. Selecting a metric for measuring the efficiency of the association rules

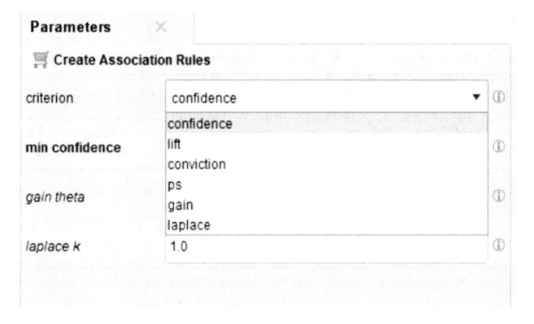

CASE STUDY

Using Data Result Analyzed With Association Rule Mining to Expand the Lifetime Value of Customers in Banking Services (Rezaei et al., 2022)

We are living in an era where the popularity of using each customer's products and services has been much shorter. There are many emerging goods and services that have become popular in their use and are rapidly deteriorating in popularity. Customer Life Time Value: CTV becomes the data that each business

Figure 9. Results from creating association rules

No.	Premises	Conclusion	Support	Confidence	LaPlace	Gain	p-s	Lift
4	Tinned goods, Bakery goods, Alcohol, Milk	Frozen foods	0.056	0.830	0.989	-0.079	0.029	2.065
5	Fresh Vegetables	Tinned goods	0.069	0.831	0.987	-0.097	0.031	1.824
6	Frozen foods, Milk	Bakery goods	0.090	0.835	0.984	-0.126	0.044	1.948
7	Bakery goods, Fresh Vegetables	Tinned goods	0.050	0.848	0.992	-0.067	0.023	1.861
8	Frozen foods, Fresh Vegetables	Tinned goods	0.043	0.850	0.993	-0.059	0.020	1.866
9	Frozen foods, Fresh Vegetables	Bakery goods	0.043	0.850	0.993	-0.059	0.021	1.982
10	Tinned goods, Alcohol, Milk	Bakery goods	0.067	0.855	0.989	-0.090	0.034	1.994
11	Frozen foods, Alcohol, Milk	Bakery goods	0.073	0.864	0.989	-0.095	0.037	2.014
12	Tinned goods, Frozen foods, Milk	Bakery goods	0.071	0.875	0.991	-0.092	0.036	2.041
13	Tinned goods, Frozen foods, Alcohol, Milk	Bakery goods	0.056	0.898	0.994	-0.069	0.029	2.094

needs to analyze to identify which groups of customers will return to buy to create value for the business so that businesses can create marketing strategies specific to these valuable customers. Technological changes have also resulted in the customer service center becoming a repair and maintenance center due to the fact that customers can visit products through the website and place orders online. The use of internet technology has destroyed international borders, and businesses are expanding to their customers worldwide. On the other hand, customers also need stores that have the ability to display their products and support their purchases via mobile devices such as Smart Phones or Tablets.

The change directly impacts the banking business, which have to provide a variety of digital channels to support the changing style of the service recipients, such as the provision of web-based applications that support the client's financial transactions, the provision of native apps installed on mobile phones to support the client's financial transactions via mobile phones. However, those marketing strategies are all so similar that the bank is unable to communicate the right marketing for the customer segments on each channel. The marketers are unable to analyze the behavior of customers on each channel and develop marketing strategies that can increase customer life time value.

The Omnichannel has become a way to get through this problem by combining business operations and online-offline marketing strategies. Such business channels have enabled marketers to identify market segmentation that overlaps between customers with consumption habits through online and offline channels. Business operations through such channels also have a similar purpose to other forms of business operations; to try to get consumers to turn their attention to their own products and services, maintaining an existing customer base, analyzing marketing data to uncover customer behavior and products or services that customers are interested in, and prolonging the time the customers stay interested in their own business by trying to promote marketing or create after-sales service that keeps customers coming back for more services.

From the transition to providing services in an online format, banking businesses have reduced the number of branches and staff in line with the popularity of online transactions by customers in order to prevent customers from moving to other banking services. The banks need to conduct a study on customer lifetime value based on three factors; When did the customer last use the banking service? How many times did the customer use the banking service? How much money have the customers spent through the bank? These three factors are variables to determine the customer lifetime value so that the bank can determine whether the customer will return to the service or change their mind to other banking services. This is the era where mobile banking is widely used among customers to transfer money, pay for goods and services to retail businesses or merchants.

In 2022, a research was conducted on the analysis of the relationship between Customer Life Time Value and omnichannel business practices (Rezaei, et. al, 2022). The research put forward a case study of agricultural banking, in which services are provided to customers both offline via bank branches and online format via mobile banking. The bank itself has made efforts to assess the satisfaction of service recipients in every touchpoint of the service process to improve the level of satisfaction and delivers a good experience to their customers. This effort has led to the issue of analyzing whether the Customer Life Time Value of omnichannel business is different from other business models. In this case study of the Agricultural Bank, the research framework environment is different from other types of banking business because the Agricultural Bank is established as a state-owned enterprise which has a higher authority to govern.

In the data exploration phase, the researchers used the data source from the transactions of customers who have used banking services for the past 2 years, then used the Association Rule Mining Technique to analyze the relationships. The relationship rules can then be analyzed as 9 types. The overall pattern revealed that the customers using the "Point of Sale" system (a retail payment system through a digital device) tend to be used to the ATM system. And lastly are the transactions at a bank branch in case the "Point of Sale" system and ATMs cannot support such transactions. In the analysis of such relationship rules, another form of relationship was found. It is the group of customers who did not receive service from the bank in the form of omnichannel. The uses only the "Point of Sale" system, not multi-channels. Therefore, service recipients can be classified into two types; Omnichannel and Non-Omnichannel. The researcher then used the T-Test Technique to prove the difference of Customer Life Time Value between the two service recipients and found that the Customer Life Time Value between these two groups is significantly different.

By segmenting customers by relationship rules model and testing the difference between Customer Life Time of customers with omnichannel and non-omnichannel relationship rules behaviors, Bank for Agriculture and Agricultural Cooperatives are cost-effective to provide digital channels along with the provision of financial services at branches because there are still groups of customers who are loyal to the bank from receiving services in multiple channels at the same time. This research suggests using omnichannel operations to extend the Customer Life Time Value by retaining existing customers to continue to buy products and services of the business without switching to competitors' products and services.

Analysis of Language Courses Based on Learner Behavior With Association Rule Mining (Chaimongkol & Meesad, 2010)

Many language schools try to provide language courses that stand out from other competing language schools. As a result, those language schools have sought to study the needs of learners to develop courses that can be used to attract those who want to improve themselves in the field of foreign languages. They can also build the loyalty of current learners to resume classes or take other courses provided by the school. The challenge in preparing those courses is that the needs of individual learners are diverse and difficult to analyze. And it is even more difficult to associate those patterns with the language courses that are appropriate for each learner. Therefore, the data mining technique is one of the ways to use the information that each school has to analyze the patterns of co-learners and analyze the linkages between the behaviors and the courses that the school currently has. To analyze such data, language schools can use data scientists to apply various forms of data mining techniques such as decision trees, neural networks, or even association rule mining techniques to analyze the data.

In 2010, there was a research attempting to analyze the correlation between learners' learning behaviors in relation to their choice of language courses (Chaimongkol & Meesad, 2010). The research extracted data about the actual needs of learners by dividing them into the fundamental needs for language use and the need to enhance their ability to use a foreign language. Data scientists have designed processes for data processing including: 1. Surveying datasets that can be used for data analysis with data mining techniques to answer the question the language schools intend to know, 2. Preparing data in a format that is ready for processing with data mining techniques; normalization or data engineering, 3. Creating models for analyzing the rules, the relationship between learner needs patterns, and language courses, and 4. Using the results from the analysis of data in the form of correlation rules to translate the results.

From such process, data scientists surveyed and collected data on language courses for students in Thailand from four language schools from January 2007 to January 2008. The features are the courses in which there are Data Objects such as Junior Courses or Advance Courses, the time of day that students choose to study, in which there are Data Objects such as 8.00 a.m., the number of registration hours in which there are Data Objects such as 400 hours and the number of days students choose to study each week in which there are Data Objects such as 3 days per week. The result of the data analysis is a set of correlation rules. For example, language schools should set the frequency of Junior Course at 3 hours per week.

From the case studies, businesses can use Association Rule Mining to analyze data to uncover hidden relationships in datasets, which leads to designing products and services that can meet different customer expectations.

CONCLUSION

Data scientists can use RapidMiner software to analyze datasets with association rules. Data suitable for analysis by such technique should be Category Data such as product type, gender and address. The association rules aim to analyze the correlation of data from the frequency of occurrence of such data to show the results of their relationship. For example, those who buy wines tend to also buy cheese. Users can apply the rules of association in business and other industry operations. However, in the process of establishing the association rules, there will appear many rules that the data scientists must consider as a strong rule that can be used for decision making by considering quantitative metrics such as Confidence, Lift and Conviction, as well as consulting Knowledge Experts. This will present the association rules that are factual and beneficial to the organizations.

EXERCISE QUESTIONS

1. Describe the purposes of data analysis with association rules.
2. Explain the difference between Confident and Support.
3. Explain the meaning of Frequency Itemsets.

4. Give an example of the problem that requires the association rules in data analysis.
5. Find a research paper that uses association rules in data analysis and summarize it briefly.

REFERENCES

Baby, S. S., & Reddy, S. L. (2021). End to End Product Recommendation system with improvements in Apriori Algorithm. *2021 Third International Conference on Inventive Research in Computing Applications (ICIRCA), Inventive Research in Computing Applications (ICIRCA), 2021 Third International Conference On*, 1357–1361.

Bing, L., Yiming, M., & Lee, R. (2001). Analyzing the interestingness of association rules from the temporal dimension. *Proceedings 2001 IEEE International Conference on Data Mining, Data Mining, 2001. ICDM 2001, Proceedings IEEE International Conference on, Data Mining*, 377–384. 10.1109/ICDM.2001.989542

Chaimongkol, N., & Meesad, P. (2010). *Association Rule Mining for Specific New Course. Mahanakorn University of Technology (MUT)*.

Glass, D. H. (2013). Confirmation measures of association rule interestingness. *Knowledge-Based Systems, 44*, 65–77. doi:10.1016/j.knosys.2013.01.021

Greco, S., Słowiński, R., & Szczęch, I. (2016). Measures of rule interestingness in various perspectives of confirmation. *Information Sciences, 346–347*, 216–235. doi:10.1016/j.ins.2016.01.056

Hodijah, A., & Setijohatmo, U. T. (2021). Analysis of frequent itemset generation based on trie data structure in Apriori algorithm. *Telkomnika, 19*(5), 1553–1564. doi:10.12928/telkomnika.v19i5.19273

Hong, G., & Nan, G. (2021). Research and Application of a Multidimensional Association Rules Mining Algorithm Based on Hadoop. *2021 IEEE Intl Conf on Parallel & Distributed Processing with Applications, Big Data & Cloud Computing, Sustainable Computing & Communications, Social Computing & Networking (ISPA/BDCloud/SocialCom/SustainCom), Parallel & Distributed Processing with Applications, Big Data & Cloud Computing, Sustainable Computing & Communications, Social Computing & Networking (ISPA/BDCloud/SocialCom/SustainCom), 2021 IEEE Intl Conf on, ISPA-BDCLOUD-SOCIALCOM-SUSTAINCOM*, 636–643.

Paruechanon, P., & Sriurai, W. (2019). Applying association rule to risk analysis for student-dropout in Information Technology Program. *Journal of Science and Science Education, 1*(2), 123-133.

Ren, X. (2021). Application of Apriori Association Rules Algorithm to Data Mining Technology to Mining E-commerce Potential Customers. *2021 International Wireless Communications and Mobile Computing (IWCMC), Wireless Communications and Mobile Computing (IWCMC), 2021 International*, 1193–1196.

Rezaei, M., Sanayei, A., Aghdaie, S. F. A., & Ansari, A. (2022). Improving the Omnichannel Customers' Lifetime Value Using Association Rules Data Mining: A Case Study of Agriculture Bank of Iran. *Iranian Journal of Management Studies, 15*(1), 49–68.

Salman, W. A. K., & Sadkhan, S. B. (2021). Proposed Association Rules Mining Algorithm for Sensors Data Streams. *2021 1st Babylon International Conference on Information Technology and Science (BICITS), Information Technology and Science (BICITS), 2021 1st Babylon International Conference On*, 76–81.

Toumi, A., Gribaa, N., & Ben Abdessalem Karaa, W. (2021). Mining biomedical texts based on statistical method and association rules. *2021 International Conference of Women in Data Science at Taif University (WiDSTaif), Women in Data Science at Taif University (WiDSTaif), 2021 International Conference Of*, 1–4.

Yingzhuo, X., & Xuewen, W. (2021). Research on Community Consumer Behavior Based on Association Rules Analysis. *2021 6th International Conference on Intelligent Computing and Signal Processing (ICSP), Intelligent Computing and Signal Processing (ICSP), 2021 6th International Conference On*, 1213–1216.

Zhang, C., & Zhang, S. (2002). *Association Rule Mining*. In Models and Algorithms. Springer Berlin Heidelberg. doi:10.1007/3-540-46027-6

Chapter 9
Recommendation System

ABSTRACT

Recommendation systems are critical tools used by marketing departments to provide customers with product recommendations. Data scientists also use recommendation system analysis to assess the effectiveness of product and service suggestions. There are two types of recommendation systems: content-based and collaborative filtering. Content-based recommendations are based on the customer's purchase history, while collaborative filtering suggests a product based on purchasing behavior. Collaborative filtering can be divided into content-based filtering, which suggests products based on similar purchasing behavior, and item-based filtering, which suggests products based on their attributes. User-based and item-based nearest-neighbor collaborative filtering and probabilistic methods are used to analyze data and provide product suggestions. Businesses rely on recommendation systems to achieve various objectives such as customer retention and increased ROI. RapidMiner can analyze data following the principles of the recommendation system, as demonstrated in this chapter, step-by-step.

INTRODUCTION

Many organizations have a set of data that can be used to support decision-making on matters such as marketing data. Such data are therefore used for the creation of an advisory system. For example, when a customer logs into an online bookstore, the recommendation system will offer books that are similar to the ones the customers have previously ordered. This is to increase the chances of a customer purchase. Recommendation System can increase a lot of sales for online stores. It is widely used in many industries such as tourism and hotels where the system advises on accommodation and attractions in line with the tastes of the customers (Aditya et al, 2021: Chen & Qin, 2021: Wayan Priscila Yuni Praditya, Erna Permanasari, Hidayah, 2021).

DOI: 10.4018/978-1-6684-4730-7.ch009

RECOMMENDATION SYSTEM

The recommendation system is divided into two types.

1. **Content-Based Recommendation:** It focuses on making recommendations using past content as a reference (Tai, Sun & Yao 2021). For example, when a customer has previously purchased Product A, the system will present Product A and other products that are similar in properties to Product A.

2. **Collaborative Filtering:** CF focuses on analyzing customer behavior (Emon et al, 2021: Khatter et al, 2021). For example, Customer A tends to buy soap and shampoo all together, so Customer B who buys soap will likely buy shampoo too. The aforementioned system is also divided into 2 forms.

   a. **Content-Based Filtering:** This is to focus on analyzing user behavior such as a group of customers with similar purchasing behavior (Yadalam et al., 2020: Kamukwamba & Chunxiao, 2021).

   b. **Item-Based Filtering:** This is to focus on analyzing product properties (Kusumawardhani, Nasrun & Setianingsih, 2019: Lourenco & Varde 2020: Padhy, Singh & Vetrivelan, 2022). For example, scooter and skateboards are different products but share similar properties.

The CF processing algorithm is a prediction of the similar data from the existing data, as in the example.

Table 1. Examples of datasets for forecasting data with recommendation system

	Data Mining Techniques	Python	Design Thinking	Technology Management
Sarawut Ramjan	5	2	5	4
Jirapon Sunkpho	2	5	?	3
Kom Campiranon	2	2	4	2
Purimprach Saengkaew	5	1	5	?

Sample dataset presents the student's satisfaction on each subject. 1 means most disliked while 5 means most liked. In CF processing algorithms, data scientists put datasets into processing to predict empty values. For example, Jirapon Sunkpho has not filled out his satisfaction in the Design Thinking course, so CF processing will use existing data to predict what extent Jirapon Sunkpho is likely to favor the course. If the forecast result is at level 5, it means most favorable. The recommendation system will recommend Design Thinking course to Jirapon Sunkpho.

Data mining techniques applied to the development of the recommendation system can be divided into 2 types: 1. Non-Probabilistic Algorithms such as K-Nearest Neighbors (KNN); both User-Based and Item-Base, and 2. Probabilistic Algorithms such as Bayesian-Network Modes.

USER-BASED NEAREST-NEIGHBOR COLLABORATIVE FILTERING

The fundamental principle of User-Based Nearest-Neighbor Collaborative Filtering is to forecast the current missing data by considering other data with a complete similar format. It starts with analyzing the similarity of the datasets, which are human opinions, and then uses that rich data to forecast the current missing data (Adeniyi, Wei & Yongquan, 2016: Riswanto, Suparyanto & Robi'In, 2019). For example, if Mr. A has evaluated his liking on the movies "Bangkok Traffic (love) Story" and "Hormones", but has not evaluated his liking of the Thai movie Nang Nak, the User-Based Nearest-Neighbor Collaborative Filtering will bring the data of others such as Mr. B, who has evaluated his liking for the movie "Bangkok Traffic (love) Story", "Hormones" and "Nang Nak" to predict Mr. A satisfaction on "Nang Nak" movie.

In this example, User-Based Nearest-Neighbor Collaborative Filtering uses the similarity of Mr. A and Mr. B's data models to predict the missing data. The significant principle of this is to calculate the similarity of the two datasets to forecast the missing data.

MEASURING USER SIMILARITY: PERSON CORRELATION

Pearson Correlation is an analysis of the relationship and similarity between two datasets with values between -1 and 1. If the value obtained from the analysis is minus, it means the relationship between the two datasets is inverse. For example, the more Mr. A likes the movie Nang Nak, the more Mr. B tends to like the movie too. In other words, if the data obtained from the analysis is positive, it means that the higher the value of one dataset, the more valuable the other dataset. By Pearson Correlation method, the similarity is calculated as follows.

a,b : Data Scientists' interests in complementing Data

$r_{a,p}$: Data that require the complement or p of the dataset a

$\overline{r}_a$: average of dataset a

$\overline{r}_b$: average of dataset b

P : datasets a and b

$$sim(a,b) = \frac{\sum_{p \in P}\left(r_{a,p} - \overline{r}_a\right)\left(r_{b,p} - \overline{r}_b\right)}{\sqrt{\sum_{p \in P}\left(r_{a,p} - \overline{r}_a\right)^2}\sqrt{\sum_{p \in P}\left(r_{a,p} - \overline{r}_a\right)^2}}$$

a is the data rating the liking for each movie, but does not assess the liking of the movie Nang Nak. So, data scientists have to calculate similarity from other datasets to predict the liking for Nang Nak of dataset a, as shown below.

From the table, data scientists can do the calculations to find similarity between Sarawut Ramjan's fondness on each movie and of others with the use of Pearson Correlation as follows.

$$\frac{\left(5 - \overline{r}_a\right)*\left(3 - \overline{r}_b\right) + \left(3 - \overline{r}_a\right)*\left(1 - \overline{r}_b\right) + \ldots + \left(4 - \overline{r}_a\right)*\left(3 - \overline{r}_b\right)}{\sqrt{\left(5 - \overline{r}_a\right)^2 + \left(3 - \overline{r}_b\right)^2} + \ldots + \sqrt{\left(4 - \overline{r}_a\right)^2 + \left(3 - \overline{r}_b\right)^2}} = 0.85$$

Table 2. Examples of datasets for forecasting data using Pearson correlation

	Hormones	The Slavery	To Irate, to Love	The Chains of Sin	Nang Nak
Sarawut Ramjan	5	3	4	4	?
Jirapon Sunkpho	3	1	2	3	3
Kom Campiranon	4	3	4	3	5
Purimprach Saengkaew	3	3	1	5	4
Tanatorn Tanantong	1	5	5	2	1

From the calculation with Pearson Correlation, which evaluates Sarawut Ramjan and Jirapon Sunkpho's fondness on the movies Hormones, The Slavery, To Irate-To love and The Chains of Sin without taking the results from the movie Nang Nak to calculate. The similarity is at 0.85. Data scientists can take the level of Sarawut Ramjan's fondness to calculate with Kom Campiranon, Purimprach Sangkaew and Tanatorn Tanantong's fondness, and the results are 0, 0.7 and − 0.79, respectively.

Therefore, the level of Jirapon Sunkpho 's fondness on the movies is most similar to Sarawut Ramjan's. Afterward, data scientists can predict the fondness level Sarawut Ramjan has on Nang Nak movie, which can be selected from Jirapon Sunkpho and Purimprach Sangkaew's fondness data on the movies. The similarity values are at 0.85 and 0.7, which are close to 1. It is to say that the more fondness Jirapon Sunkpho and Purimprach Sangkaew have for the movies, the more Sarawut Ramjan tends to like the movies. The forecast can be made using the following formula.

$$pred\left(a, p\right) = \overline{r}_a \frac{\sum_{p \in NSim\left(a,b\right)}\left(r_{b,p} - \overline{r}_b\right)}{\sum_{p \in NSim\left(a,b\right)}}$$

From the formula, scientists can predict the satisfaction Sarawut Ramjan has on Nang Nak from the liking of Jirapon Sunkpho and Purimpan Sangkaew as follows.

$$4 + \frac{0.85 * \left(3 - 2.4\right) + 0.7 * \left(4 - 3.8\right)}{0.85 + 0.7} = 4.42$$

Sarawut Ramjan's fondness on Nak Nak is 4.42, which means that the data scientists can fill in the missing values of the data set using other similar data. In this case, the scientists could choose to use the data from Jirapon Sunkpho, which shows the greatest degree of similarity without using any other dataset.

ITEM-BASED NEAREST NEIGHBOR RECOMMENDATION

When analyzing data with User-Based Nearest-Neighbor Collaborative Filtering, the greater the amount of data, the more digital resources the scientists need to prepare; memory and processing time. Therefore, Item-Based Nearest Neighbor Recommendation will not analyze the similarity which is the opinion of humans, but it analyzes the similarity of the properties such as product similarity (Gong, Ye, H-W, & Zhu, 2009). The calculation formula is as follows.

$\vec{a}, \vec{b}$: Item on which the scientists need to complement the data

$r_{u,a}$: *Data in* Item a

$r_{u,b}$: *Data in* Item b

$\bar{r}_u$: Mean of Each Item

U : Number of customers

$$sim\left(\vec{a}, \vec{b}\right) = \frac{\sum_{p \in U}\left(r_{u,a} - \bar{r}_u\right)\left(r_{u,b} - \bar{r}_u\right)}{\sqrt{\sum_{p \in U}\left(r_{u,a} - \bar{r}_u\right)^2}\sqrt{\sum_{p \in U}\left(r_{u,b} - \bar{r}_u\right)^2}}$$

The Item-Based Nearest Neighbor Recommendation analysis aims to take the weights the customers give to each item to subtract the average of each customer. The data can be analyzed as in the following example.

Table 3. Datasets for data forecasting using item-based nearest neighbor recommendation

	Soap	Toothpaste	Shampoo	Dishwasher	Bathroom Cleaner
Sarawut Ramjan	5	3	4	4	?
Jirapon Sunkpho	3	1	2	3	3
Kom Campiranon	4	3	4	3	5
Purimprach Saengkaew	3	3	1	5	4
Tanatorn Tanantong	1	5	5	2	1

Data scientists can analyze the similarity of bathroom cleaner with other products to fill in the missing data by using a similar model to forecast. The data that customers give each item weight are taken to subtract with the average value of each customer. For example, Sarawut Ramjan gives the soap weight, from scale1 to 5 of satisfaction, and he also gives other products weight; the average weight is 4. So, the difference (Mean-Adjusted Ratings Database) that Sarawut Ramjan has on soap is 1. When calculating the differences in every customer, the results are as follows:

When receiving the difference, the scientists can use data from Item 1, which is soap, to calculate the similarity with Item 5, the toilet cleaner as follows.

$$\frac{0.6 * 0.6 + 0.2 * 1.2 + \left(-0.2\right) * 0.80 + \left(-1.8\right) * \left(-1.8\right)}{\sqrt{0.6^2 + 0.2^2 + \left(-0.2\right)^2 + \left(-1.8\right)^2} * \sqrt{0.6^2 + 0.2^2 + 0.8^2 + \left(-1.8\right)^2}} = 0.80$$

Table 4. Mean-adjusted ratings database

	Soap	Toothpaste	Shampoo	Dish Washer	Bathroom Cleaner
Sarawut Ramjan	1.00	-1.00	0.00	0.00	?
Jirapon Sunkpho	0.60	-1.40	-0.40	0.60	0.60
Kom Campiranon	0.20	-0.80	0.20	-0.80	1.20
Purimprach Saengkaew	-0.20	-0.20	-2.20	2.80	0.80
Tanatorn Tanantong	-1.80	2.20	2.20	-0.80	-1.80

In the case soap has similar data format to toilet cleaner, the scientists can make predictions to complement data.

$\sum i \in ratedItem(u) Sim(i, p)$: The sum of the similarities between the item used in the calculation and the item to forecast data

$r_{u,i}$: The weight the customer gives to the item, used in the calculation

$$pred(u, p) = \frac{\sum i \in ratedItem(u) Sim(i, p) * r_{u,i}}{\sum i \in ratedItem(u) Sim(i, p)}$$

According to the formula, the scientists can predict the missing data of Sarawut Ramjan's weight on bathroom cleaner as in the following calculations.

$$prad(Sarawut\ Ramjan's, Item5) = \frac{sim(1,5) * 5 + sim(2,5) * 3 + sim(3,5) * 4 + sim(4,5) * 4}{sim(1,5) + sim(2,5) + sim(3,5) + sim(4,5)}$$

Based on the calculations, the similarity between Item 1 – 4 and Item 5, along with the weight that Sarawut Ramjan gives to every Item, is used in the calculations. The similarity of Item 1 and 5 is then multiplied by the number 5, which Sarawut Ramjan has assessed, and then divided by similarity values of Item 1 – 4 and Item 5.

PROBABILISTIC METHODS

Probabilistic Methods is one of the methods to predict the missing data. For example, the ratings that moviegoers would likely have for a particular movie can be predicted using the Bayes Theorem technique. The use of such techniques is based on calculating probability of a preceding event as in the following formula.

Y = The probability that event Y will occur
X = events that have already occurred

$$P\left(Y|X\right) = \frac{P\left(Y|X\right)*P\left(Y\right)}{P\left(X\right)}$$

The data on the probability of an event to occur are as follows.

Table 5. Examples of data sets for calculating probabilities

	Hormones	The Slavery	To Irate-To Love	The Chains of Sin	Nang Nak
Sarawut Ramjan	1	3	3	2	?
Jirapon Sunkpho	2	4	2	2	4
Kom Campiranon	1	3	3	5	1
Purimprach Saengkaew	4	5	2	3	3
Tanatorn Tanantong	1	1	5	2	1

Data scientists can calculate all cases, and the movie viewers can evaluate their liking on each movie from level 1 to 5. Therefore, the chance that Sarawut Ramjan will evaluate the film Nang Nak can be in 5 cases.

P(X|Item5 = 1)
= P(Item1 = 1|Item 5 = 1) * P(Item2 = 3| Item 5 = 1)
* P(Item3 = 3 | Item 5 = 1) * P(Item 4 = 2 | Item 5 = 1)

$$= \frac{2}{2}*\frac{1}{2}*\frac{1}{2}*\frac{1}{2}*\frac{1}{2} \approx 0.125$$

The result of the calculation in the case of Item 5 is 1, which means the probability that Sarawut Ramjan will evaluate his fondness on the movie Nang Nak is at level 1, calculated from the proportion of the fondness level in Item 5 and other items; for example, P (Item1 = 1| Item 5 = 1). When considering the data of Item 5, there are 2 users giving level1 liking, so the denominator is 2. And there are 2 Item1, so the numerator is 2, which is 2/2. By considering the proportion of Item5 and other Items, and multiplying all together, so the probability is calculated as 0.125.

Data scientists need to calculate such probability in all cases from 1 to 5, and the probabilities are then applied to predict the missing data.

EVALUATION MATRIX

Data scientists can evaluate the efficiency of data forecasting through the recommendation system which consists of

1. **Predict Accuracy:** It is the difference between the data used for teaching machines and the data received from the forecast. The lower the Root Absolute Error value, the more accurate the value obtained from the forecast. In the Recommendation System, the Evaluation Matrix from Predict Accuracy can be used to measure the efficiency and accuracy of the recommendation.
2. **Rank Accuracy:** This is the percentage of precision of the Recommendation System. For example, the system recommends 5 movies, and there are 4 movies that the user likes. This means that the percentage of recommendation accuracy is 80 percent.

RECOMMENDATION SYSTEM WITH RAPIDMINER

Data scientists can analyze the Recommendation System with RapidMiner software by downloading additional installations at Extensions and selecting Marketplace (Updates and Extensions) as shown below.

Figure 1. Accessing marketplace to download additional installation

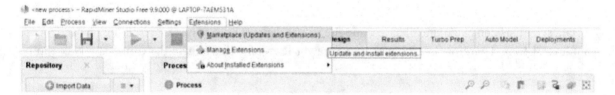

Next, the scientists can search for the Recommender Extension, select for Installation, and press the Install Packages button.

During the software installation process, RapidMiner will ask for license confirmation. The data scientists can select I accept the terms of all license agreements and then select Install packages.

After the installation, data scientists can Import Ratings.csv dataset into RapidMiner software. Within the dataset, it contains data on the fondness level each reader has on the books, totaling 10,000 instances as follows.

Afterward, the scientists can set role of each attribute, so that they can import and process with Item Recommendation as follows.

The data scientists can select Edit List (2) to Set Roles for the data within the dataset.

In the figure, the data scientists need to define rating as a label or target variable, set user_id as user identification, and set book_id as item identification, in order that such data can be processed with the Item Recommendation model.

For data recommendation, data scientists have to divide the data into two parts according to the principle of Supervised-Learning using the Split Data model.

In the figure, data scientists use Split Data to divide the data into two parts; 80% for teaching machine learning, and 20% for testing the model performance.

From the picture, the scientists can press Edit Enumeration button (2) and then determine the proportion to 0.8, which is for teaching the machine learning, and 0.2 as the proportion to test the model.

Figure 2. Recommender extension installation

In the figure, data scientists connect Split Data model, 80% of which is designated for teaching machine learning, to the User K-NN under the Recommender implementation in order to forecast the missing data. Then 20% of the data used for the test is connected to the data obtained from the forecast, and put them into the Apply Model (Item Recommendation) for analysis using Recommendation System. The results of data analysis are as presented in the picture.

Recommendation System can recommend books for each reader. For example, the system recommends 100 books to Reader 2 based on user_id number 2 and the number of books in the Item_id that the model has suggested. Then the efficiency of the recommendation can be tested using the Performance (Item Recommendation) model as follows.

Data scientists can test the efficiency of the system by connecting the machine-learning model from K-NN learning into the Performance model, then connecting the forecasted results from User K-NN to the Performance train. Then, 20 percent for testing the data is taken into Test of Performance to analyze. The efficiency testing results are as in the table below.

The result of test using a model within the RapidMiner software shows Rank Accuracy, which is the percentage of accuracy that the Recommendation System provides to the users. For example, if the prec@5 value is 0.137, it means the accuracy is 20 percent.

Figure 3. License agreement

CONCLUSION

Data scientists can develop models to provide called Recommendation System, both in the form of User-Based Recommendation which analyzes similar behaviors of each user in order to recommend products or services consistent with customer behavior, and the form of Item-Based Recommendation which focuses on the similarity of the products. Both aspects are aimed at forecasting of the missing data. The principle of data forecasting is consistent with the concept of Supervised-Learning. Data scientists still have to divide the data into two parts, for teaching machines and for testing the performance of models.

Using RapidMiner software for recommending data under the concept of Recommendation System, data scientists can use models in the Recommender Package that provides data aligned with the concept of Recommendation System such as User K-NN, Apply Model and Performance. All of them are Item-Based Recommendation data analysis. Data scientists can analyze computing efficiency in a Rank Accuracy manner, the proportion of accurate predictions or recommendations.

Figure 4. Importing ratings dataset into RapidMiner software

Import Data - Format your columns.   ×

Format your columns.

Date format _____ ▾   Replace errors with missing values ⓘ

	user_id integer		book_id integer		rating integer	
1	1		258		5	
2	2		4081		4	
3	2		260		5	
4	2		9296		5	
5	2		2318		3	
6	2		26		4	
7	2		315		3	
8	2		33		4	
9	2		301		5	
10	2		2686		5	
11	2		3753		5	
12	2		8519		5	
13	4		70		4	
14	4		264		3	
15	4		388		4	
16	4		18		5	
17	4		27		5	
18	4		21		5	

ⓞ no problems

⟵ Previous   ⟶ Next   ✖ Cancel

Figure 5. Setting roles for the dataset

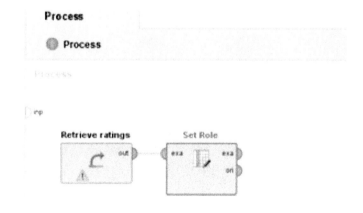

Figure 6. Setting roles on data for item recommendation processing

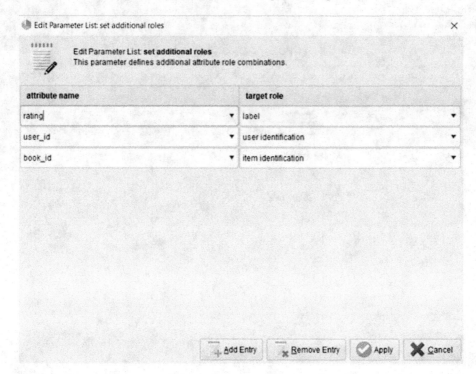

Figure 7. The data is divided into two sections: for teaching machine learning and for testing the model

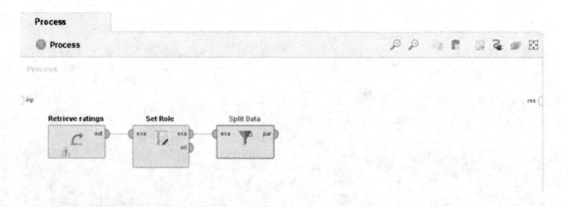

EXERCISE QUESTIONS

1. Explain the concept of Content Based Recommendation.
2. Explain the concept of Collaborative Filtering
3. Explain the difference between Content-Based Filtering and Item-Based Filter.
4. Give examples of problems that require Recommendation System to provide users with recommendations and answers.
5. Search for the research that uses Recommendation System, and summarize it.

Figure 8. Dividing the dataset into two parts using split data

Figure 9. Forecasting and testing data for recommendation

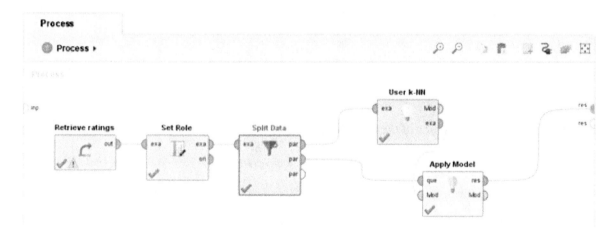

Figure 10. Results from data analysis using recommendation system

Row No.	user_id	item_id	rank
1	2	8	1
2	2	2	2
3	2	11	3
4	2	24	4
5	2	4	5
6	2	21	6
7	2	32	7
8	2	18	8
9	2	5	9
10	2	27	10
11	2	35	11
12	2	10	12
13	2	115	13
14	2	101	14
15	2	94	15
16	2	80	16

Figure 11. Testing the efficiency of the recommendation system using performance

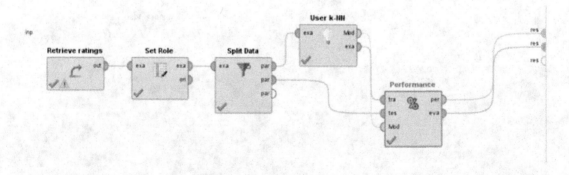

Figure 12. Results of the recommendation system efficiency

Row No.	AUC	prec@5	prec@10	prec@15	NDCG	MAP
1	0.820	0.137	0.098	0.082	0.377	0.115

REFERENCES

Adeniyi, D. A., Wei, Z., & Yongquan, Y. (2016). Automated web usage data mining and recommendation system using K-Nearest Neighbor (KNN) classification method. *Applied Computing & Informatics*, *12*(1), 90–108. doi:10.1016/j.aci.2014.10.001

Aditya, G. M., Hoode, A., Anvesh Rai, K., Biradar, G., Ajay Kumara, M., Manoj Kumar, M. V., Prashanth, B. S., Sneha, H. R., & Shivadarshan, S. L. (2021). Machine Learning Based Platform and Recommendation System for Food Ordering Services within Premises. *2021 2nd Global Conference for Advancement in Technology (GCAT), Advancement in Technology (GCAT), 2021 2nd Global Conference For*, 1–8.

Chen, Q., & Qin, J. (2021). Research and implementation of movie recommendation system based on deep learning. *2021 IEEE International Conference on Computer Science, Electronic Information Engineering and Intelligent Control Technology (CEI), Computer Science, Electronic Information Engineering and Intelligent Control Technology (CEI), 2021 IEEE International Conference On*, 225–228.

Emon, M. I., Shahiduzzaman, M., Rakib, M. R. H., Shathee, M. S. A., Saha, S., Kamran, M. N., & Fahim, J. H. (2021). Profile Based Course Recommendation System Using Association Rule Mining and Collaborative Filtering. *2021 International Conference on Science & Contemporary Technologies (ICSCT), Science & Contemporary Technologies (ICSCT), 2021 International Conference On*, 1–5.

Gong, S., Ye, H.-W., & Zhu, X. (2009). Item-based collaborative filtering recommendation using self-organizing map. *2009 Chinese Control and Decision Conference, Control and Decision Conference, 2009. CCDC '09. Chinese*, 4029–4031.

Kamukwamba, Y., & Chunxiao, L. (2021). A Novel Algorithm Using Content-Based Filtering Technology in Apache Spark for Big Data Analysis. *2021 4th International Conference on Artificial Intelligence and Big Data (ICAIBD), Artificial Intelligence and Big Data (ICAIBD), 2021 4th International Conference On*, 22–26.

Khatter, H., Arif, S., Singh, U., Mathur, S., & Jain, S. (2021). Product Recommendation System for E-Commerce using Collaborative Filtering and Textual Clustering. *2021 Third International Conference on Inventive Research in Computing Applications (ICIRCA), Inventive Research in Computing Applications (ICIRCA), 2021 Third International Conference On*, 612–618.

Kusumawardhani, N. K., Nasrun, M., & Setianingsih, C. (2019). Web Recommended System Library Book Selection Using Item Based Collaborative Filtering Method. *2019 IEEE International Conference on Engineering, Technology and Education (TALE), Engineering, Technology and Education (TALE), 2019 IEEE International Conference On*, 1–8.

Lourenco, J., & Varde, A. S. (2020). Item-Based Collaborative Filtering and Association Rules for a Baseline Recommender in E-Commerce. *2020 IEEE International Conference on Big Data (Big Data), Big Data (Big Data), 2020 IEEE International Conference On*, 4636–4645.

Padhy, S. K., Singh, A. K., & Vetrivelan, P. (2022). Item-Based Collaborative Filtering Blockchain for Secure Movie Recommendation System. *Lecture Notes in Electrical Engineering*, *792*, 937–948. doi:10.1007/978-981-16-4625-6_93

Riswanto, E., Robi'in, B., & Suparyanto. (2019). Mobile Recommendation System for Culinary Tourism Destination using KNN (K-nearest neighbor). *Journal of Physics: Conference Series*, *1201*(1), 012039. doi:10.1088/1742-6596/1201/1/012039

Tai, Y., Sun, Z., & Yao, Z. (2021). Content-Based Recommendation Using Machine Learning. *2021 IEEE 31st International Workshop on Machine Learning for Signal Processing (MLSP), Machine Learning for Signal Processing (MLSP), 2021 IEEE 31st International Workshop On*, 1–4.

Wayan Priscila Yuni Praditya, N., Erna Permanasari, A., & Hidayah, I. (2021). Designing a tourism recommendation system using a hybrid method (Collaborative Filtering and Content-Based Filtering). *2021 IEEE International Conference on Communication, Networks and Satellite (COMNETSAT), Communication, Networks and Satellite (Comnetsat), 2021 IEEE International Conference On*, 298–305.

Yadalam, T. V., Gowda, V. M., Kumar, V. S., Girish, D., & M., N. (2020). Career Recommendation Systems using Content based Filtering. *2020 5th International Conference on Communication and Electronics Systems (ICCES), Communication and Electronics Systems (ICCES), 2020 5th International Conference On*, 660–665.

Chapter 10
Case Studies on the Use of Data Mining Techniques in Data Science

ABSTRACT

This chapter presents data science research conducted by authors Sarawut Ramjan and Jirapon Sunkpho, showcasing the use of RapidMiner to gather data from social networks. The research includes the analysis of customer satisfaction for mobile applications, predicting condominium prices in Bangkok, and discovering demand and supply patterns based on Thai social media data using the association rule mining approach. Additionally, the chapter touches on other topics such as corrosion under insulation severity classification for carbon steel in a marine environment and variables that influence pilot's safe driving. The chapter is beneficial for readers without data science experience and for businesses interested in employing data mining techniques. The research highlights that software application skills are not the only important factor, but also understanding the processes of data science, such as data exploration, data pre-processing, data mining, and data presentation, which are essential and useful skills.

INTRODUCTION

This book has mentioned data mining techniques both in nature Supervised-Learning and Unsupervised Learning using RapidMiner as a data analysis tool. Several case studies from the author's researches are presented as examples for analyzing real data. They are not only the application of data mining techniques to process the data, but also cover other processes of data science work. The case studies consist of 1. Analysis of customer satisfaction in using Mobile Application, published in the journal "Thammasat Review", 2. Predicting Condominium Price in Bangkok Using Web Mining Techniques, published in the journal "Srinakharinwirot Research and Development", and 3. An Association Rule Mining Approach to Discover Demand and Supply Patterns Based on Thai Social Media Data, published in an International Journal of Knowledge and Systems Science. 4. Corrosion under Insulation Severity Classification for Carbon Steel in Marine Environment which is a part of Independent Study of Data Science Program that

DOI: 10.4018/978-1-6684-4730-7.ch010

author is advisor as well as 5. Variables Influence Pilot's Safe Driving which is a part of Independent Study of Data Science Program that author is an advisor.

THE CASE STUDY ON ANALYZING CUSTOMER SATISFACTION ON A MOBILE APPLICATION USING DATA MINING TECHNIQUES (SUNKPHO & HOFMANN, 2019)

The case study shows the analysis on customer satisfaction using mobile app services of state-owned energy enterprises in the metropolitan area of Bangkok, Thailand. The analysis follows CRSIP-DM Process, which this book has already mentioned in Chapter 1. The researcher found that Data used to reflect performance of the state energy enterprise is the satisfaction of users on services related to information technology and one important service, the Mobile App.

Mobile App is available to users as they can access the Mobile App to check the amount of energy usage each month. The app notifies important news, such as the cessation of energy services for infrastructure repairs, the area where the power is interrupted and unable to provide service, and payment channel.

Business Understanding

In the Business Understanding process, the key is that Energy enterprises have questioned the variables that effect customer satisfaction and dissatisfaction so that SOEs can develop features. Therefore, the researcher has formulated a problem for data analysis, namely Classification of data that should be used to predict customer satisfaction.

Data Understanding

After that, the researcher entered the Data Understanding process. Datasets collected customer satisfaction on mobile apps were imported into RapidMiner software to conduct surveys. The data are satisfaction level, gender, age, education, amount of mobile app usage per year, mobile app usage per month, reliability and mobile app usage in emergency situations. From the survey data, it was found that there were 81% of customers satisfied with using the mobile app at a level 4 - 5 on the Likert Scale, and 19% of the customers showed a satisfaction level of 3 or lower.

1. **Data Exploration:** The researchers then used Tableau software to perform Data Exploration for deeper data, which consists of Customer satisfaction on App Feature and User Experience. The overall satisfaction level was at a very level. However, the least satisfied part of the data was data security. As for the App Feature, the part which need to be improved and showed the least satisfaction was the Payment Feature. In the User Experience section, the overall satisfaction was at very satisfied level.
2. **Data Quality Verification:** Researchers have prepared the data by manipulating the Missing Value. It was found that the Demographic Data had a total of 26 Missing Values. There was no missing value in terms of reliability and usability of the Mobile App in emergency situations. There was 0 data because the customer had never used the Mobile App in such a manner.

3. **Correlation Analysis:** The researchers analyzed the data with Correlation Analysis to analyze the relationship of the Attribute within the data set, and found that there were data related to each other, consisting of Group 1: Data Accuracy and Data modernization, Group 2: the attractiveness of the User Interface and the Ease of Use which are considered the User Experience, and the 3rd group is Notifications and Energy History which is in the App Features group.

4. **Data Preparation:** The missing Value data in Demographic Data was filled using the Impute Missing Value technique within the RapidMiner software. The rest of the data within the Attribute was used fill the empty data with the similar data. The objective of the data analysis is to find what variables cause customer satisfaction and dissatisfaction. The researchers revised the Likert Scale data to form a binary class with only two values. Changes were made to the format of the data. For satisfaction data on a 4 - 5 scale, it was changed to satisfactory, and the level of satisfaction from 3 and lower was changed to dissatisfactory.

5. **Modeling:** The researchers used 3 data mining techniques to analyze the data: Naïve Bayes, Decision Tree and Logistic Regression, and divided the data into 2 parts according to the principle of Supervised-Learning. 80 percent was for teaching machine learning and 20 percent was for model performance testing. The researchers then created a model with all 3 data mining techniques. The data sets were imported into the model. When testing the analysis accuracy, the accuracy level of Naïve Bayes, the Decision and the Logistic Regression were 92.76%, 91.03% and 92.41%, respectively.

6. **Evaluation:** Analysis of the data showed that Naïve Bayes was slightly more accurate than Decision Tree and Logistic Regression. However, when considering Precision and Recall, the Decision Tree was the most accurate. Therefore, the researchers chose to consider the results of the Decision Tree data analysis, and it revealed that the most important variables that caused customer satisfaction and dissatisfaction were Ease of Use of Mobile App, and Payment Feature.

7. **Deployment:** After analyzing the data, the researcher advised energy enterprises to develop a new version of the mobile app, which should include improvements in ease of use and payment features in order to increase customer satisfaction and reduce dissatisfaction. After the enterprise has developed a new version of Mobile App and used for customers in the metropolitan area, the researcher will collect the data and analyze the results in a similar manner to test the performance of the new version of Mobile App to examine.

The case studies from the research paper "Analyzing Customer Satisfaction of a Mobile Application using Data Mining Techniques" can be used as a guide for data scientists who study data mining techniques and practice using RapidMiner software. The scientists are required to understand not only about the methods of data analysis and the use of the software, but they also need to understand the processes under the CRSIP-DM, so that they can prepare data and analyze results.

THE CASE STUDY ON PREDICTING CONDOMINIUM PRICE IN BANGKOK USING WEB MINING TECHNIQUES (SUNKPHO & RAMJAN, 2020)

The sales rate of condominiums in Bangkok, Thailand among the Generation Y and among condominium speculators is very high. This group of condominium buyers use variables to evaluate the appropriate condominium price, such as the distance to the sky train or subway. These variables are used to determine the price the buyer thinks appropriate for the purchase and to determine the selling price. The environment of the city where the condominium project is being built is another important variable.

Therefore, the researcher focused on analyzing variables suitable for forecasting condominium prices so that the results are accurate and appropriate to the characteristics of the city in which the condominium project is being built. The researcher therefore defined the control variables as a study of the variables related to the pricing of condominiums in Bangkok, Thailand. The research process is as follows.

Data Collection Using Web Crawling

The researchers used Web Crawling, one of Web Mining's techniques, to extract data on the condominium purchases from the website, hipflat.co.th which covers more variables than other similar websites. The data set was brought to teach machine learning under the concept of Supervised-Learning. The researchers obtained data on 1,465 condominiums and within the dataset there were a total of 15 attributes.

- Project location
- List of sky train stations near the condominium
- List of subway stations near the condominium
- The average distance from the condominium to the surrounding sky train stations
- Average distance from the condominium to the surrounding subway stations
- Name of the condominium project
- Number of floors of each project
- Number of rooms in each project
- Year the construction was completed
- Names of project owners
- Price per square meter
- The price rate that has changed since the end of the last year
- The price rate that has changed since the end of the last quarter
- Rental rate that has changed since the end of the last year
- Return on Investment

Data Exploration

The researcher used Correlation Analysis to analyze the variables related to pricing and found that the following 4 attributes affect the condominium pricing; average distance from condominium to surrounding sky train station, the average distance to the surrounding nearest subway station, return on investment, and the rental rate change since the end of last year. The number of floors and the year of completion positively influences on the price per square meter. However, the average distance from the condominium to the surrounding sky train stations, and the average distance from the condominium to the surrounding subway stations negatively influence on the price per square meter.

Data Preparation

The web-crawling dataset contained a number of missing values, so the researchers needed to manipulate the data by filling in the mean into the attribute where there was the missing value, consisting of the average distance from the condominium to the surrounding sky train stations, the average distance from condominium to surrounding subway stations, the number of floors and the number of rooms in each project.

Data Modeling

The researchers used five different data mining techniques to forecast condominium prices: Generalized Linear Model, Deep Learning, Decision Tree, Random Forest, and Gradient Boosted Trees. RapidMiner was used as a modeling and data analysis tool. The researchers then used the split test technique to divide the data into two parts: 80 percent for teaching machines learning, and 20% for testing the model's performance.

After testing the model's efficiency in forecasting five condominium prices, the researchers found that deep learning data mining technique is the most accurate in forecasting. The data scientist adjusted the model to increase efficiency by adding a Discretized Process model within the RapidMiner software to the model to classify the data of the Attribute. The average distance from the condominium to the surrounding sky train stations and the average distance from the condominium to the surrounding subway stations were divided into 4 intervals. These included distances less than 500 meters, distances between 500 and 1000 meters, distances between 1 and 2 kilometers, and distances greater than 2 kilometers. The researchers then used the Distance Measure model within the RapidMiner software to remove outlier data. Regarding the Attribute price per square meter, the researchers found that after adjusting both parts of the model, the model had a higher accuracy in forecasting condominium prices.

In the last step, the researcher transferred data from Attributes; including Return on Investment, Rates that have changed since the end of last year, the price change since the end of the last quarter, Rental rates changed since the end of last year, to teach the machine. On the contrary, it was found that after adjusting the data, the accuracy of condominium price forecasting declined.

The Research Result

Therefore, the researchers concluded that Important variables to consider when determining condominium prices. The first variable is the year of construction completion. The new condominiums have higher price per meter. Secondly, the more numbers of floors in the project, the higher the condominium price is. On the other hand, if the average distance from the condominium to the sky train station and the subway station is very far, the price of the condominium will reduce. In addition, the more numbers of rooms per project, the lower the price of condominiums. The research also found that if the names of the project owners are listed in the stock market, the prices of condominiums is higher than the condominiums whose owners' names are not listed in the stock market.

The results from this research are also consistent with other researches, such as condominium price forecasting in Japan (Diewert & Shimizu, 2016) and Singapore (Lim, et. al, 2016), which analyzed the variables used to determine condominium prices.

THE CASE STUDY ON ASSOCIATION RULE MINING APPROACH TO DISCOVER DEMAND AND SUPPLY PATTERNS BASED ON THAI SOCIAL MEDIA DATA (TANANTONG & RAMJAN, 2021)

Twitter has become a digital marketing channel for online sellers by increasing the number of Retweets on the products and services. To create a Tweet, online sellers also use Hashtags to categorize customer interests such as #KoreanArtistConcertTickets to make the Tweet appear to customers who are interested in the topic. And in many cases, the Hashtag ranks at the top which means it is the viral, such as political phenomena. Online sellers also use hashtags on the subject, so that the Tweets they generate appear alongside other Tweets of the interest of society. Therefore, the researchers used Association Rule Mining to analyze the correlation rules of demand and sales from a dataset of Tweets, Retweets, Likes and Hashtags related to goods and services on Twitter. The research process is as follows:

Data Collection

The researchers used the Twitter API along with Python to extract trading on Twitter, where online sellers and buyers interact for the 24 hours. It extracted only the buy and sell data with a total of 24,464 instances.

Data Cleansing

To prepare data for processing with affinity rules, the researchers cleaned up the data by examining the duplicates and removing them from the dataset, and then checked the tweets without comments, which means the products did not have response from customers. Researchers then deleted the data that had such characteristics from the data. In the final step, the researchers considered only the attributes involved in the analysis of the data, and removed the irrelevant attributes such as profile_image_url_https, which stored information about Twitter users, until there were only 12 attributes, with a total of 7,475 instances.

Data Labelling

Among all 12 Attributes associated with trading on Twitter, the researcher asked 3 Knowledge Experts for their opinions on which attributes to be analyzed with correlation rules. The experts recommended categorizing data into 5 groups: Demand Tweets, Supply Tweets, Demand and Supply Tweets, Comment Tweets and Other Tweets.

Hashtag Extraction

The researchers extracted 3 hashtags from the data: Demand Tweets, Supply Tweets, and Other Tweets.

Association Rule Mining

The researchers created all possible Frequent Item Sets from the dataset with the Apriori algorithm discussed in Chapter 8. The Support and Confidence Thresholds were set for Demand at 0.02, for Supply at 0.01, and for Other Tweets at 0.0001. The researchers then analyzed the data in order to create 1-itemset, 2-itemset, and 3-itemset correlation rules, and selected 2 strong correlation rules: Right-Hand-Side (RHS) which shows Demand, Supply, and Lift-Hand-Side (LHS) which doesn't show the Hashtag type. The correlation rule displays the Hashtag in LHS format along with the RHS format.

The Experimental Result

The researchers found that online sellers should offer their products and services in conjunction with the use of hashtags related to the social phenomenon or trends in order to attract the shoppers' interest. During the time of the experiment, there were Korea super stars to hold concerts in Thailand. Hashtags associated with the super stars became so popular that online sellers could present their products and services using the Hashtags. Also, the most important hashtags are buying and selling. This should be presented within the Tweet so that customers can understand and access the products or services the seller wants.

CORROSION UNDER INSULATION SEVERITY CLASSIFICATION FOR CARON STEEL IN MARINE ENVIRONMENT (THAMMASIRI & RAMJAN, 2021)

In the oil transportation industry Oil conveying equipment is made of insulated steel. Such insulators are meant to maintain the temperature of the oil transported within the pipeline. Engineers need to open the insulation to check for corrosion by continuously expanding the opening until all erosion points are found. The resulting corrosion could lead to an undersea oil spill that could contaminate the sea. destroy marine ecosystems or even cause fires that destroy nature and human life. The entire process runs on an offshore oil station, making it a difficult process for pipeline repairs and huge maintenance costs.

Data scientists need to take a dataset of rust corrosion on oil pipelines and analyze them to classify where rust may occur so that engineers can open the insulation at the location of the corroded steel from the rust. Data analysis takes existing data sets to teach machine learning and gives machines the ability to classify the degree of corrosion of steel so engineers can diagnose preliminary milling situations before deciding to open the insulator covering the duct for a real local inspection. The study and analysis of this data can help reduce the time for pipeline repairs and reduce the cost of maintenance of the pipeline.

The research used the environment to study and analyze data from an oil production platform in the Gulf of Thailand of an oil company from Thailand. Resources for collecting datasets used to study and lead to modeling in steel corrosion prediction include Pipeline Corrosion Inspection Report, Pipeline Oil Temperature Report and Plant. The researchers then took the collected data and compiled it into a dataset that could be used for analysis by data mining techniques. Data exploration process, the researchers surveyed the data to determine how appropriate the patterns of the datasets were to be analyzed using data mining techniques and to the research question. Researchers create a visualization for the data exploration consisting of bar charts, scatter plot and box plot.

Next, in the data pro-processing process, the researchers dealt with the missing value by fulfil the incomplete data, and feature engineering stage, researcher prepare a standardization of data that came from different measurement by label encoding, one hot encoding and max-min normalization. During the tuning of that data, researchers deal with the imbalanced data using a SMOTE algorithm. The researchers then divided the dataset into training set to teach machine learning. and testing set to approve the performance of the classification model. In addition, this step researchers fine-tuned the hyperparameters with the GridSeachCV technique.

This experiment aims to explore classification techniques from different data mining methods that most appropriate to the data set and research questions. Classification techniques are explored through a literature review that attempts to explore and consolidate the theories and research models involved in this research to compile possible solutions that can be applied to classify the degree of erosion of corrosives of oil pipeline. After literature review process, this research discovered a possible classification technique including decision tree, random forest, XGBoost and multilayer perceptron. The researchers compared the classification accuracy of each technique to conclude which technique is best suited for data analysis under research environments.

Experimental data set consists of 18 features and 434 instances. Features inside a data set including the plant where the pipeline was manufactured, the year the pipe was installed, the size of the pipe, the fluid inside the pipe, the year the engineer inspected it for corrosion, the equipment was inspected, the condition of the jacket, and the condition of the silicone, jacket damage scale and silicone, type of insulation, the minimum average temperature of the internal fluid, The maximum mean temperature of the internal fluid, the average temperature of the fluid inside, the altitude of the device location from sea level, location of the device in the Y-axis, location of the device in the X-axis, and the degree of corrosion severity which is a label. The data classification is divided into two sections: insulation damage assessment and pipe corrosion assessment. Insulator damage is classified into 4 classes: no damage, damage is less than 1 inch in circumference, damage is 1 inch in circumference, damage is larger than 1 inch. Corrosion in pipes is divided into 3 classes: non-corrosive, mild and severe. During the feature engineering process, the researchers created new features that could affect a label classification consists of paint age, the difference between the highest and lowest temperatures, the risk of pipe corrosion and the rate of corrosion.

From the experiment, From the experiment, this research employed a confusion matrix to be a tool for evaluate value an accuracy of each model experiment. It was found that decision tree model has an accuracy value of data classification at 71.8%, multilayer perceptron model at 72.9%, random forest model at 81.3% and XGBoost model at 82.2%. While testing for classification accuracy with machine learning is as reliable as data science theory, this research needs to prove the accuracy of real-world experiments. The researchers deployed the XGBoost classifier model to a web form to allow engineers to input parameters and then have the model classify rust corrosion levels for decision-making on oil pipeline maintenance. From real-world testing, it was found that the model has 75% accuracy in classifying corrosion data for pipelines, based on testing by engineers working in pipeline repairs.

After data analysis and research studies, the researchers found that the limitations that could be developed in data science research studies in other future research and study environments similar to this one. The data sources for this research were compiled from quantitative frequencies stored in a single sensor technology of each oil platform. If future research can collect frequency data from more than one sensor technology in each oil platform, the results of the experiments could be more accurate. In addition, in the case of other research It can collect data from different environments, such as deserts, giving machine learning the opportunity to learn features of the data goes beyond this research and may make it more accurate to classify the data.

VARIABLES INFLUENCING PILOT'S SAFE DRIVING (MANEECHAEYE & RAMJAN, 2022)

While flying is considered the safest journey out of all means, accidents can occur due to several variables. One of the interesting variables is accidents caused by pilot failure. Strict adherence to aviation standards is one of the ways to prevent human error. This research aims to study the variables that influence the safe driving behavior of pilots at the organizational, squadron and individual levels. In this research study, the researchers relied on domain expert to collect qualitative data to study the overall condition of aviation safety in Thailand and pilot behavior that does not meet aviation standards. The researchers then applied the recommendations from domain experts along with the literature review data to develop a questionnaire tool, and the result of collecting data is 610 instances.

After data collected, during data exploration process, researchers analyzed a central tendency of each feature to explore a data distribution. This research relies on exploratory factor analysis techniques to group 15 features into 4 factors consists of safety climate, knowledge of aviation safety standards, the motivation to operate safely and last factor is the pilot's compliance with aviation standards which is a label. To analyze the variables that influence the pilot's safe driving behavior, the researchers used a data mining technique which is a multiple regression to analyze a data set. Data set is split to training set at 75% to train a machine learning as well as testing set at 25% to test an accuracy of prediction model. This research evaluates an accuracy of the data mining model and found that mean absolute error (MAE) at 0.47, mean square error (MSE) at 0.42, Root mean square error (RMSE) at 0.65 and R-squared at 0.62.

The results of the data analysis revealed that the safety climate had a significant effect on pilots' compliance with aviation standards. Knowledge of aviation safety standards has a significant effect on the pilot's compliance with the aviation standards. The motivation to operate safely has a significant effect on the pilot's compliance with aviation standards.

CASE STUDY

The Design and Implementation of Attraction Guidance Systems Using Data Mining Techniques in Conjunction with Collaborative Filtering Technique (Nan et al., 2022)

Designing routes and attractions in corresponding to the personalization of tourists is an important process for tourism businesses. Understanding the conditions for each targeted tourist is critical to the design of routes and attractions. There are many ways to analyze data, and one of the methods that can be applied is the data scientist's approach to analyzing what customers are likely to be interested in for each product and service. Such an approach can be used for analyzing the sights that tourists, customers, like and dislike.

Applying Collaborative Filtering for tourist attraction analysis for, the results obtained from the analysis will help reduce the problems that can arise for tourists while traveling in various places. In 2022, there was a research paper related to the design of tourist guide systems using Collaborative Filtering (Nan, Kanato, & X, 2022). Initially, this research collects data from each traveler's search for attractions on a web browser, along with traveler opinions about tourist attractions on social media. The data were analyzed in order to recommend suitable attractions to tourists in the same market segmentation. However, once the Data Exploration process was completed, the researchers selected the features to be used in the data analysis with collaborative Filtering consisting of the current attractions that tourists are studying and the ratings that tourists have given for each tourist destination they have been to. The researchers then manipulated the missing value data and experimented it with Collaborative Filtering to increase the efficiency of data analysis. This research also brings other data for further experiments, including travel expenses, location of tourist attractions, the distance to travel to each attraction and travel time to each attraction to ensure the accuracy of suitable recommendation.

This research also suggests that in the future, other researchers can use real-time coordinates as well as real-time weather data to help make an appropriate recommendation about attractions.

Guidelines for Developing a System to Provide a Recommendation on Streaming Online with Data Mining (Liao et al., 2021)

Today, with the growth of digital utilities that are stable and supportive to high-speed loading large data, the general public can access to the Internet faster than in the past. Businesses have come up with the idea of Live stream to present their products as they can assess the customer's attitude towards the product demonstrations. Customers can place their desired products during the Live. Facebook was one of the first to use Live Feature to showcase or demonstrate their products. Customers who are also Facebook users can then view the product display in real-time or watch the demonstration that was shown earlier. They can also interact with sellers and place their order via Chat. The seller can also show the nature of the product, how it works, product prices, pros and cons of using products that are appropriate for each customer's characteristics through Facebook Live. While businesses recognize the value of offering goods and services through online streaming, businesses face challenges of collecting and analyzing customer data through customer interaction because such interactions occur only for a short time and cannot reflect long-term consumer behavior of the product.

Other e-Commerce channels, such as e-Retailer, can provide a recommendation system for customers who have experienced shopping through the website in the past. And when the customers return to make repeat purchases, the website can recommend items that customers are likely to be interested or close to the products they've used. The website can even analyze customer's market segmentation and make recommendations that are close to what customers in the same segment are interested in as well. So, the ability to analyze data in a big data will be an important variable for a website. The more information a website has on its customers, the better. The website will be accurate to analyze and recommend. The more items that correspond to the needs of the customer, the more this process incentivizes customers to choose products and make purchases instead of simply visiting the website and turning off the web browser. So, understanding and knowing the characteristics of the customer is an important condition for the recommendation system.

Choosing the right Live Platform for each business's customers is essential for selling products through Live stream. In 2021, there was research on ways to develop online streaming advisory systems (Liao, Widowati & Chang, 2021) as follows.

- Customer basic information
- Customer's online shopping habits
- Motivation to shop through customers' online channels
- Motivation to interact with sellers via Live Streaming

- Customer behavior towards the merchant's live streaming
- Variables that affect decision to purchase online
- Payment methods
- Customer behavior while watching Live streaming
- Customer behavior when interacting with sellers via Live streaming
- Reasons to watch Live streaming
- Live Stream Platform that customers choose to watch
- Types of media content that customers often watch live stream, such as politics, entertainment, etc.
- Motivation to use Stream Platform, for example, to kill time or reduce stress
- Marketing Promotion
- Activities that occur while watching Live; donations or interactions with vendors
- Marketing promotion that affects the purchase of goods, such as offering new products to customers
- Recommending items suitable for customer's needs; brand or payment method

According to the analysis of the data, it was found that customers enjoy interacting with sellers via Live too. Therefore, both the seller and the platform type affect the customer's interest. Customers also recommend their favorite streaming to their peers around them. When customers pay attention to a streamed product, they often share that content on their platform. Customers also like reading other customers' comments on Streaming. This is a hidden reason for customers changing to online shopping instead. The reputation of the Live and the overall beauty of the person who live affects the purchase decision of the customer. In addition, businesses should pay attention to the production of content that is consistent with the current popular issues and pay attention to the quality of streaming. The price reduction during live is also another variable that affects the purchasing decision of customers.

Merchants can also use Streaming to offer new products or special prices to VIP customers. Mentioning regular customers in Streaming also affect the speed of commenting by existing customers and increase interaction with other customers. This is similar to referral Item used by previous customers and affects other customers' purchasing decisions to buy this referred Item.

According to all case studies, when data scientists intend to develop a referral system for products or services, understanding the datasets in the organization or outside the organization alone may not be enough. It is necessary to consult a Domain Expert or even collect data to study the variables and factors that affect the conditions for providing advice on products and services that are suitable for each group of consumers so that the items received from the recommendation system can really affect the purchasing decision.

CONCLUSION

According to the case studies on the author's researches, data scientists need to study data mining techniques and applications of RapidMiner software, along with doing experiment throughout the data science process. It starts with collecting and extracting data from the source, surveying, pre-processing, choosing a data mining technique correspondent to the questionnaire, and finally presenting the results. Therefore, rather than focusing only on data analysis techniques from the beginning, the scientists should analyze the questions thoroughly so that other relevant processes are aligned, and ultimately led to efficient analysis.

EXERCISE QUESTIONS

1. Determine the topic used to analyze the problems.
2. From No. 1, find the Dataset on the Internet that can be used for analyzing the problems.
3. From No. 2, outline the principles and rationale for analyzing the problems, and indicate the data mining techniques used in problem analysis.
4. From No. 3, use RapidMiner software to process Data Exploration and Data Pre-Processing. The data mining techniques are then used to analyze the data.
5. From No. 4, write a report showing the results of data analysis and conclusions.

REFERENCES

Liao, S.-H., Widowati, R., & Chang, H.-Y. (2021). A data mining approach for developing online streaming recommendations. *Applied Artificial Intelligence*, *35*(15), 2204–2227. doi:10.1080/08839514.2021.1997211

Maneechaeye, P., & Ramjan, S. (2022). *Components and Indicators Development with Guidelines to Encourage Safety Behavior among Flight Crews in Thailand (Independent Study)*. Thammasat University.

Nan, X. (2022). Design and Implementation of a Personalized Tourism Recommendation System Based on the Data Mining and Collaborative Filtering Algorithm. *Computational Intelligence and Neuroscience*, 1424097. PMID:36093493

Sunkpho, J., & Hofmann, M. (2019). *Analyzing Customer Satisfaction of a Mobile Application using Data Mining Techniques*. Research Administration Division, Thammasat University.

Sunkpho, J., & Ramjan, S. (2020). Predicting Condominium Price in Bangkok using Web Mining Technique. *Srinakharinwirot Research and Development (Journal of Humanities and Social Sciences)*, *12*(24).

Tanantong, T., & Ramjan, S. (2021). An Association Rule Mining Approach to Discover Demand and Supply Patterns Based on Thai Social Media Data. *International Journal of Knowledge and Systems Science*, *12*(2), 1–16. doi:10.4018/IJKSS.2021040101

Thammasisir, S., & Ramjan, S. (2021). *Corrosion under Insulation severity Prediction for Carbon Steel in Marine Environment using Data Science Methodology (Independent Study)*. Thammasat University.

Chapter 11
Data Mining for Junior Data Scientists:
Basic Python Programming

ABSTRACT

The availability of off-the-shelf tools for data mining has made it easier to process data. However, in many cases, such software packages are not flexible enough to allow for algorithmic improvements. Therefore, data scientists need to write computer programs to customize the processing methods in tandem with the software packages. This chapter introduces Python, a programming language that provides libraries that support data science work. The content includes Python programming syntax, such as variables, structured programming, decision-making programming, recursive programming, data structure handling, and file handling. Additionally, the chapter introduces Google Colab as a tool for programming experiments. It provides a crucial foundation for data science students who are going to process data using data mining techniques in the next chapter using Python programming. Although data scientists don't need a deep understanding of computer programming, learning computer languages is essential, and this chapter caters to beginners.

INTRODUCTION

A number of industries, nowadays, focus on data science as they recognize the value of data to support decision-making (Raschka & Mirajalili, 2018). Whether it is the medical industry, automotive industry or the scientific community, data scientists have become a sought-after position for many organizations. A data scientist can either be developed from the knowledge expert within the organization itself or being adopted from outsiders. Anyhow, every organization analyzes data on the principle of questioning, seeking resources, exploring data and pre-Processing, analyzing data using data mining techniques, and presenting the results to the questioners. At present, there are many tools for exploring and preparing data, as well as machines for using data mining techniques to analyze data. One of these tools is Python, which provides a library of commands for developing visual data, exploring and preparing data, as well

DOI: 10.4018/978-1-6684-4730-7.ch011

as analyzing data with data mining techniques. In addition, data scientists can process data with Python's algorithms without limiting the size of the data. Python itself is considered an open source that allows organizations to analyze data with data mining techniques, which reduces the cost of digital resources (Sneeringer, 2016: Reges, Obourn & Stepp, 2019). Therefore, Python is a useful tool for beginners in data science (Bowles, 2015: Joshi, 2017).

INTRODUCTION TO PYTHON

Python, developed by Buido van Rossum in 1980, is a high-level language which is so close to human language, making it ideal for beginners in computer programming languages (Sunkpho & Ramjan, 2020: Tanantong & Ramjan, 2022). It also has an easy-to-remember syntax, so software developers can use Python for programming in both the Structural Programming and the Object-Oriented programming styles (Hill, 2015: Bader, 2018: Mueller, 2018: Lubanovic, 2019). Python is an open software source, so software developers worldwide can work together to develop Python without the cost of licensing (Stewart, 2017: Zelle, 2010).

Software developers can use software editors such as Google Colab to write Python and use the interpreter to translate Python in order to run the digital device with the process as shown in the following:

1. Software developers write a set of commands on a software editor.
2. The interpreter translates Python into the language that the digital devices can operate.
3. The digital devices accept the commands for processing.
4. The digital devices operate as commanded.
5. Software developers check the operation accuracy.

In the figure, software developers can write a set of commands on the Software Editor and then uses Interpreter to translate Python into the format that can be run by digital devices. The digital devices then receive the command and process it to perform the tasks as designed by the software developers. In the final step, software developers can verify whether the digital devices work as designed so that their command sets can be improved to make digital devices work more accurately.

Python is Case Sensitive, meaning lowercase and uppercase English letters are different. For example, dX and DX, when interpreted, the letters will totally be different. Although developers have different duties from data scientists, when data scientists intend to use programming for data analysis, they can begin their Python study with the following basic commands.

Variables

Data scientists can analyze data by packing it into variables within Python. The variables act as a container containing data for data transfer, processing, and display. The process goes as presented in the figure below.

Figure 1. Operation of variables

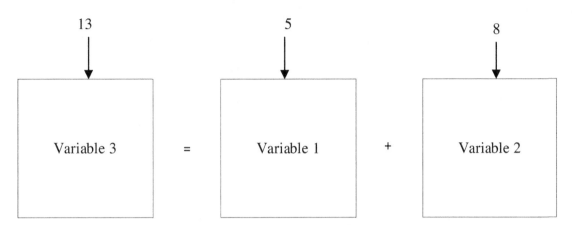

Data scientists can determine the data containing variables. In the example, the data scientists assign all 3 variables. Variable 1 stores the first data which is number 8; and variable 2 stores the second which is number 5. The numbers in variable 1 and variable 2 are then combined, so the result is 13, which is then included in the third variable. Thus, data scientists can define variables to contain the data and write Python programs based on the algorithm designed for each data mining technique.

To determine variables, letters, numbers, or underscores can be used, but it cannot begin with the number like dX or StudentCode. However, variable determination should be easy for data scientists to recall. Therefore, data scientists can begin programming in Python with the following syntax.

variable = "alphabetic data"
variable = numeric data

From the syntax, data scientists can pack alphabetic and numeric data into variables and display the data through "print" command as presented in the example below.

In the figure, the variable name contains the alphabetic data "Jirapon Sunkpho" and variable *age* contains the numeric data which is 50. The data within the variable are then output via "print" command. After the data scientists have filled the data into the variable, they can also perform mathematical operations on those variables to process the data as in this grammatical syntax.

variable = variable arithmetic operator variable

From the syntax, data scientists can pack numerical data into variables. The variables are then performed with mathematical operations to obtain the result. Then the result is displayed via the print command as shown in Figure 4.

Figure 2. Example of variable determination

```
name = "Jirapon Sunkpho"
age = 50
print(name)
print(age)
```

```
Jirapon Sunkpho
```

Figure 3. An example of using variables to perform arithmetic operation

```
num1 = 5
num2 = 8
num3 = num1 + num2
print(num3)
```

In this example, variable *num1* contains 5, variable *num2* contains 8. When the numbers of num1 and num2 are added together, it equals 13. It is then put into *num3* and output through *print* command. According to the definition of alphabetic and numeric variables, within Python the types of variables used in computation are defined as *float* which represents a real number such as 0.5, and int which represents an integer such as 5. Data scientists can examine the type of data within a variable as in the syntax.

print(type(variable))

From the syntax, data scientists can use *type* command to check the data type within the variable by working in accordance with the *print* statement, as shown below.

Figure 4. Types of variables

```
ex = 6
print(type(ex))

ed = 9.0
```

In the figure, variable *ex* contains number 6, and the variable *ed* contains number 9.0. When using *print(type())* command to display the data type, the result is an integer, which means variable *ex* contains integer-like data. And when displaying the data in variable *ed*, it is number 9.0 which is a decimal number. When data scientists intend to change the variable type for data processing, the programs can be written as in the following syntax.

print(int(variable))
print(float(variable))

From the syntax, data scientists can use *int* command to convert *float* variables into *int*, and use *float* command to convert *int* variable into *float*, as shown below.

Figure 5. Converting the data type

```
ed = 9.0
ex = 6
print(int(ed))
print(float(ex))
```

In the figure, variable *ed* contains number 9.0, which is float or real number, and variable *ex* contains 6, which is *int* or an integer. Data scientists can convert the data type; for variable *ed*, *print(int(ed))* command is used to convert the data type from *float* to *int*, changing the result is from 9.0 to 9, and for variable *ex*, *print(float(ex))* command is used to change the data type from *int* to *float*, changing the result from 6 to 6.0.

Mathematics Operation

Regarding the operation of variables with numbers within Python, mathematical operators are provided for data scientists to use in conjunction with the algorithms of data mining techniques.

Table 1. Mathematical operators in Python

Operator	Meaning	Example
+	plus	a+b
-	minus	a-b
*	multiply	a*b
/	divide	a/b
%	Modulus	a%b
**	exponentiation	a**b

Within Python, there is a sequence of interpretations of math operators, and the Interpreter performs the calculation of multiply, divide, plus and minus, respectively. Therefore, when data scientists design computational algorithms for each model, it cannot decipher the formula in usual sequence, being from left to right. Instead, it is important to consider the sequence in which the interpreter translates the language in order to obtain the correct data analysis results. The example of data sequencing is as follows.

Figure 6. An example of a mathematical operation

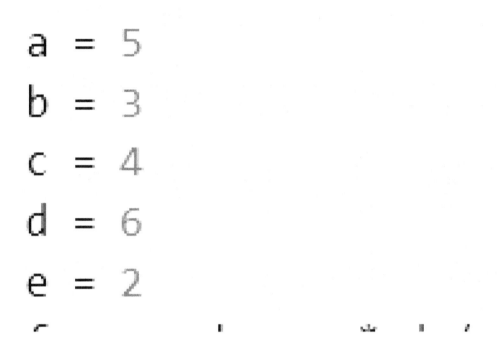

In the example, variable *a* contains number 5, variable *b* contains number 3, variable *c* contains number 4, variable *d* contains number 6, and variable *e* contains number 2. The mathematical calculations are then performed starting with multiplication, division, addition and subtraction respectively until the result is -4.0. Meanwhile, the data scientists can sort mathematical operations with parentheses to arrange the operations in addition, subtraction, multiplication, and division in sequence until the result is 12.0.

In addition to performing mathematical operations with variables, Python also provides other types of operations to reduce programming time.

From the table, data scientists can change the configuration format to reduce programming time. For example, *c = c + 3* means taking the value inside variable c to add with the number 3 and then putting it back into variable *c*. Data scientists can write programs in the form *c=+3* in order to obtain the results of the processing as in the example.

In the example, variable *h* and *g* have a starting value of 0. Then *h = h + 3*, so *h* is set as 3. The writing style is then converted to *g +=3*, and the same result is obtained; *g* equals 3. Data scientists can change their programming style in such a way to reduce programming time.

Table 2. Syntax and configuration examples within Python variables

Operators Used to Assign Variable Values	Example	Writing a Set of Commands Without Using Operators for Configuration
=	c = 3	c = 3
+=	c += 3	c = c + 3
-=	c -= 3	c = c - 3
*=	c *= 3	c = c * 3
/=	c /= 3	c = c / 3
%=	c %= 3	c = c % 3
//=	c //= 3	c = c // 3
**=	c **= 3	c = c ** 3
&=	c &= 3	c = c & 3
|=	c |= 3	c = c | 3
^=	c ^= 3	c = c ^ 3
>>=	c >>= 3	c = c >> 3
<<=	c <<= 3	c = c << 3

Figure 7. Converting the configuration style

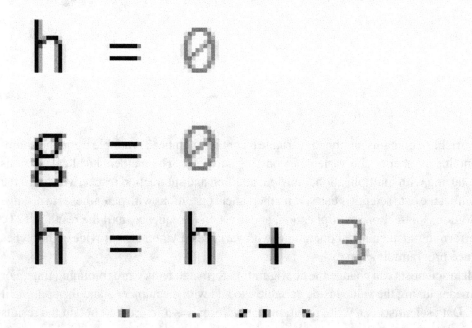

Logic Operation

Data scientists can process data within variables with logical data types or *True* and *False* data types according to the following processing conditions.

Table 3. Logical operators within Python

Logical Operators	Meaning	Example
and	True and True are resulted as True. Otherwise, it is false in all cases.	a and b
or	False or False are resulted as False Otherwise, it is true in all cases.	a or b
not	True and False values within a variable are transformed into the opposite values.	not a

From the table, when data scientists intend to process *Boolean* data, they can write a program as follows.

Figure 8. Logical data processing

```
a = True
b = True
c = a and b
```

As shown in the figure, logical value of variables *a* and *b* are assigned as *True*. The logical operator *and*, variables *a* and *b* are obtained. And then the data is put into variable *c*, and the result is presented as *True* via the *print* command, where *True* and *True* is always *true*, otherwise it is *false* in all cases. When variables *a* and *b* are executed with logical operator *or*, and the data are put into variable *d*, the result is *True* because *False or False* is *False*; otherwise, *True* in all cases. And in the last command, *not a* has changed the value *True* into *False*. It is then put into the variable *f* and output through the *print* command.

Comparation Operation

Whenever data scientists intend to compare the values contained within variables, comparative operations can be used. If the result of the comparison is true, it will get *True* value, and if the result is false, it will get *False* value as presented in the table.

Table 4. Comparative operators

Operators	Meaning	Example
>	The greater-than sign is used to compare values within variables. The result is *True* if the value in the first variable is greater than the value in the second variable; otherwise, it is *False* in all cases.	a > b
<	The less-than sign is used to compare values within variables. The result is *True* if the value in the first variable is less than the value in the second variable; otherwise, it is *False* in all cases.	a < b
==	The equals sign will get the result True when the values inside both variables are equal; otherwise, it is *False* in all cases.	a == b
!=	The not equals sign will get the result *True* when the values inside the two variables are not equal; otherwise, it is *False* in all cases.	a != b
>=	Either the greater-than sign or equal sign is used to compare values within variables. The result is *True* if the value in the first variable is greater than or equal to the value in the second variable; otherwise, it is False in all cases.	a >= b
<=	Either the less-than or equal sign is used to compare values within variables. The result is *True* if the value in the first variable is less than or equal to the value in the second variable; otherwise, it is *False* in all cases.	a <= b

From the tables, data scientists can compare values within variables by programming as presented in the example.

Figure 9. An example of using comparison operators

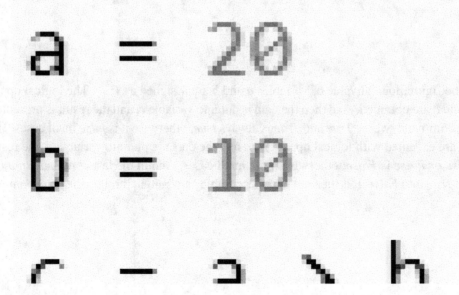

In the example, variable *a* contains number 20 and variable *b* contains 10. If *a* is greater than *b*, the result is *True* because the value in variable *a* is greater than the value in variable *b*. When *a* is less than *b*, the result is obtained as *False* because the value in variable *a* is not greater than the value in variable *b*.

CONDITIONAL OPERATION

When data scientists intend to use logical and comparative operators to command a digital device in order to perform a particular action or repeat it, they can use the following control commands.

1.   *if* Condition

When data scientists run a digital device in cases of logic and comparison operations, they can be program it according to the following syntax.

if condition:
command

From the syntax, an operation takes place when the result of a condition is **True**. The data scientists can write a program as follows.

Figure 10. Using if command

```
a = 10
if a == 10:
    print("Digital Transformation")


Digital Transformation
```

In the figure, *variable a* contains number 10, and *if* command is then used to compare whether the value in variable *a* is equal to 10 or not. When executing the command set and the result is *True*, the command after the colon is then executed. It is to display the message "Digital Transformation" through the *print* command.

In case data scientists wants run a digital device when the result is *false*, it can be programmed with the following syntax.

if condition:
command
else:
command

From the syntax, when the result is *True*, the command set will execute the command after the colon. And if it is *False*, the command set will execute the command after the *else*: command. Data scientists can write a program as follows:

Figure 11. Operation in case of getting result false

```
a = 9
if a == 10:
    print("Digital Transformation")
else:
    print("College of Innovation")

College of Innovation
```

In the figure, in case the condition result is *False,* data scientists can run a digital device by writing a set of command after the *else* command. As in the example, variable *a* has a value of 9. When the command is equal to 10, the result is *False*. The device is run after the *else* command, and the word "College of Innovation" is then displayed through the *print* command.

In case that data scientists intend to create conditions for commanding digital devices to work with more complexity, they can write a program using the following syntax.

if condition:
command
elif condition:
command
elif condition:
command
else:
command

Based on the syntax, data scientists can design multiple choices of commands. If the result of the 1st condition is *True*, the first set command set will be executed. On the other hand, if the result is *False*, the command set will compare the second condition, and if it is *True*, the second statement is executed. If the result is *False*, the instruction set will then compares the 3rd condition, and if *True*, the 3rd statement is executed. And if *False*, the last statement is executed. Data scientists can write a program as follows.

Figure 12. Example of using complex conditions

```
a = 5
if a > 10:
    print("Digital Transformation")
elif a > 8 :
    print("College of Innovation")
elif a > 6:
    print("Business Analytics")
else:
```

In this example, the data scientists determine that there are a total of 4 alternative commands, initializing variable *a* to 5. Condition 1 checks whether the value in variable *a* is greater than 10. When receiving the result as *False*, it jumps to check the 2nd condition whether the value in variable *a* is greater than 8 or not. When the result is *False*, it jumps to check the 3nd condition whether the value in variable *a* is greater than 6. And when the result is *False* again, it executes the command after ***else***: displaying the word "Design Thinking".

2.   Loop

When data scientists expect iterative operations, it can be either of loop statements within Python: the *for* statement or the *while* statement.

a.   *For* Loop

The *for* loop syntax can be divided into two; *for Loop 1* is only when within a specified range, and *for Loop 2* represents the values contained within the variable according to the following syntax.

for Loop 1: Using the *for* command along with specifying the range
for i in range(n):
command

From the syntax, the scientists are required to assign an ending so that the *for* loop repeats the specified cycles. The program can be written as in the following example.

Figure 13. Iteration using the for command, for Loop 1

```
n = 5
for a in range(n):
    print("Digital Transformation")

Digital Transformation
Digital Transformation
Digital Transformation
Digital Transformation
```

In the figure, the data scientists assign a range of data determining the variable *n* as 5, and then uses a *for loop* to render the term "Digital Transformation" for 5 times. In such this loop, the initialization does not need to be set, and the routine will repeat according to the end of the configuration cycle.

for Loop 2: Iteration to show values inside variables
for i in variable:
command

Iterating with the *for* command in *for Loop 2* method, data scientists can iterate over the amount of data within variables, and can write the program as follows.

Figure 14. Iterating using the for command, for Loop 2 method

```
n = [1,2,3,4,5]
for i in n:
    print(n)
```

In the figure, the data scientists pack 1 – 5 data into variable *n*, then using the *for* command to display the value inside variable *n* for 5 times, according to the number within variable *n*. The data scientists can also use the loop in text rendering where the command set will operate according to the loop cycle equal to the number within the variable.

b.   *While* Loop

When data scientists intend to perform the iteration while the conditional result is *True*, the *while* command can be used for iteration with the following syntax.

Initialization of variables
while variable default condition:
command
Increasing or decreasing the value of the initialized variables

From the syntax, the data scientists initialize the variables used for iteration control. Then the *while* command is used to check the condition. If the result of the condition is *True*, the given command is executed. Then the value within the variable is increased or decreased in order to check the condition again. If the result of the conditional check appears to be *False*, it exits the loop. The program can be written as in the example below.

Figure 15. Using the while statement

```
i = 1


while i <= 10:
```

As in the example, data scientists initialize variable *i*. The *while* command then checks if the value inside variable *i* is less than or equal to 10. If the result is *True*, it displays the value inside variable *i* through the *print* command. Then the variable *i* value is increased in order to create loops until the value inside variable *i* is not greater than or equal to 10. If the result of the condition is *False*, it will exit the iteration.

c.   Exiting the loops with the *Break* command

When data scientists use the *while* command for iterative operations. If the data scientists intend to exit the loops, the *break* command can be used as in the following syntax.

```
while True:
command
adding the iterative value
if condition:
break
```

From the syntax, data scientists can run a digital device to iterate while the value obtained through the *while* command is *true*, and incrementally increment the value to perform iteration. To exist the loop command is when the *while* command is checked and the value is *False*. If data scientists intend to exit the loop by adding conditions, they can create conditions with *if* command and then use the *break* command to exit the loop if the value checked through the *if* command is *True*. A program can be written as follows.

Figure 16. Exiting the loops with the break command

```
i = 1

while i <= 10:
```

In this example, the data scientists initialize the variable *i* to 1 by repeating the value inside the variable *i* while the value inside the variable *i* is less than or equal to 10. The value is continually increased until the value inside *i* is obtained as *False*. However, data scientists can exit the loop with the break command when the value inside the variable *i* equals 5.

d.   Excluding processing within the loop with the *Continue* command

When data scientists use the *for loop* command, some loops can be skipped. If the aforementioned loops meet the defined conditioned, to skip, they can use the *continue* command as in the following syntax.

if condition:
continue
command

From the syntax, the data scientists can skip the execution of the command set if the value received from the condition is *True*. And they can skip the execution of the command with the *continue* command, and execute the command when the condition is *false*. The program can be written as follows.

Figure 17. Skipping the loops with the continue command

```
for i in range(10):
    if i == 5:
        continue
    print(i)
```

As in the example, the data scientists use the *for loop* to represent numbers from 0 to 9. It iterates to represent the value in variable *i* only if the value obtained in the *for loop* is *True*, which is in the specified data range. And the *continue* command is used to skip the execution of the commands when the value inside the variable *i* is 5. Therefore, when executing the command set, displaying numbers 0 to 9 except 5. It corresponds to the exception of executing the command set using of the *continue* command.

BASIC OF DATA STRUCTURE

When data scientists intend to store multiple data within a single variable; importing a data set from a computer into Python command set, each variable needs to put a large amount of data into a single variable. Scientists need to manage and access data within different types of data structures.

List

Data scientists can pack multiple amounts of data into *List* variable. The syntax for creating *List* is as follows.

variable = [data, data, …, data]

From the syntax, a single variable acts as *List* by storing multiple data in square brackets. Data scientists can create *List* as follows.

Figure 18. Creating list

```
i = [1, 3, 5, 7, 9 ]
print(i)
```

As in the example, data scientists can create the variable *i* to store all five numeric data; consisting of 1, 3, 5, 7, and 9 respectively, and then display them via the *print* command.

Managing Data Within *List*

Data scientists can use commands to access and manipulate data within List, either by adding data to a list, replacing existing data or deleting data with the following syntax.

Syntax 1: Adding data to *list*, Method 1
variable += ['data', 'data']

According to Syntax 1, data scientists can use *list* variable to add new data into the *list* using *symbol* +=. The newly added data will come after the previously added data.

Syntax 2: Adding data to *list*, Method 2
variable.append('data')

According to Syntax 2, data scientists can add data to the end of the current data by using the *.append* command. Data scientists can choose to use either syntax 1 or 2 in their programming.

Syntax 3: Replacing the existing data
variable[data location] = "data"

According to Syntax 3, when data scientists intend to replace existing data within *list*, they can refer to the data location within the *list* and insert the new data into it.

Syntax 4: Deleting data within the list
variable[data range] = [ ]

According to Syntax 4, the data scientists can specify the location of the data to be deleted, and fill in a blank value to replace that location. Then, the appended data of the deleted data will be replaced the empty position.

Data scientists can program all the four syntaxes as follows:

Figure 19. Managing data within list

```
staffs = ['Jirapon', 'Sarawut', 'Chayakrit', 'Kannapa']
print(staffs)

staffs += ['Kom', 'Noppol']
print(staffs)

staffs.append('Jiroj')
print(staffs)

staffs[5] ="Jibby"
print(staffs)

staffs[1:3] = []
print(staffs)
```

In the example, data scientists create variables that act as *list* called *staffs*, containing *Jirapon* data in position 0, *Sarawut* data in position 1, *Chayakrit* data in position 2, and *Kannapa* data in position 3. Data are then displayed through the *print* command.

Kom data is then added to position 4 and *Noppol* data to position 5 with +=, and the data is displayed with the *print* command. The *Kom* and *Noppol* data are appended to the preceding data within *List*.

In the next operation, data scientists add *Jiroj* data to position 6 with the *.append* command, and then display it via the *print* command. When the data scientists intend to replace the data in position 5, formerly *Noppol*, with the data *Jibby*, so they can refer the position of the data and put the new data to replace it and display it through the *print* command.

When the data scientists determine that the location of data to be deleted is positions 1 and 2. Next, the data is then replaced. As shown by the *print* command, the deletion of an item from a *list* is performed to the position before the deletion's final digit.

Dictionary Key and Values

When data scientists want to provide a variable that packs multiple types of data into one variable, they can write a program with the following syntax.

Syntax 1: Creating a dictionary
variable = {key: value}, …, {key: value}

According to Syntax 1, data scientists can create a dictionary consisting of a set of data that acts as keys and values, both of which can be either numeric or alphabetic.

Syntax 2: Adding data into the dictionary
variable[key] = value

From syntax 2, data scientists can add key and value data to the dictionary by appending the existing data.

Syntax 3: Removing data from the dictionary
del variable[key]

From syntax 3, data scientists can delete data within a dictionary using the *del* command, and refer the keys needed to delete. After execution, the referred keys and values are deleted from the dictionary.

Syntax 4: Displaying data of all keys and values within a dictionary
variable.keys()
variable.values()

From syntax 4, data scientists can display all data in a dictionary. It displays all keys and all values via the *print* command.

With these four syntaxes, data scientists can write programs to manipulate dictionaries as in the example.

As in the example, data scientists create a dictionary by filling the data into the *students* variable consisting of 3 sets of letter keys and numeric values, and the result is displayed. Then, a new set of data is added into the variables before displaying them again. The newly added data is appended to the existing data.

Figure 20. Manipulating the dictionary

```python
students = {"Jirapa": 123, "Janira": 567, "Yonrada": 891}
print(students)

students["Jirakan"] = 345
print(students)

del students['Jirapa']
print(students)

print(students.keys())

print(students.values())
```

Data scientists can then delete the data from the dictionary by referring the keys using the *del* command. As seen in the example, the data scientists referred the *Jirapa* key, so after re-rendering the data, the *Jirapa* key and the value 123 are then removed from the dictionary.

The data scientists can render all key data within a dictionary using *.keys()* and returns only the values of all data within a dictionary using *.values()*.

Searching for Data With Keywords

Where scientists store large amounts of data in variables that function as *list* or a dictionary, they can search for the data using the following syntax.

Syntax 1: Searching for data from the list
"keyword" in variable

According to syntax 1, data scientists can search for data within a list and display it via the *print* command.

Syntax 2: Searching for data from the dictionary
'keyword' in variable

Using syntax 2, the data scientists can search for data within a dictionary and display it through the *print* command.

With both syntaxes, data scientists can program the search of data in the list and the dictionary as follows.

Figure 21. Searching data with keywords

```
staffs_list = ["Sunkpho", "Ramjan", "Campiranon"]

print("Ramjan" in staffs_list)

staffs_dict = {"Sunkpho":1, "Ramjan":2, "Campiranon":3}

print('Sunkpho' in staffs_dict)



True
True
```

As in the example, data scientists create the list containing *Sunkpho, Ramjan, and Campiranon* data respectively. Then, it searches for *Ramjan* within the *staffs_list* variable and displays it through the *print* command, and the result is *True*, which means the data is contained within the list. Then a dictionary is created. It contains data including *Sunkpho:1, Ramjan:2,* and *Campiranon:3*. Then *Sunkpho* data is searched within the *staffs_dict* variable, which acts as a dictionary, and the result is *True*, which means the data is actually contained in the dictionary.

IMPORTING DATA INTO A COMMAND SET (FILE I/O)

When data scientists intend to put data into a set of instructions for processing with various techniques, they can use commands within Python to read the data by inputting data via the keyboard and creating *.txt* format files.

Importing Data Into the Command Set via a Keyboard

In the case that data scientists intend to input data into the command set via a keyboard, they can write a program with the following syntax.

variable = input("alt text")

From the syntax, data scientists can write a program to input data into the command set via the keyboard as in the example.

Figure 22. Importing data into the command set via keyboard

```
aa = input("Please enter number")
print(aa)
```

```
Please enter number20
20
```

In this example, data scientists input data into variables via a keyboard using the *input* command, where number 20 is inserted into variable *aa,* and the value is displayed inside variable *aa* on the keyboard.

Creating and Manipulating Text Files

Data scientists can create *a .txt, Text File*, which supports writing data into that file. It can also bring the written data into the file displayed on the screen. The syntax for writing and reading data within the file is as follows.

Syntax 1: Writing data into the *text file*
file variable = open("file name *.txt", "w+"*)
file variable *.write*("data")
file variable. *close*()

Based on syntax 1, data scientists can create *.txt* file by naming the file and using *w+* mode for writing data into *text file* with the *open* function. The file is then put into the file-holding variables. Data scientists can use the *.write()* method to write data and the *.close()* method to close the file.

Syntax 2: Reading data from the *text file*
file variable = open("file name *.txt", "r+*")
variable = file variable.*read*(character count)
print (variable)
File variable.*close*()

According to syntax 2, data scientists can open a file with *open* function, using *r+* mode to read the data from the *Text File*. The data are then imported from the *Text File* into a variable using the. *read* method, and the data are displayed through *Print* command, The file can be closed with the *close( )* method.

Data scientists can write a program to create a file, write data and read text file as shown in the example below.

Figure 23. Creating a File, writing and reading data from text file

```
aa = open("aa.txt", "w+")
aa.write( "Digital Transformation and Innovation")
aa.close()


bb = open("aa.txt","r+")
str = bb.read(40)
print("Output are : ", str)
bb.close()



Output are :  Digital Transformation and Innovation
```

In the figure, data scientists can create a file named *aa* using the *open* function. And *w+* mode is used to write data into the *Text File* via the *.write* method. As in the example, data scientists can write the Digital Transformation and Innovation data on the *Text File*, and then close the file with the *.close( )* detach method.

After that, data scientists reopen the *aa* file, use *r+* mode to read the data in the *text file*, load the file into the *bb* variable, and then execute the *.read* command, which reads all 40 characters. Later the data are filled into the *str* variable, which sdisplay the data through the *print* statement. Then the file is closed again with the *.close( )* method.

EXCEPTION HANDLING

In case an error occurs during processing, it causes the program to stop working. When the command set does not find the files or data required to process, data scientists can use *Exception Handling* to skip the error, so that the command set can continue processing. The syntax is as follows.

Try:
command
except, type of exception:
command
else:
command

According to the syntax, data scientists put all commands to be processed inside *try:* After that, if during processing occurs any error, process it inside *except*. And if there is no error, process it inside *else:*

The *except* processing occurs only when there is an error as specified; an *IOError* which occurs the command set is unable to open the file, or *SyntaxError* which is caused by a syntax error whiling writing a program. Within a command set, the *except* command can be written in a number of cases; when checking for both *IOError* and *SyntaxError* after processing *with try:* Data scientists can write a command set covered by *Exception Handling*, as in the example.

Figure 24. Using exception handling in case the command fails to open the text file

```
try:
    aa = open("dd.txt", "r+")
    aa.write("Test")
except IOError:
    print("I could not find a text file")
else:
    print("Everything Correct")
    aa.close()

I could not find a text file
```

As in the example, data scientists write a command set with *try:* to open and read a *text* file called *dd.txt*, which hasn't been created before. Therefore, the *IOError* exception condition is met, so the command executes the *print* statement *"I could not find a text file"* and terminates it. In another case, if the statement under *try:* is valid, it will be displayed as follows.

Figure 25. Using exception handling in case the command set can open files

```
try:
    aa = open("aa.txt", "r+")
    aa.write("Test")
except IOError:
    print("I could not find a text file")
else:
    print("Everything Correct")
    aa.close()
```

As shown in the figure, the command can open *Text File* named *aa.txt*, which is a pre-written file. The command is then executed after *else:* which is to display the statement *"Everything Correct"* and close the file with the. *close ()* method.

USING GOOGLE COLAB

Data scientists can choose from a wide variety of software editors either by installing on the computer or in processing through the web such as Google Colab. Google Colab also has an Interpreter set ready to translate any Python language with no additional setup required. And all files are stored on Google Colab's memory without the need to store them on a computer.

Data scientists can access Google Colab by registering for gmail such as ramjan77@gmail.com, then login to use Google services, then enter Google Colab through the link is https://colab.research.google.com, and enter to open the file for programming as seen in the picture below.

Figure 26. Creating a programming file

Examples	Recent	Google Drive	GitHub	Upload

Filter notebooks

Title	Last opened ▼	First opened ▼	🗑
⊙ Welcome To Colaboratory	4:37 PM	Jan 28, 2020	↗
▲ Untitled67.ipynb	4:01 PM	4:01 PM	⬛ ↗
▲ File I/O	10:52 AM	May 12	⬛ ↗
▲ Test	May 11	May 11	⬛ ↗
▲ Untitled63.ipynb	April 18	Nov 16, 2020	⬛ ↗

From the figure, data scientists select NEW NOTEBOOK to create a file for programming. And if intending to continue working from the created file, they can select the file name that appears or search from Google Drive and start working, as shown in the picture below.

Figure 27. Getting started with Google Colab

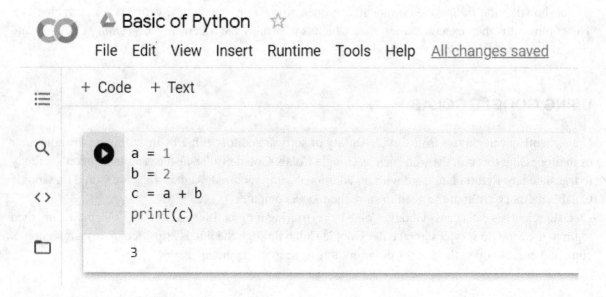

Once data scientists enter a file created by Google Colab, they can write a command set in Python. Then the command set is tested by pressing the Run Cell key or using the *Ctrl + Enter* key to execute the command with the *Interpreter* in Google Colab. The result is presented below the command set. To write additional commands without creating new files, data scientists can press the *+ Code* button.

Figure 28. Writing additional commands

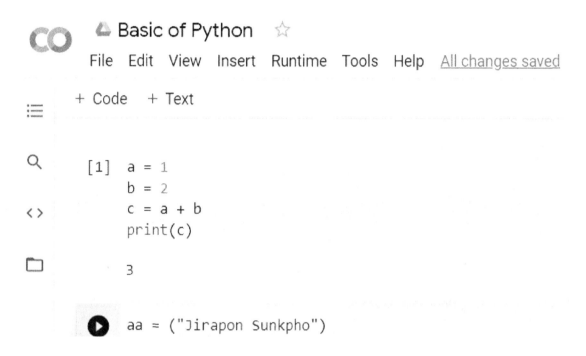

As in the figure above, data scientists can write multiple commands in a single file without affecting previously programmed commands. Another outstanding use of Google Colab is the display of possible commands. For example, if the scientists type *Ex* into Google Colab, it will show possible commands for data scientists to choose, which is to reduce programming errors.

When data scientists intend to create a new file or access the file stored on Google Drive, they can go to the *file* menu and select New Notebook to create a new file and select Open Notebook to access the old file.

Once logging into Google Colab, data scientists can share the created files with other data scientists, and those who have shared the files can also edit them along with those who own the original files. The results of processing with Google Colab are very nice for visualization, making Google Colab a popular software editor in data science.

Figure 29. Showing possible commands by Gogole Colab

Figure 30. Creating new files and accessing the old files

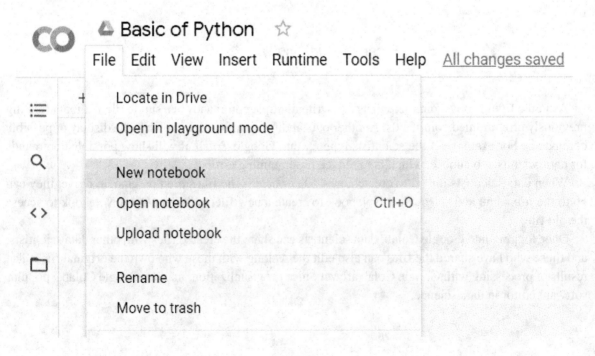

CONCLUSION

Data scientists can use Python's as an open source to process big data while reducing the cost of digital resource investments. Python also provides libraries, providing a set of commands for data processing. As a result, Python has become a powerful tool in data science and a computer language that scientists should study as a foundation for future studies. This book introduces the basic commands that data scientists need to study before writing a program to put data into a set of commands, and displaying data in various formats.

Google Colab is a software editor that can be used to write commands in Python. It also provides libraries that store command sets for data mining processing. Data scientists can do experiments, write command sets and test them via the web, without installing software on a computer.

EXERCISE QUESTIONS

1. Write a program in Python to get 2 numbers from the keyboard, then add, subtract, multiply, divide and display the result through the screen.
2. Write a program in Python to get the pork weight from the keyboard, then multiply the weight by $2 to calculate the pork price that the customer has to pay the pork shop.
3. Write a program for a hamburger restaurant to serve customers.
    ◦   If the customer wants a beef hamburger, press number 1.
        ▪   Have the customer enter the number of hamburgers on the keyboard. Then multiply the number of hamburgers by 4 dollars and show the price that the customer has to pay on the screen.
    ◦   If the customer wants a pork hamburger, press the number 2.
        ▪   Have the customer enter the number of hamburgers on the keyboard. Then multiply the number of hamburgers by 3 dollars and show the price that the customer has to pay on the screen.
    ◦   If the customer presses another number, it will alert "Choose between numbers 1 and 2".
4. Write a program to get scores from the keyboard.
    ◦   If the score is between 80 - 100, show the letter *A* on the screen.
    ◦   If the score is between 70 - 79, show the letter *B* on the screen.
    ◦   If the score is between 60 - 69, show the letter *C* on the screen.
    ◦   If the score is between 50 - 59, show the letter *D* on the screen.
    ◦   If the score is between 0 - 49, show the letter *F* on the screen.
    ◦   If the score is more than 100 or less than 0, display a message "Please enter your score from 0 – 100"
    ◦   If the user wants to redo, press Y, and to exit, press Q using While Loop

REFERENCES

Bader, D. (2018). *Python tricks: The book*. Dan Bader.

Bowles, M. (2015). *Machine learning in Python: essential techniques for predictive analysis*. Wiley. doi:10.1002/9781119183600

Hill, C. (2015). *Learning scientific programming with Python*. Cambridge University Press. doi:10.1017/CBO9781139871754

Joshi, P. (2017). *Artificial intelligence with Python: a comprehensive guide to building intelligent apps for Python beginners and developers*. Packt Publishing Ltd.

Lubanovic, B. (2019). *Introducing Python: modern computing in simple packages* (2nd ed.). O'Reilly Media, Inc.

Mueller, J. (2018). *Beginning programming with Python* (2nd ed.). John Wiley & Sons.

Raschka, S., & Mirajalili, V. (2018). *Python machine learning: machine learning and deep learning with Python, scikit-learn, and TensorFlow* (2nd ed.). Packt Publishing.

Reges, S., Obourn, A., & Stepp, M. (2019). *Building Python programs* (1st ed.). Pearson.

Sneeringer, L. (2016). *Professional Python*. WROX/John Wiley & Sons.

Stewart, J. (2017). *Python for scientists* (2nd ed.). Cambridge University Press. doi:10.1017/9781108120241

Sunkpho, S., & Ramjan, S. (2020). *Introduction to Python Programming for Data Science*. Thammasat Press.

Tananatong, T., & Ramjan, S. (2022). *Data Visualization Design and Development for Data Science*. Thammasat Press.

Zelle, J. M. (2010). *Python programming: an introduction to computer science* (2nd ed.). Beedle & Associates.

Chapter 12
Data Mining for Junior Data Scientists:
Data Analytics With Python

ABSTRACT

It is crucial for junior data scientists to learn computer programming as data science software packages may not always cater to the requirements of data analysis. Python provides a vast library of algorithms for data analysis, including NumPy, Pandas, Matplotlib, Seaborn, and Scikit-learn. NumPy and Pandas aid in organizing datasets as part of the pre-processing stage, while Matplotlib and Seaborn offer a range of data visualization commands. These visualization tools are instrumental in data exploration processes, such as creating histograms and scatter plots, and displaying data mining results like cluster analysis outcomes. Scikit-learn is a popular library in the data science industry that offers various data mining commands for regression, decision constructs, and cluster analysis, covering both supervised and unsupervised learning. Therefore, junior data scientists must learn Python programming for data science applications, especially when using software packages that require editing the model using Python commands.

INTRODUCTION

Nowadays, there are tools used for analyzing data during the workflow; the data extraction tools, data survey tools, data preparation tools, Data Analysis Tools with Data Mining Techniques and Data Visualization tools. Each step has a ready-to-use software in both instant software and language programming software. Python is a tool that supports the entire workflow as it can be used for data analysis purposes; manipulating datasets, importing routines, developing data visualization, and data analysis with data mining techniques using libraries (Massaron & Mueller, 2015: Mueller & Massaron, 2019).

DOI: 10.4018/978-1-6684-4730-7.ch012

NumPy Library

The NumPy library provides a set of commands that data scientists can execute to manipulate imported datasets and then process them within Python's command set. The library focuses on compiling data into the format ready to process with data mining techniques:

Array

Python supports storing data in arrays, which are in rows and columns. Array variables can store data of one to more dimensions. The structure is as follows:

Table 1. Dimension array

	Column 0
Row 0	0,0
Row 1	1,0
Row 2	2,0
Row.	.
Row.	.
Row n	n,0

From the table, data scientists can store data as a 1-dimensional array with records starting from 1 row and 1 column. Inside array variables, the location of the data is specified at row 0 and columns 0. For example, the number 2 might be contained in row 0 and column 0. When data scientists store more than 1 column, a 2-dimensional array variable can be created with the following structure:

Table 2. Dimension array

	Column 0	Column 1	Column 2	Column .	Column .	Column n
Row 0	0,0	0,1	0,2	0,.	0,.	0,n
Row 1	1,0	1,1	1,2	1,.	1,.	1,n
Row 2	2,0	2,1	2,2	2,.	2,.	2,n
Row .	.,0	.,1	.,2	.,.	.,.	.,n
Row .	.,0	.,1	.,2	.,.	.,.	.,n
Row n	n,0	n,1	n,2	n,.	n,.	n,n

From the table, data scientists can store data in multiple rows and columns simultaneously. For example, the numeric data 25 may be positioned in Row 5, Column 3. By storing data in this manner, the data scientists can design data structures with good memory management.

Therefore, when manipulating with datasets that require array variables to store data, data scientists can run commands from the *NumPy* library with the following syntax:

import numpy as the variable that executes command sets
    Array variable = the variable that executes the *.array* command([data,data..data])

From the syntax, data scientists can invoke *.array* commands from the *NumPy* library to create array variables, which can be programmed as in the example.

Figure 1. Using commands to create array variables

```
import numpy as mm
a = mm.array([5,6,7])
print(a)


[5 6 7]
```

In the figure, the data scientist invokes an *.array* command from *NumPy* library where variable *mm* executes the command to generate array data of 5, 6, and 7, respectively. Then the data are packed into variable *a* and displayed via *print* command

When data scientists intend to store data as a 2-dimension array, they can also use the *.array* command from the *NumPy* library. The syntax is as follows:

import numpy as the variable that executes command sets
    Array variable = the variable that executes the *.array* command([(data,data..data), (data,data..data)])

From the syntax, data scientists can add the second data. In Python, the data inside the parentheses is counted as 1 row.

Figure 2. Using commands to create a two-dimensional array

```
import numpy as mm
a = mm.array([(5,6,7),(8,9,10)])
print(a)


[[ 5  6  7]
 [ 8  9 10]]
```

In the figure, data scientists use variable *mm* to invoke the *.array* command from the *NumPy* library and generate two datasets; 5, 6, 7 as in set 1, and 8, 9, 10 as in set 2. Then, the data is put into variable *a* and displayed through the *print* command.

Creating Array Data With .arange

Within the *NumPy* library, there is also a set of *.arange* commands that data scientists can use to create a series of numbers, the array variables, for other usages. The syntax is as follows:

import numpy as the variable that executes command sets
    print(variable that executes the *.arange* command(number of numbers))

Based on the syntax, the data scientists get the variable to invoke *.arange* command from the *NumPy* library and then specify a number to display via the *print* command. The set of numbers starts from 0 to the previous of the specified number. The data scientists can write a program as in the example.

Figure 3. Creating an array dataset with arange

```
import numpy as np
print(np.arange(5))



[0 1 2 3 4]
```

In the figure, the data scientists get an *np* variable to invoke *.arange* command from *NumPy* library, then create a dataset of 5 arrays starting from 0 – 4 and display them via the *print* command.

The .reshape Command

After data scientists have created an array dataset with *.arange* command, they can arrange the data into the specified row and column sizes by using *.reshape* command from *NumPy* library, as in the following syntax.

import numpy as the variable that executes command sets
    print(variable to execute *.arange*(numbers*).reshape*(numbers of rows, numbers of columns)

After creating a dataset with *.arange* command, data scientists can adjust the data into the specified row and column format using *.reshape* command.

Figure 4. Compiling data with reshape

```
import numpy as np
a = np.arange(10).reshape(5,2)
print(a)

[[0 1]
 [2 3]
 [4 5]
 [6 7]
 [8 9]]
```

By creating a dataset containing 10 numbers, from 0 to 9, with *.arange*, the scientists compile the data with *.reshape* command to have 5 rows and 2 columns, pack the data into variable *a*, and then display it via *print* command. In order to compile data with *.reshape* command, data scientists must take into account the data size.

The .linspace Command

Not only the *.arange* statement can be used to create an array of datasets, *the .linspace* command from *NumPy* library can also be used to create periodic datasets.

import numpy as the variable that executes a set of instructions
    the variables that execute *.linspace* (initial number, end number, data frequency)

From the syntax, the data scientists invoke *.linspace* command, defining the initial number and the end number of the created datasets, and defining the frequency of the data amount to be generated in the data range. The program is written as follows.

Figure 5. Creating a dataset with linspace command

```
import numpy as np
print(np.linspace(7, 15, 3))

[ 7. 11. 15.]
```

In the figure, data scientists use *np* variable to invoke *.linsapce* command from *NumPy* library and generate a data range starting from 7 to 15 with the frequency of 3 times. So, the created data are 7, 11 and 15, respectively.

Changing Data Types in Array Variables

When data scientists prepare the array data, they can use *dtype* command to change data types within *array* variables. If the data type is an integer to be changed to a real number, it can be specified as *float*. If the data type is a real number to be changed to an integer number, it can be specified as an *int* with the following syntax:

import numpy as the variable that executes a set of commands
    array variables = the variables that execute .*array*([[(data,data..data), (data,data..data)]], dtype=
        'data type')

From the syntax, after the scientists create an array-like dataset, they can change the data type with *dtype* by writing a program as in the example below.

Figure 6. Changing the data type

```
import numpy as mm
ee = mm.array([[5.8,6.2],[7.1,8.3]],dtype='int')
print(ee.dtype)
print(ee)



int64
[[5 6]
 [7 8]]
```

Based on the figure, data scientists create an array dataset where the internal data is all real numbers, then use *dtype* command to change a real number into an integer. When checking using *dtype* command via *print* command, the result is *int64*, meaning the data inside the variable have been converted into an integer, and the entire results are re-rendered through *print* statement.

Mathematical Operations Within Array

When data scientists intend to transform data with mathematical operation methods, they can take *array* variable containing a dataset to perform the operations as in the following syntax.

import numpy as the variable that executes command sets
    Array variables = the variable that executes .*array*([data])
    Array variables = the variable that executes .*array*([data])
    variable = array variable mathematical operators *array* variables

From the syntax, the scientists can take the created array variables to perform the mathematical operation such as addition, subtraction, multiplication, and division by writing the following program.

Figure 7. Mathematical operation of array variables

```
import numpy as mm
ee = mm.array([7,4])
cc = mm.arange(2)
c = ee - cc
print(c)

[7 3]
```

After the data scientists create the 1ˢᵗ array variable containing the datasets 7 and 4, and create the 2ⁿᵈ array variable containing the datasets 0 and 1, the data in the array variables are mathematical operated, subtracting, through the variables containing the two datasets. The result is then added into variable c. Number 7 is to subtract with 0 to get the result as 7, and number 4 is to subtract with 1 to get the result as 3, respectively.

Creating Array Variables With .random Command

Data scientists can also create datasets with *.random* from *NumPy* library with a range of 0 – 1 as in the syntax below.

import numpy as the variable that executes the command
  variable = the variable that executes the *.random.random* command([number of rows, number of columns])

From the syntax, the scientists can create datasets with values between 0 and 1 within *array* variable using *.random* command, and then specify the number of rows and columns. Data scientists can experiment with programming by the following example.

Figure 8. Creating a dataset with random command

```
import numpy as np
a = np.random.random([3,4])
print(a)

array([[0.52256213, 0.88143325, 0.52947593, 0.04102454],
       [0.01393007, 0.5033998 , 0.18646051, 0.31449915],
       [0.74056756, 0.42395087, 0.12502817, 0.93248877]])
```

In the figure, the data scientists use *np* variable, invoke *.random* command from *NumPy* library, create a dataset ranging from 0 to 1 with 3 rows and 4 columns, and then output the data via *print* command.

Summarizing Array Data

After data scientists have created array datasets, they can summarize that data with commands such as *.sum* to combine numeric data within *array* variable; *.min* to find the smallest number within thearray variable, and *.max* to find the largest number in the array variable, as seen in the following syntax.

import numpy as the variable that executes a set of commands
    Array variable = the variable that executes *.array*([data,data..data])
      print(array variable.sum())
      print(array variable.min())
      print(array variable.max())

From the syntax, data scientists can sum up and find the largest and the smallest values from the *array* variable. The program can be written according to the example.

Figure 9. Summarizing data in array variables

```
import numpy as np
a = np.array([1,3,5,7,9])
print(a.sum())
print(a.min())
print(a.max())

25
1
9
```

In the figure, data scientists create *array* variable consisting of 1, 3, 5, 7, and 9, respectively, then use *.sum* command to sum the data, and get the result as 25. The *.min* command is then used to find the smallest value which is 1, and the *.max* command is used to find the largest value which is 9.

Indexing and Slicing

When data scientists intend to access data by indexing, they can refer to the location to store the data, and the can sort the data by slicing it according to the following syntax:

import numpy as the variable that executes a set of commands
    Array variable = the variable that executes *.array*([data,data..data])
    Array variable[location of data]

Array variable[start position:end position:display frequency)

From the syntax, the scientists can refer the location in order to access the data within that location and manipulate them by displaying in intervals. The program can be written as in the example.

Figure 10. Accessing data locations and intermittent displays

```
import numpy as mm
a = mm.array([5,4,3,2,1,5,4,3,2,1])
print(a[3])
print(a[1:7:2])

2
[4 2 5]
```

Based on the figure, the scientists create *array* variable. The data consist of 5, 4, 3, 2, and 1 respectively, and specify the location in position 3, which is the number 2. The result is displayed through *print* command.

Then, the data is accessed in positions 1-7, and the output is displayed in every 2 positions, resulting via *print* command as 4, 2 and 5 respectively.

10.   Vectorization

When data scientists perform *Attribute Transformation* in the preparation process, they can use *.vectorize* command from *NumPy* library. *Vectorization* is to use small data called *Broadcast* to perform calculations on the dataset in order to change the data. The syntax is as follows.

import numpy as the variable that executes the command
        variable = the variable that executes *.vectorize*(computing function)

From the syntax, the data scientists invoke **.vectorize** command to calculate a small dataset. The program can be written as in the following example.

In the figure, the data scientists get *np* variable to execute *vectorize* command from *NumPy* library. Inside the command, the *abc* function is executed, packing all the data into the *mm* variable, then passing the values 4, 3, 2, and 1 to the *d* parameter, and passing the value 2 to the *e* parameter. If the value inside variable *d* is greater than the value in variable *e*, then subtract the returned values. If it is not greater, then add them. And the result of the calculation is 2, 1, 4 and 3, respectively. In this way, the *vectorize* command can be used to process the data.

Figure 11. Vectorization

```
def abc(d, e):
  if d > e:
    return d - e
  else:
    return d + e

import numpy as np
mm = np.vectorize(abc)
print(mm([4, 3, 2, 1], 2))



[2 1 4 3]
```

PANDAS LIBRARY

When data scientists manipulate and process data with mining techniques, *Pandas* is a critical library used for storing command sets.

Series and Data Frames

Whenever data scientists import data or create datasets within Python, the datasets will be then called a *Data Frame*, and the columns within the dataset are so called *Series*. Data in each raw are called *Instances*, and individual data is called *Data Object*. Data scientists can create a *Series* with the following syntax:

Import pandas as series variables
Series variables.Series([data,data, ….])

From the syntax, the scientists invoke *.Series* command to generate a single column of data by writing the following syntax.

Figure 12. Creating a series

```
import pandas as pd
pd.Series(['Jirapon Sunkpho', 'Sarawut Ramjan', 'Kanapan Pongponrat'])



0        Jirapon Sunkpho
1         Sarawut Ramjan
2     Kanapan Pongponrat
dtype: object
```

In the figure, data scientists use the *pd* variable to invoke a *.Series* command from the pandas library to generate the data within the Series. Then, when the scientists intend to create multiple Series and combine them into a Data Frame, they can writing the program as in the following syntax.

Import pandas as the variable that invokes commands
variables that invoke *.DataFrame*({ column name: series variable})

From the syntax, data scientists can use *.DataFrame* command from the pandas library by naming the column and the generated series variable. The program can be written as follows.

Figure 13. Creating a data frame

```
import pandas as pd
c = pd.Series(['Digital Transformation', 'Service Innovation', 'Creative Industry'])
stu = pd.Series([60, 60, 120])

pd.DataFrame({ 'Curiculums': c, 'Number of Students': stu })
```

	Curiculums	Number of Students
0	Digital Transformation	60
1	Service Innovation	60
2	Creative Industry	120

In the figure, data scientists have created a series of two columns containing the data on the three courses and the number of students in each academic year. Then, the *.DataFrame* command is used to name the Series and connect it with the Series, which is created by referring to variables that store the Series data and combining all the Series into a Data Fame.

Importing Data Into the Command Set

The *Pandas* Library supports data import by importing computer dataset into Python and by importing an Internet dataset into Python command set. To import data from a computer into a command set can be programmed according to the following syntax:

import pandas as the variable that invokes commands
Data Frame variables = Variables that invoke *csv*('file source address')

From the syntax, data scientists can take *.csv* files by accessing the file address and then importing the data into the data frame variables. They can be programmed with *Google Colab* as follows:

Figure 14. Importing data from computer into command set

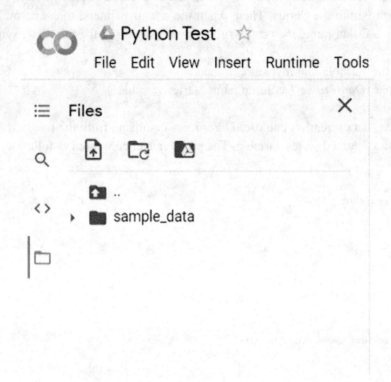

In the figure, the scientists select *Upload to Session Storage*, and then *Google Colab* enters the file address. The scientists can then choose the file intended to import into *Google Colab*. In the example, the file named *chol.txt* is chosen.

From the figure, data scientists can right click on *chol.txt* file and bring the file address to write the program as shown in the example.

In the figure, data scientists use *.read_csv* command to import the dataset from *chol.txt* file into *Google Colab*, then pack all datasets into *cc* variable and display the data via the *print* command.

In case the scientists intend to import any dataset available on the Internet, they can import the file address into *Google Colab* without uploading it. The program can be written according to the following syntax.

import pandas as the variable that invokes commands
Data Frame variable = Variable that invoke *csv*('Internet file source address')

From the syntax, data scientists can refer to the source address of a dataset on the Internet to process the data by writing a program according to the example.

In the figure, data scientists copy the address of the dataset using *read_csv* command from the *Pandas* library.

Figure 15. Entering the file address

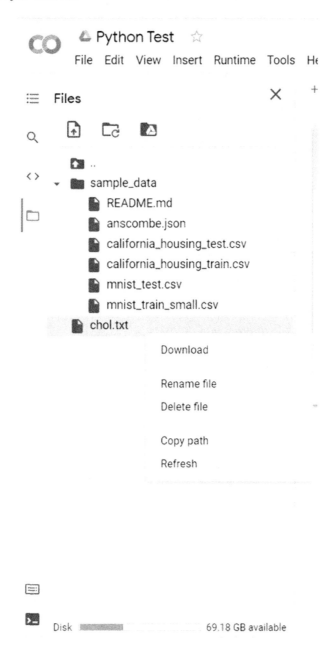

Figure 16. Importing data from a computer into Google Colab

```
import pandas as pd
cc=pd.read_csv("/content/chol.txt")
print(cc)

     AGE HEIGHT WEIGHT CHOL SMOKE BLOOD MORT
0              20 176 77 195 nonsmo b alive
1              53 167 56 250 sigare o dead
2              44 170 80 304 sigare a dead
3              37 173 89 178 nonsmo o alive
4              26 170 71 206 sigare o alive
..                                      ...
195            35 174 57 222 pipe a alive
196            38 172 91 227 nonsmo b alive
197            26 170 60 167 sigare a alive
198            39 165 74 259 sigare o alive
199            49 178 81 275 pipe b alive

[200 rows x 1 columns]
```

Figure 17. Importing data on the Internet into datasets

```
import pandas as pd
cc=pd.read_csv("https://download.mlcc.google.com/mledu-datasets/california_housing_train.csv")
print(cc)

        longitude latitude ... median_income median_house_value
0        -114.31    34.19  ...        1.4936            66900.0
1        -114.47    34.40  ...        1.8200            80100.0
2        -114.56    33.69  ...        1.6509            85700.0
3        -114.57    33.64  ...        3.1917            73400.0
4        -114.57    33.57  ...        1.9250            65500.0
...          ...      ...  ...           ...                ...
16995    -124.26    40.58  ...        2.3571           111400.0
16996    -124.27    40.69  ...        2.5179            79000.0
16997    -124.30    41.84  ...        3.0313           103600.0
16998    -124.30    41.80  ...        1.9797            85800.0
16999    -124.35    40.54  ...        3.0147            94600.0

[17000 rows x 9 columns]
```

Indexing, Selecting, and Filtering

After data scientists import a dataset into Python's programming language, the scientists can begin manipulating the data by referring to each Series within the Data Frame according to the syntax.

variable = the variable that executes command ["named *Series*"]

From the syntax, data scientists can refer to the name *Series* within a data frame, then place all *Instances* from that *Series* into variables and render them as in the example.

Figure 18. Data accessibility (indexing)

```
import pandas as pd
cc=pd.read_csv("/content/sample_data/california_housing_test.csv")
ff=cc["median_income"]
print(ff)


0        6.6085
1        3.5990
2        5.7934
3        6.1359
4        2.9375
          ...
2995     1.1790
2996     3.3906
2997     2.2895
2998     3.2708
2999     8.5608
Name: median_income, Length: 3000, dtype: float64
```

The figure shows how the scientists can be indexing or accessing the series named *median_income* in order to display the data from all *Data Frames*. In other cases, the scientists can access multiple *Series* from the same *Data Frame* in the meantime.

Figure 19. Selecting data

```
import pandas as pd
cc=pd.read_csv("/content/sample_data/california_housing_test.csv")
ff=cc[["median_income","total_bedrooms","population"]]
print(ff)


      median_income  total_bedrooms  population
0            6.6085           661.0      1537.0
1            3.5990           310.0       809.0
2            5.7934           507.0      1484.0
3            6.1359            15.0        49.0
4            2.9375           244.0       850.0
...             ...             ...         ...
2995         1.1790           642.0      1258.0
2996         3.3906          1082.0      3496.0
2997         2.2895           201.0       693.0
2998         3.2708            14.0        46.0
2999         8.5608           263.0       753.0

[3000 rows x 3 columns]
```

According to the figure, data scientists can add the *Series* intended to display using an extra layer of square brackets so that they can cover multiple *Series* in the meantime. As in the example, the data scientists access the *Series* including *median_income, toal_bedrooms,* and population.

When displaying all data, the scientists can also perform filtering to select only the data involved in processing. The program can be written as presented in the following example:

Figure 20. Filtering

```
import pandas as pd
cc=pd.read_csv("/content/sample_data/california_housing_test.csv")
ff = cc[cc['population'] > 1429]
print(ff)
```

```
      longitude  latitude  ...  median_income  median_house_value
0      -122.05     37.37   ...         6.6085            344700.0
2      -117.81     33.78   ...         5.7934            270500.0
8      -122.84     38.40   ...         3.6696            194400.0
9      -118.02     34.08   ...         2.3333            164200.0
13     -117.03     32.97   ...         4.5625            231200.0
...       ...       ...    ...           ...                 ...
2982   -118.28     34.08   ...         3.1607            182000.0
2984   -117.59     33.88   ...         2.6111            107000.0
2987   -121.97     37.29   ...         5.3294            300300.0
2990   -118.23     34.09   ...         2.6923            150000.0
2996   -118.14     34.06   ...         3.3906            237200.0

[1103 rows x 9 columns]
```

From the figure, the scientists are able to filter data to select only instances with the *Series* named *population* greater than 1,429. From the sample, the number of instances has dropped from a total of 3,000 to 1,103.

Data Processing in the Data Frame

Data Processing Within the Data Frame

When data scientists intend operate the data within the *Series* and the variables that act as broadcast or small data, they can access that series variable and create *Broadcast* variables and perform mathematical operations by writing the following program.

In the figure, the scientists access the *Series* named *population*, create a *Broadcast* variable with a value of 1000, place it inside variable *b*, then take all *Data Objects* within the *Series* to subtract from variable *b*, and present the result through *print* commands.

Sorting Data Within a Data Frame

In the data survey process, data scientists can sort all instances within a dataset with a particular *Series* to explore trends and patterns in the data. The program can be written as in the example.

In the figure, data scientists can use *.sort_values* command to sort instances from a particular series to explore data patterns and trends. Based on the example, all data within the dataset are sorted according to Series named *median_hosue_value*, sorting from the smallest to the largest number.

Figure 21. Using Broadcast along with series variables

```
import pandas as pd
cc=pd.read_csv("/content/sample_data/california_housing_test.csv")
ff = cc['population']
b = 1000
c = ff - b
print(c)
```

```
0          537.0
1         -191.0
2          484.0
3         -951.0
4         -150.0
            ...
2995       258.0
2996      2496.0
2997      -307.0
2998      -954.0
2999      -247.0
Name: population, Length: 3000, dtype: float64
```

Figure 22. Sorting instances with series

```
import pandas as pd
cc=pd.read_csv("/content/sample_data/california_housing_test.csv")
cc.sort_values(by='median_house_value')
```

	longitude	latitude	housing_median_age	total_rooms	total_bedrooms	population	households	median_income	median_house_value
2001	-117.16	32.71	52.0	845.0	451.0	1230.0	375.0	1.0918	22500.0
1031	-123.08	40.40	10.0	365.0	102.0	140.0	49.0	1.7969	37500.0
2740	-119.97	36.44	18.0	1128.0	237.0	772.0	220.0	2.1771	39200.0
734	-117.65	35.00	36.0	1184.0	316.0	672.0	241.0	1.9107	39800.0
2555	-122.06	37.39	22.0	1236.0	290.0	413.0	274.0	3.6875	40000.0
...	...	...	...	...	...	...	...	...	...
1563	-118.44	33.98	21.0	18132.0	5419.0	7431.0	4930.0	5.3359	500001.0
1561	-122.06	37.27	16.0	1612.0	221.0	567.0	208.0	10.5793	500001.0
1510	-122.43	37.79	52.0	6186.0	1566.0	2065.0	1374.0	5.8543	500001.0
2738	-118.45	33.96	24.0	3097.0	791.0	1075.0	639.0	5.7230	500001.0
2999	-119.63	34.42	42.0	1765.0	263.0	753.0	260.0	8.5608	500001.0

Dealing With Missing Values

Before analyzing data with data mining techniques, data scientists need to survey and prepare data, by considering whether the *Data Objects* are missing values. Data scientists can write a program to detect data objects that are missing values, then perform manipulation of the missing values, such as eliminating the Data Object or filling the incomplete Data Object with another value. The program can be written according to the following syntax.

import numby

from numpy import nan as NA

Based on the syntax, data scientists run *NaN* command from the *NumPy* library, working with other commands from the *Panda* library to check for data containing NA or the missing values, and then replace those values with *NaN* as in the example.

Figure 23. Verifying missing values

```
import pandas as pd
import numpy
from numpy import nan as NA

a = pd.Series([2,NA,4,5])
b = pd.Series([6,7,8,NA])
c = pd.Series([10,NA,12,13])

data = pd.DataFrame({'A':a,'B':b,'C':c})
data
```

	A	B	C
0	2.0	6.0	10.0
1	NaN	7.0	NaN
2	4.0	8.0	12.0
3	5.0	NaN	13.0

In the figure, the data scientists run the *NaN* command from the *NumPy* library. When examining data containing NA text or the missing value and replacing it with *NaN* as seen in the sample, the scientists create a total of 3 series, each of which contains data in the form of *NA,* then create a *Data Frame* from that series and display it. All data in *NA* format are replaced with *NaN*.

Programming in such a way allows data scientists to determine whether there is missing value within the dataset. To survey and prepare data, data scientists can consider dealing with those missing values, such as eliminating incomplete data from the dataset or complementing such data with other values. It can be programmed according to the syntax.

variable = dataset variable.*dropna( )*

variable = variable.*reset_index*(drop=True)

From the syntax, data scientists use *.dropna()* command to remove *NaN*-formatted data. Then, the *.reset_index(drop=True)* command is used to rearrange the purged dataset, which can be written as in the example.

Figure 24. Eliminating incomplete data

```
import pandas as pd
import numpy
from numpy import nan as NA

a = pd.Series([2,NA,4,5])
b = pd.Series([6,7,8,NA])
c = pd.Series([10,NA,12,13])

data = pd.DataFrame({'A':a,'B':b,'C':c})
dataclean = data.dropna()
dataclean = dataclean.reset_index(drop=True)
dataclean
```

	A	B	C
0	2.0	6.0	10.0
1	4.0	8.0	12.0

In the figure, data scientists extract the *NaN*-formatted data from the *Data Frame* contained in the data variable, and then use the *.dropna()* command to remove the *NaN*- data from the data frame. The data frame is then loaded into the *dataclean* variable. At the next step, the scientists reformat the data frame using *.rest_index(drop=True)* and leave only the complete data command. It is then rendered for a result.

In this case, the data scientists determine that the incomplete data should be filled, such as replacing with the mean or substituting with nominal values. The syntax for filling incomplete data with the mean is as follows.

variable = fillna(data.mean())variable.

From the syntax, data scientists use the *.fillna(data.mean)* command to fill incomplete data with the mean, which can be programmed as in the example.

In the figure, the data scientists generate an average from the mean of each series, and then fill that average into the missing values of each series by running the *fillna.(data.mean)* command and then display all data.

Figure 25. Filling missing values with the mean

```
import pandas as pd
import numpy
from numpy import nan as NA

a = pd.Series([2,NA,4,5])
b = pd.Series([6,7,8,NA])
c = pd.Series([10,NA,12,13])

data = pd.DataFrame({'A':a,'B':b,'C':c})
datamean = data.fillna(data.mean())
datamean
```

	A	B	C
0	2.000000	6.0	10.000000
1	3.666667	7.0	11.666667
2	4.000000	8.0	12.000000
3	5.000000	7.0	13.000000

Dealing With Duplicate Data

In the process of surveying and preparing data, another thing that the scientists need to consider is how to deal with duplicate data. Therefore, the first step to take is to verify whether the dataset, imported into the Python command, contains duplicate data. It can be written with the following syntax.

variable.duplicated(keep=False)

From the syntax, data scientists can use the *.duplicated(keep=False)* command to check whether the data object inside the data frame is duplicate or not. If the value is True, it is duplicate. And if the value is False, it means that it is normal. The program can be written as follows.

In the figure, after data scientists create a data frame from a series, check for duplicate data using the *.duplicated(keep=False)* command, display the result through the *print* statement, and execute the dataset, they have found a total of 4 duplicates. The duplicate value is shown as True.

After the scientists examine the duplicate data, in the data preparation process the data scientists can reduce this duplication while maintaining the integrity of the data frame structure. The program can be written as the following syntax.

variable.drop_uplicates(inplace=True)

Figure 26. Verifying duplicate data

```
import pandas as pd              0    False              A   B   C
import numpy                     1    True       0   1   2   3
                                 2    True       1   4   5   6
a = pd.Series([1,4,4,7,7,10,10,13,16])   3  False   2   4   5   6
b = pd.Series([2,5,5,8,18,11,11,14,17])  4  False   3   7   8   9
c = pd.Series([3,6,6,9,9,12,12,15,9])    5  True    4   7   18  9
                                 6    True       5   10  11  12
data = pd.DataFrame({'A':a,'B':b,'C':c}) 7  False   6   10  11  12
print(data.duplicated(keep=False))       8  False   7   13  14  15
                                 dtype: bool        8   16  17  9
```

From the syntax, data scientists can use the *.drop_duplicates(inplace=True)* command to reduce duplicate data. The program can be written as in the following example.

Figure 27. Reducing duplicate data

```
import pandas as pd                     A   B   C
import numpy                    0   1   2   3

a = pd.Series([1,4,4,7,7,10,10,13,16])  1   4   5   6
b = pd.Series([2,5,5,8,18,11,11,14,17]) 3   7   8   9
c = pd.Series([3,6,6,9,9,12,12,15,9])   4   7   18  9

data = pd.DataFrame({'A':a,'B':b,'C':c})5   10  11  12
data.drop_duplicates(inplace=True)      7   13  14  15
data                                    8   16  17  9
```

In the figure, data scientists reduce data duplication by using *.drop_duplicates(inplace=True)* command. After executing the command set, duplication is reduced, but the structure of the data frame is still preserved. The aim is to reduce the duplication of the data that lack integrity to be analyzed.

Dealing With Outliers

Data scientists can investigate outliers from the datasets imported into Python command, such as excessive-valued data or deficient-valued data. These data can cause the average value of the entire feature to change, affecting the patterns and trends of the analyzed data, leading to the inaccuracy of the data analysis.

Thus, data scientists can compute *z*-values, which reshape the entire data object's feature to the form of data under *Normal Curve*. If the data falls within the Standard deviation (SD) of over 3 or – 3, those data objects are considered outliers. You can write a program as in the example below.

Figure 28. Detecting outliers

```python
import pandas as pd
import numpy as np
df = pd.read_csv("http://www.mosaic-web.org/go/datasets/galton.csv")

def z_score(high):
  outlierlimit = 3
  m = np.mean(high)
  sd = np.std(high)
  z = [(x - m) / sd for x in high]
  return np.where(np.abs(z) > outlierlimit)

for i in z_score(df.height)[0]:
  print(df[i:i+1])
print()
```

	family	father	mother	sex	height	nkids
125	35	71.0	69.0	M	78.0	5
	family	father	mother	sex	height	nkids
288	72	70.0	65.0	M	79.0	7
	family	father	mother	sex	height	nkids
672	155	68.0	60.0	F	56.0	7

Data scientists import data into a command set and check the data object inside the data frame to verify whether it is an outlier when the data is transformed to *z*-value and it is in the normal curve region with a standard deviation greater than 3. In other words, the program does not use commands from the Python library; rather it is programming based on the normal *z*-value algorithm. And then the result value is checked whether it is greater than 3. And if the scientists intend to check whether the Data Object is deficient-valued or not, this can be done by changing the number 3 to – 3 and re-establishing the verification conditions.

Finally, the command set displays only instances with the *z* value greater than 3, so that the scientists can determine whether the value is outliers. However, the scientists should consult with a knowledge expert to consider the context in order to reassure.

Developing Data Visualization With *Matplotlib* and *Seaborn* **Libraries**

Data scientists can develop data visualizations in response to data survey purposes and data presentation (Healy, 2018: Pajankar, 2021). By developing data visualizations, data scientists can explore patterns of data both in terms of trends and distribution. Within Python, the Matplotlib and Seaborn libraries, whose commands the scientists can use to develop useful visualizations for data exploration, are provided.

Line Chart

Data scientists can create line graphs made up of two data sets using the *.plot* command from the *Matplotlib* library.

import matplotlib.pyplot as variable that executes a command set
Variable that executes the .plot([axis data x],[y-axis data])
Variables that run the .show() routine.

From the syntax, the scientists get the variable to run *.plot* command in the *matplotlib.pyplot* library in order to create a line graph. Then the result is displayed with the *.show()* command. You can write a program to create a graph as follows.

Figure 29. Creating a line graph

```
import matplotlib.pyplot as cc
cc.plot([2,5,6,7,9,12],
        [3,2,8,3,7,8])
cc.show()
```

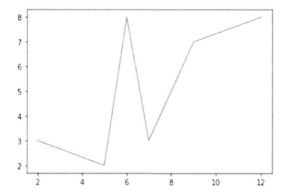

In the figure, data scientists use the variable *cc* to run the *.plot* command in the *matplotlib.pyplot* library, then prepare the data for the *x* and *y* axes to create a line graph, and display it through the *.show*() command. In case data scientists intend to develop a line graph by adding the visual guideline and describing each part of the graph, they can write the program as in the syntax below.

import matplotlib.pyplot as variable that executes a command set
from matplotlip import style
style.use("ggplot")
Variable that executes .plot([axis data x],[y-axis data])
plt.title("Graphic label")
plt.xlabel("x-axis alt label")
plt.ylable("y-axis alt label")

Based on the syntax, the scientists import the *style* command from the *matplotlib* library and assign the *ggplot* format in order to run the *plt.title* command to create the graph label, run *plt.xlable* command to create the x-axis label, and run *plt.ylable* command to create y-axis label as well as the visual guideline. The program is as mentioned in the following example.

Figure 30. Creating a ggplot patterned line graph

```
import matplotlib.pyplot as cc
from matplotlib import style
style.use("ggplot")
cc.plot([2,5,6,7,9,12],
        [3,2,8,3,7,8])
plt.title("Relationship of COVID-19 with Tourism")
plt.xlabel("COVID-19")
plt.ylabel("Tourism")

Text(0, 0.5, 'Tourism')
```

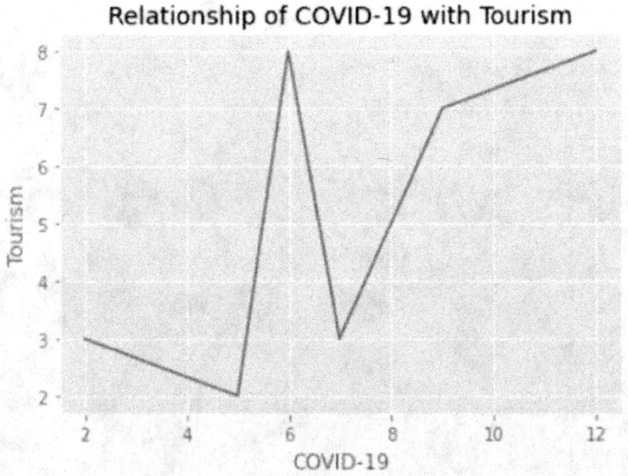

From the figure, data scientists can use the *ggplot* pattern to create guide lines, and provide the graph titles and labels for the x- and y-axis. From the graph, the scientists can also apply quantitative data that is presented based on clustered data. For instance, it can be used to show the relationship of the incidence of COVID-19 with the number of tourism, which is quantitative data presented in 2020 and 2021 as follows:

Figure 31. Presenting quantitative data by clustering

```
import matplotlib.pyplot as cc
from matplotlib import style
style.use("ggplot")
cc.plot([2,5,6,7,9,12],
        [3,2,8,3,7,8],
        label = 2020)
cc.plot([4,7,8,9,12,14],
        [5,4,10,5,9,10],
        label = 2021)
plt.title("Relationship of COVID-19 with Tourism")
plt.xlabel("COVID-19")
plt.ylabel("Tourism")
plt.legend()
```

```
<matplotlib.legend.Legend at 0x7fef66419750>
```

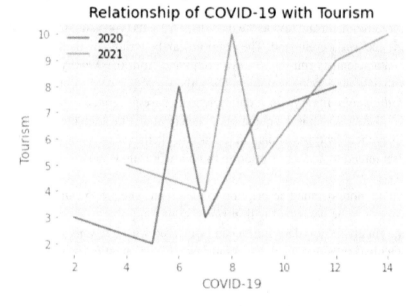

In the figure, data scientists create two data clusters, year 2020 and 2021, to compare the correlation of COVID-19 with tourism rates. In each data set, a label can be specified to assign data to the *plt. legend( )* command, which is used to create data labels. The line graph for 2020 is orange and the line graph for 2021 is blue.

Bar Chart

Data scientists can develop bar charts from quantitative data combined with data used for classification. The program is as mentioned in the following syntax:

import numpy as nv
import matplotlib.pyplot as a variable that runs the command to create a graph
Series acting as the x-axis = [data]
Series acting as the y-axis = [data]
variable that control graphing = variable that executes the graphing command (len(Series acting as the y-axis)
variables that run commands to create graphs .bar(variables that control graph creation, Series that act as axes)
variables that run commands to create graphs .xticks(variables that control graphing, Series acting on the x-axis)
variables that execute the command to create graphs .show()

From the syntax, data scientists can create a Series for the x and y axes, and then use the *.arange(len())* command to count the number of data from Series acting as the x-axis. Data scientists can create quantitative data using the *.bar* command and divide the data display by its type using the *.xticks()* command, and then render it using the *.show* command. The program can be written by the following example.

In the figure, the data scientists run the *.arange* command from the *NumPy* library to count and compile a bar chart with data-classifying variables. Then, the variable *p* runs a command to create a bar graph from the *matplotlib.pyplot* library. Once data scientists have generated data for the *x*-axis which is the types of animal and the *y* which is the quantity of each animal, they then create a bar based on the data in the *y*-axis, display them by types of data in the x-axis via the *.show()* command.

When data scientists intend to add description to the bar chart, they can write a program as in the example.

Data scientists can add more-detailed description to the graph. The graph can be named using *.title* command, then the *x*-axis can be described with *p.xlabel* command, the *y*-axis can be described with *p.ylable* command, and finally the bar description can be created with *p.legend()* command.

In cases that the scientists intend to display a comparison of the quantitatively-divided data and the data used in two classifications; for example, the number of Zoo animals in 2020 and 2021, and animal species, they can write programs to display the result as follows.

In the figure, data scientists create two data sets of: number of animals according to their types in 2020 and 2021. The year 2020 is represented in green as 2021 data is represented by purple. As the 2021 data is designated in purple and the color intensity is 0.5, the 2020 data is seen as being less volume and green even though the bar showing the data for both 2020 and 2021 are displayed overlapped.

Figure 32. Creating a bar chart

```python
import numpy as cc
import matplotlib.pyplot as p
x = ['Cat','Dog','Lion','Monkey']
y = [30,40,50,60]
ee = cc.arange(len(x))
p.bar(ee,y)
p.xticks(ee,x)
p.show()
```

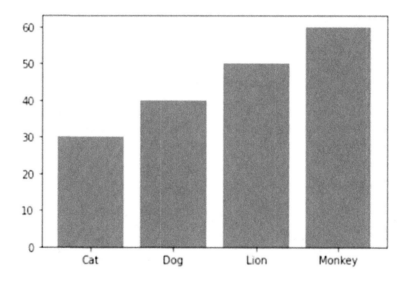

Pie Chart

When data scientists intend to make a quantitative comparison of data in percentage by dividing the display by data types. The program to create a Pie Chart can be written with the following syntax:

import matplotlib.pyplot as variables that execute the command
storage variable for categorization = [data used for categorization]
quantitative storage variables = [quantitative data]
variables that use pie command (quantitative storage variables,
labels = storage variables for categorization
autopct = "data display in percentage")
p.title("chart explaining Data")
p.show()

Figure 33. Adding details to the bar chart

```
import matplotlib.pyplot as cc
cc.bar(
['cat','dog','lion','monkey'],
[30,40,50,60],
label = "Animal Quantity",
align = "center"
)
p.title("Animal in a Zoo")
p.xlabel("Animal Types")
p.ylabel("Quantity")
p.legend()
```

<matplotlib.legend.Legend at 0x7fd82ccc6ed0>

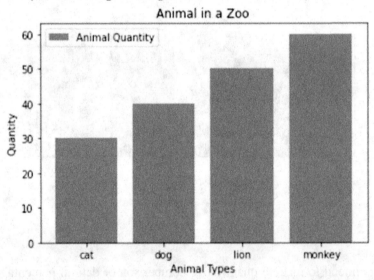

From the syntax, the scientists create a variable that run the *.pie* command to create a pie graph from the *matplotlib.pyplot* library. It then generates the categorization data and the quantitative data to create a pie graph by using the quantitative storage variables, then packing the categorization storage variables into *labels*, and displaying them in percentage with *autopct*.

Data scientists can name a graph with the *p.title* command and display the graph with the *p.show()* command.

From the figure, the scientists generate the data for categorization and putting into the ***song*** variable, and then generate the quantitative data to pack into the variable *r*. The pie graph aims to show the proportion of the total data in percentage. Therefore, when the quantitative data and the classification data are used to create a pie chart, the data are converted into a proportional form and the result is displayed in percentage with the *autopct* command.

Figure 34. Creating two data sets to compare in the bar chart

```
import matplotlib.pyplot as cc
cc.bar(
['cat','dog','lion','monkey'],
[30,40,50,60],
label = "Animal Quantity 2020",
color = 'g',
align = "center",
alpha = 0.5
)

cc.bar(
['cat','dog','lion','monkey'],
[60,80,100,120],
label = "Animal Quantity 2021",
color = 'm',
align = "center",
alpha = 0.5
)

p.title("Animal in a Zoo")
p.xlabel("Animal Types")
p.ylabel("Quantity")
p.legend()
```

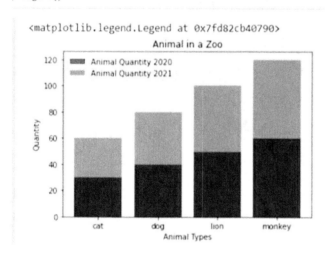

The sample pie graph shows the ratio of popular classical songs in the world. In case the scientists intend to focus on a particular proportion on a pie chart, they can write a program as follows.

From the figure, data scientists can determine the position on the pie graph further away from the other proportions so that they can focus on the desired display. To create a pie graph, the distance of the data proportion can be specified with *explode*. When the scientists intend to represent data types with *legends* to communicate graph details, they can write a program according to the following example.

In this figure, data scientists can use the classification datasets to describe a pie graph with the *.legend()* command. In the example, a *Legend* is created showing the color that represents the proportion which it is classified with the datasets.

Figure 35. Creating a pie chart

```
import matplotlib.pyplot as cc
song = ["Mozart","Beethoven","Chopin","Wagner"]

r = [90,80,70,60]
cc.pie(r,
        labels = song,
        autopct="%.1f%%")

p.title("Popular Song in the World")
p.show()
```

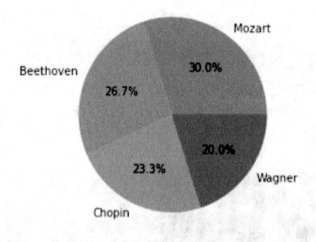

Histogram

Histograms are used to explore the distribution of data where the *x*-axis is created from the frequency of the data in a range, and the axis *y* is created from the quantitative values of the data of the same feature. Therefore, the histogram is generated from the 1 feature data.

import matplotlib.pyplot as variable that executes the command
data containing variable = [data]
variable that executes *.hist*(data containing variable)

From the syntax, data scientists can insert data into variables and use *.hist* command from the *matplotlib.pyplot* library to create a histogram. The following example shows how to write the program.

Figure 36. The focus display of a particular aspect in the pie chart

```
import matplotlib.pyplot as cc
song = ["Mozart","Beethoven","Chopin","Wagner"]

r = [90,80,70,60]
e = [0,0.3,0,0.1]
cc.pie(r,
        labels = song,
        explode = e,
        autopct="%.1f%%")

p.title("Popular Song in the World")
p.show()
```

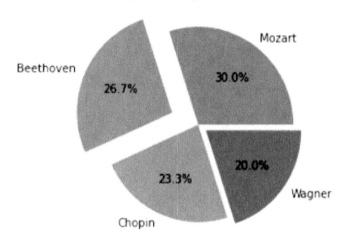

From the figure, data scientists insert the data set named *california_housing_train.csv* into the *.read_csv* command from the *pandas* library, and then access the feature named *median_income*. Later it is inserted into variable *x* to create a histogram with *.hist* command. In the example, the data frequency range is created from the feature named *median_income* as the x-axis, and then the y-axis is created from the quantitative data in the same feature. The scientists can determine the distribution of data during the survey process.

Figure 37. Adding a legend to the pie chart

```
import matplotlib.pyplot as cc
song = ["Mozart","Beethoven","Chopin","Wagner"]

r = [90,80,70,60]
e = [0,0.3,0,0.1]
cc.pie(r,
        labels = song,
        explode = e,
        autopct="%.1f%%")

p.title("Popular Song in the World")
p.legend()
p.show()
```

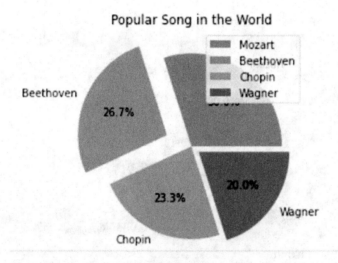

When data scientists intend to display a histogram in conjunction with a line dispersion display, the *Seaborn* library provides *.distplot* command to create a graph with such a pattern with the following syntax.

import seaborn as graphing variable
variable = data
graphing variable.displot(variable, kde=True)

In the figure, the scientists construct a histogram showing the distribution of the data together with the lines by inserting the data set named *California_housing_test.csv* into the command, then add a feature named *median_income* to the variable *x*, and create a histogram with *.displot* command to explore the distribution of data in both bar and line formats.

Figure 38. Creating a histogram

```
import pandas as pd
import matplotlib.pyplot as plt
cc = pd.read_csv("/content/sample_data/california_housing_train.csv")
x = cc['median_income']
plt.hist(x)

(array([1833., 6100., 5020., 2466.,  891.,  368.,  152.,   79.,   42.,
          49.]),
 array([ 0.4999 ,  1.94992,  3.39994,  4.84996,  6.29998,  7.75   ,
          9.20002, 10.65004, 12.10006, 13.55008, 15.0001 ]),
 <a list of 10 Patch objects>)
```

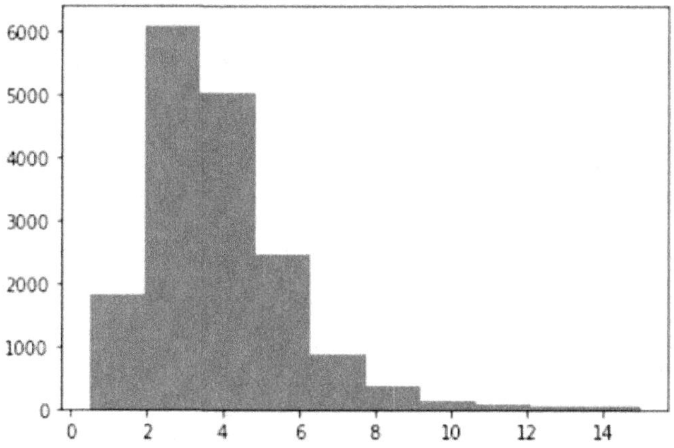

Density Plot

Not only histograms can be used to explore data, the Density Plot can also be used to explore the data in order to determine the distribution of the data. The y-axis, which is created by the Density Plot, using the *Probability* of the feature, is considered a measure of how data is displayed. Data scientists can write programs in the following syntax.

import seaborn as graphing variable
variable = data
graphing variable.kdeplot(variable)

From the syntax, data scientists can create Density Plot from the *.kdeplot* command from the *seaborn* library.

From the figure, data scientists can create Density Plot for data exploration by having the *mi* variable run the *.kdeplot* command from the *seaborn* library. As in the example, the *california_housing_train. csv* dataset is imported into the command set, and the feature named *median_income* is inserted into the *x* variable to create Density Plot. The x-axis is created from the data frequency, and the y-axis is from *Probability* of the same feature.

Figure 39. Creating a density plot along with a histogram

```
import pandas as pd
import seaborn as mi
cc = pd.read_csv("/content/sample_data/california_housing_test.csv")
x = cc['median_income']
mi.displot(x,kde=True)
```

```
<seaborn.axisgrid.FacetGrid at 0x7fd812998690>
```

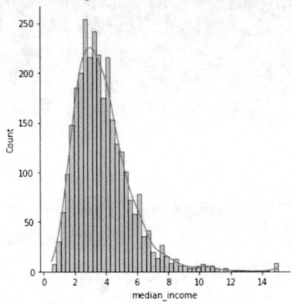

Creating Box Plot

Data scientists can preliminarily explore five data: Min Value *25% Value, Mid Value, 75% Value, and Maximum Value,* from the explored feature. Such data can also be expressed in the form of Box Plot, which displays quantitative data along with the classification data.

import seaborn as variable that executes a command set
storage variable = command executing variable(data).
data.boxplot(x= 'x-axis Feature', y= 'y-axis Feature', data = storage variable, order = [display of each type]

From the syntax, data scientists can write a program to create Box Plot using the *.boxplot* command stored in the *Seaborn* library, and then specify the feature used for creating the x-axis, which is the classification data used for identifying the feature to create the y-axis, which is quantitative data. The dataset is then taken into the Box Plot and finally rendered.

Figure 40. Creating density plot

```
import pandas as pd
import seaborn as mi
cc = pd.read_csv("/content/sample_data/california_housing_train.csv")
x = cc['median_income']
mi.kdeplot(x)
```

```
<matplotlib.axes._subplots.AxesSubplot at 0x7fd81e82a1d0>
```

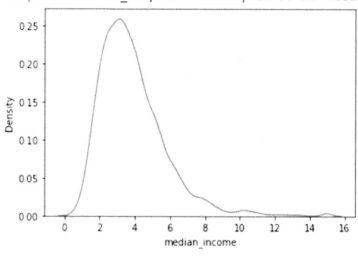

Figure 41. Creating box plot

```
import seaborn as mi
ee = mi.load_dataset('iris')
mi.boxplot(x='species', y = 'sepal_length', data = ee, order=["virginica","setosa","versicolor"] )
```

```
<matplotlib.axes._subplots.AxesSubplot at 0x7fd811e23650>
```

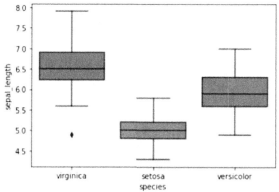

In the figure, the scientists retrieve a sample dataset in *Python* called *iris* by running *load_dataset* from the *Seaborn* library, loading it into the *ee* variable, and creating Box Plot. The x-axis displays the feature named *species* as the names of Iris flower species, and the y-axis displays the feature named *sepal_length* as the length of the Iris flower petal. The data from the *ee* variable are then entered into the Box Plot, in the order of the Iris species; virginicia, setosa, and versicolor, respectively.

The Box Plot displays data for each Iris flower species, showing the *outlier*, the smallest value, the 25th percentile, the middle 75th percentile, and the largest value for the Iris width of each cultivar. It allows data scientists to see the distribution of data before categorizing it with data mining techniques.

Scatter Plot

In the survey process, data scientists can use quantitative data from two or more features to create a scatter plot to show the relationship between the two data. Scatter plots can also represent data that are the *outlier*.

import seaborn as variable that executes the command
variable = variable that executes the command(data)
data.regplot(x= Feature that creates the x-axis, y =Feature that creates the y-axis)

From the syntax, data scientists can create a scatter Plot to determine the relationship of data using the *.regplot* commands provided in the *Seaborn* library, graphing them from the quantitative data of two or more features.

In the figure, the scientists create a scatter plot from two features, *sepal_length* and *sepal_width*, contained within the *iris* sample dataset by running the *.regplot* command from the *Seaborn* library. The Scatter Plot creates a data point from 2 features to show the relationship of data. Data scientists can also determine the *outlier* from scatter plots.

FEATURE ENCODING

When data scientists insert a dataset into a command set to prepare the data for processing, they can use *Label Encoding* and *One Hot Encoding*.

1. *Label Encoding* by adding feature names and monitoring for incomplete data.

In some cases, data scientists find that the datasets obtained from the data exploration process lack the feature names to use for data analyzing programming, and those datasets may contain incomplete data. The scientists can write a program to solve such a problem with the following syntax:

import pandas as the variable that executes commands
variable = [feature name data]
dataset storage variable = (header = None, names = variables, na_values= "?")
the variable that holds dataset.head()

Figure 42. Creating scatter plot

```
import seaborn as mi
ee = mi.load_dataset('iris')
mi.regplot(x=ee["sepal_length"], y = ee["sepal_width"])
```

```
<matplotlib.axes._subplots.AxesSubplot at 0x7fd811d37690>
```

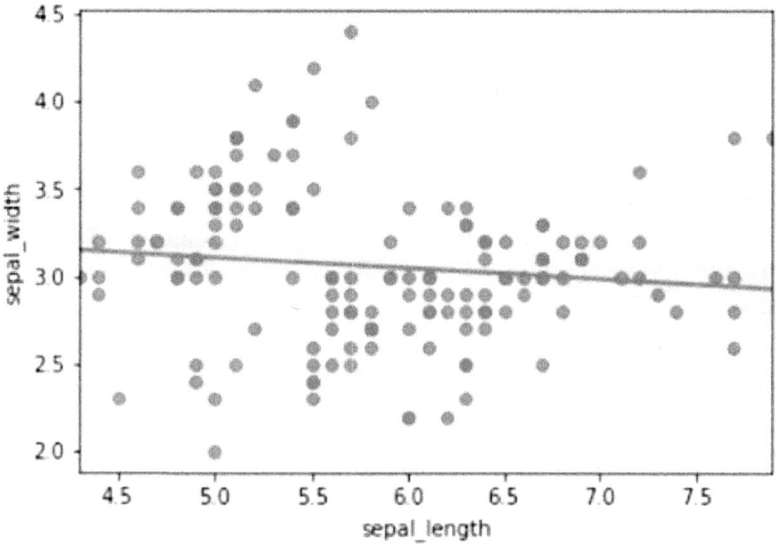

From the syntax, data scientists use a variable to run the *.read_csv* command from the *pandas* library, then assign the data within the variable as the feature in the dataset with *names*, and then assign the Data Object within the dataset *?* to be replaced with *NaN*. The program can be written as follows.

Figure 43. Adding a feature name and monitoring for incomplete data

```
import pandas as pd
h = ["Number1", "Number 2", "Normalization"]

df = pd.read_csv("https://archive.ics.uci.edu/ml/machine-learning-databases/autos/imports-85.data",
                header = None, names = h,na_values="?")
df.head()
```

			Number1	Number 2	Normalization						
9.0	111.0	5000.0	21	27	13495.0	3	NaN	alfa-romero	gas	std	two
		5000.0	21	27	16500.0						
9.0	154.0	5000.0	19	26	16500.0	1	NaN	alfa-romero	gas	std	two
10.0	102.0	5500.0	24	30	13950.0	2	164.0	audi	gas	std	four
8.0	115.0	5500.0	18	22	17450.0						

In the figure, the data scientists use the *pd* variable to run the *.read_csv* command from the *panda* library in order to insert the dataset *imports-85.data* into the command set. Then a dataset to be used to name a Feature is created and put into the *names* so that the created dataset can be used as the feature name. It is also determined as *na_values = "?"*, which means that whenever the data object which resembles a question mark is encountered, the data object has to be replaced with *NaN*.

When displaying a dataset with *.head()* command, it is found that the data created to name the feature is used for naming. However, before the data scientists name a feature, it is important to explore both the number of feature and the nature of the data object in each feature for the great benefit of programming.

2.   Label Encoding by converting letters to numbers

In many cases, data scientists receive datasets that are textual, used for classification such as gender, province and region. However, data mining techniques use computation to analyze the data. Therefore, data scientists have to turn those letters into numbers while retaining the classification properties. It can be written as in the following syntax.

replacement data storage variable = {"Text Data Object": Number}
dataset variable.replace(replacement data storage variable)

From the syntax, data scientists can identify a text data object that classifies the data and identifies the numbers to replace the text so that those numbers remain classifiable. The program can be written as follows:

Figure 44. Turning texts into numbers

```
import pandas as pd
da = pd.DataFrame(["Cat","Lion","Dog"])
print(da)
convert = {"Cat": 1,"Lion": 2, "Dog": 3}
da.replace(convert)
```

```
        0
0    Cat
1    Lion
2    Dog

        0

0  1

1  2

2  3
```

In the figure, the scientists get the variable *pd* to run the *.DataFrame* command from the *Pandas* library to create a dataset consisting of *Cat, Lion, and Dog*, respectively. Then, the data is packed into the *da* variable and outputs it via the *print* command. The next step is to specify the number to replace a text Data Object and put it into the *convert* variable. Then that variable is changed from text to number with the *.replace* command.

3.   One Hot Encoding

Changing text to numbers with *Label Encoding* cannot reflect quantitative data but still retain the data properties for classification. *One Hot Encoding* is therefore used to count the number of text data in the form of numbers, which can be used in quantitative analysis. It resembles *Dummy* data consisting of the numbers 0 and 1. Data scientists can write a program according to the following syntax.

Import pandas as dataset variables
data storage variable = dataset variable.DataFrame({'data category':[data]})
dataset variable.get_dummies(data storage variable, prefix=['data category'])

From the syntax, data scientists can create *Data Frame* that stores data categories that cover all Data Objects, and then quantify the text to be counted as the quantitative data. Then the Dummy is created with numbers consisting of 0 which means no data, and 1 which means data. The program can be written in the following example:

Figure 45. Creating dummy data set from text

```
import pandas as pd
da = pd.DataFrame({'Animal': ['Cat', 'Dog', 'Lion','Lion','Lion']})
print(da)
pd.get_dummies(da,prefix=['Animal'])
```

```
   Animal
0     Cat
1     Dog
2    Lion
3    Lion
4    Lion
```

	Animal_Cat	Animal_Dog	Animal_Lion
0	1	0	0
1	0	1	0
2	0	0	1
3	0	0	1
4	0	0	1

In the figure, the scientists create a data frame, which contains the animal categories; Cat, Dog, Lion, Lion, and Lion, respectively, and then present the result via the *print* command. When all data are created from the animal categories in the form of a dummy dataset with the *.get_dummies* command, the result is a table that counts the frequency of each format encounter. For instance, in the original data, Lion is found 3 times. When it is changed into the form of dummy dataset, then the frequency of encountering the word Lion is created as 3 of number 1. By creating the dummy data in this manner, Text data is quantitatively valuable through counting the frequency of text occurrences.

4.   Scikit-Learn Library

Python provides the *Scikit Learn* library, in which there is a command set for data mining. Data scientists can insert the data set into the command set and then run a mining command from the *Scikit-Learn* library to analyze it. Data analysis with machine learning (ML) can be divided into two ways:

- **Supervised-Learning:** Is to divide the data set into 2 sets. The first set is used to teach the machine to recognize the nature of the data. The second set is used for testing machine accuracy by Supervised-Learning, which is used in conjunction with various data mining techniques such as regression, neural networks, and deep learning. When processing with data mining techniques, the obtained results do not only forecast or classify data, but it can also show the accuracy of forecasting and classification as well as compare the result with the actual data, resulting more closely to the facts.
- **Unsupervised-Learning:** Is to bring data into data mining without teaching the machine to learn. Data mining techniques are classified as Unsupervised-Learning, such as Clustering and Association Rule Mining.

The *Scikit-Learn* library provides a command set for data mining in both forms; Supervised-Learning and Unsupervised-Learning. Data scientists can experiment with the commands from

Scikit-Learn library as shown below.

Linear Regression Analysis is an analysis of the relationship of two features organized in a supervised learning model where data scientists have to divide the data of the two features into two sets consisting of the data for Train Set and Test Set (Sonu & Suyampulingam, 2021). The sample questions will put forward the analysis of the relationship of height and weight by assigning the weight variable to the target variable (Label). Data scientists can write a program according to the following syntax.

```
import matplotlib.pyplot as variable that runs the graph command
from sklearn.linear_model import LinearRegerssion
Feature variable = data
Target variable = data
Variable that invokes the graph command.scatter(variable Feature, target variable)
Variable that invokes the graph command.title('graph title')
Variable that invokes the graph command.xlabel('x-axis label')
Variable that invokes the graph command.ylabel('y-axis label')
```

```
Data mining model variable = LinearRegerssion()
Data mining model variables.fit(X=Feature variable, y=target variable)
target variable = data mining model variable.predict([data to predict]])
print(target variable)
Variable that invokes the graph command.plot(Feature variable, model variable.predict(Feature variable))
```

From the syntax, data scientists can run regression analysis techniques with *LinearRegerssion* command from the *Scikit-Learn* library, then create feature to analyze data and target variables, and generate a *scatter plot* from the actual data set.

The machine is taught to learn by importing the dataset into regression analysis model with the *.fit* command and inserting the required values to predict the outcome for the model to analyze the data. In the last step, all the values obtained from the forecast are used to create *Prediction Line* onto the *Scatter Plot* that has been created. To compare the accuracy of the values obtained from the forecast with the actual data, data scientists can use the *Scikit-Learn* library, by writing the program as presented in the example.

From the graph above, the scientists create the feature *height* and the target variable *weight*. A Scatter Plot is then created, displaying the data as a data point that intersects the x-axis which is the height, and the weight in the y-axis. The *LinearRegression()* command from the *Scikit-Learn* library is run and then the height and weight datasets are to teach machine learning.

Using supervised learning regression analysis, the scientists can predict the weight from a height of 175 cm. The result, 75.97 kg, is displayed via the *print* command. All forecast data are then used to create the *Prediction Line* to show the closeness of the data obtained from the forecast with the actual data.

CLASSIFICATION

Data classification is a type of supervised learning among all data mining techniques in which data scientists divide data into two parts: the data used to teach machines and the data used for testing. The target variables are set as the result of data classification. The questions are consistent with techniques used in data analysis, such as classifying the bank customers who have ability-to-repay if refinancing the loan or classifying the coffee shop customers who show possibility to go to other coffee shops. There are data mining techniques that are characterized as data classification techniques such as decision trees (Cheewaprakobkit, 2019).

Data scientists can program for analyzing data with decision tree techniques as in the syntax below.

```
from sklearn.datasets import sample dataset
from sklearn import tree
from sklearn.model_selection import train_test_split
from sklearn.metrics import accuracy_score
Model = tree.DecisiontreeClassifier()
Feature using Train, Feature using Test, Target variables using Train, Target variables using Test =
    train_test_split(sample dataset.data, sample dataset.target, test_size = 0.4)
model.fit(Feature using Train, Target data using Train)
Result variables from the actual test = Target variable using Test
```

Result variables from data classification= model.predict(Feature using Test)
Accuracy result = accuracy_score(Target variables using Test,Result variables from data classification)
print(accuracy result)
tree.plot_tree(model.fit(Feature using Train, target variables using Train))

Figure 46. Linear regression analysis

```
import matplotlib.pyplot as p
from sklearn.linear_model import LinearRegression

h = [[160], [165], [170], [173], [180]]
w = [[60], [65], [72], [75], [80]]
p.scatter(h, w)
p.title('Relationship of high and weight of 5 students')
p.xlabel('Student hight')
p.ylabel('Student weight')


model = LinearRegression()
model.fit(X=h, y=w)

w = model.predict([[175]])
print(w)

p.plot(h,model.predict(h))
```

```
[[75.97598628]]
[<matplotlib.lines.Line2D at 0x7fb6af4a6080>]
```

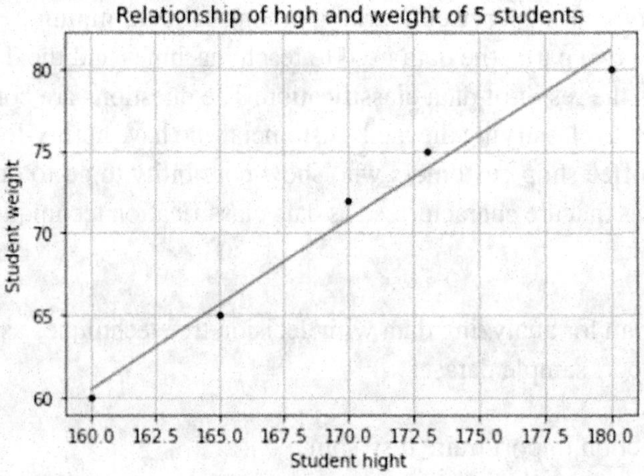

From the syntax, data scientist can use the sample dataset from *sklearn.datasets* to experiment with programming for large data processing, then classify the data to import tree to run a set of *.Decision-TreeClassifier()* command in order to classify data with decision trees. This is to divide the data into datasets; for teaching machine learning and for testing. The *train_test_split* command from *sklearn. model_selection* can be run for testing the accuracy of data analysis when the data scientists can use *accuracy_score* command from *sklearn.metrics*.

While processing the data, scientists pack decision tree techniques into variables. Then, the sample data set is divided into 2 sets. The 1st set is the features used to teach machine learning and target variables that teach machine learning, 60 percent of all instances. The 2nd set is the features used to test and target variables, 40 percent of all instances.

The data are then categorized by the decision tree technique, importing the data for machine learning into the model *via .fit* commands, and then classifying the data from the feature used for testing together with the model being taught to learn through the *.predict* command. Then the efficiency of data classification is tested with the *accuracy_score* command, with the test target variables and with the data classification. The results are then presented via the *print* command in the last step. The data scientists can display the results of data classification with decision trees using the *tree.plot.tree* command. The scientists can program by running the iris dataset, which stores attributes including the width of the petals, the length of the petals, the width of the sepals and the length of the sepals, totaling 150 instances. Then the program can be written to identify the Iris cultivars, including Setosa, Versicolor and Virginica, which are assigned as target variables. The program is in the following example.

Figure 47. Programming for data analysis with decision trees

```
from sklearn.datasets import load_iris
from sklearn import tree
from sklearn import metrics
from sklearn.externals.six import StringIO
from sklearn.model_selection import train_test_split
from sklearn.metrics import accuracy_score
import seaborn as sns
import pandas as pd
import pydotplus
from IPython.display import Image


iris = load_iris()
sns.set
df = pd.DataFrame(iris.data)
df.columns = iris.feature_names
df.loc[:,'target'] = pd.Series(iris.target_names[iris.target])
sns.pairplot(df, hue='target')


model = tree.DecisionTreeClassifier()

x_trian, x_test, y_trian, y_test = train_test_split(iris.data,iris.target,test_size = 0.4)

model.fit(x_trian,y_trian)
expected = y_test
predicted = model.predict(x_test)
acc=accuracy_score(y_test,predicted)
print(acc)


dot_data = StringIO()
tree.export_graphviz(model, out_file=dot_data,
                    feature_names=iris.feature_names,
                    class_names=iris.target_names,
                    filled = True, rounded =True,
                    special_characters = True)
graph = pydotplus.graph_from_dot_data(dot_data.getvalue())
Image(graph.create_png())
```

From the figure, data scientists have divided programming into 3 parts: 1. Developing visual data in the Scatter Matrix for surveying the data, 2. Analysis of data using decision tree technique, and 3. Accuracy display of data analysis and data classification results with decision trees.

Part 1: The data scientists retrieve the iris dataset from *load_iris( )*, then create a data frame from the iris dataset, and create a Scatter Matrix visualization through the *.pairplot* command by graphing it from the features; the petal width, the petal length, the petal width and the sepal length, and the target variables; the Iris flower species. The result of Execute is shown in the picture.

Figure 48. Scatter matrix visualization for data exploration

Part 2: The data scientists pack decision tree techniques into the model variable with *tree.Decision-TreeClassifiter* command, and then divide the dataset used to teach machine learning which is *iris.data* and the dataset used for testing which is *irist.target* into 2 parts, 60% for machines learning and 40 percent for testing. The data in each set also includes the characteristic features of the Iris flowers and the cultivars.

The machine learning dataset is then imported into the model *via .fit*, and the data is categorized with *.predict* command, processing the test features with the data, loaded into the model. The classification accuracy is tested by *accuracy_score* command by using the target variable data for testing together with the results obtained from the classification data. When executing the command set, the accuracy of the model is obtained as follows:

Figure 49. Accuracy of data analysis with decision trees

```
0.9166666666666666
```

From the figure, the accuracy of the data analysis is 91.66%, which means that the data obtained from the classification has a high degree of accuracy and closeness to the facts.

In Part 3, the scientists build decision trees obtained from data analysis, using the *tree.export_graphviz* command to create a graph from the data obtained from the analysis in Part 2. The graph can be used to describe how Iris flower cultivars are classified based on the features and target variables.

REGRESSION

When the scientists are asked for a data analysis aimed at predicting quantitatively correlated data, such as customer revenue and product sales, they can use regression analysis to analyze the relationship and predict it. The variables used for data analysis can have one or more features for the analysis of target variables (Labels). Therefore, regression is a type of data mining technique, Supervised-Learning, which must be divided into 2 sets: data for the machine learning and data for model testing.

In addition, this book has already introduced programming for simple regression analysis. The discussion of regression analysis in this section, therefore, covers programming for multiple linear regression and polynomial regression.

1.   Multiple Linear Regression

In this case, when the scientists intend to predict the outcome of the target variables using two or more feature data, the multiple regression analysis is used (Rathaur, Kamath, & Ghanekar, 2020). The programming syntax is as follows.

```
from pandas as dataset variables
import numpy as combined variables Feature
from sklearn.linear_model import LinearRegression
from sklearn.model_selection import train_test_split
dataset storage variables = dataset variables read_csv('data source')
storage data Feature = dataset variables.DataFrame(combined variables Feature.c_[df['Feature'],
df['Feature'], columns = ['Feature', 'Feature'])
```

target variables = df['Label']

Feature using Train, Feature using Test, target variables using Train, target variables using Test = train_test_split(storage variables Feature, target variables, test_size = 0.3)

Model variables = LinearRegression()

Model variables.fit(Feature using Train, target variables using Train)

Forecast results = model variables.predict(Feature using Test)

print(forecast results)

model variables.score(Feature using Test, target variables using Test)

Figure 50. Decision tree model

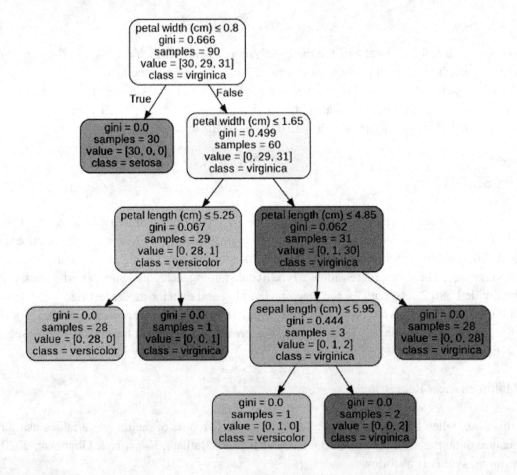

From the syntax that uses multiple regression analysis techniques to predict target variables with two or more features, data scientists can experiment with programming. The sample program is divided into 3 parts: 1. Feature Selection to select variables suitable for data analysis, 2. Graphing in 3D Scatter Plot format to survey data from variables obtained from the section 1, and 3. Using multiple regression analysis techniques to analyze the data of the target variables.

The goal of this analysis is to analyze which features influence daily rental pricing, and how much the accommodation should be priced each day. The scientist can write a program as in this example.

Figure 51. Multiple regression analysis

```
import matplotlib.pyplot as plt
import numpy as np
import pandas as pd
from sklearn.linear_model import LinearRegression
from sklearn.model_selection import train_test_split

df = pd.read_csv('/content/AB_NYC_2019.csv')
print(df.corr().abs().nlargest(3,'price').index)

fig = plt.figure(figsize=(18,15))
ax = fig.add_subplot(111, projection='3d')
ax.scatter(df['availability_365'],df['longitude'],df['price'],c='b')
ax.set_xlabel("availability_365")
ax.set_ylabel("longitude")
ax.set_zlabel("price")
plt.show()

x = pd.DataFrame(np.c_[df['availability_365'], df['longitude']],
                 columns = ['availability_365','longitude'])
y = df['price']
x_train, x_test, y_train, y_test = train_test_split(x,y,test_size=0.3)

model = LinearRegression()
model.fit(x_train,y_train)

price_perday = model.predict(x_test)
print(price_perday)

print('R-Sqaured: %.4f' % model.score(x_test,y_test))

Index(['price', 'longitude', 'availability_365'], dtype='object')
```

As you can see, the data scientists write a program in three parts.

Part 1: Data scientists run the *read_csv* command from the *pandas* library to import the dataset into the instruction set, and then perform a correlation analysis between all features and the target variable, which is the rental price per day by using *the .corr()* command to analyze the top 3 correlated features. As a result, price which is the target variable, and Feature which is longitude, the property's location, and availability_365 which is the number of days of service per year. This feature selection process is known as feature selection. Data scientists can use this approach along with consulting knowledge experts, data subjects, or questioners who intend to analyze them in order to obtain the features that are effective in their performance. Then, the results of the data analysis are obtained as follows.

Figure 52. Feature selection operation

```
Index(['price', 'longitude', 'availability_365'], dtype='object')
```

Part 2: After data scientists have acquired the features that can be used to predict target variables, the scientists can take both features and target variables to survey the data to determine the distribution of the data. To observe outlier data and show the relationship of data in 3D format that creates a Data Point from data on the x, y and z axes with 3D Scatter Plot visualization data, data scientists can bring the feature named availability_365 to build on the x-axis, and the longitude to build on the y-axis. Then, the target variable, price, is generated on the z-axis, resulting from the development of the visualization data.

Figure 53. Surveying data with 3D scatter plot

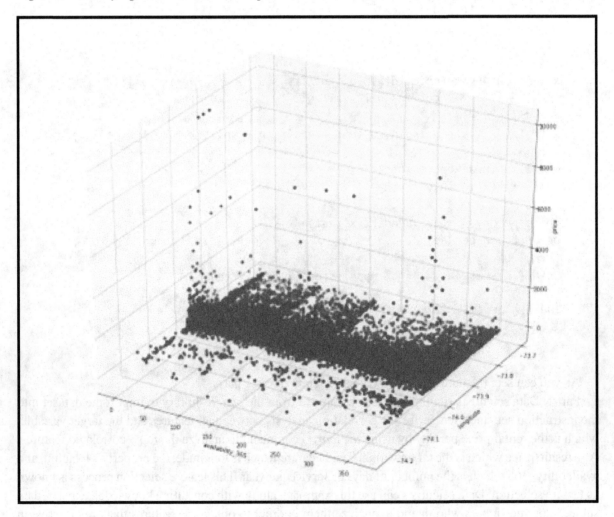

Part 3: Data Analysis with Multiple Regression Analysis

Data scientists take features named availability_365 and longitude to create a data frame, and populate into the observation variable *x*. To program for data analysis with multiple regression analysis techniques, it uses a method of combining features by creating Data Frame before analyzing the data together with the target variables.

The target variable, price, is then inserted into the *y* variable, and the data within the variables x and y are divided into two parts: Part 1 is 60% for machine learning, and Part 2 is 40% for model testing. Then the model variable is assigned to used LinearRegression(), and the machine is taught to learn by applying a Train-based feature and a Train-based target variable into the model.

Data scientists forecast daily accommodation prices. The *.predict* command is used in conjunction with the Test-based feature, and all forecasts are rendered via the *print* command, and the precision of the data is analyzed in the R Squared format. The result is 0.0274, which is still very accurate. Accuracy is considered a low level, which means that the data received from the forecast is not closely related to the facts as shown in the figure.

Figure 54. Forecast results and model accuracy values

```
[175.51704094 157.10322755 131.13947656 ...  84.28931985 131.47634801
  200.62518158]
R-Sqaured: 0.0274
```

To analyze data using multiple regression analysis techniques, Python uses the LinearRegression() command similarly to a simple regression analysis. Only the method of combining multiple features to create a data frame is done before analyzing with the target variables.

2.   Polynomial Regression

In the case of data scientists survey the data through the creation of a scatter plot, and the data is not linear, data scientists can use polynomial regression analysis techniques for predictions which is more closely tied to real data (Gong & Zhang, 2021). The syntax is as follows.

import matplotlib.pyplot as graph making variables
from sklearn.linear_model import LinearRegression
from sklearn.model_selection import train_test_split
from sklearn.preprocessing import PolynomialFeatures
polynomial variables= PolynomialFeatures(degree = number of Matrix)
Feature variables= [data]
Target variables = [data]
Polynomial storage variables = polynomial variables.fit_transform(Feature variables)
print(Polynomial storage variables)
Model variables = LinearRegression()
Model variables.fit(Polynomial storage variables, target variables)

Forecast results = model variables.predict(Polynomial storage variables)
print(forecast result)
graph making variables.scatter(Feature variables,target variables)
graph making variables.plot(Feature variables, forecast result)
model variables.score(Polynomial storage variables, target variables)

From the syntax, data scientists can define a matrix used to adjust a Data Object within a Feature variable by setting the number of Degrees for PolynomialFeatures, then use the *.fit_transform* command to transforms the Data Object into a Matrix form in order to bring the values to forecast the target variable's value. Therefore, they can create a graph showing the intersection of the actual data together with the Prediction Line obtained from the forecast with high accuracy. Data scientists can write a program as follow.

Figure 55. Programming with polynomial regression analysis technique

```
import matplotlib.pyplot as plt
from sklearn.linear_model import LinearRegression
from sklearn.model_selection import train_test_split
from sklearn.preprocessing import PolynomialFeatures

polynomail_features = PolynomialFeatures(degree = 2)

h = [[1.5],[2],[3],[4],[5],[6]]
w = [[1.5],[2.5],[4],[4],[4.5],[5]]

h_poly = polynomail_features.fit_transform(h)
print(h_poly)

model = LinearRegression()
model.fit(h_poly,w)

weight = model.predict(h_poly)
print(weight)

plt.scatter(h,w)
plt.plot(h, weight)
plt.show()

print('R-Sqaured: %.4f' % model.score(h_poly,w))
```

In the figure, the data scientists transform the normal data into the Matrix form with the *Polynomail-Features* command, based on the equation $Y = B0+B1X+B2X2$. In the example, *Degree* is set as 2, which means the matrix with the number 0. – 2 sums to 3, and then the values inside the variable h are converted into such forms before putting into the variable *h_poly*. The result of the data transformation is as follows:

Figure 56. Results of data processing with polynomial features

```
[[ 1.     1.5    2.25]
 [ 1.     2.     4.  ]
 [ 1.     3.     9.  ]
 [ 1.     4.    16.  ]
 [ 1.     5.    25.  ]
 [ 1.     6.    36.  ]]
```

Data scientists combine the *h_poly* variable, which acts as a feature, together with the variable w, which acts as a target variable. The machine is taught to learn through the *.fit* command. Data is then analyzed with *LinearRegression()* command then predicted with the variable *h_poly*. The forecast result is presented via the *print* command.

Figure 57. Forecast results with polynomial regression analysis

```
[[1.71496131]
 [2.40472915]
 [3.52566638]
 [4.30180567]
 [4.73314703]
 [4.81969046]]
```

To show the efficiency of data analysis, data scientists create a *scatter plot* based on the data of the initial variables *h* and *w*. A *Prediction Line* is then created from the data obtained from the forecast together with the variable *h_poly* which is generated from the data within the variable *h* transformed by *PolynomailFetures* to demonstrate the affinity of facts. The *.score* command is used to analyze the accuracy. The result is 94.74% which is high accuracy, as shown in the figure.

Polynomial regression analysis is the transformation of data into matrix format, which is suitable for using non-linear features to analyze target variable data with *LinearRegression()* command. According to the samples, the forecast results show high accuracy.

FEATURE EXTRACTION

Data mining techniques use computational methods to process datasets in order to obtain results that can be used to answer a given question. Therefore, the data that can be used in data mining techniques must be numerical. However, data scientists often receive datasets that are either text or images, which cannot be imported into data mining techniques directly. Data scientists therefore need to use Feature Extraction to transform data from text or images into a numeric form so that it can be used for computation during the data preparation process. The library Scikit-Learn provides the datasets that data scientists can apply for Feature Extraction

Figure 58. Results of data analysis by polynomial regression analysis technique

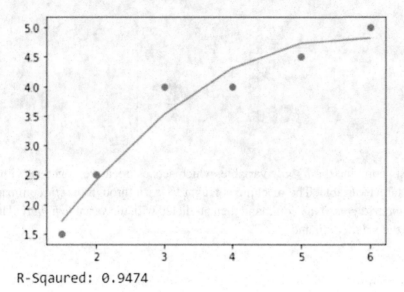

R-Sqaured: 0.9474

1.   Sklearn.Feature_Extraction

The Scikit-Learn library provides a package named Sklearn.Feature_Extraction which stores a set of commands for feature extraction to convert text into numbers in an array format as in the following syntax:

from sklearn.feature_extraction import DictVectorizer
data processing variables = DictVectorizer
dataset variables = text data
data processing variables. fit_transform(data variables).toarray()
data processing variables. get_feature_name()

From the syntax, data scientists run the *DictVectorizer* command from *sklearn.feature_extraction*, create variables that perform data processing using *DicVectorizer* command, and then create a text data set.

Data scientists can use *.fit_transform* command in combination with the dataset and the *.toaary()* command to convert all text into numbers in the form of an array, and display the *feature* names within the dataset with the *.get_feature_name()* command. You can write a program for *Feature Extraction* as in the example.

In the figure, data scientists determine the *vec* variable to manipulate the data using *DicVectorizer()* command, then create a dataset consisting of text and numbers, pack them into variable *m*, and convert them into numbers as an array by taking the variable *m* to process in the *.fit_transform().toaary()* command. And the result of the *Execute* command is a whole numeric array. The feature name is then displayed with the *get_feature_names* command. The result of the execution is the text Covid=19, and the list of provinces includes Bangkok, Chiang Mai and Lampang, which is the text data.

Figure 59. Using the DicVectorizer command

```
from sklearn.feature_extraction import DictVectorizer

vec = DictVectorizer()

m = [{'Province':'Bangkok','Covid-19':200},
     {'Province':'Chiang Mai','Covid-19':300},
     {'Province':'Lampang','Covid-19':10}]

print(vec.fit_transform(m).toarray())
print(vec.get_feature_names())


[[200.    1.    0.    0.]
 [300.    0.    1.    0.]
 [ 10.    0.    0.    1.]]
['Covid-19', 'Province=Bangkok', 'Province=Chiang Mai', 'Province=Lampang']
```

2.   Sklearn.Featue_Extraction.Text

Where data scientists receive long text or sentence datasets and intend to transform them into a text, they can run *CountVectorizer* command from package *sklearn.feature_extraction.text*, as in the following syntax.

from sklearn.feature_extraction.text import CountVectorizer
dataset variables = ['data']
data processing variables = CountVectorize(analyzer= 'word')
data processing variables. fit_transform(dataset variables).toarray()
data processing variables.get_feature_names()

From the syntax, data scientists run *CountVectorizer* command from *sklearn.faeture_extraction.text* package and then create a variable that transforms text into numeric data using the *CountVectorizer(analyzer= 'word')* command. Then the variables are used to process the data within the dataset with the *.fit_transform(). toarry()* command, and the feature names within the dataset are displayed with the *.get_feature_name()* command. Data scientists can write the syntax as in the example.

In the figure, the scientists run *CountVectorizer(analyzer= 'word')* command to define vec variable to process the data. The variable that stores the dataset is then inserted into *.fit_transform.toarray()* command in order to convert text into numeric data in an array format. The *.get_featuer_names()* command is then used to present feature names from the source dataset, and then displayed through the *print* command.

Figure 60. Using CounVectorizer command

```
from sklearn.feature_extraction.text import CountVectorizer
d = ['College of Innovation is the leader of innovation',
     'in Thailand. Besides, There are many Professor',
     ' who expert in digital transformation and ',
     'service design.']
vec = CountVectorizer(analyzer='word')
print(vec.fit_transform(d).toarray())
print(vec.get_feature_names())
```

```
[[0 0 0 1 0 0 0 0 2 1 1 0 2 0 0 0 1 0 0 0]
 [0 1 1 0 0 0 0 1 0 0 0 1 0 1 0 1 0 1 0 0]
 [1 0 0 0 0 1 1 1 0 0 0 0 0 0 0 0 0 0 1 1]
 [0 0 0 0 1 0 0 0 0 0 0 0 0 0 1 0 0 0 0 0]]
['and', 'are', 'besides', 'college', 'design', 'digital', 'expert', 'in'
```

3.   Feature Hashing

In case data scientists intend to determine the number of Data Objects converted from text into numeric data within the *sklearn.feature_extraction* package, the *FeatureHasher* command is available to use.

from sklearn.feature_extraction import FeatureHasher
data transforming variables = FeatureHashwer(n_features=number of Data Object)
dataset variables = [{data}]
data after transformation = data transforming variables.transform(dataset variables)
data after transformation. toarray()

From the syntax, the scientists run *FeatureHasher* command from *sklearn.feature_extraction* package by specifying the number of Data Objects after processing, then use the *.transform* command to transform the data, and then display it in the form of an array using the *.toarray()* command.

Figure 61. Using FeatureHasher

```
from sklearn.feature_extraction import FeatureHasher
hash = FeatureHasher(n_features=10)
Animal = [{'Lion': 1, 'Tiger':2, 'Cat':4}]
data = hash.transform(Animal)
data.toarray()
```

```
array([[-1.,  0.,  4., -2.,  0.,  0.,  0.,  0.,  0.,  0.]])
```

From the figure, data scientists runs *FeatureHasher* command from *sklean.feature_extraction* package by defining the *hash* variable to process the data and assigning *n_feature* as value of 10. After processing the data, there will be 10 numeric Data Objects. Then the dataset is packed into *Animal* variable, and the data is transformed into numeric data with *.transform( )* command. The data is then packed into the data variable and displayed as an array with *.toarray( )* command.

CONCLUSION

When data scientists begin to study Python for big data analysis, they first need to realize that Python provides a number of libraries that can be used to support data analysis, including Pandas, NumPy, SciPy, and Scikit-Learn. Besides studying about the commands and programming methods, knowledge of data mining is also something that data scientists need to explore in order to be able to choose the right data mining technique for the given problem. Python also supports data exploration through visualization and data preparation. Python is a tool that supports data science processes and big data analytics as it reduces the use of digital resources. In addition, this book also uses *Google Colab* tools where data scientists can write and test Python commands through a Web Brower without the need to install the *Software Editor* and *Interpreter* for libraries on their computers.

EXERCISE QUESTIONS

1. Write a program to create a data frame from a data set like this:
2. Write a program to create a data frame from a data consists of 16, 20 and NA then compensate NA by mean of 16 and 20.
3. Write a program with one-hot encoding from Table 1.

Table 1.

Colors
Red
Red
Yellow
Green
Pink

4. Explain the difference in data analysis between *Supervised-Learning* with *Unsupervised-Learning*
5. From the dataset includes mileage and oil. Apply polynomial regression analysis to predict oil from distance.

Distance [2.5,4.6,5.6,3.2,6.6,3.1,3.2,3.3,4.5]
   Oil [2.2,5.5,5.2,4.1,4.2,4.4,3.2,2.2,1.4]

REFERENCES

Cheewaprakobkit, P. (2019). *Predicting Student Academic Achievement by Using the Decision Tree and Neural Network Techniques*. Asia-Pacific International University.

Gong, Y., & Zhang, P. (2021). Predictive Analysis and Research Of Python Usage Rate Based on Polynomial Regression Model. *2021 3rd International Conference on Artificial Intelligence and Advanced Manufacture (AIAM), Artificial Intelligence and Advanced Manufacture (AIAM), 2021 3rd International Conference on, AIAM*, 266–270.

Healy, K. (2018). *Data visualization: a practical introduction*. Princeton University Press.

Massaron, L., & Mueller, J. (2015). *Python for data science for dummies*. John Wiley and Sons, Inc.

Mueller, J., & Massaron, L. (2019). *Python for data science* (2nd ed.). John Wiley & Sons, Inc.

Pajankar, A. (2021). *Practical Python data visualization: a fast track approach to learning data visualization with Python*. Apress. doi:10.1007/978-1-4842-6455-3

Rathaur, S., Kamath, N., & Ghanekar, U. (2020). Software Defect Density Prediction based on Multiple Linear Regression. *2020 Second International Conference on Inventive Research in Computing Applications (ICIRCA), Inventive Research in Computing Applications (ICIRCA), 2020 Second International Conference On*, 434–439.

Sonu, S. B., & Suyampulingam, A. (2021). Linear Regression Based Air Quality Data Analysis and Prediction using Python. *2021 IEEE Madras Section Conference (MASCON), Madras Section Conference (MASCON)*, 1–7.

Glossary

A

Administrator: Internal executives who establish the questions that data scientists use for data mining analysis.

Agglomerative Clustering Algorithm: A clustering method that supports Hierarchical Clustering by analyzing data from 2 or more attributes.

Apriori Algorithm: An algorithm used for analyzing correlation rules, using Confident values, Support values, and Support and Confidence Thresholds values as a measure for generating correlation rules in the form of Frequency Itemset.

Artificial Neural Network or ANN: A data mining technique that has both classification and numerical prediction capabilities. It can be classified as Supervised Learning.

Association Rule: Rules for the relationship of data or events. When one event occurs, another event will always follow.

Association Rule Mining: An analysis of the relationship rules of data or events from a dataset related to that data or event.

Attribute: The data attributes such as gender, education, income.

Attribute Transformation: Changing data formats to support data analysis with data mining techniques.

Authentication: Authentication of a user in any form, such as authentication with User Name or Password.

Average Pooling: Taking all the numbers in each part of the image data to create an average or mean.

Aviation Function: Adjusting data from Linear to Non-Linear with values between 0 - 1, which makes the data obtained from the calculation more closely attached to the facts until getting the output from calculation.

B

Back Propagation Artificial Neural Network (BP-ANN): Teaching machines to learn and test data with a neural network, which focuses on adjusting the weights of each link.

Bayesian Classifier: Classification of data based on the probability that data will be classified into a particular type.

Bias: A careful selection of data analysis to reduce the tendency of the data from the concentrated opinions.

Big Data: Big data can grow from customer transactions connected over the Internet until it acquires a large dataset that hides customer behavior patterns.

Binominal: Data Characteristics within RapidMiner with values of 0 and 1.

Box Plot: A graph showing the lowest value, 25% value, middle value, 75% value, highest value and abnormal data as well as showing multiple groups of data simultaneously.

Branch: Results in data classification within the Decision Tree.

Business Understanding: Understanding the issues of each business, the business environment and context of the industry.

C

C-Index: Clustering performance analysis that can avoid discrepancies from data points, characterized by noise.

Categorial Data: Data Categories such as gender, education, flower species.

Centroid: The center of the clustered data.

Class Label: Identifying the types of data that can be classified within the decision tree.

Classification: Data mining techniques used to classify data such as Decision Tree or k-NN.

Classification Rule: Classification is possible only if there is a result of a variable that supports the classification efficiency.

Cloud Technology: Technology to provide software services, processing, and memory without installing any hardware or software.

Cluster: Data groups such as groups of customers with different purchasing behaviors.

Clustering: Grouping the data, segmenting customers from the available data sets in order to know how differently each customer behaves.

Collaborative Filtering or CF: The focus on analyzing the behavior of customers with similar interests.

Confidence: The frequency as a percentage of the availability of rules-based data within the dataset.

Confusion Matrix: Measurement of the efficiency of data classification.

Content-Based Filtering: The focus on user behavior analysis.

Content-Based Recommendation: The focus on recommendations based on past content as references.

Continuous Data: Data that shows actual numbers such as height, distance, salary.

Convolutional Neural Networks: One of the deep learning techniques used to analyze large amounts of data, especially image data.

Convolutional Operation: Image data analysis in numeric form.

CRISP-DM: A process that enables data scientists to understand the problem and choose the right data mining techniques, which leads to the correct answer to the determined questions.

Cross Validation: Determination of the number of data division cycles by dividing the data into 2 parts in every round.

D

Data Analytics: The use of the Data Mining Technique for analyzing big data from the business sectors or other industries through classifying, forecasting or analyzing correlation rules to answer determined questions.

Data Collection: Collecting or even extracting data from outside the organization such as Social Network.

Data Exploration: Exploring data patterns and trends as well as surveying unusual and incomplete data.

Data Labeled: Target variables that data scientists need for forecasting or classifying data from the existing datasets, where the target variable is one of the components of the Supervised-Learning processing.

Data Mining: The techniques for analyzing data from large datasets, divided into Supervised-Learning and Unsupervised-Learning. The results obtained from the analysis are in the form of data classification, data segmentation, data forecasting and correlation rules.

Data Object: The data within the attributes of a dataset.

Data Point: The intersection that occurs when the data of 2 Attributes are plotted on the Scatter Plot.

Data Pre-Processing: Changing the data format to be standardized until the data can be processed by data mining techniques.

Data Preparation: The preparation of data by dealing with outliers and incomplete data.

Data Science: Knowledge on algorithms development to analyze data from large datasets. The result of development is in the form of Data Mining.

Data Scientist: The person who analyzes problems, explore and prepare data, analyze data with data mining techniques and present the results obtained from the analysis.

Data Selection: A selection of data to support the analysis of data with data mining techniques, and to answer the determined questions.

Data Set: The data set locates inside and outside the organization. It is consistent with data analysis.

Data Sources: A source of data sets that can be stored either internally or externally, such as a business partner's data store.

Data Store: To store data, data scientists should duplicate the data used for analysis without altering the original data.

Data Understanding: Understanding the nature of the data whether it can be used to analyze the data to answer the determined questions.

Data Visualization: Creating graphs to understand data patterns, data trends and abnormal data during the survey process.

Date: Data characteristics within RapidMiner covering the information on day, month, year.

Date_time: Data characteristics within RapidMiner which include day, month, year, and duration.

Davies-Bouldin Index: An analysis of the performance of clusters using data from the center of every cluster (Centroid).

DBSCAN: Clustering data by defining the radius from the center from every Data Point and setting the minimum number of Data Points that must be within the radius in order to determine the density of data within each cluster.

Decision Tree: A technique to classify the resulting data in a tree diagram. Data scientists can use the diagram to classify data or target variables.

Deep Learning: A data mining technique that can be used to analyze non-projected data; including images, sounds, and text. There are two types of deep learning; convolutional neural networks and recurrent neural networks. The deep learning model modulates the pre-configuration data for processing in conjunction with neural network techniques.

Deployment: The use of the results obtained from the analysis to respond to the problem.

Descriptive Statistics: The statistics that focuses on quantitative analysis of data. It could be an analysis of the data to answer a given question, such as testing the average between two populations.

Dimensionality: The number of attributes within the data set.

Discreate: The data that indicates a clustering or a data type.

Domain Expert: A data specialist who is familiar with data sets that can be used to analyze problems. Data scientists must consult with the expert to understand the data and ensure that the results obtained from the analysis are consistent with the corporate environment.

Dunn Index: The determination of the minimum distance from the data point to the data point in other clusters (Intercluster) divided by the distance of the largest data point within the cluster.

Duplicate Data: Duplicate data within the same data set.

E

Entropy: The uncertainty of the data.

Epochs: Iterative analysis of the data to teach the machine to learn each time.

Euclidean Distance: The Calculation of the distance between the data point and the center of each cluster within a K-Mean clustering. Within the data set, there is still the movement of the data object while clustering the data in multiple direction.

F

Feature: Features in database textbooks is also called an Attribute.

Feature Extraction: Image transformation process to be in numeric format.

Feature Selection: Selecting appropriate features to be used in data analysis, using quantitative analysis techniques or consulting a Domain Expert.

Filter Matrix: It is used to examine patterns in each part of the image to obtain data within the feature that preserves the distinctive characteristics of the image.

Forecasting: Numerical forecasting of outcomes. In some data mining techniques, such as logistic regression, it may result in data classification.

Frequency: The frequency at which an event occurs or similar information is encountered.

Fully Connected: The merging of data segments in a feature that is ready to be used to process data with neural networks for classifying image data.

G

Generalized: Organizing data in a format suitable for classification.

H

Hashtag: Text used to characterize content within Twitter, preceded by the # sign.

Hidden Layer: Nodes and layers that enhance neural network processing efficiency.

Hierarchical Clustering: The division of data into cluster according to the order of clusters to determine which sub-clusters belong to each large cluster.

Histogram: A graph used to explore the distribution of data by generating the spectral values of the data.

I

Impurity Measure: A value at which each class can be divided into more classes. The better the class can be divided, the lower the impurity measure.

Inconsistency Data: The data gathered from multiple but conflicting sources.

Inferential Statistics: A statistical analysis once receiving the results of a test on a sample. It can be used to represent the entire population.

Information Gain: Selecting the features appropriate for creating a decision tree.

Information Security: Information security, which includes data integrity, data confidentiality, and data availability. This can be done both in terms of security policy and the provision of effective defense technology.

Input Neural: The number of input nodes dependent on the number of variables or features analyzed with the model.

Instance: Number of records formed by a combination of multiple features.

Integer: Data attributes within RapidMiner which are integers.

Interpretation: Translating the results of data mining analysis into an easy-to-understand format.

Item-Based Filtering: It focuses on analyzing product properties.

Item-Based Nearest Neighbor Recommendation: An analysis on similarity of a dataset, which is a human opinion and the similarity of the properties of the subject.

Itemset: The number of features to be analyzed in the correlation rule.

K

K-Means: Clustering and defining according to the objectives of the data analysis. It is a type of Unsupervised-Learning datamining techniques.

Knowledge Discovery: The discovery of knowledge in various forms, such as the use of data mining techniques to analyze the correlation rules of customer buying behavior.

Knowledge Discovery Process: The process of analyzing data using data mining techniques, focusing on data extraction, data processing using data mining and interpretation techniques to answer the questions.

L

Label: Target variables that are set for forecasting or classifying data.

Leaf Node: The result of classifying data from each class within the decision tree.

Long Short-Term Memory (LSTM): The ability to memorize values from the previous step that are very distant from the current node. Those values are then computed with the current node to obtain results from sorting related data within deep learning data mining techniques.

M

Machine Learning: A machine that has the ability to recognize characteristics of data for data forecasting, data classification, data segmentation and correlation rule analysis.

Manhattan Distance: A method for calculating the distance for quantitative data by subtracting the data objects from each instance and gathering the results of all data objects.

Max Pooling: Selecting the largest number in each part of the image data.

Missing Value: Incomplete data within the dataset.

Mode: Frequency analysis from the largest amount of duplicate data.

Model Evaluation: Analysis of efficiency to assure how accurately data processing can predict, classify, and analyze correlation rules.

Modeling: Data analysis with data mining techniques without programming. The tools within software packages such as RapidMiner can be used to create a schematic data analysis process.

N

Naïve Bayes: Classification of data using probabilistic analysis as to what classification the data should be.

Nearest Neighbor: Matching the closest neighbors by identifying how the data is classified from the neighboring data.

Nominal Scale: Data in the form of clusters, such as gender; female, male and others.

Normalization: Making data to the same standard.

Numerical Prediction: Forecasting numeric data by defining target variables used for forecasting.

O

Objective Measurement: Using data from quantitative analysis that can be used to reflect the efficiency of correlation rules obtained from data mining analysis.

Open Source: Non-licensed software that allows developers from all over the world to collaborate on the development of the software.

Ordinal Scale: Representing an Abstraction with ordinal numbers.

Outlier: Outliers, either too many or too few, can affect the average of the entire feature. It may be due to data entry errors.

Output Neural: The results obtained from the processing. There can be one or more results depending on the data analysis question.

P

Pattern Recognition: A system for recognizing and distinguishing data from the learned patterns, such as photo recognition.

Pearson Correlation: Analysis of the relationship between two sets of data for similarity analysis.

Polynomial: Characteristics of data within RapidMiner that can be numeric data or text data.

Polynomial Regression: Data analysis for forecasting. Data obtained from this analysis is more closely related to facts than linear data analysis.

Precision: Displays of the accuracy of data classification.

Predict Accuracy: The difference in data that data scientists use to teach machines to learn.

Prediction: Results from data analysis using data mining techniques to predict the outcomes based on data from existing datasets.

Probabilistic Method: One of the methods for forecasting missing data using Bayes Theorem.

Pruning the Tree: The reduction of the feature number used in data analysis in order to ease its use in data classification.

R

Rank Accuracy: The percentage accuracy of the recommendation that Recommendation System provides for users.

RapidMiner: The software that allows data scientists to process data with data mining techniques by creating schematic models.

Real: The data within RapidMiner as real numbers.

Recall: The displays of the accuracy of data classification in accordance with the actual data.

Recommendation System: The system that analyzes data from a dataset. It can be used to support decision-making in a variety of matters.

Recurrent Neural Networks: One of the deep learning data mining techniques aiming at analyzing the relationships of sequential and time series data.

Regression: A data mining technique used to forecast numerical data.

Resolution: A measure used to store data objects in each feature.

Retweet: Repeating the Tweets that others have Tweeted in their Twitter Account.

Rule Interestingness: Determining the strength or value of correlation rules, or applying the results of the analysis to make decisions in businesses or industries.

S

Scalability: The size of data that keeps growing from updates of global users on social networks or data that grows from the updates from business partners.

Scatter Plot: A graph that creates intersections from 2 or more features by plotting graphs on the x and y axes.

Set Role: Assigning a feature within RapidMiner software as a target variable for Supervised-Learning datamining process.

Similarity: Calculation of similarity.

Split Data: Splitting data into two parts: 1 for teaching machine learning and 2 for testing the performance of the model.

Stopping Conditions: The neural network model will stop computation in order to teach the machine learning. Data scientists can then calculate weight to obtain the appropriate error level.

Stride: Moving the Filter Matrix to inspect the image data one by one.

Strong Association Rule: A strong correlation rule, used as a rule for data analysis. It is useful for making decision.

Subjective Measurement: Using opinions or Domain Expert suggestions to decide which correlation rules are helpful for decision making.

Supervised-Learning: Teaching machines to have the ability to recognize the features to classify, forecast, and analyze the correlation rules.

Support: The frequency as a percentage of the availability of rules-based data within the entire dataset.

Support and Confidence Thresholds: A measure of whether each correlation rule can be used in data analysis.

T

Tensor Object: The model used to transform image data into numeric format.

Test Set: A data sets for testing the performance of a data mining model.

Time: A characteristic of data within RapidMiner, characterized by duration.

Time Series: Data that occurs continuously over time.

Training Set: A data set for teaching machines to learn.

Tweet: Commenting or presenting products and services within Twitter.

Twitter: A social network where users can comment and reproduce the opinions of others.

Twitter API: A tool used for extracting data from Twitter for the purpose of data analysis.

U

Unsupervised-Learning: Analyzing data with data mining techniques, that do not require machine learning. Those datasets can be processed directly, such as Cluster Analysis and Association Rule Mining.

User-Based Nearest-Neighbor Collaborative Filtering: Forecasting current missing data based on other data of a similar and complete form.

W

Web Mining: Data Extraction used for data analysis from web-based resources to obtain a dataset that corresponds to the questions.

Compilation of References

Abbas, A., Prayitno, P., Butarbutar, F., Nurkim, N., Prumanto, D., Dewadi, F. M., Hidayati, N., & Windarto, A. P. (2021). Implementation of clustering unsupervised learning using K-means mapping techniques. *IOP Conference Series. Materials Science and Engineering, 1088*(1), 012004. doi:10.1088/1757-899X/1088/1/012004

Abbasnasab Sardareh, S., Brown, G. T. L., & Denny, P. (2021). Comparing Four Contemporary Statistical Software Tools for Introductory Data Science and Statistics in the Social Sciences. *Teaching Statistics: An International Journal for Teachers, 43*.

Abdul Aziz, A., & Starkey, A. (2020). Predicting Supervise Machine Learning Performances for Sentiment Analysis Using Contextual-Based Approaches. *IEEE Access : Practical Innovations, Open Solutions, 8*, 17722–17733. doi:10.1109/ACCESS.2019.2958702

Abu-Soud, S. M. (2019). A Novel Approach for Dealing with Missing Values in Machine Learning Datasets with Discrete Values. *2019 International Conference on Computer and Information Sciences (ICCIS)*, 1-5. 10.1109/ICCISci.2019.8716430

Adeniyi, D. A., Wei, Z., & Yongquan, Y. (2016). Automated web usage data mining and recommendation system using K-Nearest Neighbor (KNN) classification method. *Applied Computing & Informatics, 12*(1), 90–108. doi:10.1016/j.aci.2014.10.001

Aditya, G. M., Hoode, A., Anvesh Rai, K., Biradar, G., Ajay Kumara, M., Manoj Kumar, M. V., Prashanth, B. S., Sneha, H. R., & Shivadarshan, S. L. (2021). Machine Learning Based Platform and Recommendation System for Food Ordering Services within Premises. *2021 2nd Global Conference for Advancement in Technology (GCAT), Advancement in Technology (GCAT), 2021 2nd Global Conference For*, 1–8.

Aggarwal, C. C. (2018). *Neural networks and deep learning: a textbook.* Springer. doi:10.1007/978-3-319-94463-0

Almasoud, A. M., Al-Khalifa, H. S., & Al-Salman, A. S. (2019). Handling Big Data Scalability in Biological Domain Using Parallel and Distributed Processing: A Case of Three Biological Semantic Similarity Measures. *BioMed Research International, 2019*, 1–20. doi:10.1155/2019/6750296 PMID:30809545

Andrews, F. M., & Messenger, R. C. (1973). *Multivariate nominal scale analysis; a report on a new analysis technique and a computer program.* University of Michigan.

Angiulli, F., & Fassetti, F. (2021). Uncertain distance-based outlier detection with arbitrarily shaped data objects. *Journal of Intelligent Information Systems, 57*(1), 1–24. doi:10.100710844-020-00624-7

Atanasovski, M., Kostov, M., Arapinoski, B., & Spirovski, M. (2020). K-Nearest Neighbor Regression for Forecasting Electricity Demand. *2020 55th International Scientific Conference on Information, Communication and Energy Systems and Technologies (ICEST), Information, Communication and Energy Systems and Technologies (ICEST), 2020 55th International Scientific Conference On*, 110–113.

Baby, S. S., & Reddy, S. L. (2021). End to End Product Recommendation system with improvements in Apriori Algorithm. *2021 Third International Conference on Inventive Research in Computing Applications (ICIRCA), Inventive Research in Computing Applications (ICIRCA), 2021 Third International Conference On*, 1357–1361.

Bader, D. (2018). *Python tricks: The book.* Dan Bader.

Başarslan, M. S., & Argun, İ. D. (2018). Classification Of a bank data set on various data mining platforms. *2018 Electric Electronics, Computer Science, Biomedical Engineerings' Meeting, 2018*, 1–4.

Bayram, E., & Nabiyev, V. (2020). Image segmentation by using K-means clustering algorithm in Euclidean and Mahalanobis distance calculation in camouflage images. *2020 28th Signal Processing and Communications Applications Conference (SIU), Signal Processing and Communications Applications Conference (SIU), 2020 28th*, 1–4.

Bean, R. (2022). Why Becoming a Data-Driven Organization Is So Hard. *Harvard Business Review Digital Articles*, 1–6.

Bell, J. (2015). *Machine learning: hands-on for developers and technical professionals. John Wiley & Sons.*

Ben Ncir, C.-E., Hamza, A., & Bouaguel, W. (2021). Parallel and scalable Dunn Index for the validation of big data clusters. *Parallel Computing*, *102*, 102. doi:10.1016/j.parco.2021.102751

Beohar, D., & Rasool, A. (2021). Handwritten Digit Recognition of MNIST dataset using Deep Learning state-of-the-art Artificial Neural Network (ANN) and Convolutional Neural Network (CNN). *2021 International Conference on Emerging Smart Computing and Informatics (ESCI), Emerging Smart Computing and Informatics (ESCI), 2021 International Conference On*, 542–548.

Berman, J. J. (2018). Principles and practice of big data: preparing, sharing, and analyzing complex information (2nd ed.). Academic Press/Elsevier.

Bing, L., Yiming, M., & Lee, R. (2001). Analyzing the interestingness of association rules from the temporal dimension. *Proceedings 2001 IEEE International Conference on Data Mining, Data Mining, 2001. ICDM 2001, Proceedings IEEE International Conference on, Data Mining*, 377–384. 10.1109/ICDM.2001.989542

Bowles, M. (2015). *Machine learning in Python: essential techniques for predictive analysis.* Wiley. doi:10.1002/9781119183600

Bramer, M. (2016). *Principle of Data Mining* (3rd ed.). Springer-Verlag London Ltd.10.1007/978-1-4471-7307-6

Cai, S., Sun, R., Hao, S., Li, S., & Yuan, G. (2016). An efficient outlier detection approach on weighted data stream based on minimal rare pattern mining. *China Communications, 16*(10), 83-99.

Carlson, K., Livermore, M. A., & Rockmore, D. N. (2020). The Problem of Data Bias in the Pool of Published U.S. Appellate Court Opinions. *Journal of Empirical Legal Studies*, *17*(2), 224–261. doi:10.1111/jels.12253

Chaimongkol, N., & Meesad, P. (2010). *Association Rule Mining for Specific New Course. Mahanakorn University of Technology (MUT).*

Chavan, A. (2020). *RapidMiner Installation on Windows.* Retrieved 15 December 2021 from https://www.youtube.com/watch?v=4RpepmDH-7s

Cheewaprakobkit, P. (2019). *Predicting Student Academic Achievement by Using the Decision Tree and Neural Network Techniques.* Asia-Pacific International University.

Chen, Q., & Qin, J. (2021). Research and implementation of movie recommendation system based on deep learning. *2021 IEEE International Conference on Computer Science, Electronic Information Engineering and Intelligent Control Technology (CEI), Computer Science, Electronic Information Engineering and Intelligent Control Technology (CEI), 2021 IEEE International Conference On*, 225–228.

Chiarini, T. M., Kohli, R., & Forsgren, N. (2021). Theories in Flux: Reimagining Theory Building in the Age of Machine Learning. *Management Information Systems Quarterly*, *45*(1), 455–459.

Chinnarasri, C., Nonsawang, S., & Supharatid, S. (2012). *Application of Artificial Neural Networks for River Stage Forecasting in Hatyai. King Mongkut's University of Technology Thonburi*. KMUTT.

Chisholm, A. (2013). *Exploring Data with RapidMiner: Explore, Understand, and Prepare Real Data Using Rapidminer's Practical Tips and Tricks*. Packt Publishing.

Chow, T. W. S., & Cho, S.-Y. (2007). *Neural networks and computing: learning algorithms and applications*. Imperial College Press. doi:10.1142/p487

Curry, E., Heintz, F., Irgens, M., Smeulders, A. W. M., & Strmigioli, S. (2022). Partnership on AI, Data, and Robotics. *Communications of the ACM*, *65*(4), 54–55. doi:10.1145/3513000

Dai, H., Zhang, S., Wang, L., & Ding, Y. (2016). Research and implementation of big data preprocessing system based on Hadoop. *2016 IEEE International Conference on Big Data Analysis (ICBDA)*, 1-5. 10.1109/ICBDA.2016.7509802

Desale, K. S., Kumathekar, C. N., & Chavan, A. P. (2015) Efficient Intrusion Detection System Using Stream Data Mining Classification Technique. *2015 International Conference on Computing Communication Control and Automation*, 469-473. 10.1109/ICCUBEA.2015.98

Emon, M. I., Shahiduzzaman, M., Rakib, M. R. H., Shathee, M. S. A., Saha, S., Kamran, M. N., & Fahim, J. H. (2021). Profile Based Course Recommendation System Using Association Rule Mining and Collaborative Filtering. *2021 International Conference on Science & Contemporary Technologies (ICSCT), Science & Contemporary Technologies (ICSCT), 2021 International Conference On*, 1–5.

Erdoğmuş, Z. İ., & Arslan, M. K. (2022). Engaging with Social Media Influencers on Youtube: A Cluster Analysis. *Istanbul University Journal of the School of Business Administration*, *51*(1), 359–373.

Fadlil, A., Umar, R., & Gustina, S. (2019). Mushroom Images Identification Using Order Statistics Feature Extraction with Artificial Neural Network Classification Technique. *Journal of Physics: Conference Series*, *1373*(1), 012037. doi:10.1088/1742-6596/1373/1/012037

Fernando, T., Gammulle, H., Denman, S., Sridharan, S., & Fookes, C. (2021). Deep Learning for Medical Anomaly Detection - A Survey. *ACM Computing Surveys*, *54*(7), 1–37. doi:10.1145/3464423

Ghorpade, V. G., & Koneru, V. S. (2021). Pattern recognition neural networkmodel for experimental based compressive strength graded self compacting concrete. *Materials Today: Proceedings*, *43*(Part 2), 795–799. doi:10.1016/j.matpr.2020.06.175

Ghous, H., & Kovács, L. (2020). Efficiency Comparison of Python and Rapidminer. *Multidiszciplináris Tudományok*, *10*(3), 212–220. doi:10.35925/j.multi.2020.3.26

Ginting, S. W., Hartati, R. S., Sudarma, M., & Swamardika, I. B. A. (2021). Clustering of Earthquake and Volcanic Eruption Trauma Survivor Groups using K-Means Algorithm. *2021 International Conference on Smart-Green Technology in Electrical and Information Systems (ICSGTEIS), Smart-Green Technology in Electrical and Information Systems (ICSGTEIS), 2021 International Conference On*, 69–73.

Giri, C., & Chen, Y. (2022). Deep Learning for Demand Forecasting in the Fashion and Apparel Retail Industry. *Forecasting*, *4*(2), 565–581. doi:10.3390/forecast4020031

Glass, D. H. (2013). Confirmation measures of association rule interestingness. *Knowledge-Based Systems*, *44*, 65–77. doi:10.1016/j.knosys.2013.01.021

Global Mindset University. (2020). *RapidMiner Data Exploration demo | Data Analysis - Using the Iris Data | Data Mining*. Retrieved 15 December 2021 from https://www.youtube.com/watch?v=EfQkqcj3MIk

Gong, S., Ye, H.-W., & Zhu, X. (2009). Item-based collaborative filtering recommendation using self-organizing map. *2009 Chinese Control and Decision Conference, Control and Decision Conference, 2009. CCDC '09. Chinese*, 4029–4031.

Gong, Y., & Zhang, P. (2021). Predictive Analysis and Research Of Python Usage Rate Based on Polynomial Regression Model. *2021 3rd International Conference on Artificial Intelligence and Advanced Manufacture (AIAM), Artificial Intelligence and Advanced Manufacture (AIAM), 2021 3rd International Conference on, AIAM*, 266–270.

Görtler, J., Hohman, F., Moritz, D., Wongsuphasawat, K., Ren, D., Nair, R., Kirchner, M., & Patel, K. (2021). *Neo: Generalizing Confusion Matrix Visualization to Hierarchical and Multi-Output Labels*. Academic Press.

Govindaraj, V., Thiyagarajan, A., Rajasekaran, P., Zhang, Y., & Krishnasamy, R. (2020). Automated unsupervised learning-based clustering approach for effective anomaly detection in brain magnetic resonance imaging (MRI). *IET Image Processing*, *14*(14), 3516–3526. doi:10.1049/iet-ipr.2020.0597

Greco, S., Słowiński, R., & Szczęch, I. (2016). Measures of rule interestingness in various perspectives of confirmation. *Information Sciences*, *346–347*, 216–235. doi:10.1016/j.ins.2016.01.056

Grutter, R. (2019). A framework for assisted proximity analysis in feature data. *Journal of Geographical Systems*, *21*(3), 367–394. doi:10.100710109-019-00304-3

Guo, C., Zhang, M., & Chen, H. (2021). Suitability of low-field nuclear magnetic resonance (LF-NMR) combining with back propagation artificial neural network (BP-ANN) to predict printability of polysaccharide hydrogels 3D printing. *International Journal of Food Science & Technology*, *56*(5), 2264–2272. doi:10.1111/ijfs.14844

Gupta, A., Sahayadhas, A., & Gupta, V. (2020). Proposed Techniques to Design Speed Efficient Data warehouse Architecture for Fastening Knowledge Discovery Process. *2020 IEEE Third International Conference on Artificial Intelligence and Knowledge Engineering (AIKE)*.

Hannah, S., Deepa, A. J., Chooralil, V. S., BrillySangeetha, S., Yuvaraj, N., Arshath Raja, R., Suresh, C., Vignesh, R., YasirAbdullahR, Srihari, K., & Alene, A. (2022). Blockchain-Based Deep Learning to Process IoT Data Acquisition in Cognitive Data. *BioMed Research International*, *2022*, 1–7. doi:10.1155/2022/5038851 PMID:35187166

Haviluddin, I. M., Putra, G. M., Puspitasari, N., Setyadi, H. J., Dwiyanto, F.A., Wibawa, A. P., & Alfred, R. (2020). A Performance Comparison ofEuclidean, Manhattan and Minkowski Distances in K-Means Clustering. *2020 6th International Conference on Science in Information Technology (ICSITech), Science in Information Technology (ICSITech), 2020 6th International Conference On*, 184–188.

Healy, K. (2018). *Data visualization: a practical introduction*. Princeton University Press.

Hernandez-Suarez, A., Sanchez-Perez, G., Toscano-Medina, K., Martinez-Hernandez, V., Sanchez, V., & Perez-Meana, H. (2018). *A Web Scraping Methodology for Bypassing Twitter API Restrictions*. Academic Press.

Hill, C. (2015). *Learning scientific programming with Python*. Cambridge University Press. doi:10.1017/CBO9781139871754

Hodijah, A., & Setijohatmo, U. T. (2021). Analysis of frequent itemset generation based on trie data structure in Apriori algorithm. *Telkomnika*, *19*(5), 1553–1564. doi:10.12928/telkomnika.v19i5.19273

Hong, G., & Nan, G. (2021). Research and Application of a Multidimensional Association Rules Mining Algorithm Based on Hadoop. *2021 IEEE Intl Conf on Parallel & Distributed Processing with Applications, Big Data & Cloud Computing, Sustainable Computing & Communications, Social Computing & Networking (ISPA/BDCloud/SocialCom/ SustainCom), Parallel & Distributed Processing with Applications, Big Data & Cloud Computing, Sustainable Computing & Communications, Social Computing & Networking (ISPA/BDCloud/SocialCom/SustainCom), 2021 IEEE Intl Conf on, ISPA-BDCLOUD-SOCIALCOM-SUSTAINCOM*, 636–643.

Hongboonmee, N., & Trepanichkul, P. (2019). *Comparison of Data Classification Efficiency to Analyze Risk Factors that Affect the Occurrence of Hyperthyroidusing Data Mining Techniques. Mahanakorn University of Technology (MUT).*

Hume, E., & West, A. (2020). Becoming a Data-Driven Decision Making Organization: Seven Challenges Facing Not-for-Profits. *The CPA Journal*, *90*(4), 32.

Hyrmet, M., & Arbana, K. (2021). The Data Mining Approach: A Case Study - Clustering Algorithms for After Sales Service. *10th Mediterranean Conference on Embedded Computing (MECO)*, 1-6.

Inmon, W. H., & Lindstedt, D. (2015). *Data architecture: a primer for the data scientist : big data, data warehouse and data vault*. Morgan Kaufmann/Elsevier.

Ironfrown. (2016). *RapidMiner Stats (Part 5): Boxplots*. Retrieved 15 December 2021 from https://www.youtube.com/watch?v=IJ180B4ZiLo

Jamalludin, M. D. M,, Fajar Shidik, G., Zainul Fanani, A., Purwanto, & Al Zami, F. (2021). Implementation of Feature Selection Using Gain Ratio Towards Improved Accuracy of Support Vector Machine (SVM) on Youtube Comment Classification. *2021 International Seminar on Application for Technology of Information and Communication (ISemantic), Application for Technology of Information and Communication (ISemantic), 2021 International Seminar On*, 28–31.

Jiang, S., Jiang, T., & Wang, L. (2020). Secure and Efficient Cloud Data Deduplication with Ownership Management. *IEEE Transactions on Services Computing*, *13*(6), 1152–1165.

Johnny, O., & Trovati, M. (2020). Big data inconsistencies and incompleteness: a literature review. *International Journal of Grid and Utility Computing, 5*, 705. 10.1504/IJGUC.2020.110057

Joshi, P. (2017). *Artificial intelligence with Python: a comprehensive guide to building intelligent apps for Python beginners and developers*. Packt Publishing Ltd.

Junaidi, A., Ferani Tanjung, N. A., Wijayanto, S., Lasama, J., & Iskandar, A. R. (2021). Overfitting Problem in Images Classification for Egg Incubator Using Convolutional Neural Network. *2021 9th International Conference on Cyber and IT Service Management (CITSM), Cyber and IT Service Management (CITSM), 2021 9th International Conference On*, 1–7.

Jyothi, P. N., Lakshmi, D. R., & Rao, K. V. S. N. R. (2020). A Supervised Approach for Detection of Outliers in Healthcare Claims Data. *Journal of Engineering Science & Technology Review*, *13*(1), 204–213. doi:10.25103/jestr.131.25

Kamukwamba, Y., & Chunxiao, L. (2021). A Novel Algorithm Using Content-Based Filtering Technology in Apache Spark for Big Data Analysis. *2021 4th International Conference on Artificial Intelligence and Big Data (ICAIBD), Artificial Intelligence and Big Data (ICAIBD), 2021 4th International Conference On*, 22–26.

Karthik, M. G., & Krishnan, M. B. M. (2021). Detecting Internet of Things Attacks Using Post Pruning Decision Tree-Synthetic Minority Over Sampling Technique. *International Journal of Intelligent Engineering & Systems*, *14*(4), 105–114. doi:10.22266/ijies2021.0831.10

Keles, M. K. (2019). Breast Cancer Prediction and Detection Using Data Mining Classification Algorithms: A Comparative Study. *Tehnicki Vjesnik - Technical Gazette, 26*(1), 149.

Khan, S. A., & Ali Rana, Z. (2019). Evaluating Performance of Software Defect Prediction Models Using Area Under Precision-Recall Curve (AUC-PR). *2019 2nd International Conference on Advancements in Computational Sciences (ICACS), Advancements in Computational Sciences (ICACS), 2019 2nd International Conference On,* 1–6.

Khatter, H., Arif, S., Singh, U., Mathur, S., & Jain, S. (2021). Product Recommendation System for E-Commerce using Collaborative Filtering and Textual Clustering. *2021 Third International Conference on Inventive Research in Computing Applications (ICIRCA), Inventive Research in Computing Applications (ICIRCA), 2021 Third International Conference On,* 612–618.

Klinkenberg, R., & Hofmann, M. (2014). *RapidMiner: data mining use cases and business analytics applications.* CRC Press.

Kotu, V., & Deshpande, B. (2014). *Predictive analytics and data mining: concepts and practice with RapidMiner.* Elsevier Ltd.

Kumar, P., Ganapathy, G., & Kang, J.-J. (2021). A Hybrid Mod K-Means Clustering with Mod SVM Algorithm to Enhance the Cancer Prediction. International Journal of Internet. *Broadcasting and Communication, 13*(2), 231–243.

Kusumawardhani, N. K., Nasrun, M., & Setianingsih, C. (2019). Web Recommended System Library Book Selection Using Item Based Collaborative Filtering Method. *2019 IEEE International Conference on Engineering, Technology and Education (TALE), Engineering, Technology and Education (TALE), 2019 IEEE International Conference On,* 1–8.

Kyaw, K. S., & Limsiroratana, S. (2019). Case Study: Knowledge Discovery Process using Computation Intelligence with Feature Selection Approach. *2019 17th International Conference on ICT and Knowledge Engineering (ICT&KE), ICT and Knowledge.*

Lakshmi Devi, R., & Samundeeswari, V., V. (2021). Detection and Automated Classification of Brain Tumor Types in MRI Images using Convolutional Neural Network with Grid Search Optimization. *2021 Fifth International Conference on I-SMAC (IoT in Social, Mobile, Analytics and Cloud) (I-SMAC), I-SMAC (IoT in Social, Mobile, Analytics and Cloud) (I-SMAC), 2021 Fifth International Conference On,* 1280–1284.

Lawal, M. M., Ibrahim, H., Sani, N. F. M., & Yaakob, R. (2020). Analyses of Indexing Techniques on Uncertain Data With High Dimensionality. *IEEE Access : Practical Innovations, Open Solutions, 8,* 74101–74117. doi:10.1109/ACCESS.2020.2988487

LeCun, Y., Cortes, C., & Burges, J. C. C. (2021). *The MNIST Database of Handwritten Digits.* Retrieved from: http://yann.lecun.com/exdb/mnist/

Li, J., Horiguchi, Y., & Sawaragi, T. (2020). Data Dimensionality Reduction by Introducing Structural Equation Modeling to Machine Learning Problems. *2020 59th Annual Conference of the Society of Instrument and Control Engineers of Japan (SICE), Instrument and Control Engineers of Japan (SICE), 2020 59th Annual Conference of the Society Of,* 826–831.

Liao, S.-H., Widowati, R., & Chang, H.-Y. (2021). A data mining approach for developing online streaming recommendations. *Applied Artificial Intelligence, 35*(15), 2204–2227. doi:10.1080/08839514.2021.1997211

Li, K., Li, J., Liu, S., Li, Z., Bo, J., & Liu, B. (2019). GA-iForest: An Efficient Isolated Forest Framework Based on Genetic Algorithm for Numerical Data Outlier Detection. *Transactions of Nanjing University of Aeronautics & Astronautics, 36*(6), 1026–1038.

Liu, L. (2021). Design of Human Resource Management Information System Based on Decision Tree Algorithm. *2021 Global Reliability and Prognostics and Health Management (PHM-Nanjing), Reliability and Prognostics and Health Management (PHM-Nanjing), 2021 Global*, 1–6.

Liu, Y.-Y., Li, L., Liu, Y.-S., Chan, P.-W., Zhang, W.-H., & Zhang, L. (2021). Estimation of precipitation induced by tropical cyclones based on machine-learning-enhanced analogue identification of numerical prediction. *Meteorological Applications*, 28(2). Advance online publication. doi:10.1002/met.1978

Lou, N. (2022). Analysis of the Intelligent Tourism Route Planning Scheme Based on the Cluster Analysis Algorithm. *Computational Intelligence and Neuroscience*, 2022, 1–10. doi:10.1155/2022/3310676 PMID:35800698

Lourenco, J., & Varde, A. S. (2020). Item-Based Collaborative Filtering and Association Rules for a Baseline Recommender in E-Commerce. *2020 IEEE International Conference on Big Data (Big Data), Big Data (Big Data), 2020 IEEE International Conference On*, 4636–4645.

Lubanovic, B. (2019). *Introducing Python: modern computing in simple packages* (2nd ed.). O'Reilly Media, Inc.

Mandhare, H. C., & Idate, S. R. (2017). A comparative study of cluster based outlier detection, distance based outlier detection and density based outlier detection techniques. *2017 International Conference on Intelligent Computing and Control Systems (ICICCS)*, 931-935. 10.1109/ICCONS.2017.8250601

Maneechaeye, P., & Ramjan, S. (2022). *Components and Indicators Development with Guidelines to Encourage Safety Behavior among Flight Crews in Thailand (Independent Study)*. Thammasat University.

Maslan, A., Mohamad, K. M. B., & Mohd Foozy, F. B. (2020). Feature selection for DDoS detection using classification machine learning techniques. *IAES International Journal of Artificial Intelligence*, 9(1), 137–145. doi:10.11591/ijai.v9.i1.pp137-145

Massaron, L., & Mueller, J. (2015). *Python for data science for dummies*. John Wiley and Sons, Inc.

Mat, T. M., Lajis, A., & Nasir, H. (2018). Text Data Preparation in RapidMiner for Short Free Text Answer in Assisted Assessment. *2018 IEEE 5th International Conference on Smart Instrumentation, Measurement and Application (ICSIMA)*, 1-4.

Mesner, O. C., & Shalizi, C. R. (2021). Conditional Mutual Information Estimation for Mixed, Discrete and Continuous Data. *IEEE Transactions on Information Theory*, 67(1), 464–484. doi:10.1109/TIT.2020.3024886

Mishra, A., & Vats, A. (2021). Supervised machine learning classification algorithms for detection of fracture location in dissimilar friction stir welded joints. *Frattura e Integrita Strutturale*, 15(58), 242–253. doi:10.3221/IGF-ESIS.58.18

Mladenova, T. (2021). A Feature-Weighted Rule for the K-Nearest Neighbor. *2021 5th International Symposium on Multidisciplinary Studies and Innovative Technologies (ISMSIT), Multidisciplinary Studies and Innovative Technologies (ISMSIT), 2021 5th International Symposium On*, 493–497.

Mnich, K., Polewko-Klim, A., Kitlas Golinska, A., Lesinski, W., & Rudnicki, W. R. (2020). Super Learning with Repeated Cross Validation. *2020 International Conference on Data Mining Workshops (ICDMW), Data Mining Workshops (ICDMW), 2020 International Conference on, ICDMW*, 629–635.

Mohan, L., Jain, S., Suyal, P., & Kumar, A. (2020). Data mining Classification Techniques for Intrusion Detection System. *2020 12th International Conference on Computational Intelligence and Communication Networks (CICN)*, 351-355.

Montesdeoca, B., Luengo, J., Maillo, J., García-Gil, D., García, S., & Herrera, F. (2019). A first approach on big data missing values imputation. *IoTBDS 2019 - Proceedings of the 4th International Conference on Internet of Things, Big Data and Security*, 315–323. 10.5220/0007738403150323

Mueller, J. (2018). *Beginning programming with Python* (2nd ed.). John Wiley & Sons.

Mueller, J., & Massaron, L. (2019). *Python for data science* (2nd ed.). John Wiley & Sons, Inc.

Munlika, H. (2019). *Machine Learning with Clustering Model.* Retrieved June 17, 2021, from https://medium.com/tniuniversity/%E0%B8%81%E0%B8%B2%E0%B8%A3%E0%B8%97%E0%B8%B3-machine-learning-%E0%B8%94%E0%B9%89%E0%B8%A7%E0%B8%A2-clustering-model-2a3c392e7faa

Nan, X. (2022). Design and Implementation of a Personalized Tourism Recommendation System Based on the Data Mining and Collaborative Filtering Algorithm. *Computational Intelligence and Neuroscience,* 1424097. PMID:36093493

Naparat, D. (2020). *Data Mining with Rapidminer - Getting RapidMiner Educational License.* Retrieved 15 December 2021 from https://www.youtube.com/watch?v=hBxjN1YYXXU

Nigam, H., Biswas, P., Raj, J. S., Iliyasu, A. M., Bestak, R., & Baig, Z. A. (2021). *Web Scraping: From Tools to Related Legislation and Implementation Using Python.* Academic Press.

Nuttavut Thongjor. (2017). *Understanding the data classification: k-Nearest Neighbours.* Retrieved 9 August, 2021, from https://www.babelcoder.com/blog/articles/k-nearest-neighbors

Padhy, S. K., Singh, A. K., & Vetrivelan, P. (2022). Item-Based Collaborative Filtering Blockchain for Secure Movie Recommendation System. *Lecture Notes in Electrical Engineering,* 792, 937–948. doi:10.1007/978-981-16-4625-6_93

Pajankar, A. (2021). *Practical Python data visualization: a fast track approach to learning data visualization with Python.* Apress. doi:10.1007/978-1-4842-6455-3

Paruechanon, P., & Sriurai, W. (2019). Applying association rule to risk analysis for student-dropout in Information Technology Program. *Journal of Science and Science Education,* 1(2), 123-133.

Peungvicha, P., Tubtiang, A. & Sattayaaphitan, T. (2019). Clustering of Jewellery Purchasing Behaviour through Social Network. *Journal of Humanities and Social Sciences, Rajapruk University,* 5, 212-224.

Phan, Q.-T., Wu, Y.-K., & Phan, Q.-D. (2021). An Overview of DataPreprocessing for Short-Term Wind Power Forecasting. *2021 7th International Conference on Applied System Innovation (ICASI), Applied System Innovation (ICASI), 2021 7th International Conference On,* 121–125.

Punhani, R., Arora, V. P. S., Sabitha, S., & Kumar Shukla, V. (2021). Applicationof Clustering Algorithm for Effective Customer Segmentation in E-Commerce. *2021 International Conference on Computational Intelligence and Knowledge Economy (ICCIKE), Computational Intelligence and Knowledge Economy (ICCIKE), 2021 International Conference On,* 149–154.

Puspasari, B. D., Damayanti, L. L., Pramono, A., & Darmawan, A. K. (2021). Implementation K-Means Clustering Method in Job Recommendation System. *2021 7th International Conference on Electrical, Electronics and Information Engineering (ICEEIE), Electrical, Electronics and Information Engineering (ICEEIE), 2021 7th International Conference On,* 1–6.

Puspitasari, D. I., Riza Kholdani, A. F., Dharmawati, A., Rosadi, M. E., & Mega Pradnya Dhuhita, W. (2021). Stroke Disease Analysis and Classification Using Decision Tree and Random Forest Methods. *2021 Sixth International Conference on Informatics and Computing (ICIC), Informatics and Computing (ICIC), 2021 Sixth International Conference On,* 1–4.

Rabiul Alam, M. G., Hussain, S., Islam Mim, M. M., & Islam, M. T. (2021). Telecom Customer Behavior Analysis Using Naïve Bayes Classifier. *2021 IEEE 4th International Conference on Computer and Communication Engineering Technology (CCET), Computer and Communication Engineering Technology (CCET), 2021 IEEE 4th International Conference On,* 308–312.

Rahman, B., Hendric Spits Warnars, H. L., Subirosa Sabarguna, B., & Budiharto, W. (2021). Heart Disease Classification Model Using K-Nearest Neighbor Algorithm. *2021 Sixth International Conference on Informatics and Computing (ICIC), Informatics and Computing (ICIC), 2021 Sixth International Conference On*, 1–4.

Ramirez-Hernandez, J., Juarez-Sandoval, O.-U., Hernandez-Gonzalez, L., Hernandez-Ramirez, A., & Olivares-Dominguez, R.-S. (2020). Voltage Control Based on a Back-Propagation Artificial Neural Network Algorithm. *2020 IEEE International Autumn Meeting on Power, Electronics and Computing (ROPEC), Power, Electronics and Computing (ROPEC), 2020 IEEE International Autumn Meeting On, 4*, 1–6.

RapidMiner, Inc. (2020). *How to Import Data into a Repository | RapidMiner Studio*. Retrieved 15 December 2021 from https://www.youtube.com/watch?v=DS-tYhgA5lA

Raschka, S., & Mirajalili, V. (2018). *Python machine learning: machine learning and deep learning with Python, scikit-learn, and TensorFlow* (2nd ed.). Packt Publishing.

Rathaur, S., Kamath, N., & Ghanekar, U. (2020). Software Defect Density Prediction based on Multiple Linear Regression. *2020 Second International Conference on Inventive Research in Computing Applications (ICIRCA), Inventive Research in Computing Applications (ICIRCA), 2020 Second International Conference On*, 434–439.

Reges, S., Obourn, A., & Stepp, M. (2019). *Building Python programs* (1st ed.). Pearson.

Ren, X. (2021). Application of Apriori Association Rules Algorithm to Data Mining Technology to Mining E-commerce Potential Customers. *2021 International Wireless Communications and Mobile Computing (IWCMC), Wireless Communications and Mobile Computing (IWCMC), 2021 International*, 1193–1196.

Rezaeijo, S. M., Hashemi, B., Mofid, B., Bakhshandeh, M., Mahdavi, A., & Hashemi, M. S. (2021). The feasibility of a dose painting procedure to treat prostate cancer based on mpMR images and hierarchical clustering. *Radiation Oncology (London, England), 16*(1), 1–16. doi:10.118613014-021-01906-2 PMID:34544468

Rezaei, M., Sanayei, A., Aghdaie, S. F. A., & Ansari, A. (2022). Improving the Omnichannel Customers' Lifetime Value Using Association Rules Data Mining: A Case Study of Agriculture Bank of Iran. *Iranian Journal of Management Studies, 15*(1), 49–68.

Riswanto, E., Robi'in, B., & Suparyanto. (2019). Mobile Recommendation System for Culinary Tourism Destination using KNN (K-nearest neighbor). *Journal of Physics: Conference Series, 1201*(1), 012039. doi:10.1088/1742-6596/1201/1/012039

Rogers, S., & Kalinova, E. (2021). Big Data-driven Decision-Making Processes, Real-Time Advanced Analytics, and Cyber-Physical Production Networks in Industry 4.0-based Manufacturing Systems. *Economics, Management, and Financial Markets, 16*(4), 84. doi:10.22381/emfm16420216

Romero, M. P., Parry, J., Prosser, A., Upton, P., Rees, E., Tearne, O., Arnold, M., Chang, Y.-M., Brunton, L. A., Stevens, K., & Drewe, J. A. (2019). Decision tree machine learning applied to bovine tuberculosis risk factors to aid disease control decision making. *Preventive Veterinary Medicine, 175*. PMID:31812850

Sabau Popa, C. D., Popa, D. N., Bogdan, V., & Simut, R. (2021). Composite Financial Performance Index Prediction — A Neural Networks Approach. *Journal of Business Economics and Management, 22*(2), 277–296. doi:10.3846/jbem.2021.14000

Salman, W. A. K., & Sadkhan, S. B. (2021). Proposed Association Rules Mining Algorithm for Sensors Data Streams. *2021 1st Babylon International Conference on Information Technology and Science (BICITS), Information Technology and Science (BICITS), 2021 1st Babylon International Conference On*, 76–81.

Samasiri, P. (2020). Visual representations of different family structures using an interactive data exploration technique. *2020 1st International Conference on Big Data Analytics and Practices (IBDAP), Big Data Analytics and Practices (IBDAP), 2020 1st International Conference On*, 1–5.

Samsani, S. (2016). An RST based efficient preprocessing technique for handling inconsistent data. *2016 IEEE International Conference on Computational Intelligence and Computing Research (ICCIC)*, 1-8. 10.1109/ICCIC.2016.7919591

Shao, L., Mahajan, A., Schreck, T., & Lehmann, D. J. (2017). Interactive Regression Lens for Exploring Scatter Plots. *Computer Graphics Forum*, *36*(3), 157–166. doi:10.1111/cgf.13176

Sharma, M., Joshi, S., Sharma, S., Singh, A., & Gupta, R. (2021). Data Mining Classification Techniques to Assign Individual Personality Type and Predict Job Profile. *2021 9th International Conference on Reliability, Infocom Technologies and Optimization (Trends and Future Directions) (ICRITO)*, 1-5.

Shrestha, R. B., Razavi, M., & Prasad, P. W. (2020). An Unsupervised Machine Learning Technique for Recommendation Systems. *2020 5th International Conference on Innovative Technologies in Intelligent Systems and Industrial Applications (CITISIA), Innovative Technologies in Intelligent Systems and Industrial Applications (CITISIA), 2020 5th International Conference On*, 1–9.

Sneeringer, L. (2016). *Professional Python*. WROX/John Wiley & Sons.

Snineh, S. M., Amrani, N. E. A., Youssfi, M., Bouattane, O., & Daaif, A. (2021). Detection of traffic anomaly in highways by using recurrent neural network. *2021 Fifth International Conference On Intelligent Computing in Data Sciences (ICDS), Intelligent Computing in Data Sciences (ICDS), 2021 Fifth International Conference On*, 1–6.

Soft, N. (2020). *RapidMiner Tutorial For Beginners | Download & Install | Introduction to RapidMiner*. Retrieved 15 December 2021 from https://www.youtube.com/watch?v=im11NBJfjhM

Song, H., Fu, Y., Saket, B., & Stasko, J. (2021). Understanding the Effects of Visualizing Missing Values on Visual Data Exploration. *2021 IEEE Visualization Conference (VIS), Visualization Conference (VIS), 2021 IEEE, VIS*, 161–165.

Song, J., Yu, Q., & Bao, R. (2019). The Detection Algorithms for Similar Duplicate Data. *2019 6th International Conference on Systems and Informatics (ICSAI), Systems and Informatics (ICSAI), 2019 6th International Conference On*, 1534–1542.

Sonu, S. B., & Suyampulingam, A. (2021). Linear Regression Based Air Quality Data Analysis and Prediction using Python. *2021 IEEE Madras Section Conference (MASCON), Madras Section Conference (MASCON)*, 1–7.

SPSS Inc. and International Consortium Publish CRISP-DM 1.0; Free Document Offers Step-By-Step Guidance for Data Mining Projects. (2000). *Business Wire*.

Sriwiboon, N. (2020). Improvement the Performance of the Chest X-ray Image Classification with Convolutional Neural Network Model by Using Image Augmentations Technique for COVID-19 Diagnosis. *The Journal of King Mongkut's University of Technology North Bangkok, 31*(1).

Stewart, J. (2017). *Python for scientists* (2nd ed.). Cambridge University Press. doi:10.1017/9781108120241

Sunkpho, J. & Ramjan, S. (2020). Predicting Condominium Price in Bangkok Using Web Mining Techniques. *Srinakharinwirot Research and Development (Journal of Humanities and Social Sciences), 12*(24).

Sunkpho, J., & Ramjan, S. (2020). Predicting Condominium Price in Bangkok using Web Mining Technique. *Srinakharinwirot Research and Development (Journal of Humanities and Social Sciences), 12*(24).

Sunkpho, J., & Hofmann, M. (2019). *Analyzing Customer Satisfaction of a Mobile Application using Data Mining Techniques*. Research Administration Division, Thammasat University.

Sunkpho, S., & Ramjan, S. (2020). *Introduction to Python Programming for Data Science*. Thammasat Press.

Susanti, S. P., & Azizah, F. N. (2017). Imputation of missing value using dynamic Bayesian network for multivariate time series data. *2017 International Conference on Data and Software Engineering (ICoDSE)*, 1-5. 10.1109/ICODSE.2017.8285864

Tai, Y., Sun, Z., & Yao, Z. (2021). Content-Based Recommendation Using Machine Learning. *2021 IEEE 31st International Workshop on Machine Learning for Signal Processing (MLSP), Machine Learning for Signal Processing (MLSP), 2021 IEEE 31st International Workshop On*, 1–4.

Tananatong, T., & Ramjan, S. (2022). *Data Visualization Design and Development for Data Science*. Thammasat Press.

Tanantong, T. (2021). *Data Mining*. Retrieved from: https://www.skilllane.com/courses/tuxsa-Data-Mining-Algorithms/chapter

Tanantong, T., & Ramjan, S. (2021, April-June). An Association Rule Mining Approach to Discover Demand and Supply Patterns Based on Thai Social Media Data. *International Journal of Knowledge and Systems Science*, *12*(2), 1–16. doi:10.4018/IJKSS.2021040101

Tanantong, T., & Ramjan, S. (2022). *Data Visualization for Data Science* (1st ed.). Thammasat Press.

Telikani, A., Shahbahrami, A., & Gandomi, A. H. (2021). High-performance implementation of evolutionary privacy-preserving algorithm for big data using GPU platform. *Information Sciences*, *579*, 251–265. doi:10.1016/j.ins.2021.08.006

Thammasisir, S., & Ramjan, S. (2021). *Corrosion under Insulation severity Prediction for Carbon Steel in Marine Environment using Data Science Methodology (Independent Study)*. Thammasat University.

Thangakumar, J., & Kommina, S. B. (2020). Ant colony optimization based feature subset selection with logistic regression classification model for education data mining. *International Journal of Advanced Science and Technology*, *29*(3), 5821–5834.

Thankachan, T., Prakash, K. S., & Jothi, S. (2021). Artificial neural network modeling to evaluate and predict the mechanical strength of duplex stainless steel during casting. *Sadhana*, *46*(4), 1–12. doi:10.100712046-021-01742-w

Torrens, M., & Tabakovic, A. (2022). A Banking Platform to Leverage Data Driven Marketing with Machine Learning. *Entropy (Basel, Switzerland)*, *24*(3), 347. doi:10.3390/e24030347 PMID:35327858

Toumi, A., Gribaa, N., & Ben Abdessalem Karaa, W. (2021). Mining biomedical texts based on statistical method and association rules. *2021 International Conference of Women in Data Science at Taif University (WiDSTaif), Women in Data Science at Taif University (WiDSTaif), 2021 International Conference Of*, 1–4.

Tuition, D. (2021). *RapidMiner Tutorial, Learn Data Cleaning, Data Visualization & Data Analysis with Rapidminer*. Retrieved 15 December 2021 from https://www.youtube.com/watch?v=r27eUHJtIFs

Van der Ark, L. A., Croon, M. A., & Sijtsma, K. (2005). *New developments in categorial data analysis for the social and behavioral sciences*. Lawrence Erlbaum Associates Publishers.

Vasudevan, S. (2021). *Rapid Miner Installation - Step by Step explanation*. Retrieved 15 December 2021 from https://www.youtube.com/watch?v=Wp42fV4q66Y

Vichi, M., Ritter, G., & Giusti, A. (2013). *Classification and data mining*. Springer Verlag.

Wafa, H. A., Aminuddin, R., Ibrahim, S., Mangshor, N. N. A., & Wahab, N. I. F. A. (2021). A Data Visualization Framework during Pandemic using the Density-Based Spatial Clustering with Noise (DBSCAN) Machine Learning Model. *2021 IEEE 11th International Conference on System Engineering and Technology (ICSET), System Engineering and Technology (ICSET), 2021 IEEE 11th International Conference On*, 1–6.

Wang, G., & Chen, Y. (2022). Enabling Legal Risk Management Model for International Corporation with Deep Learning and Self Data Mining. *Computational Intelligence and Neuroscience*, *2022*, 6385404. doi:10.1155/2022/6385404 PMID:35432517

Wang, J., Sato, K., Guo, S., Chen, W., & Wu, J. (2019). Big Data Processing With Minimal Delay and Guaranteed Data Resolution in Disaster Areas. *IEEE Transactions on Vehicular Technology*, *68*(4), 3833–3842. doi:10.1109/TVT.2018.2889094

Wayan Priscila Yuni Praditya, N., Erna Permanasari, A., & Hidayah, I. (2021). Designing a tourism recommendation system using a hybrid method (Collaborative Filtering and Content-Based Filtering). *2021 IEEE International Conference on Communication, Networks and Satellite (COMNETSAT), Communication, Networks and Satellite (Comnetsat), 2021 IEEE International Conference On*, 298–305.

Wijaya, Y. A., Kurniady, D. A., Setyanto, E., Tarihoran, W. S., Rusmana, D., & Rahim, R. (2021). Davies Bouldin Index Algorithm for Optimizing Clustering Case Studies Mapping School Facilities. *TEM Journal*, *10*(3), 1099–1103. doi:10.18421/TEM103-13

Xu, B., Chen, C., & Yang, J.-H. (2022). Application of Cluster Analysis Technology in Visualization Research of Movie Review Data. *Computational Intelligence and Neuroscience*, *2022*, 1–11. doi:10.1155/2022/7756896 PMID:35880060

Yadalam, T. V., Gowda, V. M., Kumar, V. S., Girish, D., & M., N. (2020). Career Recommendation Systems using Content based Filtering. *2020 5th International Conference on Communication and Electronics Systems (ICCES), Communication and Electronics Systems (ICCES), 2020 5th International Conference On*, 660–665.

Yager, R. R. (2020). Ordinal scale based uncertainty models for AI. *Information Fusion*, *64*, 92–98. doi:10.1016/j.inffus.2020.06.010

Yang, F.-J. (2019). An Extended Idea about Decision Trees. *2019 International Conference on Computational Science and Computational Intelligence (CSCI)*, 349-354. 10.1109/CSCI49370.2019.00068

Yang, H., Zheng, Z., & Sun, C. (2022). E-Commerce Marketing Optimization of Agricultural Products Based on Deep Learning and Data Mining. *Computational Intelligence and Neuroscience*, *2022*, 2022. doi:10.1155/2022/6564014 PMID:35634060

Yingzhuo, X., & Xuewen, W. (2021). Research on Community Consumer Behavior Based on Association Rules Analysis. *2021 6th International Conference on Intelligent Computing and Signal Processing (ICSP), Intelligent Computing and Signal Processing (ICSP), 2021 6th International Conference On*, 1213–1216.

Zadeh, A. H., Zolbanin, H. M., & Sharda, R. (2021). Incorporating Big Data Tools for Social Media Analytics in a Business Analytics Course. *Journal of Information Systems Education*, *32*(3), 176–198.

Zagatti, F. R., Silva, L. C., Dos Santos Silva, L. N., Sette, B. S., Caseli, H. de M., Lucredio, D., & Silva, D. F. (2021). MetaPrep: Data preparation pipelines recommendation via meta-learning. *2021 20th IEEE International Conference on Machine Learning and Applications (ICMLA), Machine Learning and Applications (ICMLA), 2021 20th IEEE International Conference on, ICMLA*, 1197–1202.

Zelle, J. M. (2010). *Python programming: an introduction to computer science* (2nd ed.). Beedle & Associates.

Zhang, H., Zhang, L., & Jiang, Y. (2019). Overfitting and Underfitting Analysis for Deep Learning Based End-to-end Communication Systems. *2019 11th International Conference on Wireless Communications and Signal Processing (WCSP), Wireless Communications and Signal Processing (WCSP), 2019 11th International Conference On*, 1–6.

Zhang, C., & Zhang, S. (2002). *Association Rule Mining*. In Models and Algorithms. Springer Berlin Heidelberg. doi:10.1007/3-540-46027-6

Zhou, Y., Yan, S., Wang, C., Zheng, K., & Zhu, L. (2021). Position Monitoring System Based on Hierarchical Clustering. *2021 26th IEEE Asia-Pacific Conference on Communications (APCC), Communications (APCC), 2021 26th IEEE Asia-Pacific Conference On*, 111–114.

Zhu, H., Samtani, S., Brown, R. A., & Chen, H. (2021). A Deep Learning Approach for Recognizing Activity of Daily Living (Adl) for Senior Care: Exploiting Interaction Dependency and Temporal Patterns. *Management Information Systems Quarterly*, 45(2), 859–895. doi:10.25300/MISQ/2021/15574

Zuo, L., & Guo, J. (2019). Customer Classification of Discrete Data Concerning Customer Assets Based on Data Mining. *2019 International Conference on Intelligent Transportation, Big Data & Smart City (ICITBS)*. 10.1109/ICITBS.2019.00093

About the Authors

Sarawut Ramjan is a highly accomplished academician with a Ph.D. in Computer and Engineering Management, which he earned from Assumption University in 2013. In 2017, he joined the College of Innovation at Thammasat University as an Associate Professor, where he currently conducts cutting-edge research at the Thammasat University AI Center. Dr. Ramjan is a renowned expert in data science, with a strong focus on teaching and research in this field. His remarkable contributions to the academic world have made him a prominent figure in the academic community.

Jirapon Sunkpho is a distinguished scholar with a passion for academic excellence. He holds a Ph.D. in Civil and Environmental Engineering (Computer-Aided Engineering) from the esteemed Carnegie Mellon University, earned in 2001, as well as an MSc in Applied Data Science and Analytics from Technological University Dublin, which he completed in 2021. Dr. Sunkpho is a visionary leader and currently serves as the Vice Rector in Information Technology at Thammasat University, where he plays a key role in shaping the institution's technological direction. He is also a Board of Director at Airport of Thailand, where his expertise is valued. As an accomplished Associate Professor, Dr. Sunkpho is widely recognized for his teaching excellence and his research in data science. His contributions to this field have been profound, and he remains committed to advancing knowledge in this area. With his unique combination of academic prowess and leadership abilities, Dr. Sunkpho is a true asset to the academic and professional communities.

Index

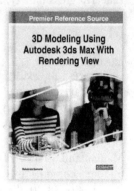
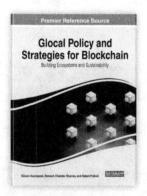

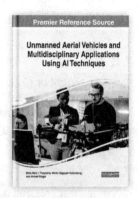

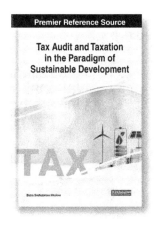

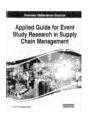

Printed in the United States
by Baker & Taylor Publisher Services